尾田栄一郎

Um...Right now, it's the seventh month of the year 1999, going by the western calendar. It's the month that Brother Nostra[damus] predicted would see "the destruction of the world by the great king of Anglemois." And so the world governments have taken the opportunity to put the great king of Anglemois on the most wanted list. His royal mug appears above. ⬆ His punishment: "Confinement until the eighth month." If you should find him, please refrain from using any rolling savate or piledriver attack moves. (Signed, the world governments.)

-Eiichiro Oda, 1999

Eiichiro Oda began his manga career at the age of 17, when his one-shot cowboy manga **Wanted!** won second place in the coveted Tezuka manga awards. Oda went on to work as an assistant to some of the biggest manga artists in the industry, including Nobuhiro Watsuki, before winning the Hop Step Award for new artists. His pirate adventure **One Piece**, which debuted in **Weekly Shonen Jump** in 1997, quickly became one of the most popular manga in Japan.

ONE PIECE VOL. 9
EAST BLUE PART 9

SHONEN JUMP Manga Edition

This graphic novel contains material that was originally published in English in **SHONEN JUMP** #32–35.

STORY AND ART BY EIICHIRO ODA

English Adaptation/Lance Caselman
Translation/Naoko Amemiya
Touch-up Art & Lettering/Mark McMurray
Additional Touch-up/Josh Simpson and Walden Wong
Design/Sean Lee
Editors/Megan Bates and Yuki Takagaki

Published by VIZ Media, LLC
P.O. Box 77010
San Francisco, CA 94107

10 9 8 7
First printing, December 2005
Seventh printing, April 2011

www.viz.com

THE WORLD'S MOST POPULAR MANGA
www.shonenjump.com

SHONEN JUMP MANGA

ONE PIECE

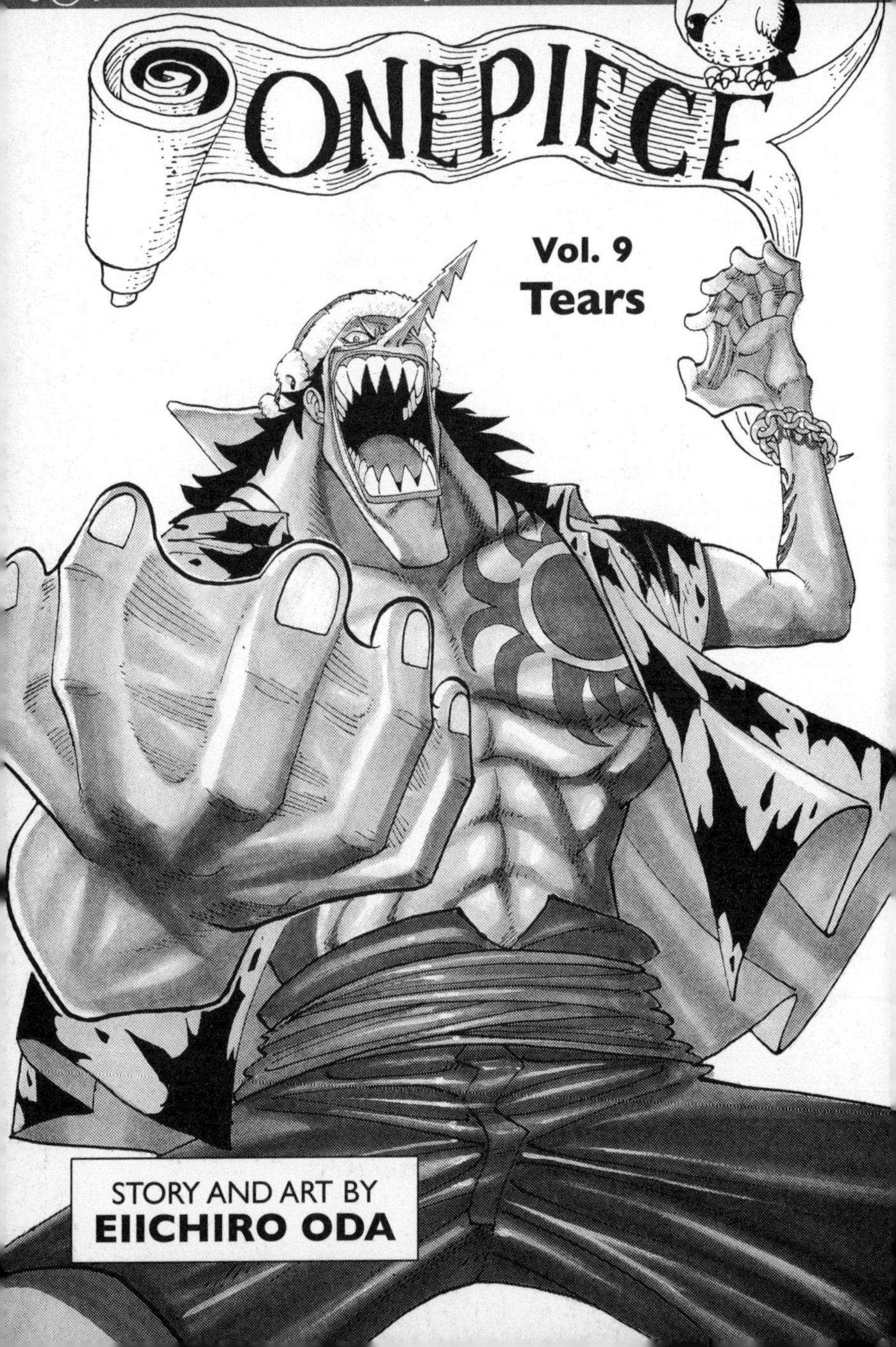

Vol. 9
Tears

STORY AND ART BY
EIICHIRO ODA

Monkey D. Luffy
Boundlessly optimistic and
able to stretch like rubber,
he is determined to
become King of the Pirates.

Roronoa Zolo
A former bounty hunter and
master of the "three-sword"
fighting style.

Usopp
Usopp's known for his tall tales,
but he has a way with a slingshot
and a heart of gold. His father,
Yasopp, is part of Shanks's crew.

Nami
A thief who specializes in
robbing pirates. Nami hates
pirates, but Luffy convinced her
to join his crew as navigator.

Sanji
A compassionate cook (and
ladies' man) whose dream is
to find the legendary sea,
the "All Blue."

THE STORY OF ONE PIECE

Volume 9

Monkey D. Luffy started out as just a kid with a dream — and that dream was to become the greatest pirate in history! Stirred by the tales of pirate "Red-Haired" Shanks, Luffy vowed to become a pirate himself. That was before the enchanted Devil Fruit gave Luffy the power to stretch like rubber, at the cost of being unable to swim — a serious handicap for an aspiring sea dog. Undeterred, Luffy set out to sea and recruited some crewmates: lying sharp-shooter Usopp, master swordsman Zolo, treasure-hunting thief Nami and the sous-chef Sanji.

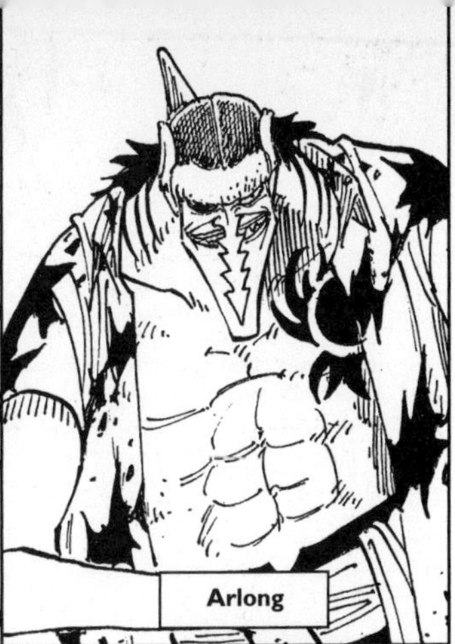
Arlong

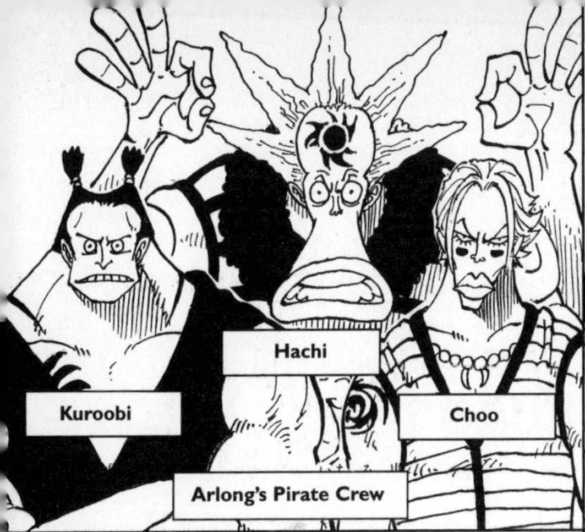
Hachi
Choo
Kuroobi
Arlong's Pirate Crew

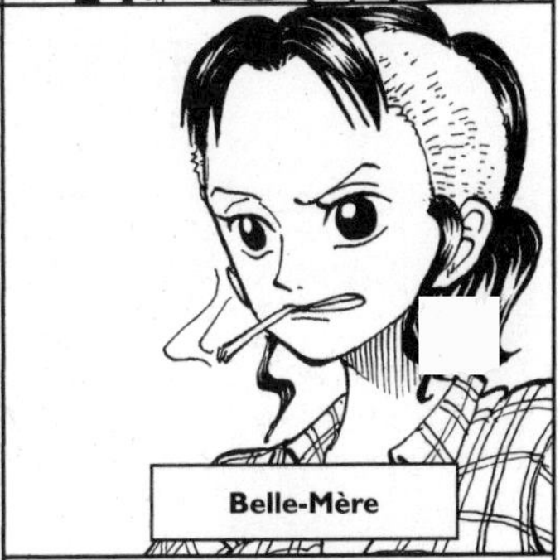
Belle-Mère

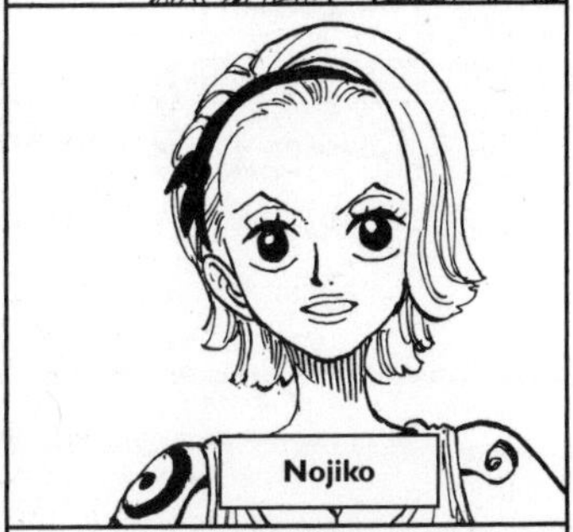
Nojiko

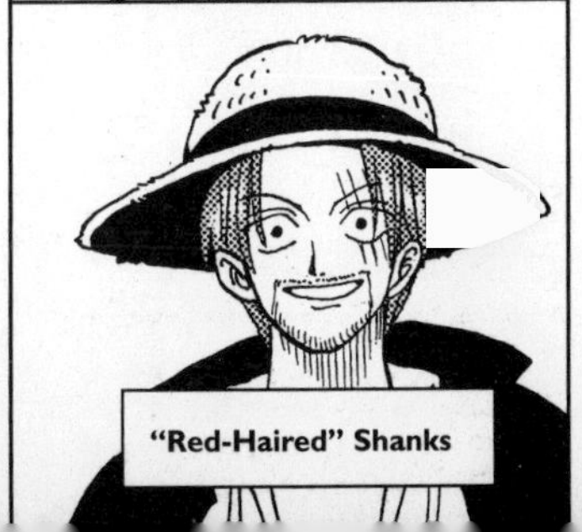
"Red-Haired" Shanks

While working off the damage he caused aboard the oceangoing restaurant Baratie, Luffy meets Sanji the sea cook and asks him to join his crew. But Sanji, for reasons only he knows, refuses to leave the restaurant ship. Before that mystery can be solved, Don Krieg and his pirates try to capture the Baratie, triggering a ferocious battle. In the end, Luffy and Krieg face off, and Luffy proves that courage is sometimes more than a match for overwhelming firepower.

After the battle, Luffy again asks Sanji to sail with him, and once more Sanji refuses, until Chef Zeff and his fighting cooks conspire to convince Sanji that he should follow his dream. Touched by their extremely tough brand of love, Sanji says a tearful goodbye and sets off with Luffy!

Meanwhile, Zolo and Usopp sail ahead in pursuit of Nami and arrive at an island ruled by the Fish-Man warlord, "Saw-Tooth" Arlong. Scarcely have they arrived when, to their shock, they find Nami—consorting with the pirates!!

EAST BLUE

ONE PIECE

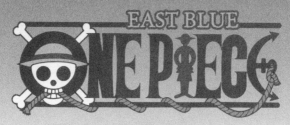

Vol. 9
TEARS

CONTENTS

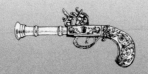

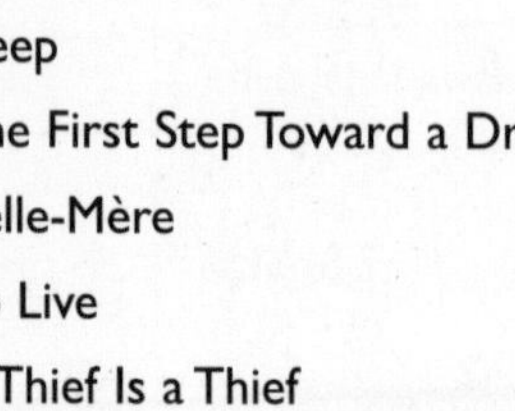

Chapter 72:
PROPER LIVING

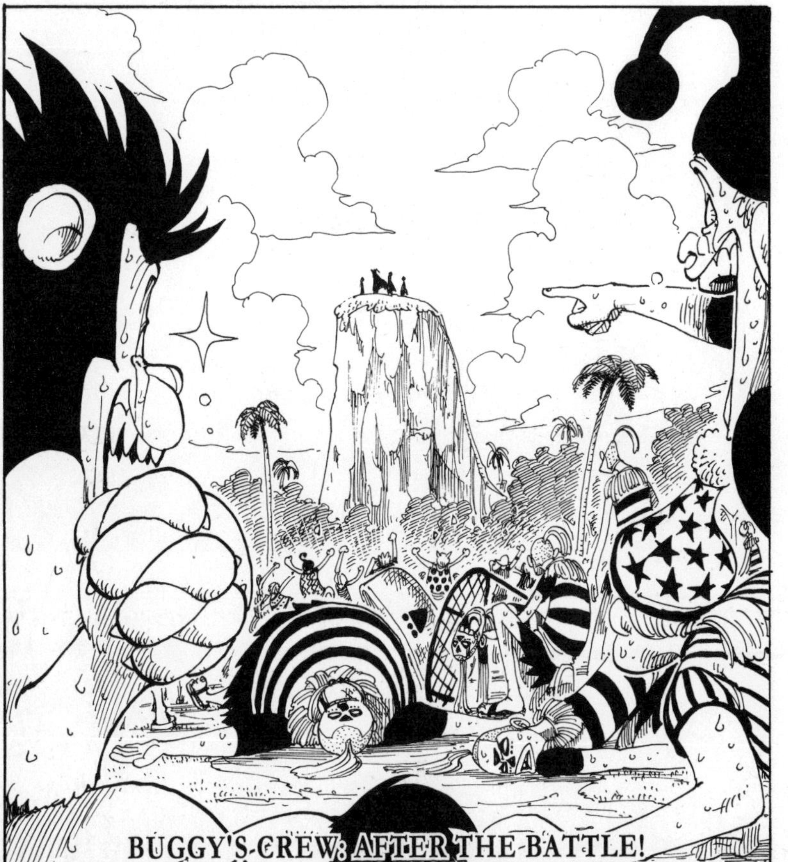
BUGGY'S CREW: AFTER THE BATTLE!
PART 25: "MYSTERIOUS FIGURES IN THE EAST"

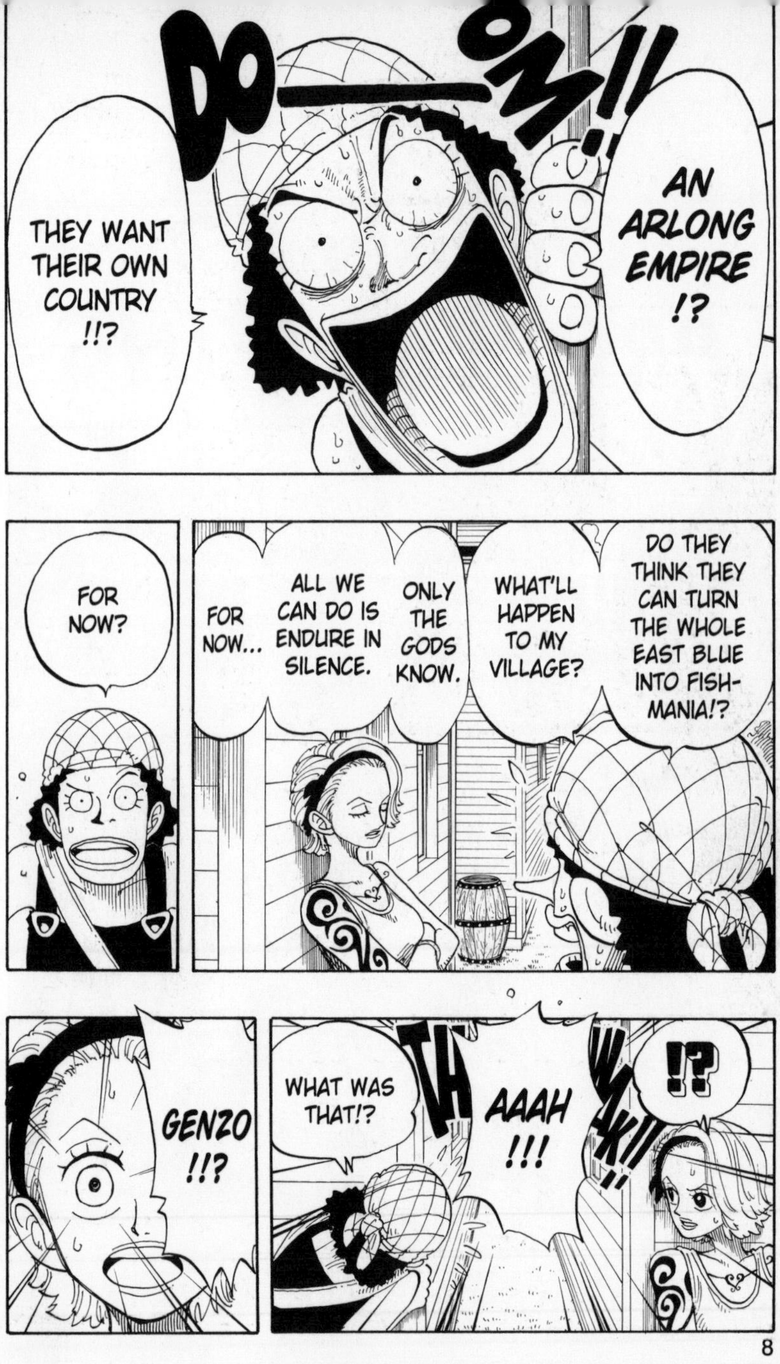
DO—OM!!
AN ARLONG EMPIRE !?
THEY WANT THEIR OWN COUNTRY !!?
DO THEY THINK THEY CAN TURN THE WHOLE EAST BLUE INTO FISH-MANIA!?
WHAT'LL HAPPEN TO MY VILLAGE?
ONLY THE GODS KNOW.
FOR NOW... ALL WE CAN DO IS ENDURE IN SILENCE.
FOR NOW?
!?
TH
WAK!!
AAAH !!!
WHAT WAS THAT!?
GENZO !!?

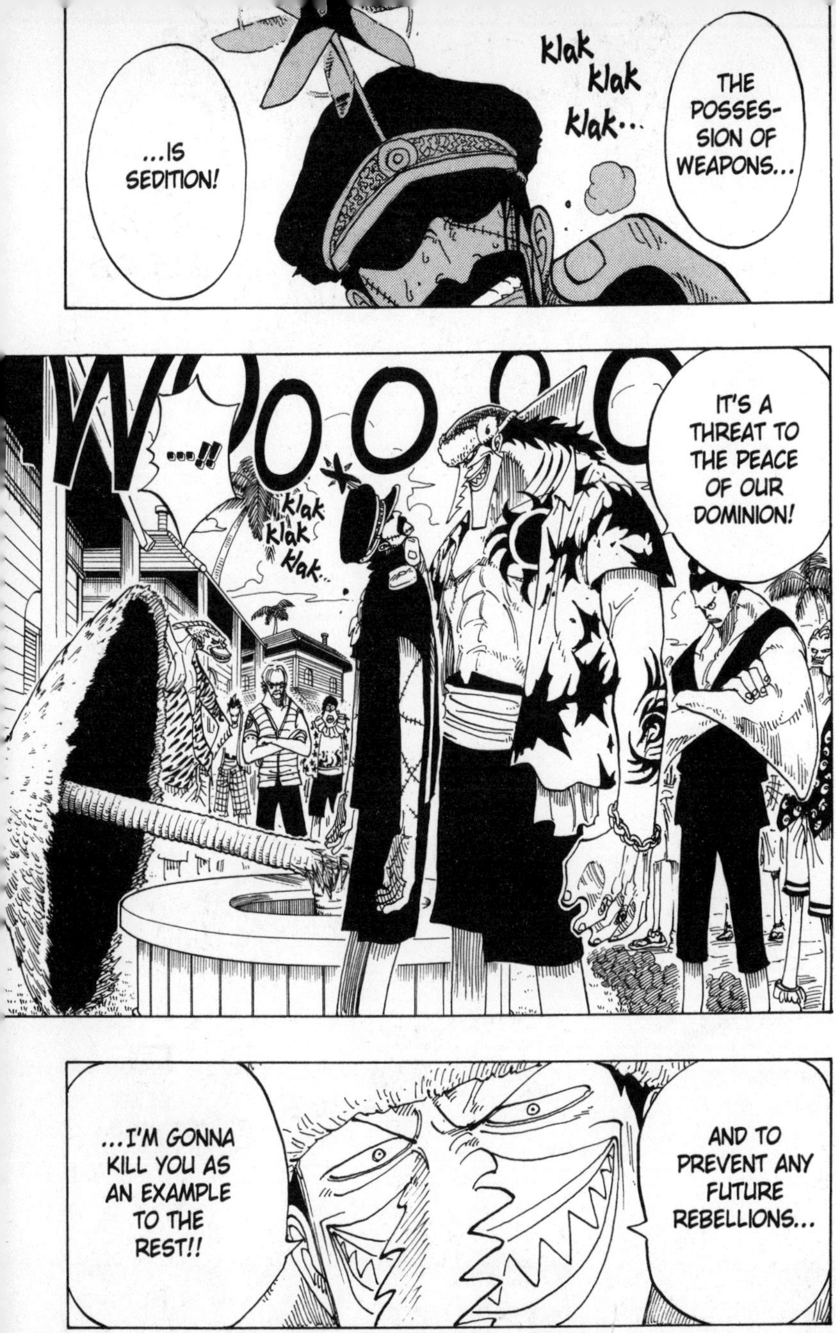
THE POSSESSION OF WEAPONS...
klak klak klak...
...IS SEDITION!
IT'S A THREAT TO THE PEACE OF OUR DOMINION!
WOOOO
...!!
klak klak klak...
AND TO PREVENT ANY FUTURE REBELLIONS...
...I'M GONNA KILL YOU AS AN EXAMPLE TO THE REST!!

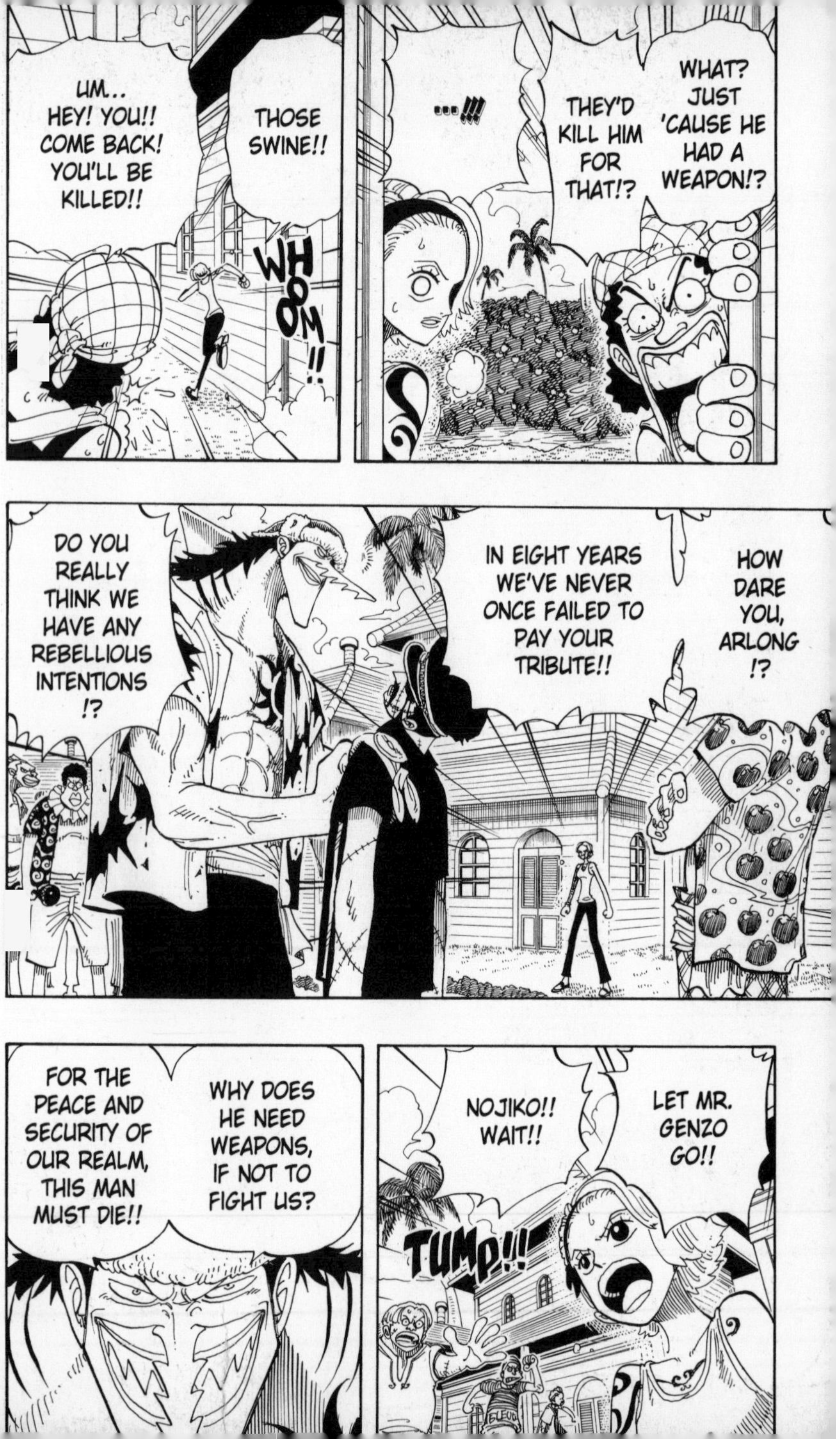
WHAT? JUST 'CAUSE HE HAD A WEAPON!?
THEY'D KILL HIM FOR THAT!?
...!!!
THOSE SWINE!!
UM... HEY! YOU!! COME BACK! YOU'LL BE KILLED!!
WHOOM!!
HOW DARE YOU, ARLONG !?
IN EIGHT YEARS WE'VE NEVER ONCE FAILED TO PAY YOUR TRIBUTE!!
DO YOU REALLY THINK WE HAVE ANY REBELLIOUS INTENTIONS !?
LET MR. GENZO GO!!
NOJIKO!! WAIT!!
TUMP!!
WHY DOES HE NEED WEAPONS, IF NOT TO FIGHT US?
FOR THE PEACE AND SECURITY OF OUR REALM, THIS MAN MUST DIE!!

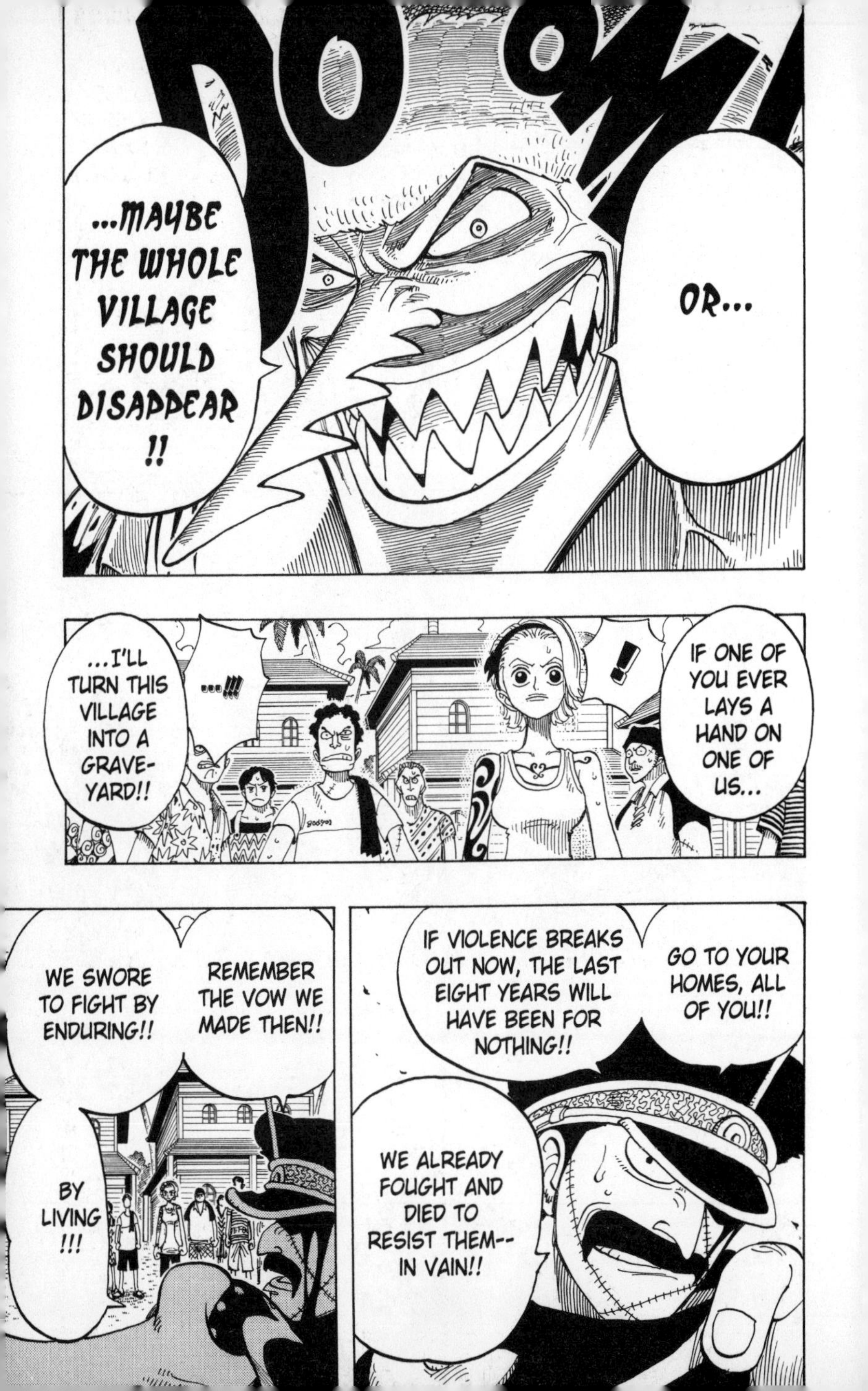
DOOM
OR...
...MAYBE THE WHOLE VILLAGE SHOULD DISAPPEAR!!
IF ONE OF YOU EVER LAYS A HAND ON ONE OF US...
!
...!!!
...I'LL TURN THIS VILLAGE INTO A GRAVEYARD!!
GO TO YOUR HOMES, ALL OF YOU!!
IF VIOLENCE BREAKS OUT NOW, THE LAST EIGHT YEARS WILL HAVE BEEN FOR NOTHING!!
WE ALREADY FOUGHT AND DIED TO RESIST THEM-- IN VAIN!!
REMEMBER THE VOW WE MADE THEN!!
WE SWORE TO FIGHT BY ENDURING!!
BY LIVING!!!

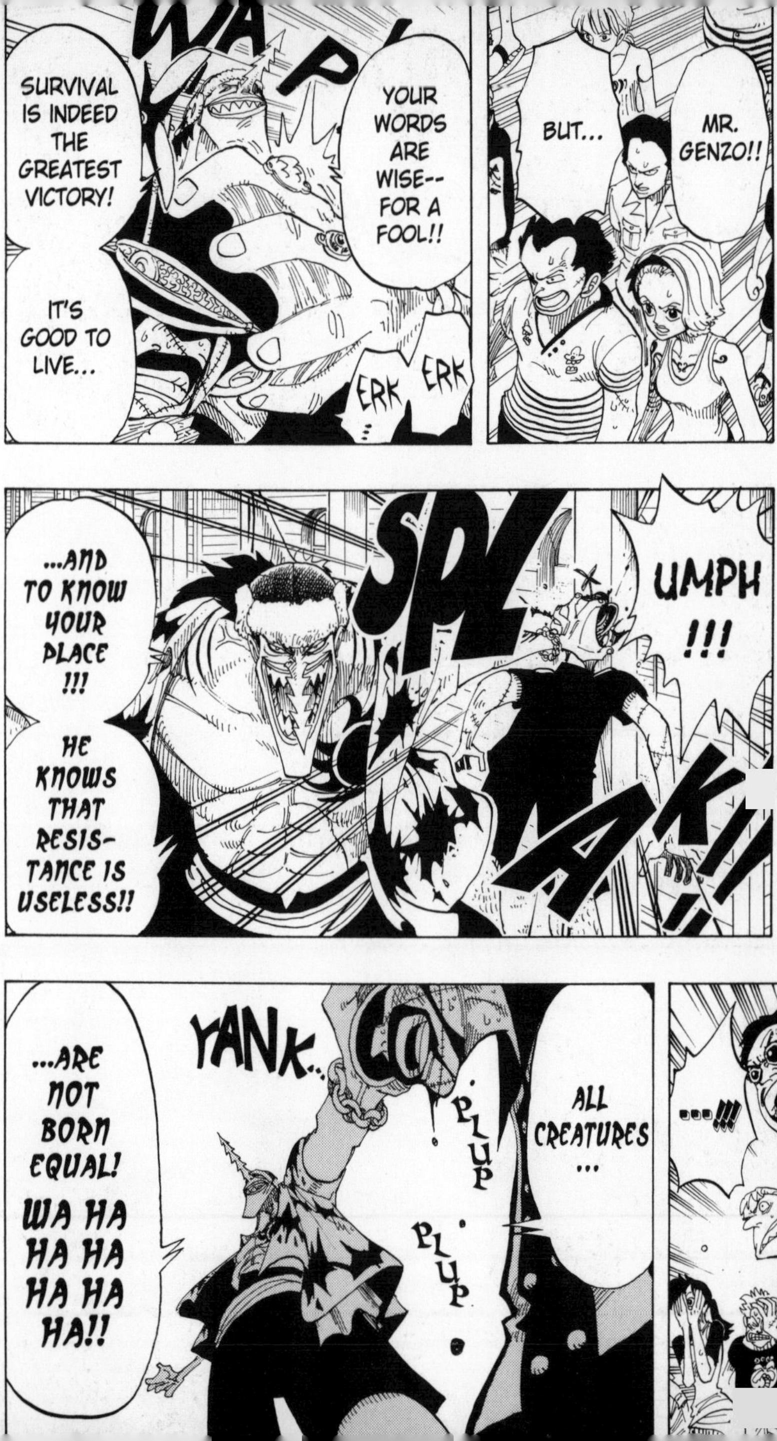
MR. GENZO!!
BUT...
WAP
YOUR WORDS ARE WISE-- FOR A FOOL!!
SURVIVAL IS INDEED THE GREATEST VICTORY!
IT'S GOOD TO LIVE...
ERK
ERK
UMPH !!!
SPLAK!!
...AND TO KNOW YOUR PLACE !!!
HE KNOWS THAT RESIS-TANCE IS USELESS!!
...!!!
ALL CREATURES ...
YANK...
PLUP
PLUP
...ARE NOT BORN EQUAL!
WA HA HA HA HA HA HA!!

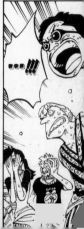

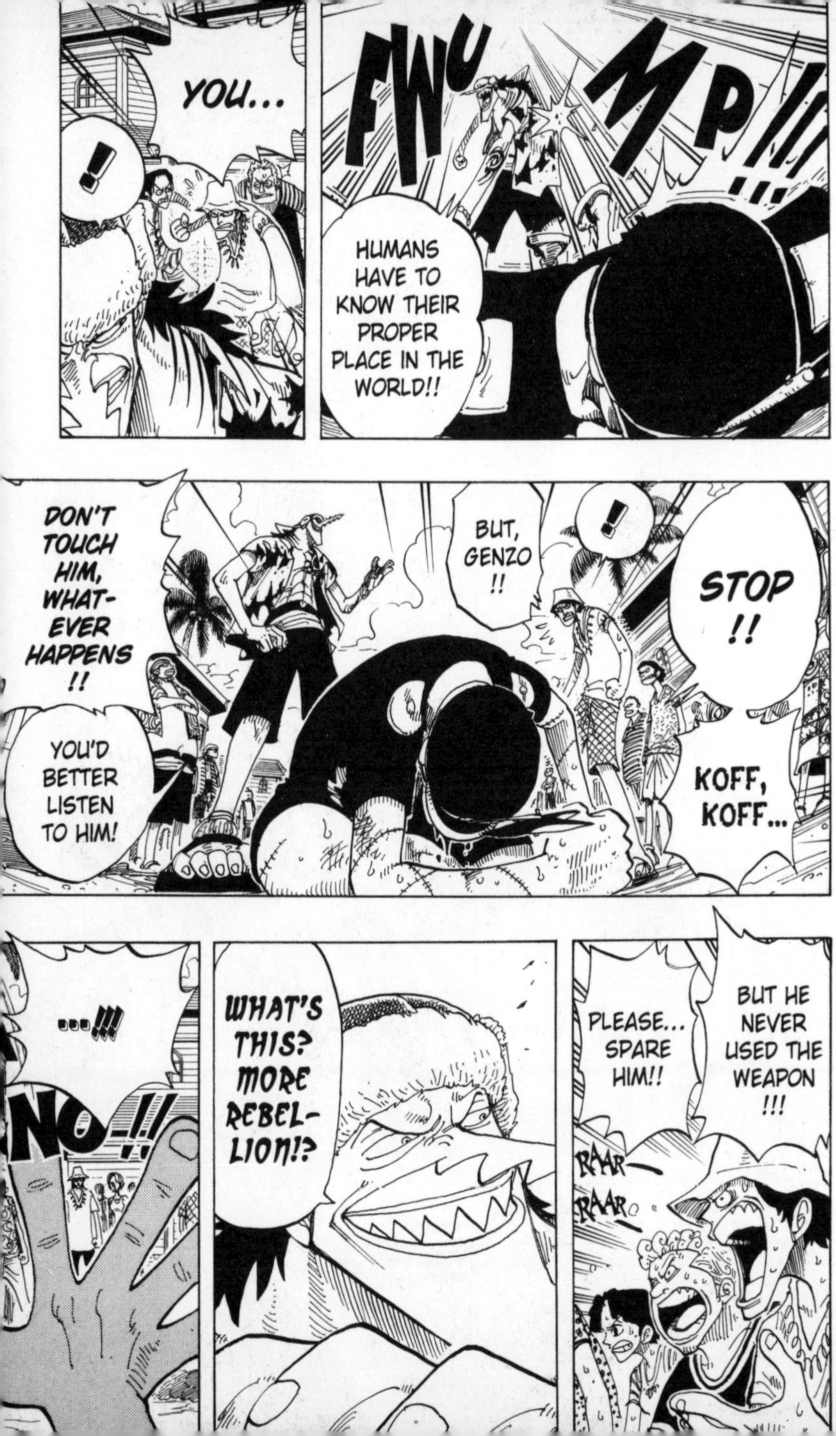
FWUMP!!!
HUMANS HAVE TO KNOW THEIR PROPER PLACE IN THE WORLD!!
YOU...
!
STOP!!
!
BUT, GENZO!!
KOFF, KOFF...
DON'T TOUCH HIM, WHAT-EVER HAPPENS!!
YOU'D BETTER LISTEN TO HIM!
BUT HE NEVER USED THE WEAPON!!!
PLEASE... SPARE HIM!!
RAAR—
RAAR
WHAT'S THIS? MORE REBEL-LION!?
...!!!
NO-!!

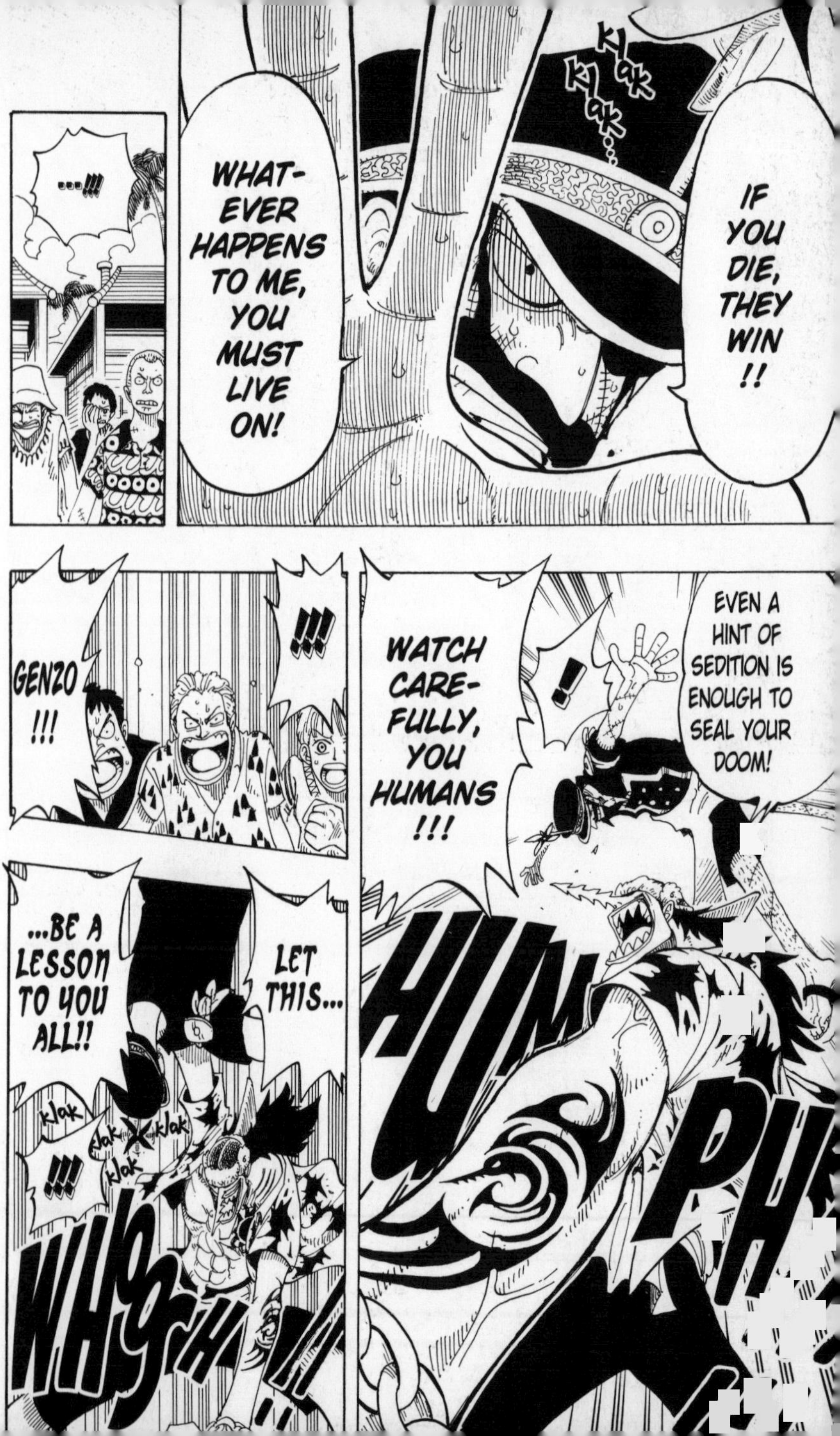

klak klak...
IF YOU DIE, THEY WIN!!
WHATEVER HAPPENS TO ME, YOU MUST LIVE ON!
...!!!
EVEN A HINT OF SEDITION IS ENOUGH TO SEAL YOUR DOOM!
!
WATCH CAREFULLY, YOU HUMANS!!!
HUM
PH
!!!
GENZO!!!
LET THIS...
...BE A LESSON TO YOU ALL!!
klak klak klak klak
!!!
WHOOSH!!

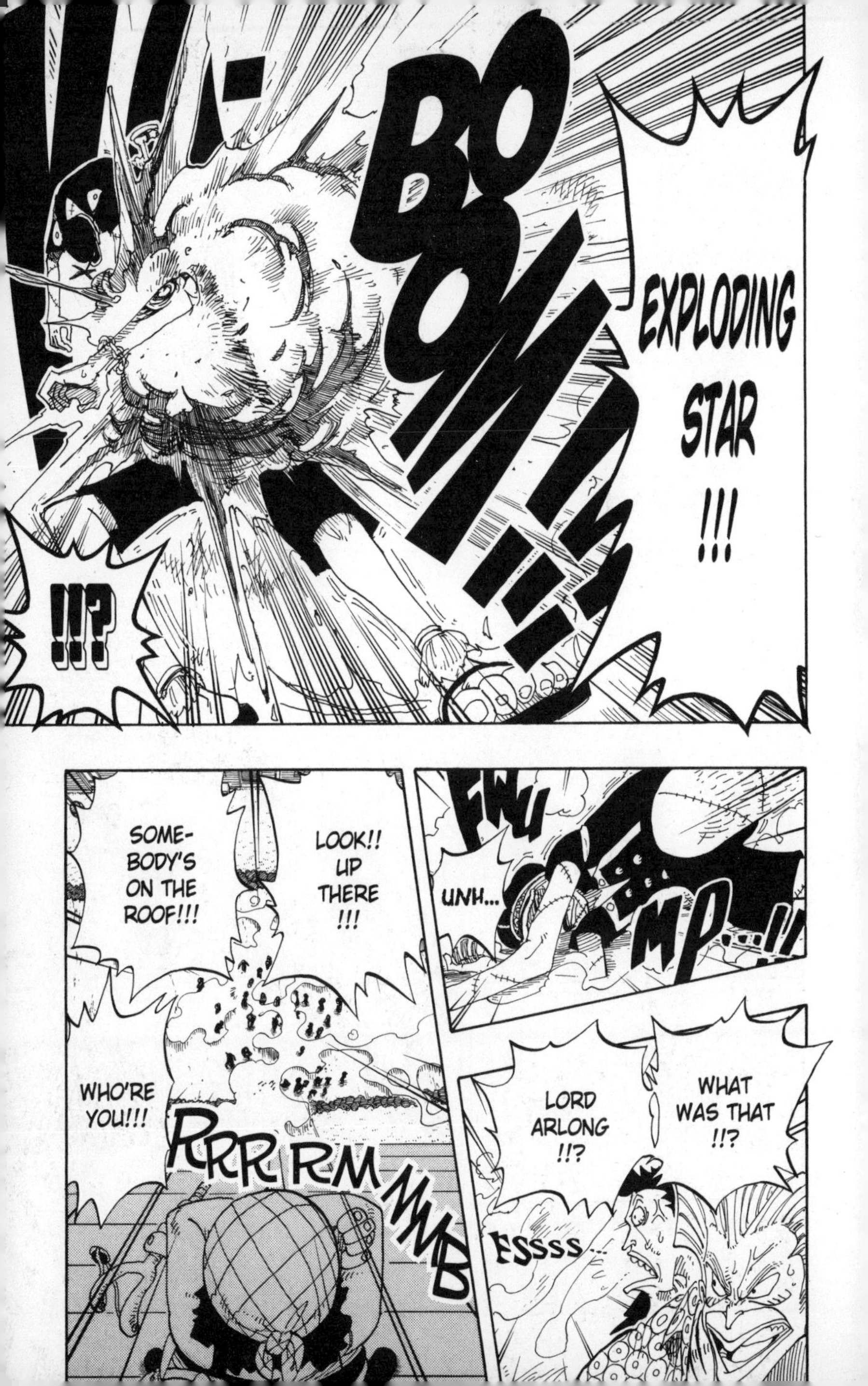
EXPLODING STAR !!!
BOOM!!
!!?
FWU
UNH...
MP...!!
WHAT WAS THAT !!?
LORD ARLONG !!?
ESSSS...
LOOK!! UP THERE !!!
SOME-BODY'S ON THE ROOF!!!
WHO'RE YOU!!!
RRR RM MMB

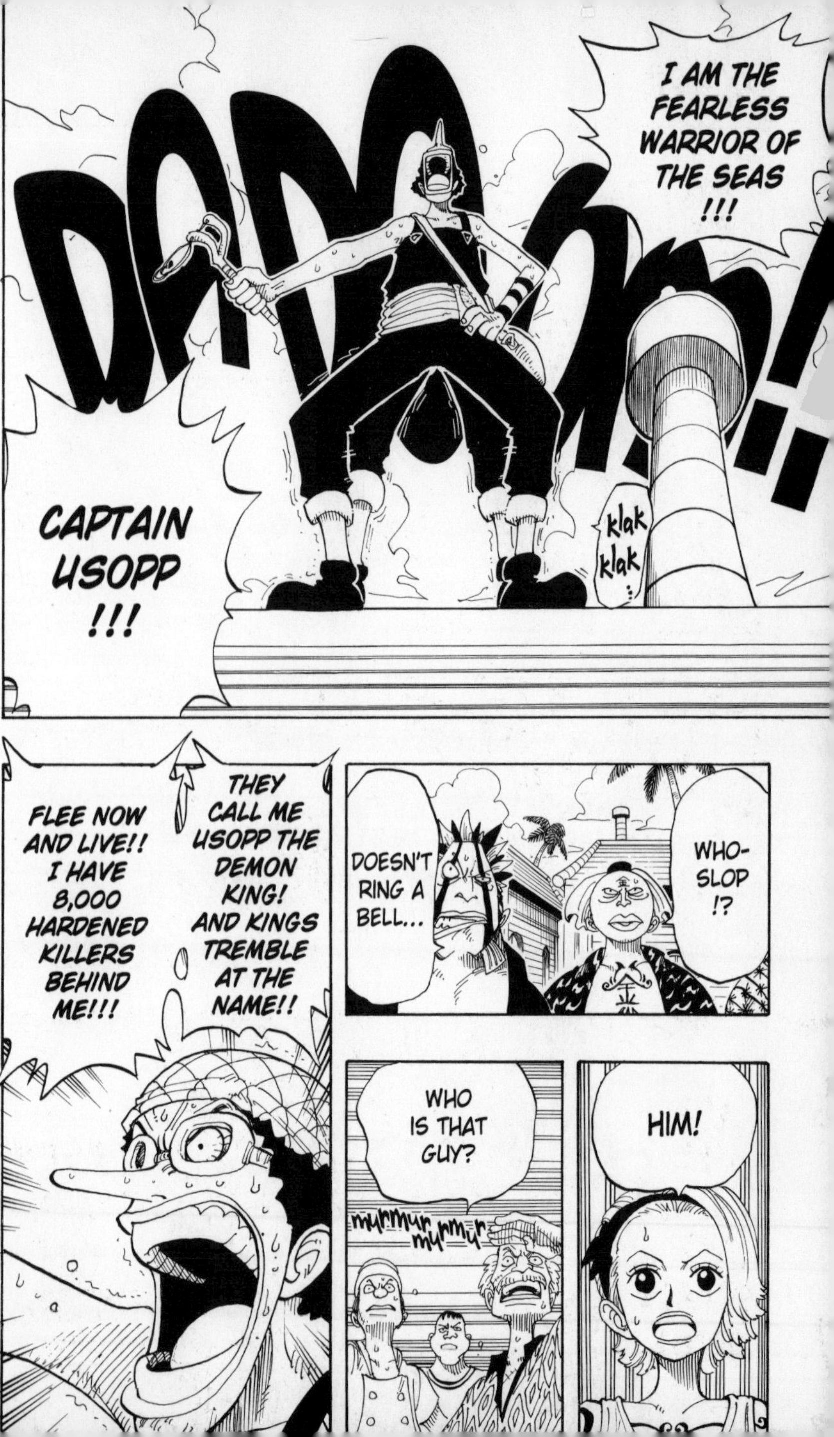
I AM THE FEARLESS WARRIOR OF THE SEAS !!!
klak klak
CAPTAIN USOPP !!!
WHO-SLOP !?
DOESN'T RING A BELL...
HIM!
WHO IS THAT GUY?
murmur murmur murmur
THEY CALL ME USOPP THE DEMON KING! AND KINGS TREMBLE AT THE NAME!!
FLEE NOW AND LIVE!! I HAVE 8,000 HARDENED KILLERS BEHIND ME!!!

READ THIS WAY

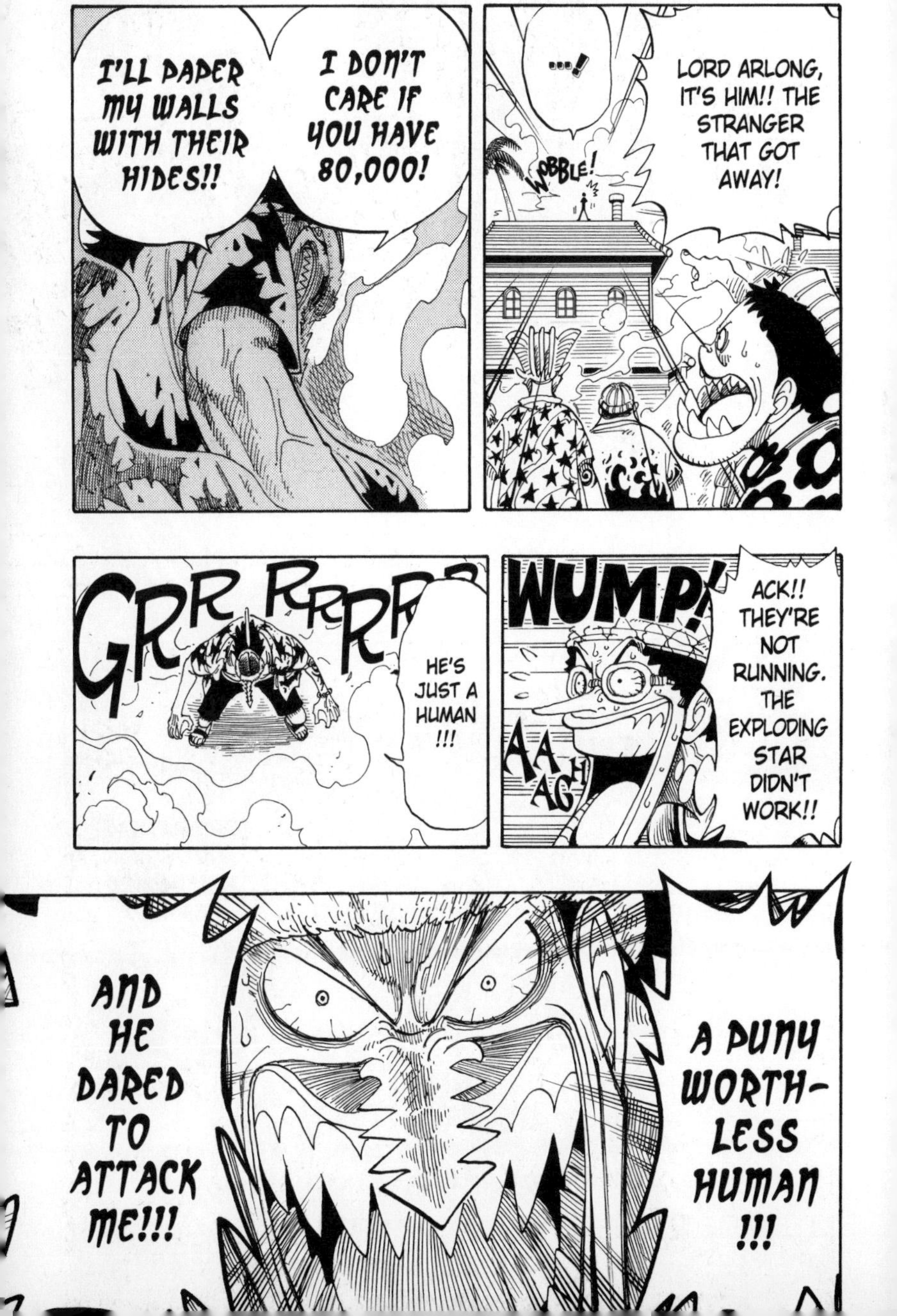
...!
WOBBLE!
LORD ARLONG, IT'S HIM!! THE STRANGER THAT GOT AWAY!
I DON'T CARE IF YOU HAVE 80,000!
I'LL PAPER MY WALLS WITH THEIR HIDES!!
WUMP!
ACK!! THEY'RE NOT RUNNING. THE EXPLODING STAR DIDN'T WORK!!
AAAGH!
HE'S JUST A HUMAN!!!
GRR RRRRR
A PUNY WORTH-LESS HUMAN!!!
AND HE DARED TO ATTACK ME!!!

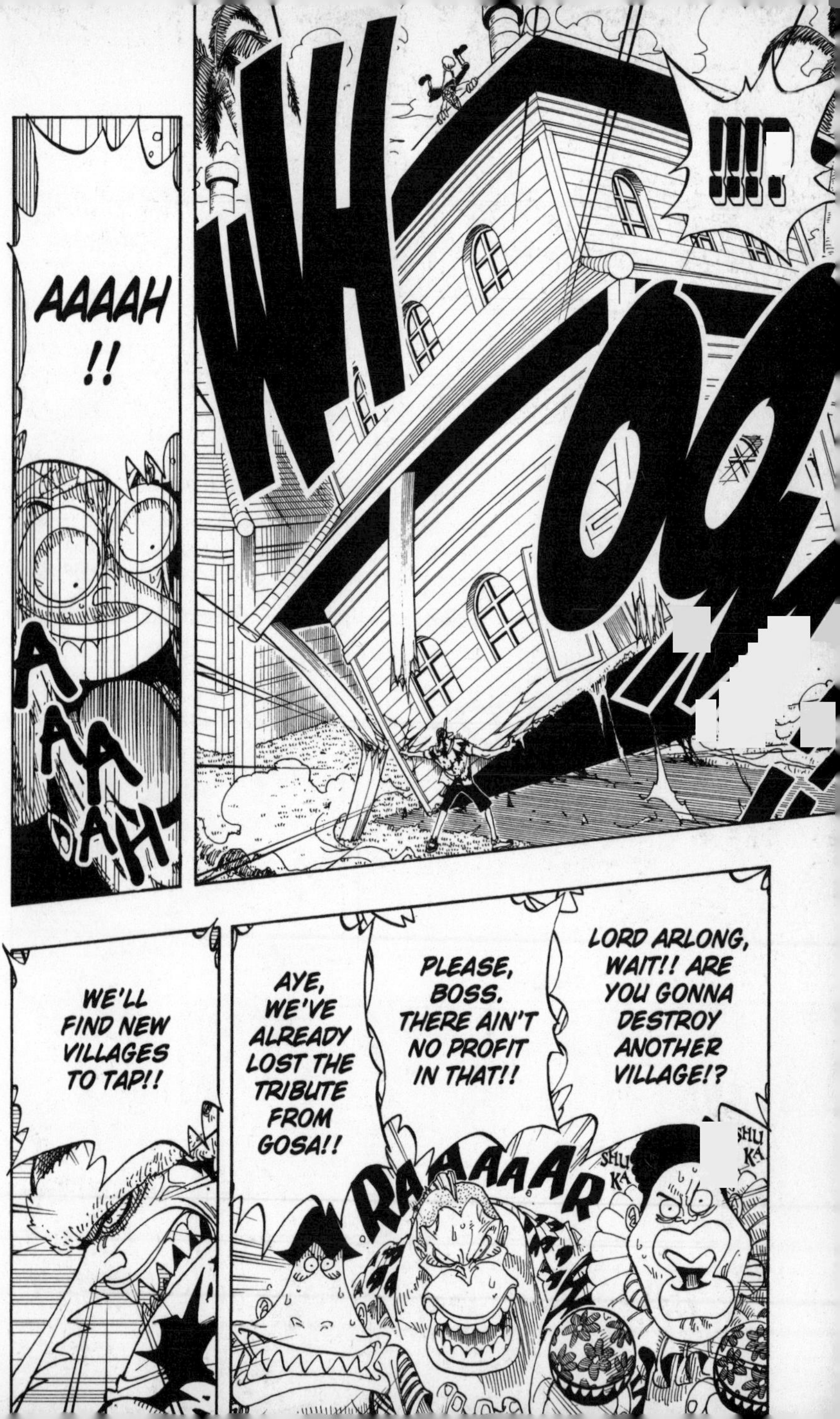
!!!?
AAAAH !!
AAAAH
LORD ARLONG, WAIT!! ARE YOU GONNA DESTROY ANOTHER VILLAGE!?
PLEASE, BOSS. THERE AIN'T NO PROFIT IN THAT!!
AYE, WE'VE ALREADY LOST THE TRIBUTE FROM GOSA!!
SHU KA
SHU KA
RAAAAAAR
WE'LL FIND NEW VILLAGES TO TAP!!

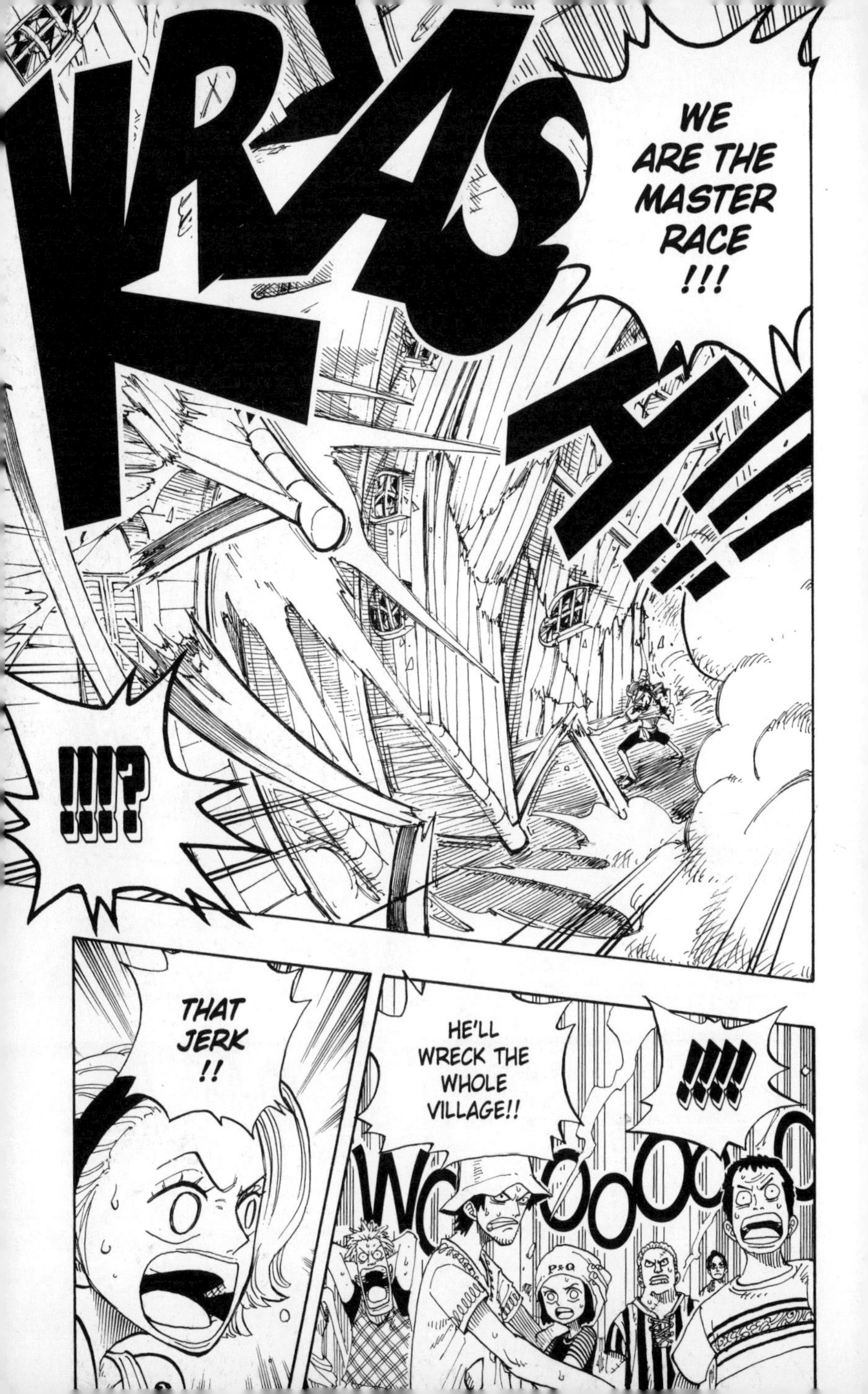

KRASH!!!
WE ARE THE MASTER RACE!!!
!!!?
!!!!
HE'LL WRECK THE WHOLE VILLAGE!!
WOOOOOO
THAT JERK!!

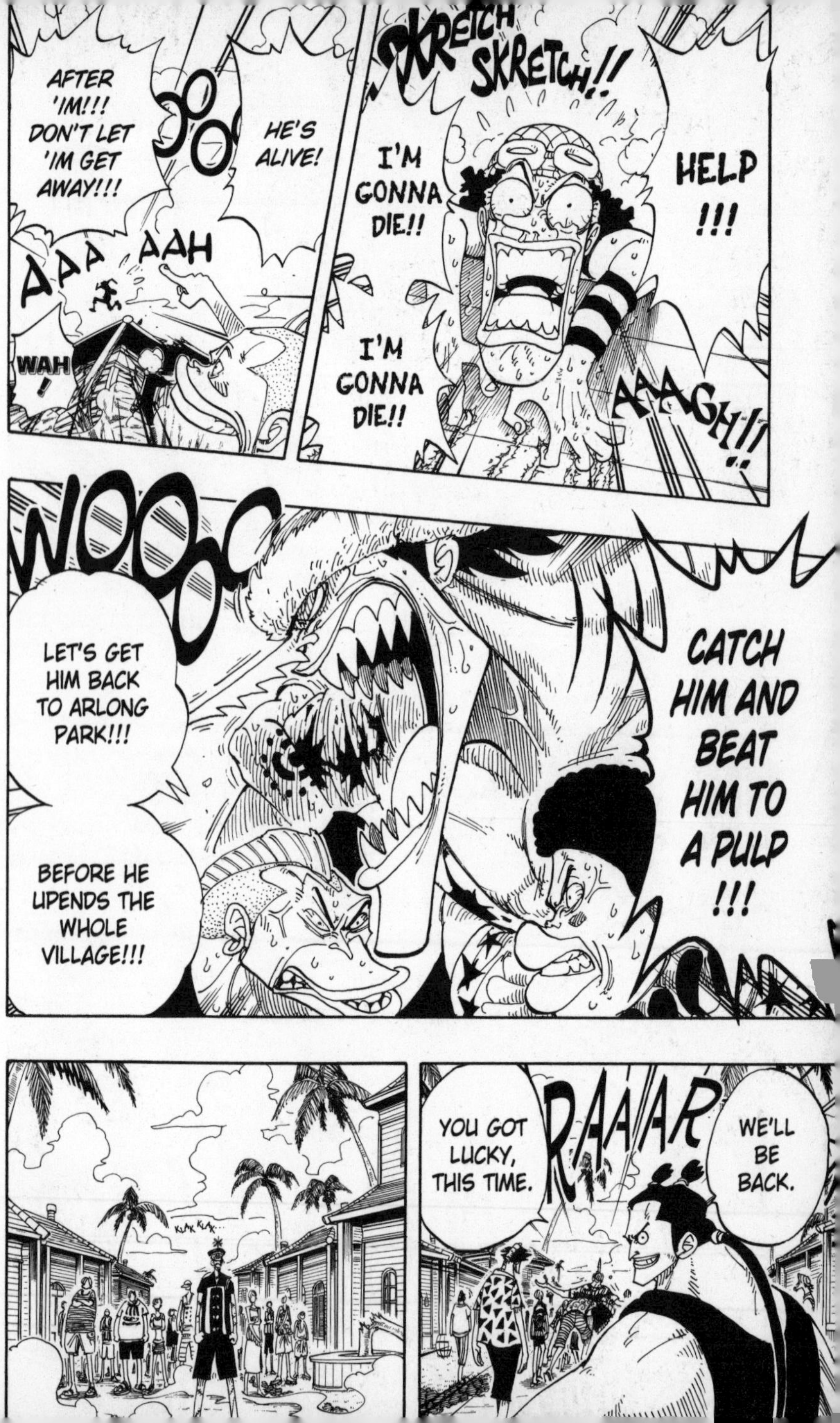
SKRETCH SKRETCH!!
HELP!!!
I'M GONNA DIE!!
I'M GONNA DIE!!
AAAGH!!!
HE'S ALIVE!
AFTER 'IM!!! DON'T LET 'IM GET AWAY!!!
AAH
WAH!
WOOO
CATCH HIM AND BEAT HIM TO A PULP!!!
LET'S GET HIM BACK TO ARLONG PARK!!!
BEFORE HE UPENDS THE WHOLE VILLAGE!!!
WE'LL BE BACK.
RAAAR
YOU GOT LUCKY, THIS TIME.
KLAK KLAK...

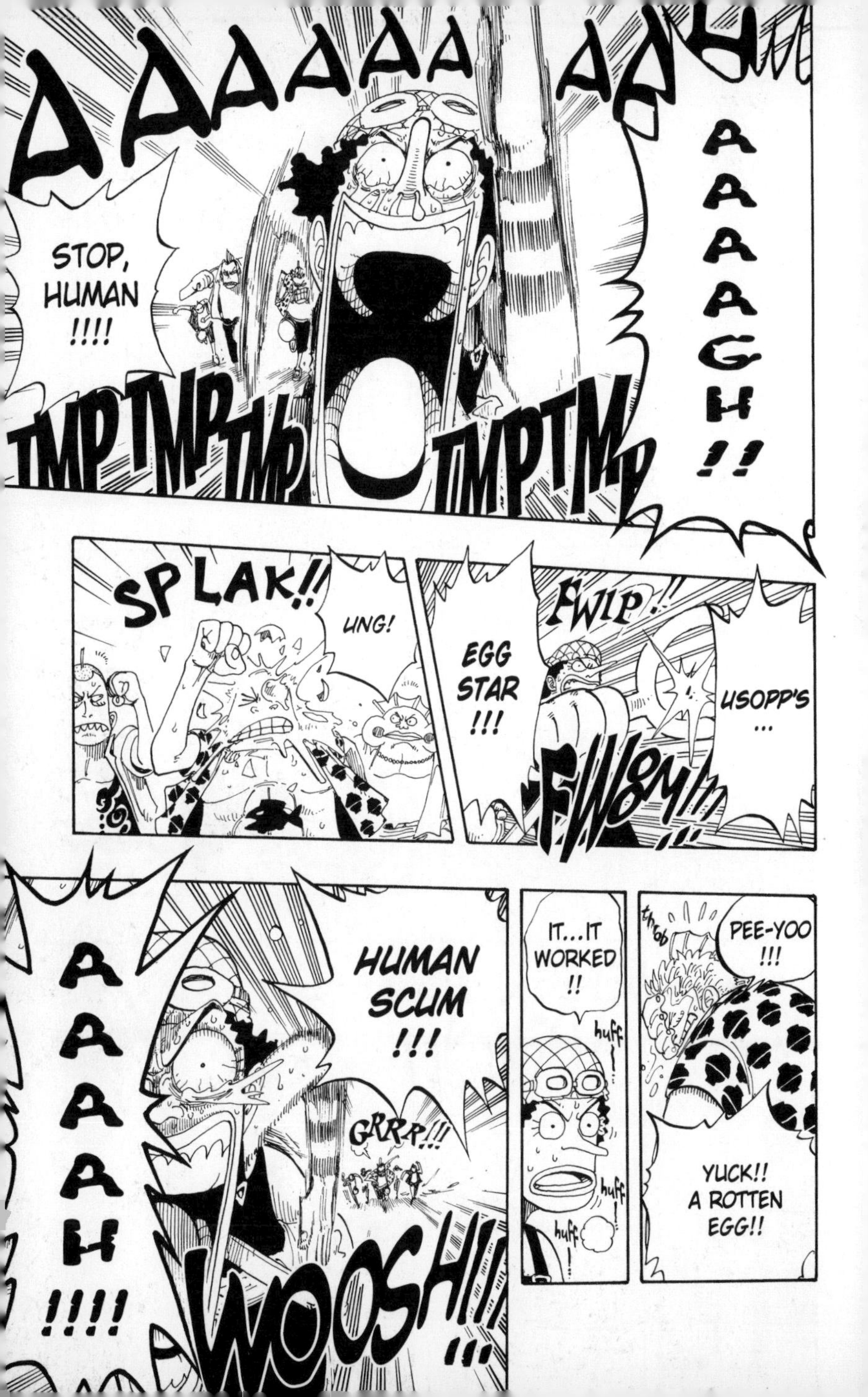
AAAAAA AAY
AAAAGH!!
STOP, HUMAN!!!!
TMP TMP TMP TMP
TMPTMP
USOPP'S...
EGG STAR!!!
FWIP!!
FWOM!!
SPLAK!!
UNG!
PEE-YOO!!!
throb
YUCK!! A ROTTEN EGG!!
IT...IT WORKED!!
huff
huff
huff
AAAAAH!!!!
HUMAN SCUM!!!
GRRR!!!
WOOSH!!!

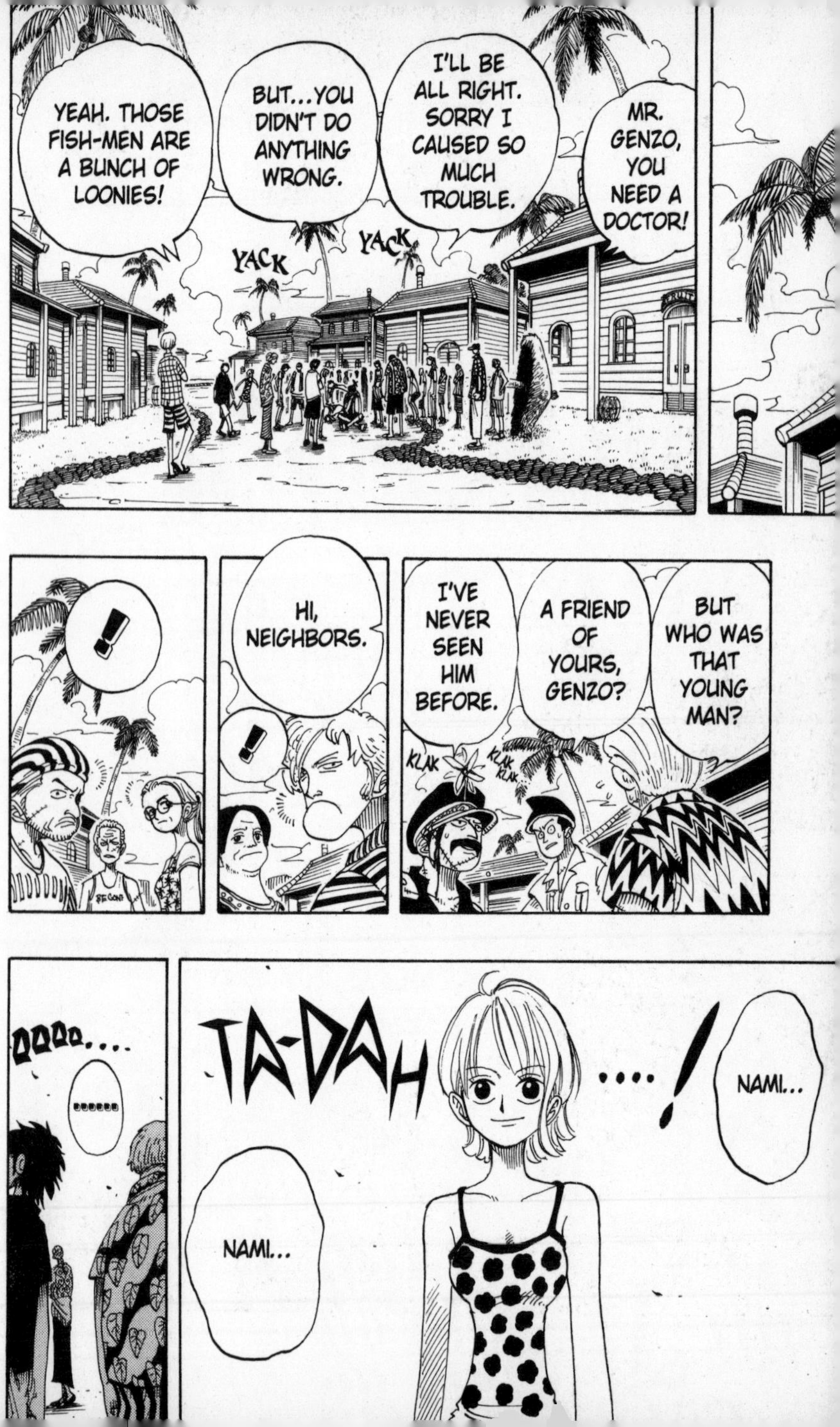
MR. GENZO, YOU NEED A DOCTOR!
I'LL BE ALL RIGHT. SORRY I CAUSED SO MUCH TROUBLE.
YACK
YACK
BUT...YOU DIDN'T DO ANYTHING WRONG.
YEAH. THOSE FISH-MEN ARE A BUNCH OF LOONIES!
BUT WHO WAS THAT YOUNG MAN?
A FRIEND OF YOURS, GENZO?
KLAK KLAK
I'VE NEVER SEEN HIM BEFORE.
KLAK
HI, NEIGHBORS.
!
!
NAMI...
....!
TA-DAH
NAMI...
OOOO....
......

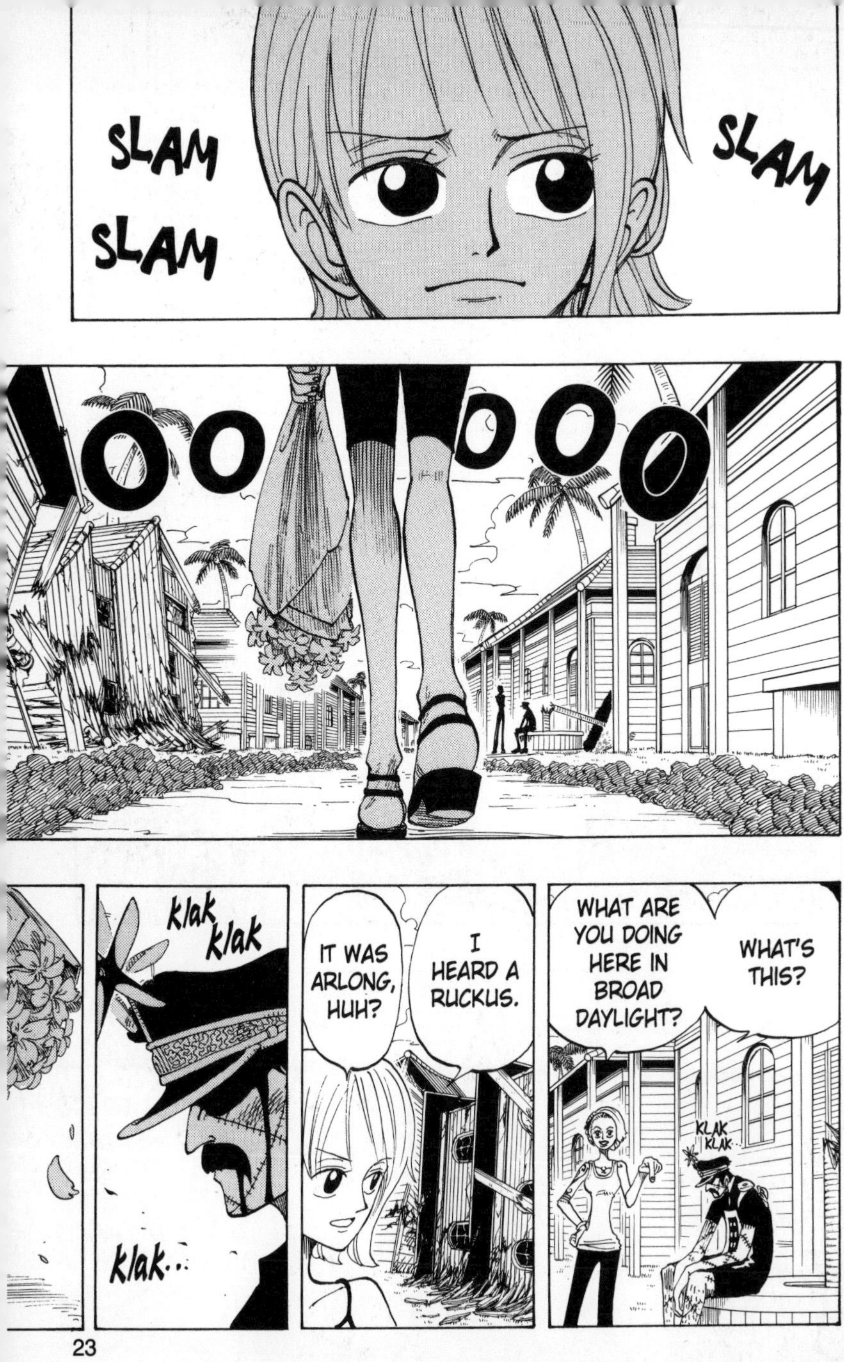
SLAM
SLAM
SLAM
DOOO
WHAT'S THIS?
WHAT ARE YOU DOING HERE IN BROAD DAYLIGHT?
KLAK KLAK...
I HEARD A RUCKUS.
IT WAS ARLONG, HUH?
klak klak
klak...

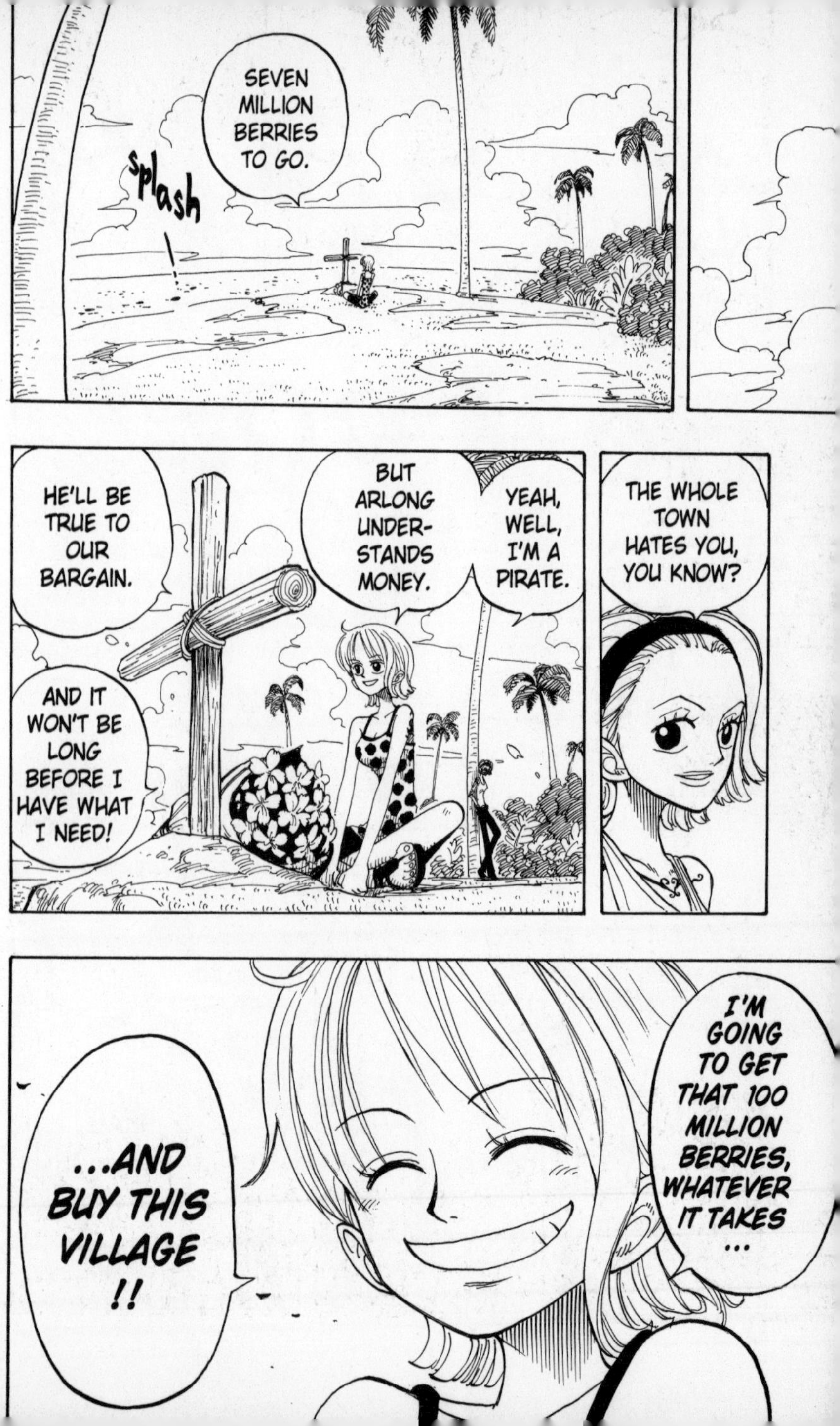
SEVEN MILLION BERRIES TO GO.
splash
THE WHOLE TOWN HATES YOU, YOU KNOW?
YEAH, WELL, I'M A PIRATE.
BUT ARLONG UNDER-STANDS MONEY.
HE'LL BE TRUE TO OUR BARGAIN.
AND IT WON'T BE LONG BEFORE I HAVE WHAT I NEED!
I'M GOING TO GET THAT 100 MILLION BERRIES, WHATEVER IT TAKES ...
...AND BUY THIS VILLAGE !!

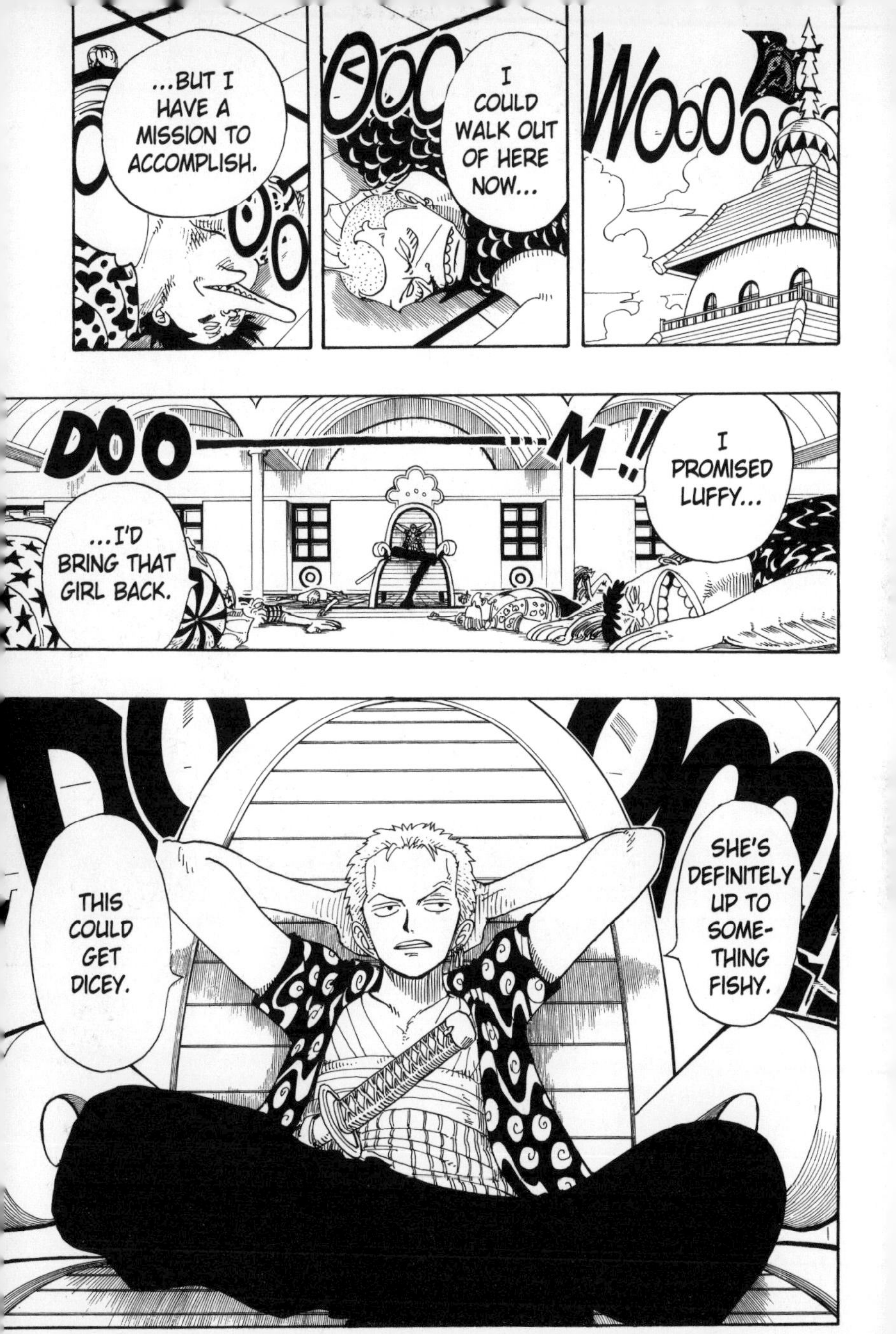
WOOOO
I COULD WALK OUT OF HERE NOW...
...BUT I HAVE A MISSION TO ACCOMPLISH.
DOO—M!!
I PROMISED LUFFY...
...I'D BRING THAT GIRL BACK.
SHE'S DEFINITELY UP TO SOME-THING FISHY.
THIS COULD GET DICEY.

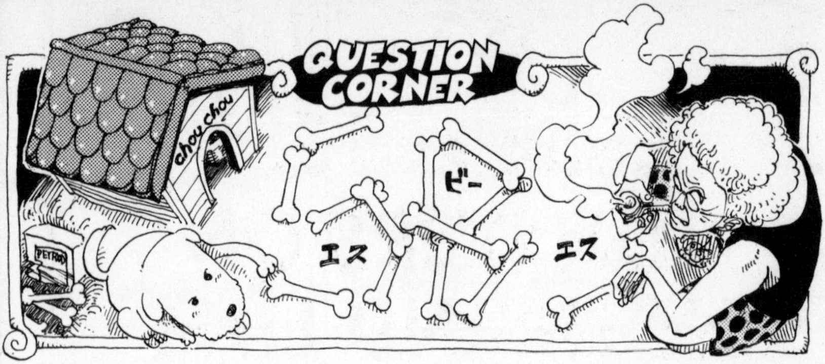
QUESTION CORNER
chou chou
エス
ビー
エス

Q: Sensei, Zeff's mustache-braids won't stop growing! Please tell me how to make them stop.

A: Don't worry!! Sit back and enjoy Question Corner!!

Q: Dear Oda Sensei, I always enjoy **One Piece** very much! By the way, in the third panel on page 18 of Volume 7, there seems to be some writing on the knife that Sanji is holding, but I can't make out what it says. What's written there? Please tell me!!

A: You couldn't read it because I wrote it so that no one could read it. Still, I'm impressed that you spotted it. I'll confess. I did in fact write **Fist of the North Star**. It's a great manga that I was crazy about in elementary school. Do you know it?

Q: One day I was seized by a sudden strong urge to participate in SBS Question Corner!! So please read this. Oda Sensei, are you "crap"-crazy? You have Sanji say it an awful lot!!

A: Heavens! What a filthy, nasty word! I'm embarrassed to even read it!! Please stop!!

Q: When reading Usopp's tale, Merry's words moved me so that I unexpectedly found myself crying like a strong man (even though I'm a girl). The tears ran down my cheeks and got in my mouth. Know what they tasted like?

A: Eyes cream?

Q: I heard that Sanji's favorite snack is cake.

A: It is?

Chapter 73: MONSTERS OF THE GRAND LINE

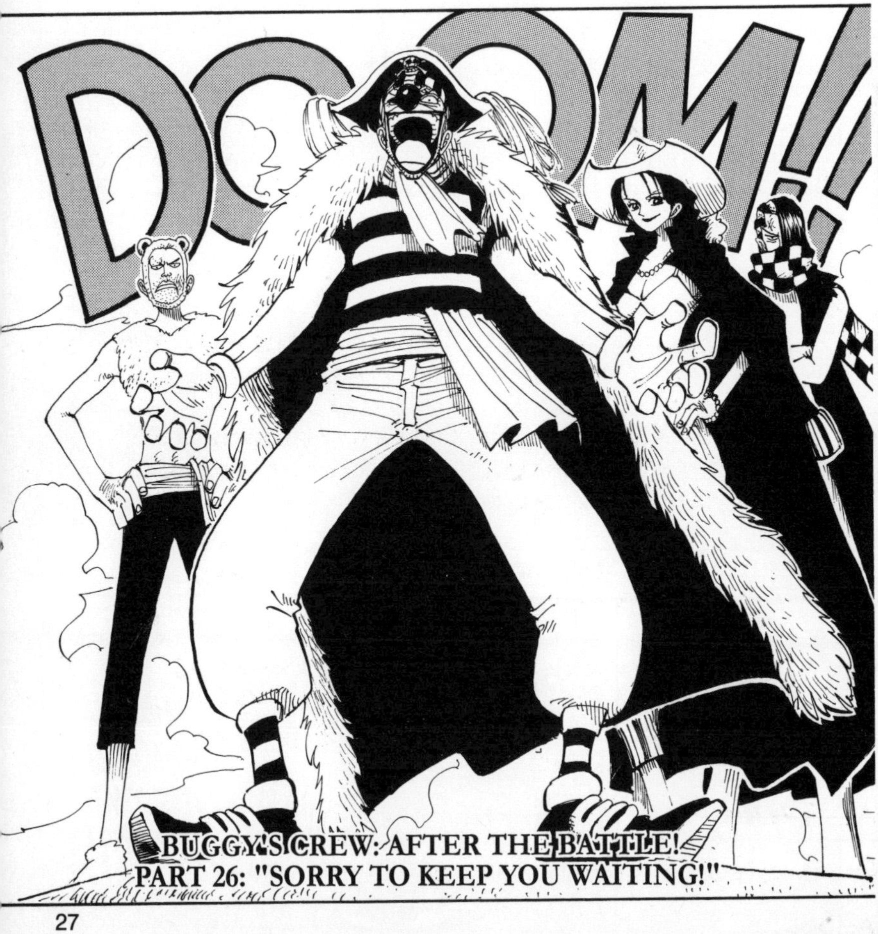
DOOM!!
BUGGY'S CREW: AFTER THE BATTLE!
PART 26: "SORRY TO KEEP YOU WAITING!"

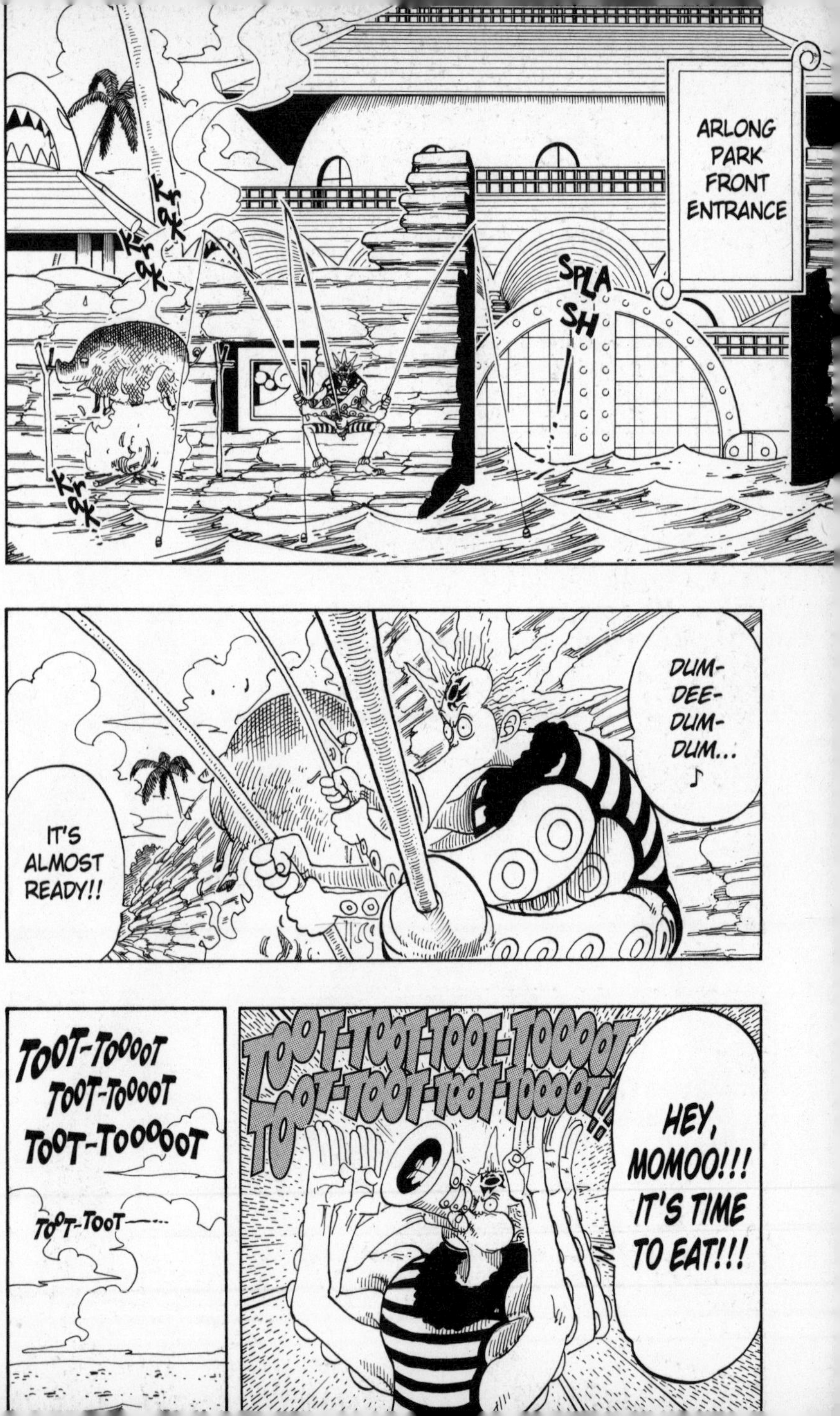
ARLONG PARK FRONT ENTRANCE
SPLASH
KRAK
KRAK
KRAK
DUM-DEE-DUM-DUM... ♪
IT'S ALMOST READY!!
HEY, MOMOO!!! IT'S TIME TO EAT!!!
TOOT-TOOT-TOOT-TOOOOT
TOOT-TOOT-TOOT-TOOOOT!!
TOOT-TOOOOT
TOOT-TOOOOT
TOOT-TOOOOOT
TOOT-TOOT---

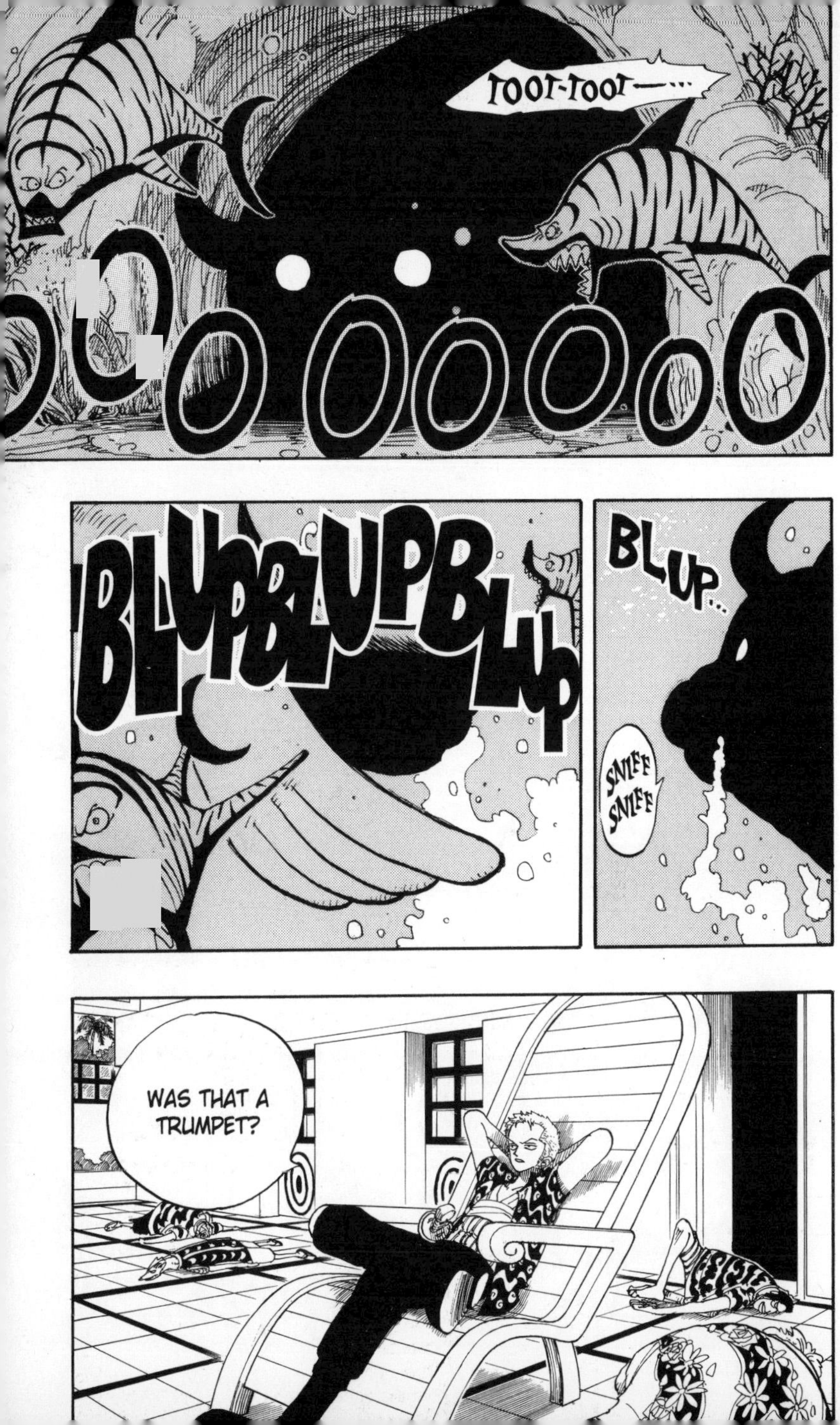
TOOT-TOOT—...
OOOOOOOO
BLUP...
SNIFF SNIFF
BLUPBLUPBLUP
WAS THAT A TRUMPET?

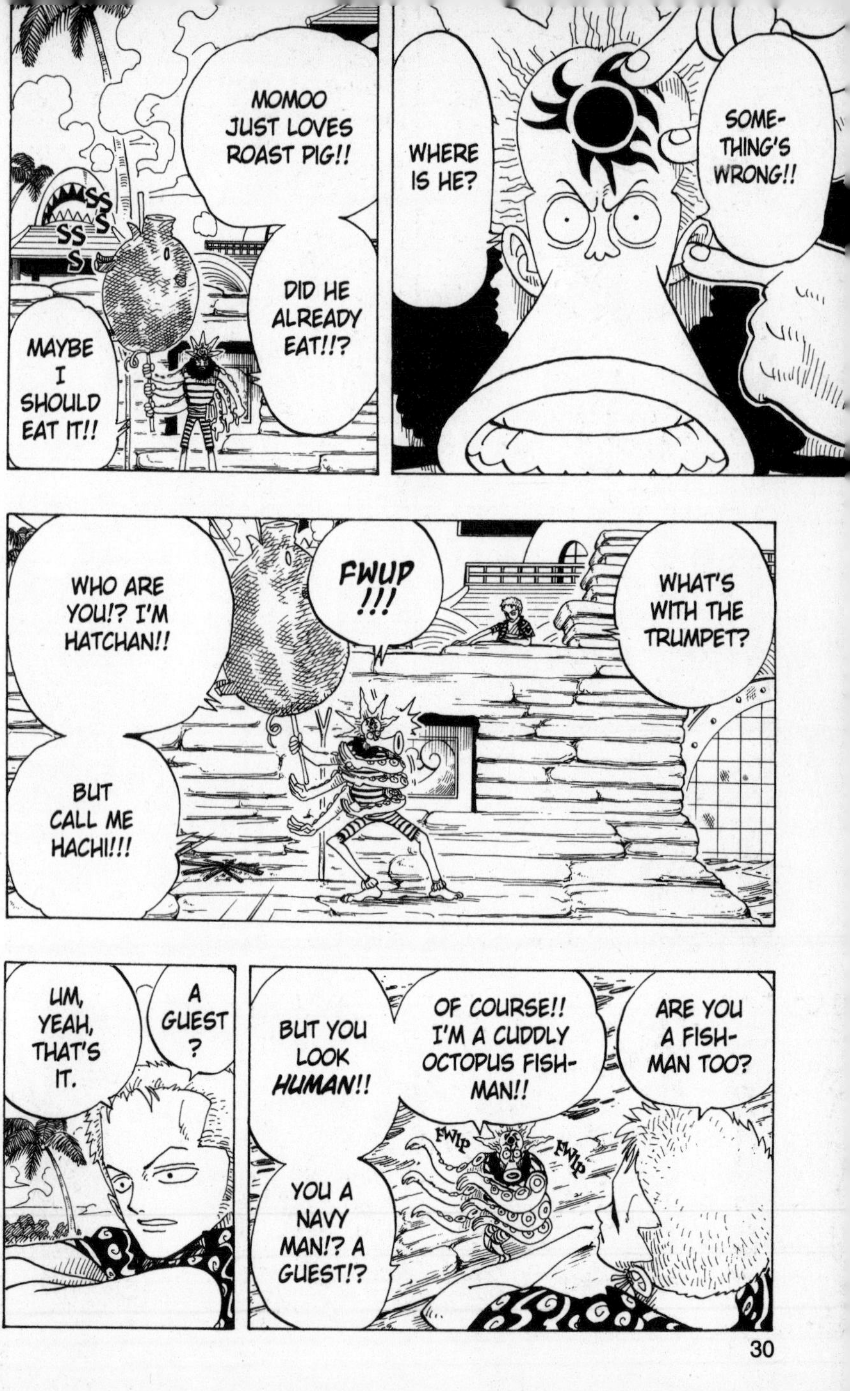
SOMETHING'S WRONG!!
WHERE IS HE?
MOMOO JUST LOVES ROAST PIG!!
DID HE ALREADY EAT!!?
SSSSS
MAYBE I SHOULD EAT IT!!
WHAT'S WITH THE TRUMPET?
FWUP!!!
WHO ARE YOU!? I'M HATCHAN!!
BUT CALL ME HACHI!!!
ARE YOU A FISH-MAN TOO?
OF COURSE!! I'M A CUDDLY OCTOPUS FISH-MAN!!
BUT YOU LOOK *HUMAN*!!
FWIP FWIP
YOU A NAVY MAN!? A GUEST!?
A GUEST?
UM, YEAH, THAT'S IT.

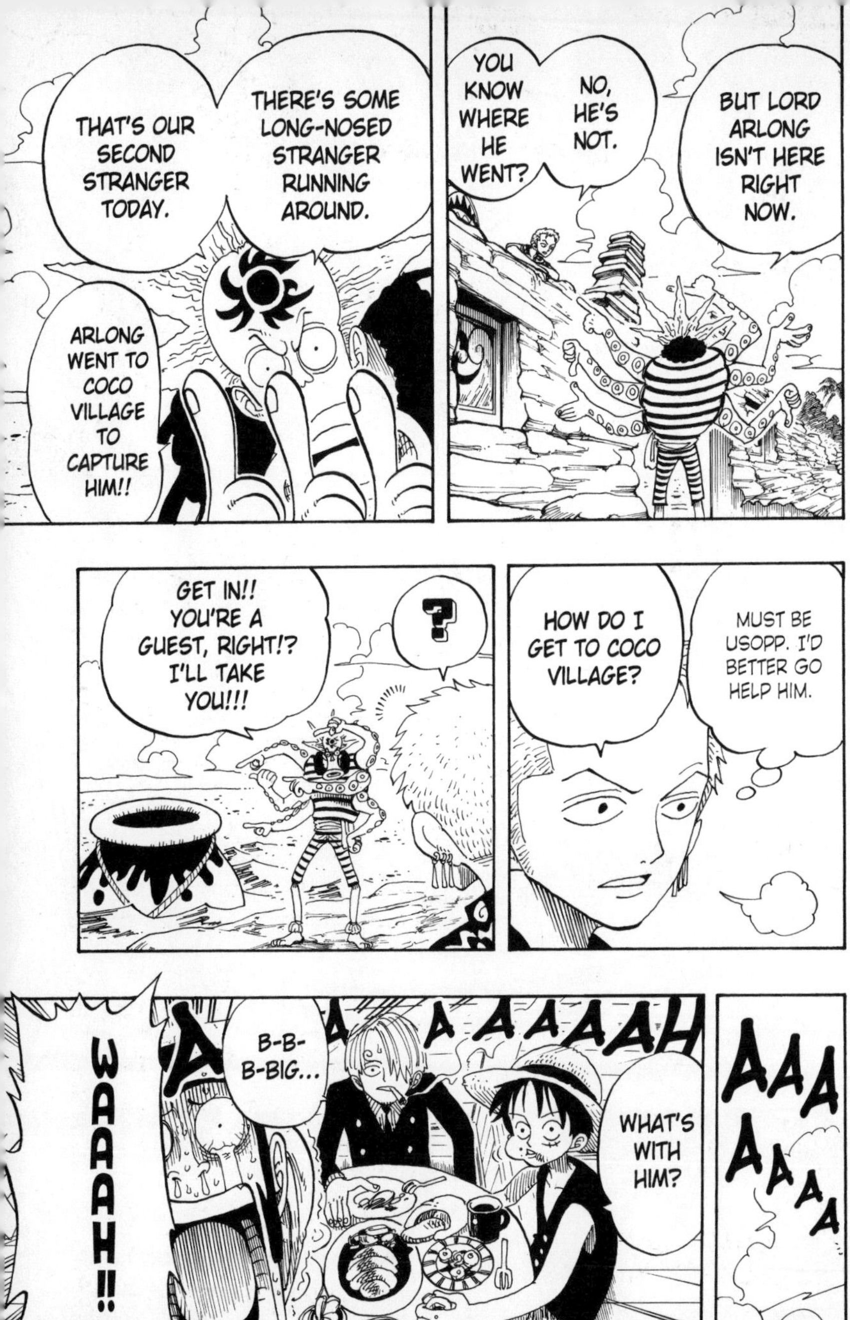
BUT LORD ARLONG ISN'T HERE RIGHT NOW.
NO, HE'S NOT.
YOU KNOW WHERE HE WENT?
THERE'S SOME LONG-NOSED STRANGER RUNNING AROUND.
THAT'S OUR SECOND STRANGER TODAY.
ARLONG WENT TO COCO VILLAGE TO CAPTURE HIM!!
MUST BE USOPP. I'D BETTER GO HELP HIM.
HOW DO I GET TO COCO VILLAGE?
?
GET IN!! YOU'RE A GUEST, RIGHT!? I'LL TAKE YOU!!!
AAAAAAA
AAAAAAH
WHAT'S WITH HIM?
B-B-B-BIG...
WAAAAH!!

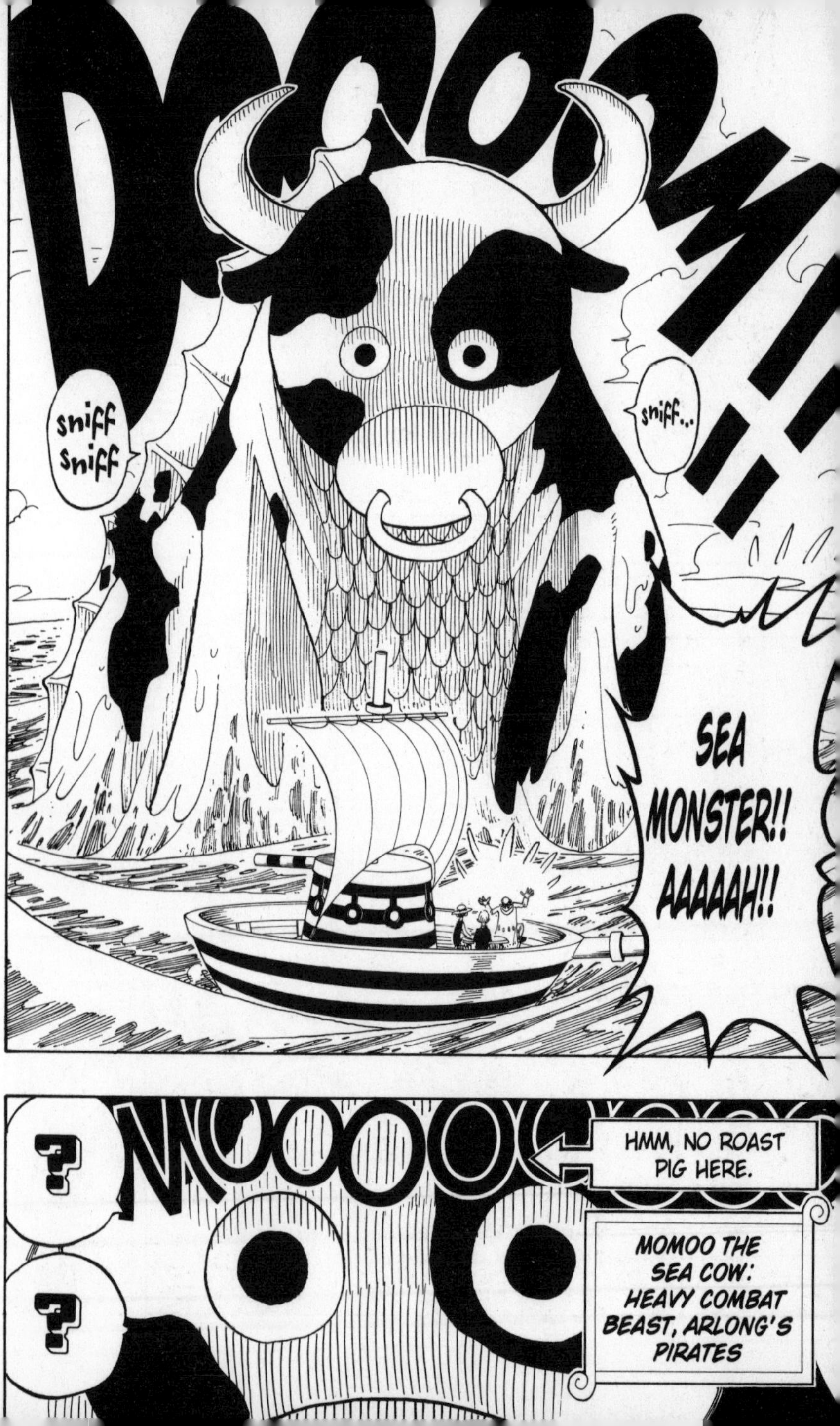
DOOOOM!!!
SEA MONSTER!! AAAAAH!!
sniff...
sniff sniff
HMM, NO ROAST PIG HERE.
MOMOO THE SEA COW: HEAVY COMBAT BEAST, ARLONG'S PIRATES
MOOOO
?
?

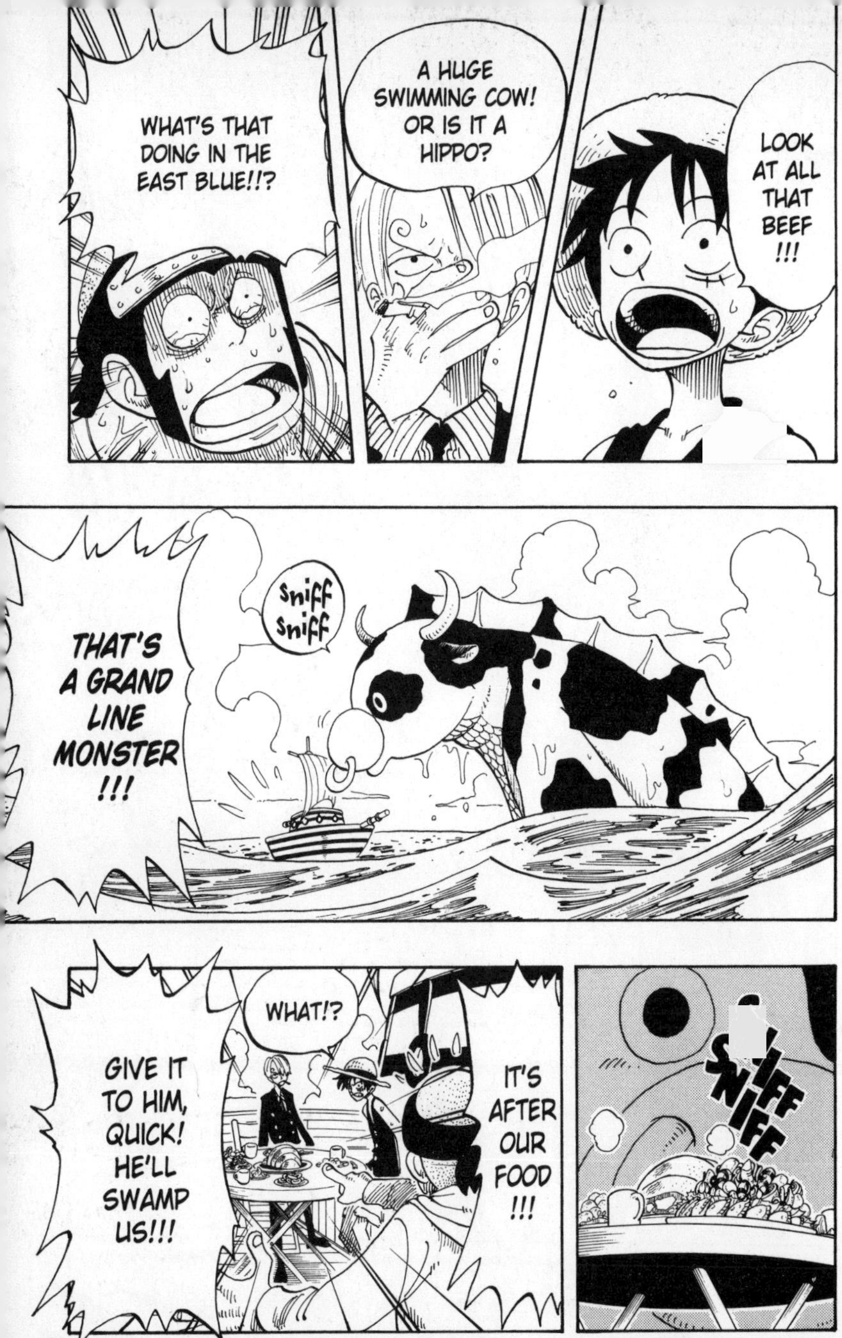
LOOK AT ALL THAT BEEF!!!
A HUGE SWIMMING COW! OR IS IT A HIPPO?
WHAT'S THAT DOING IN THE EAST BLUE!!?
Sniff sniff
THAT'S A GRAND LINE MONSTER!!!
SNIFF SNIFF
WHAT!?
IT'S AFTER OUR FOOD!!!
GIVE IT TO HIM, QUICK! HE'LL SWAMP US!!!

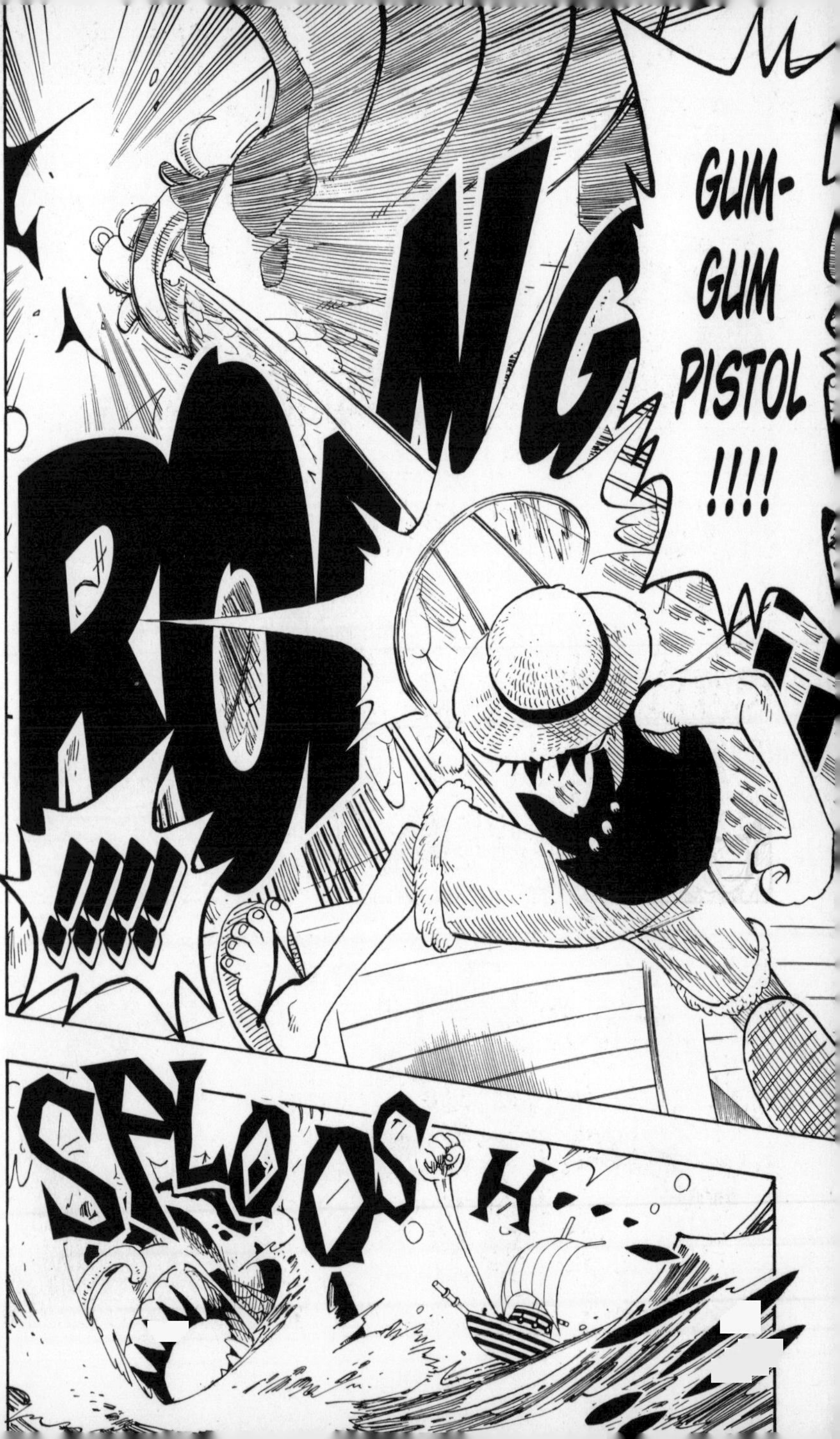
GUM-GUM PISTOL!!!!
BOING!!!!
SPLOOSH

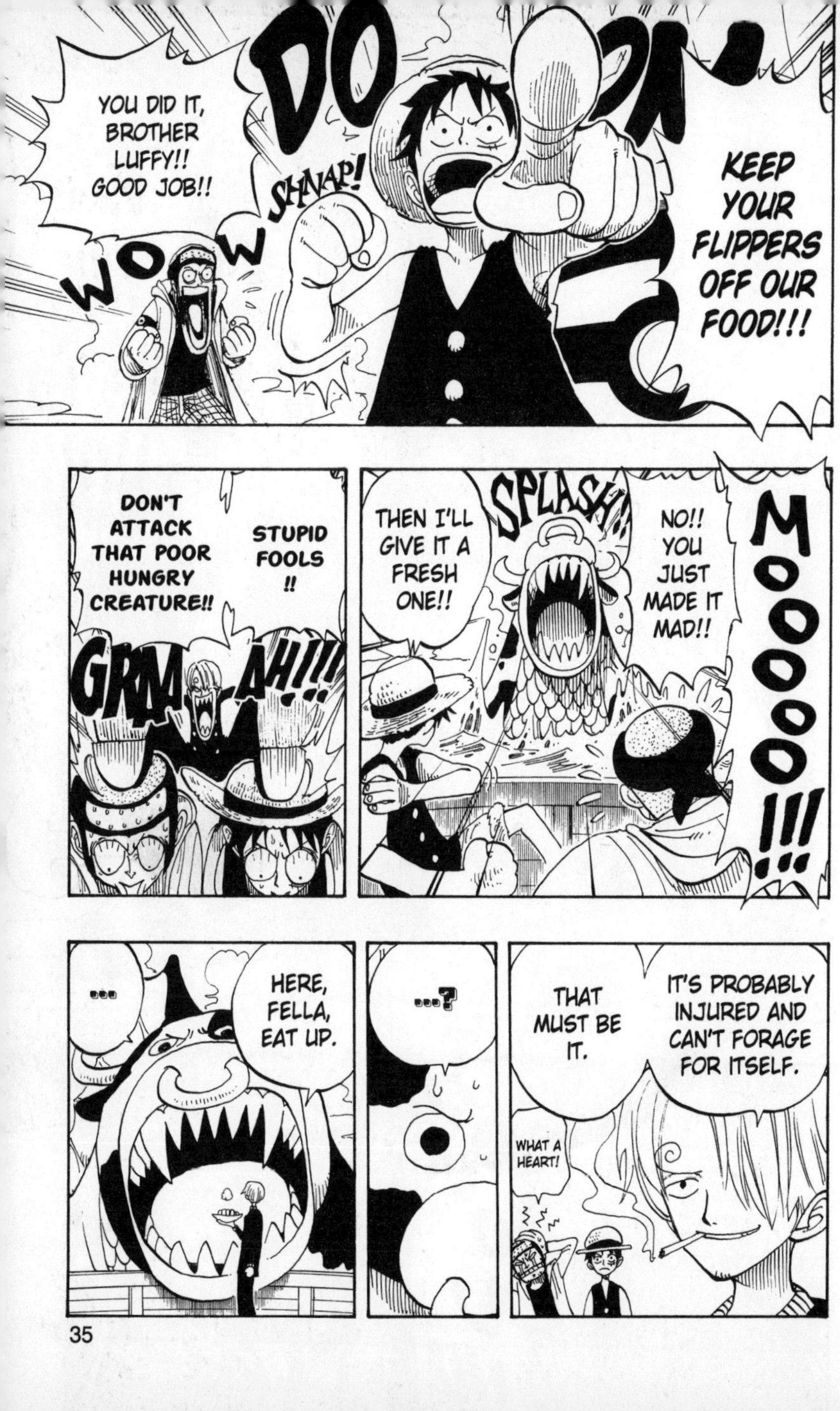
DOOM!
KEEP YOUR FLIPPERS OFF OUR FOOD!!!
SHNAP!
YOU DID IT, BROTHER LUFFY!! GOOD JOB!!
WOW
MOOOOO!!!
NO!! YOU JUST MADE IT MAD!!
SPLASH!!
THEN I'LL GIVE IT A FRESH ONE!!
STUPID FOOLS!!
DON'T ATTACK THAT POOR HUNGRY CREATURE!!
GRAAAH!!!
IT'S PROBABLY INJURED AND CAN'T FORAGE FOR ITSELF.
THAT MUST BE IT.
WHAT A HEART!
...?
HERE, FELLA, EAT UP.
...

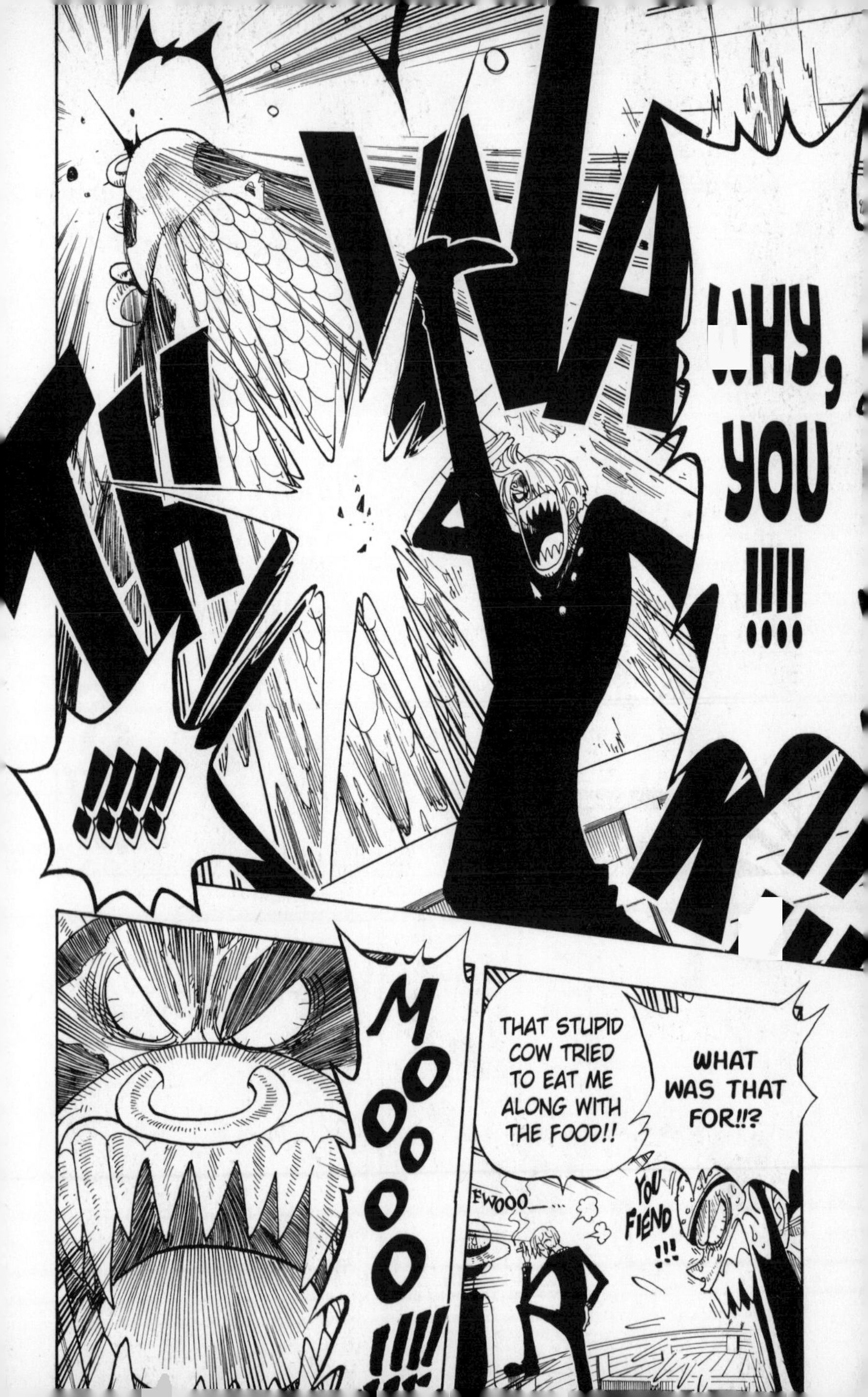

WHY, YOU!!!!
THWAK!!!!
WHAT WAS THAT FOR!!?
THAT STUPID COW TRIED TO EAT ME ALONG WITH THE FOOD!!
YOU FIEND!!!
FWOOO_...
MOOOOOO!!!!

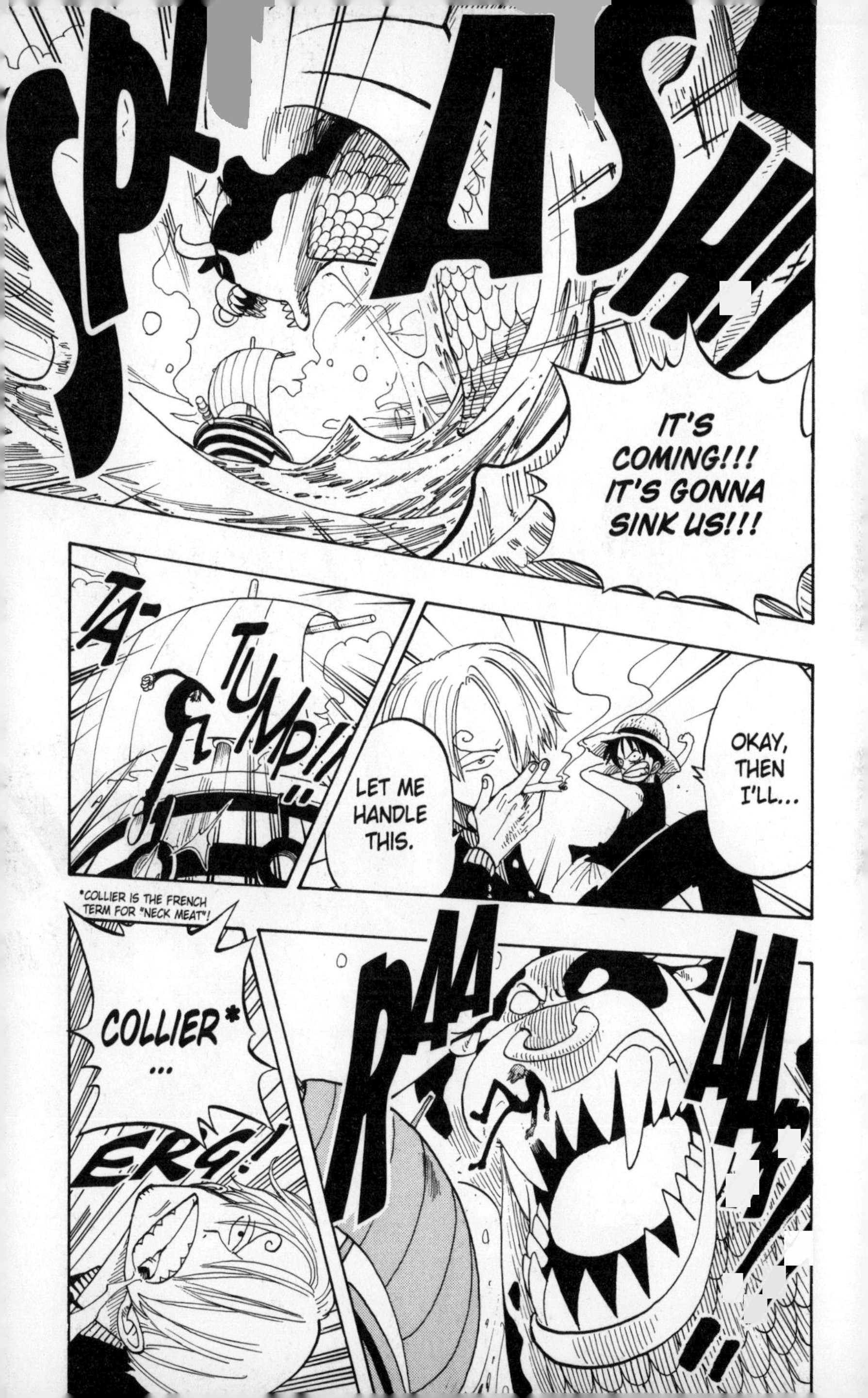
SPLASH!!
IT'S COMING!!! IT'S GONNA SINK US!!!
OKAY, THEN I'LL...
LET ME HANDLE THIS.
TA-TUMP!!
RAAAA!!
COLLIER* ...
ERG!
*COLLIER IS THE FRENCH TERM FOR "NECK MEAT"!

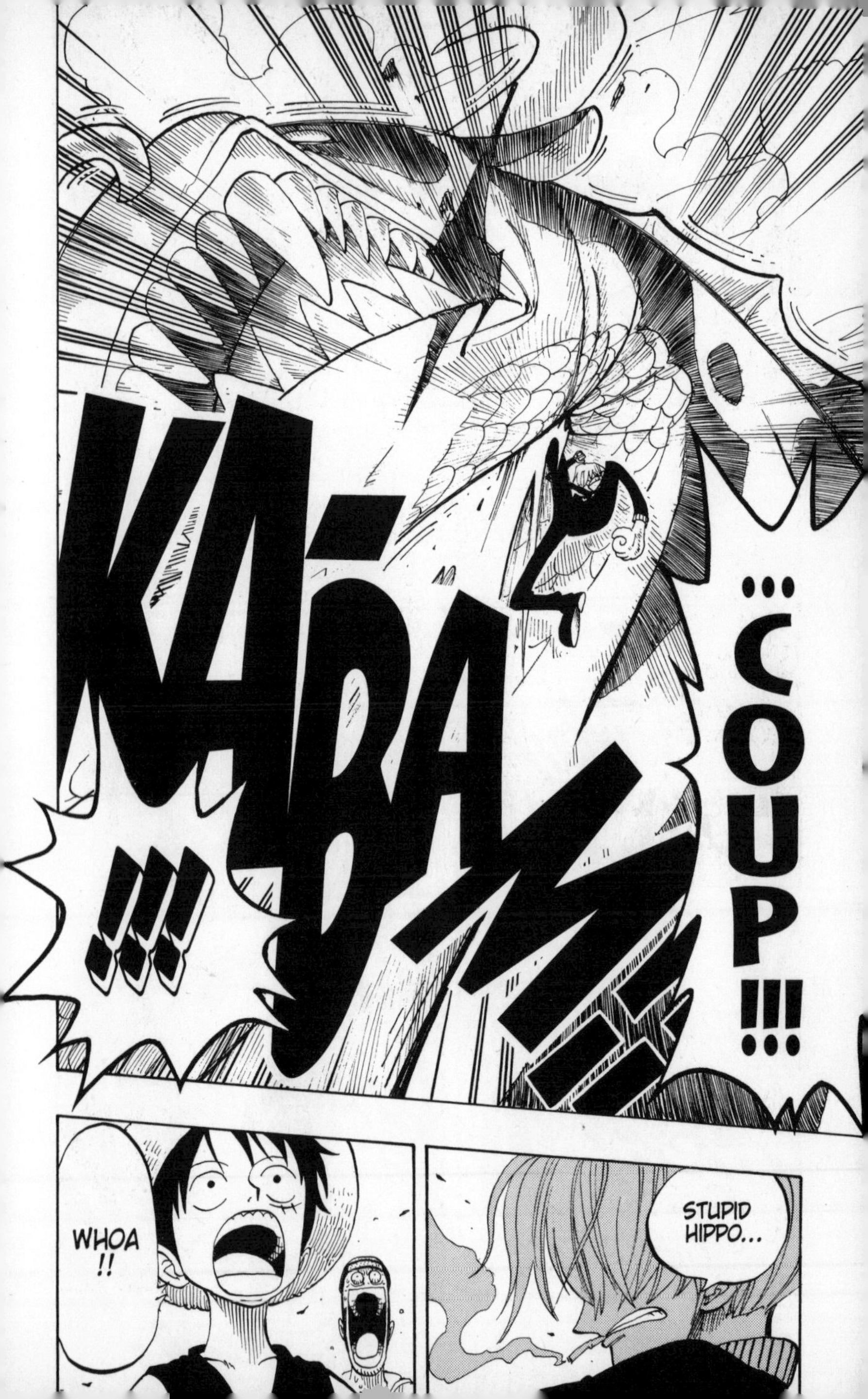
...COUP!!!
KABAM!!!
STUPID HIPPO...
WHOA !!

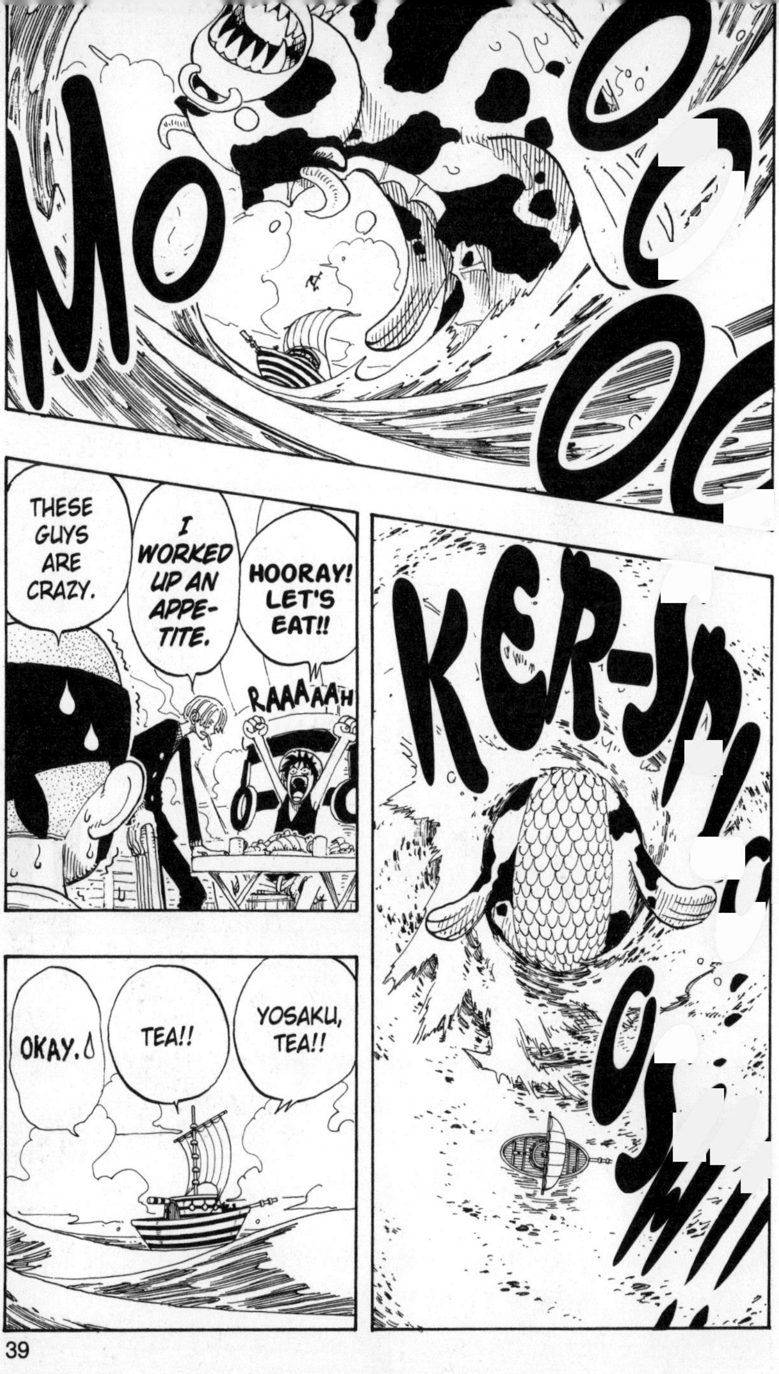
MOOOO
KER-SPLOOSH!!
HOORAY! LET'S EAT!!
RAAAAAH
I WORKED UP AN APPE-TITE.
THESE GUYS ARE CRAZY.
YOSAKU, TEA!!
TEA!!
OKAY.

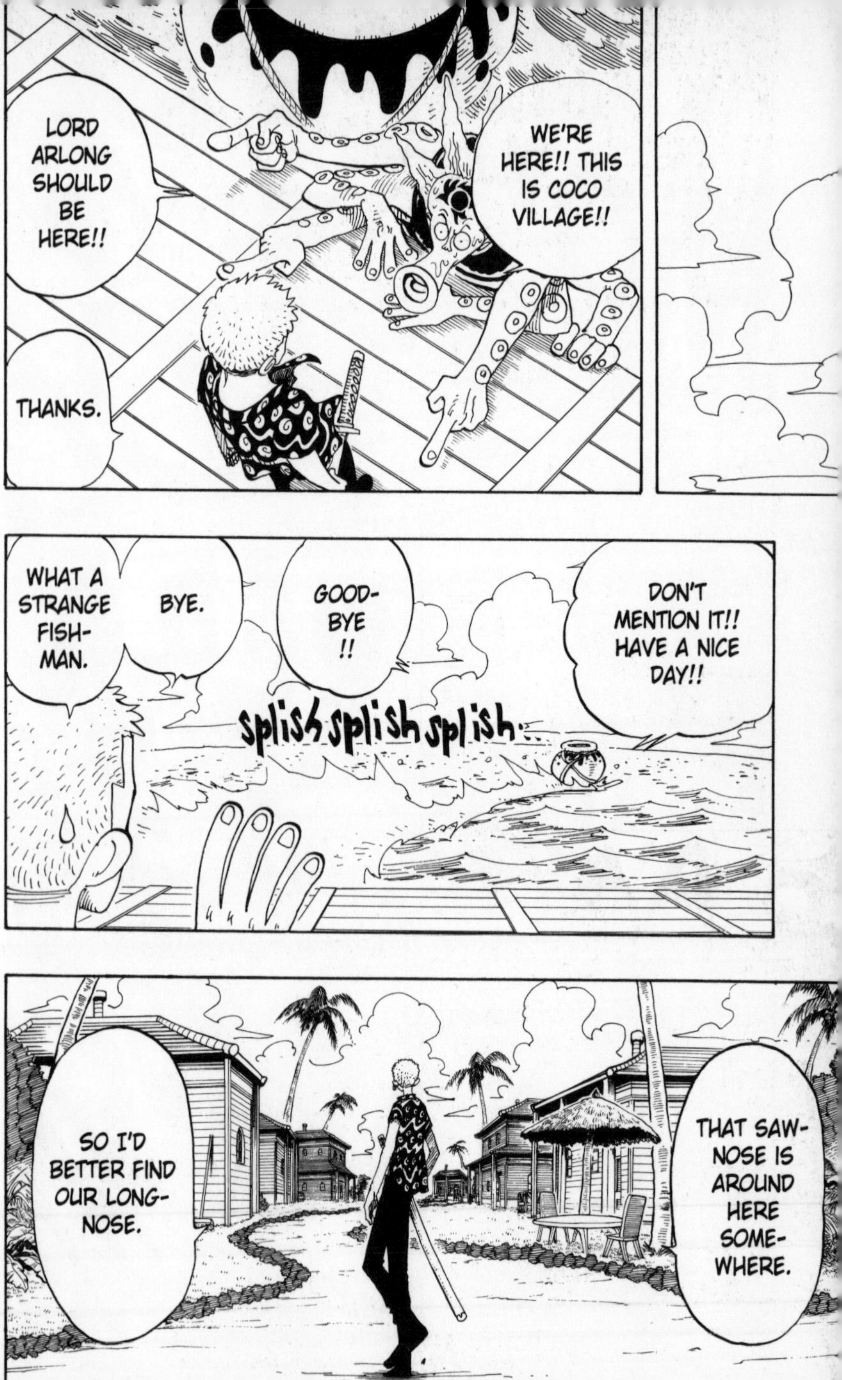
WE'RE HERE!! THIS IS COCO VILLAGE!!
LORD ARLONG SHOULD BE HERE!!
THANKS.
DON'T MENTION IT!! HAVE A NICE DAY!!
GOOD-BYE !!
BYE.
WHAT A STRANGE FISH-MAN.
splish splish splish
THAT SAW-NOSE IS AROUND HERE SOME-WHERE.
SO I'D BETTER FIND OUR LONG-NOSE.

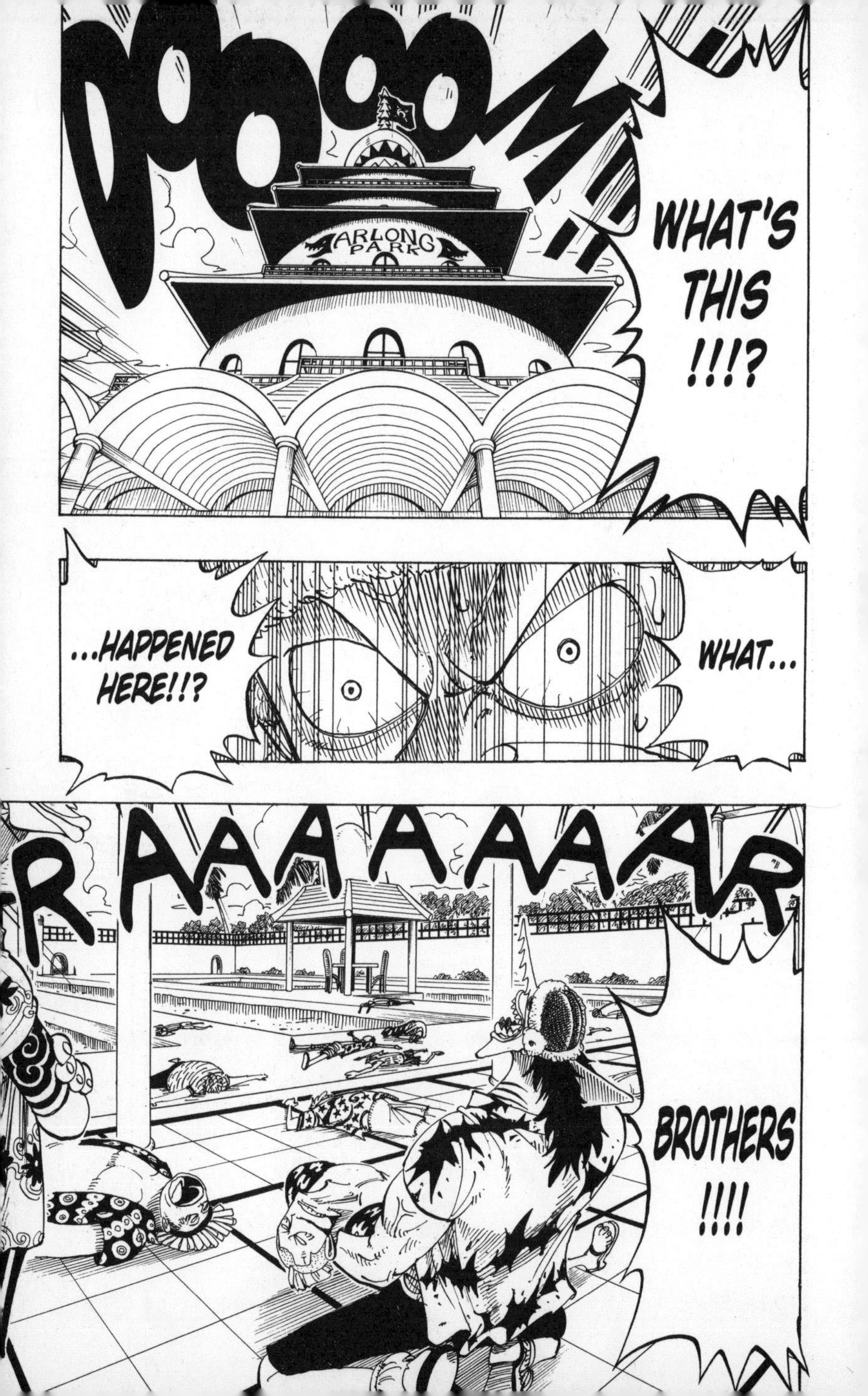
DOOOOM!!
WHAT'S THIS!!!?
WHAT...
...HAPPENED HERE!!?
RAAAAAAAR
BROTHERS!!!!

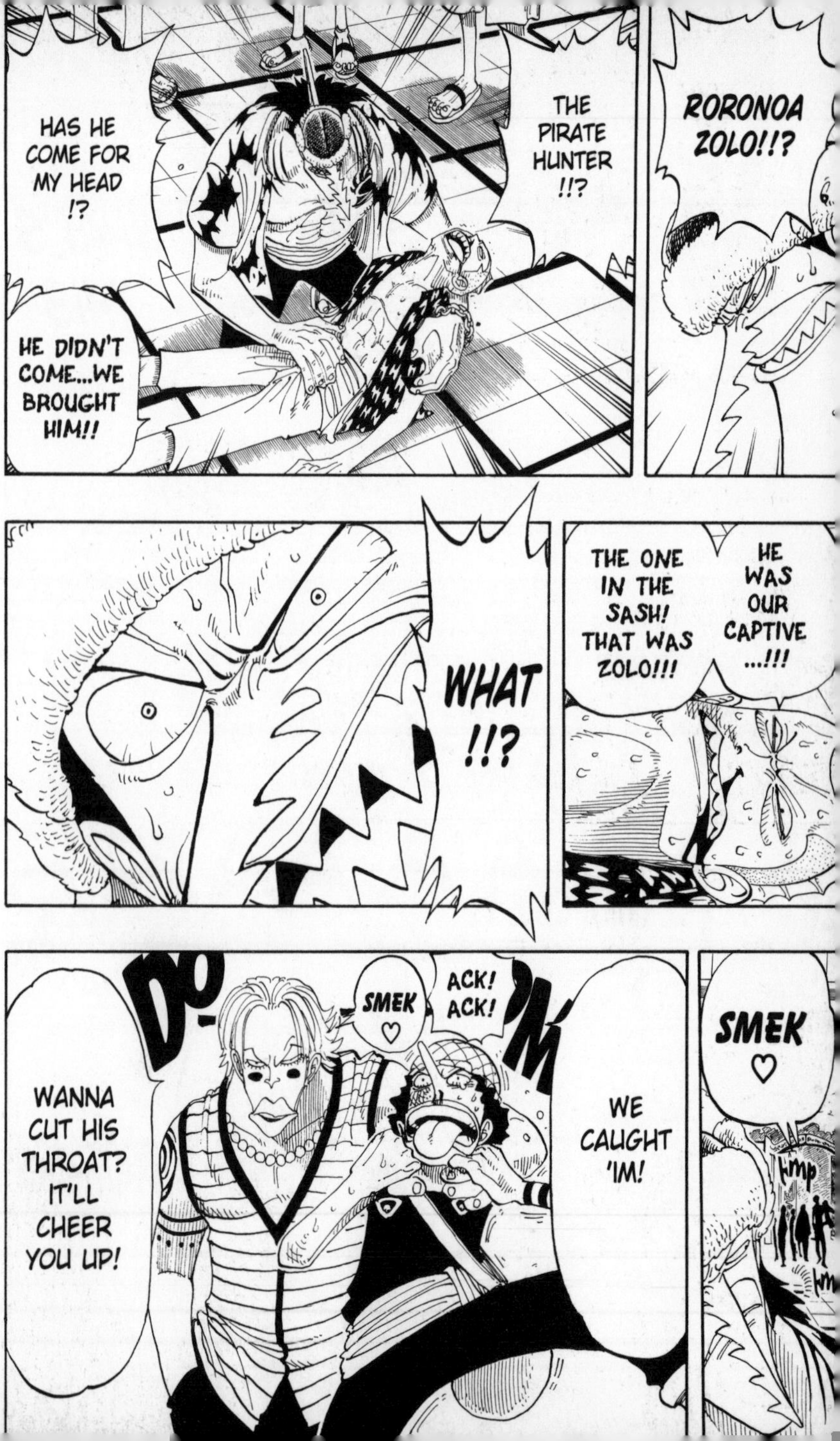

RORONOA ZOLO!!?
THE PIRATE HUNTER !!?
HAS HE COME FOR MY HEAD !?
HE DIDN'T COME...WE BROUGHT HIM!!
HE WAS OUR CAPTIVE ...!!!
THE ONE IN THE SASH! THAT WAS ZOLO!!!
WHAT !!?
SMEK ♡
WE CAUGHT 'IM!
ACK! ACK!
SMEK ♡
WANNA CUT HIS THROAT? IT'LL CHEER YOU UP!

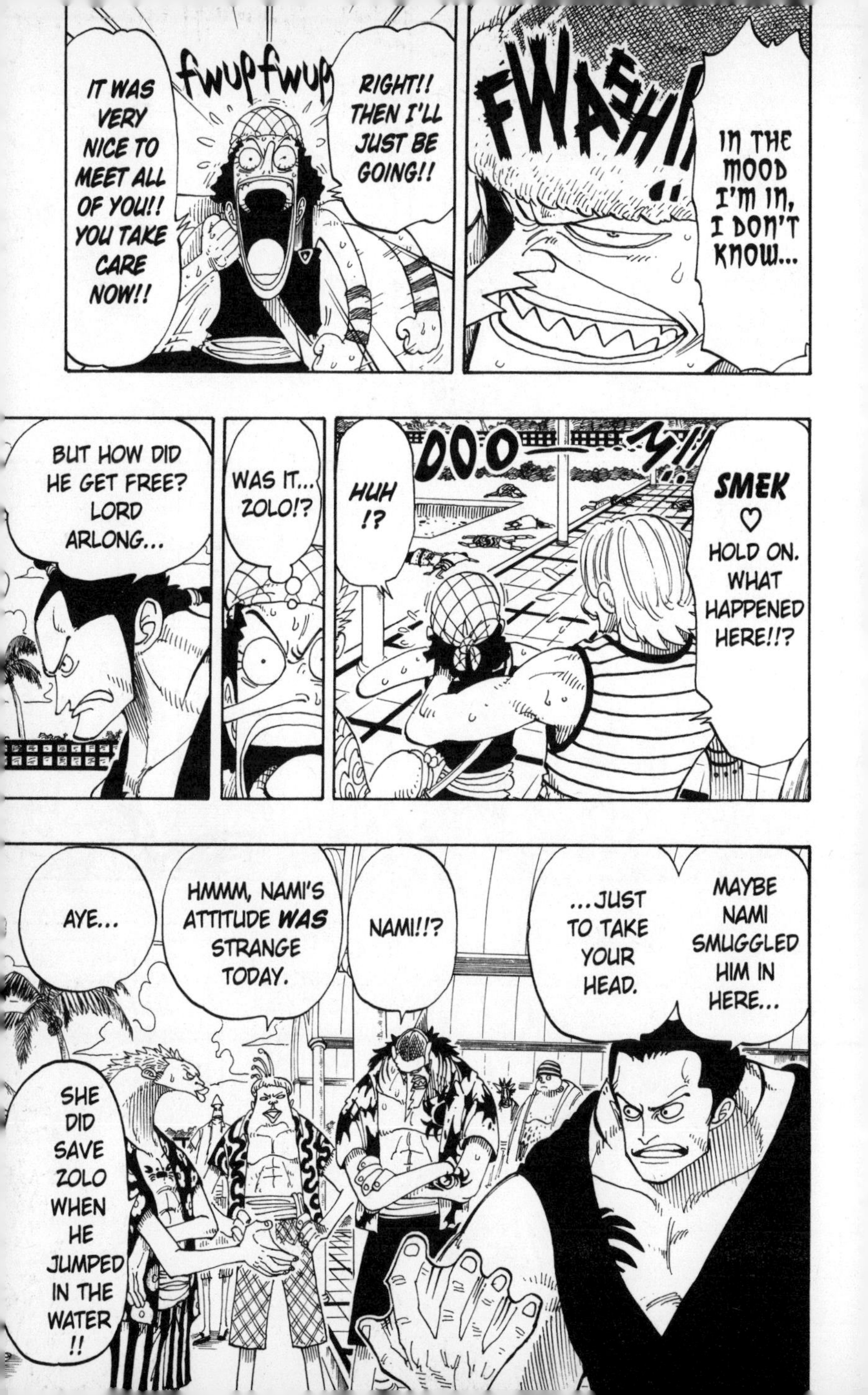
FWASH!!
IN THE MOOD I'M IN, I DON'T KNOW...
RIGHT!! THEN I'LL JUST BE GOING!!
fwupfwup
IT WAS VERY NICE TO MEET ALL OF YOU!! YOU TAKE CARE NOW!!
SMEK ♡ HOLD ON. WHAT HAPPENED HERE!!?
DOO—M!!
HUH !?
WAS IT... ZOLO!?
BUT HOW DID HE GET FREE? LORD ARLONG...
MAYBE NAMI SMUGGLED HIM IN HERE...
...JUST TO TAKE YOUR HEAD.
NAMI!!?
HMMM, NAMI'S ATTITUDE **WAS** STRANGE TODAY.
AYE...
SHE DID SAVE ZOLO WHEN HE JUMPED IN THE WATER!!

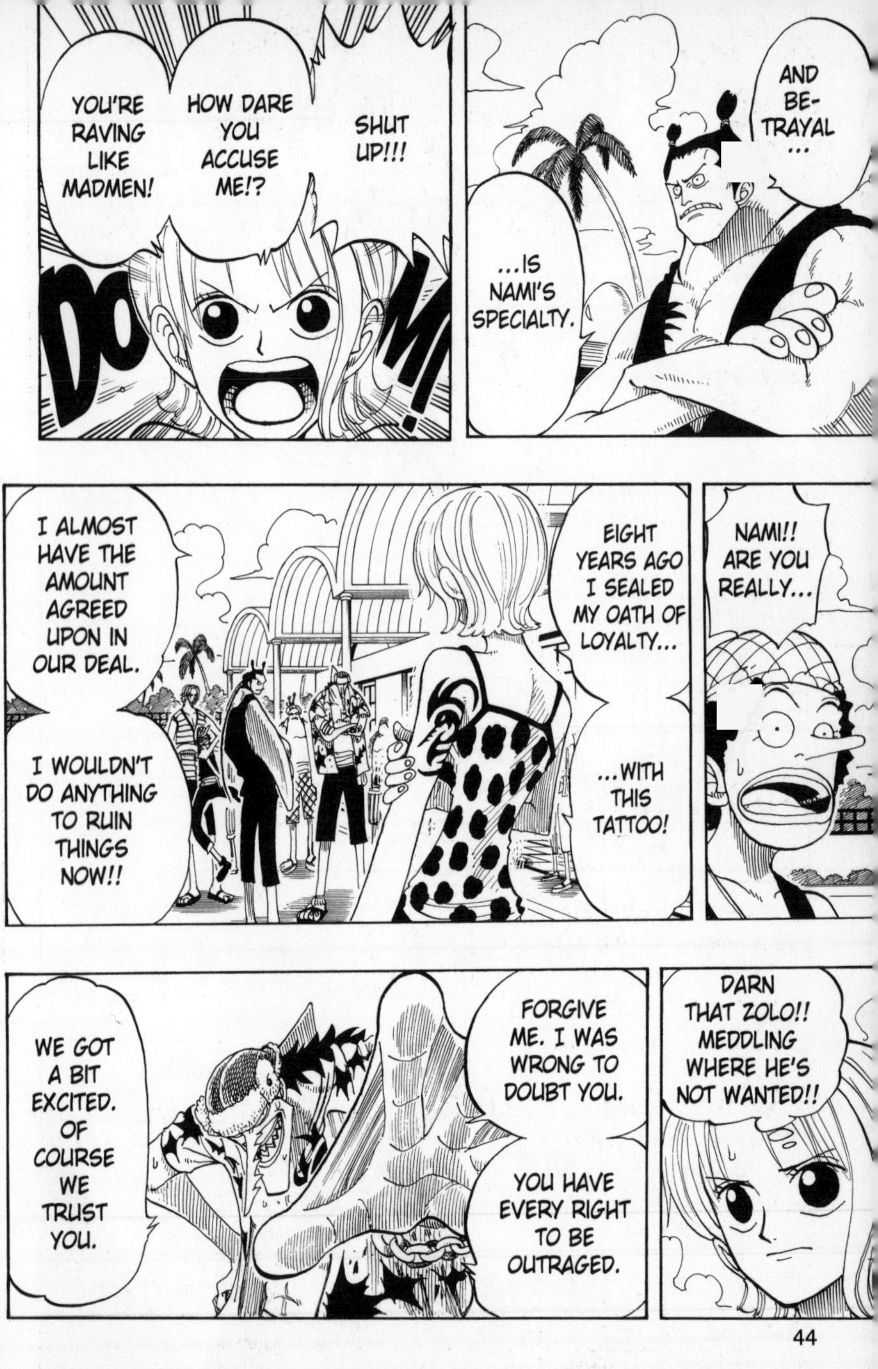
AND BE-TRAYAL...
...IS NAMI'S SPECIALTY.
SHUT UP!!!
HOW DARE YOU ACCUSE ME!?
YOU'RE RAVING LIKE MADMEN!
DOM!
NAMI!! ARE YOU REALLY...
EIGHT YEARS AGO I SEALED MY OATH OF LOYALTY...
...WITH THIS TATTOO!
I ALMOST HAVE THE AMOUNT AGREED UPON IN OUR DEAL.
I WOULDN'T DO ANYTHING TO RUIN THINGS NOW!!
DARN THAT ZOLO!! MEDDLING WHERE HE'S NOT WANTED!!
FORGIVE ME. I WAS WRONG TO DOUBT YOU.
YOU HAVE EVERY RIGHT TO BE OUTRAGED.
WE GOT A BIT EXCITED. OF COURSE WE TRUST YOU.

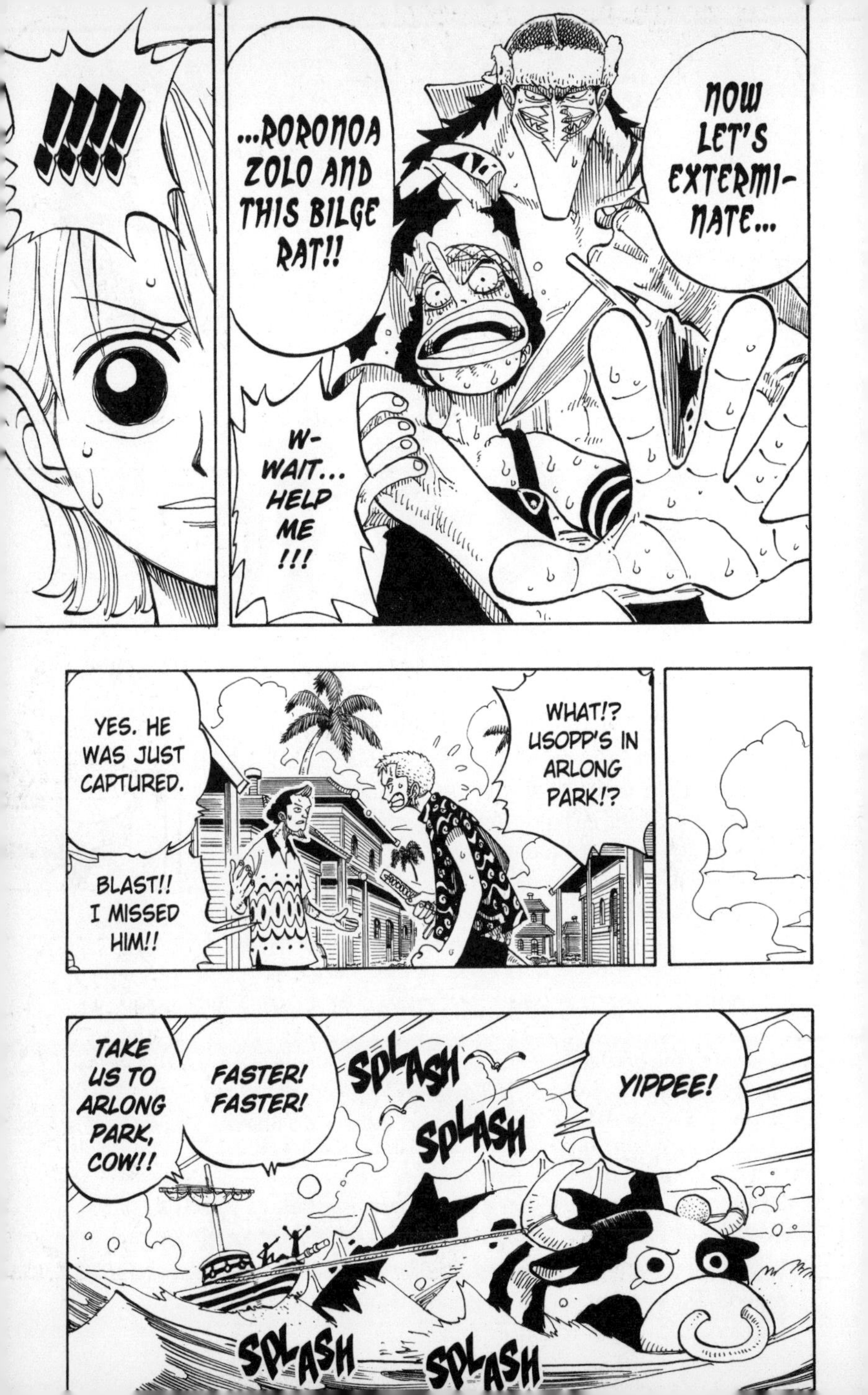
NOW LET'S EXTERMINATE...
...RORONOA ZOLO AND THIS BILGE RAT!!
W-WAIT... HELP ME!!!
!!!!
WHAT!? USOPP'S IN ARLONG PARK!?
YES. HE WAS JUST CAPTURED.
BLAST!! I MISSED HIM!!
YIPPEE!
SPLASH
SPLASH
FASTER! FASTER!
TAKE US TO ARLONG PARK, COW!!
SPLASH
SPLASH

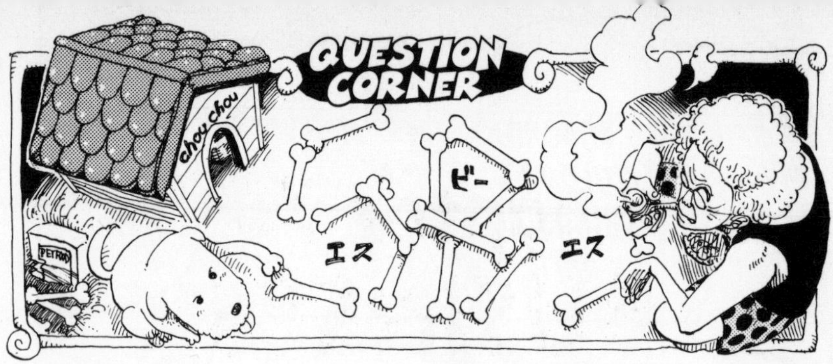
QUESTION CORNER
chou chou
ビー
エス
エス

Q: Oda Sensei, this is spirit, right? (pen name: Arunya)

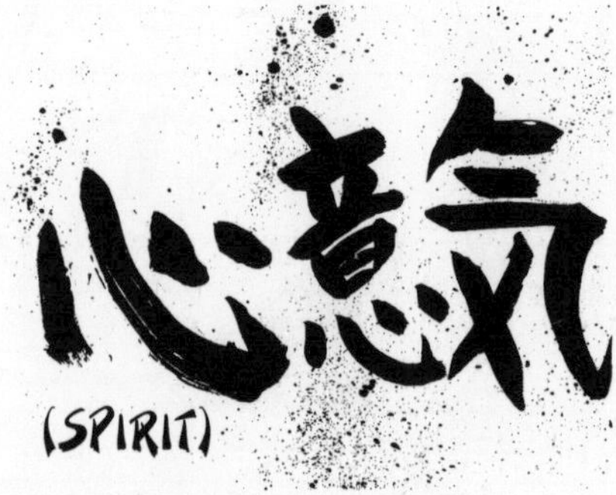
心意気
(SPIRIT)

A: Yes, you show true spirit.

Q: Nobunaga: If the cuckoo won't sing, kill it.
Hideyoshi: If the cuckoo won't sing, make it sing.
Ieyasu: If the cuckoo won't sing, wait until it does.
^ These haiku capture the philosophies of three men who wanted to rule Japan. What would yours be?

A: Oda: If the cuckoo won't sing, buy me a cola.
Meaning: "I want a cola right now." (And not a diet cola.)

Q: I went to the barbershop and said, "I want a manly haircut!!" The barber said, "Okay!!" and shaved all my hair off. It wasn't at all what I had in mind. Sensei, do I have what it takes to be like Zolo? Please tell me!! Sob sob.

A: Don't cry!! Stand up!! There are some battles in which a man must retreat!! So what if he shaved your head!! When your hair grows back, challenge that barber again!! Think of it as a rematch!! Though personally, I wouldn't do it. (Wild laughter)

Chapter 74: BUSINESS

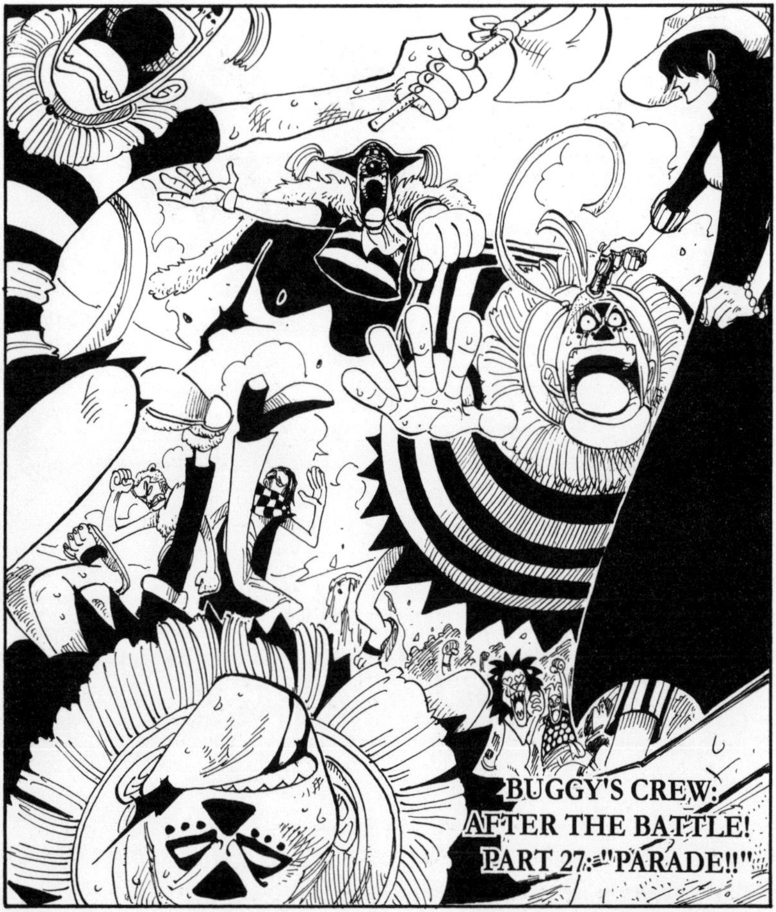
BUGGY'S CREW: AFTER THE BATTLE! PART 27: "PARADE!!"

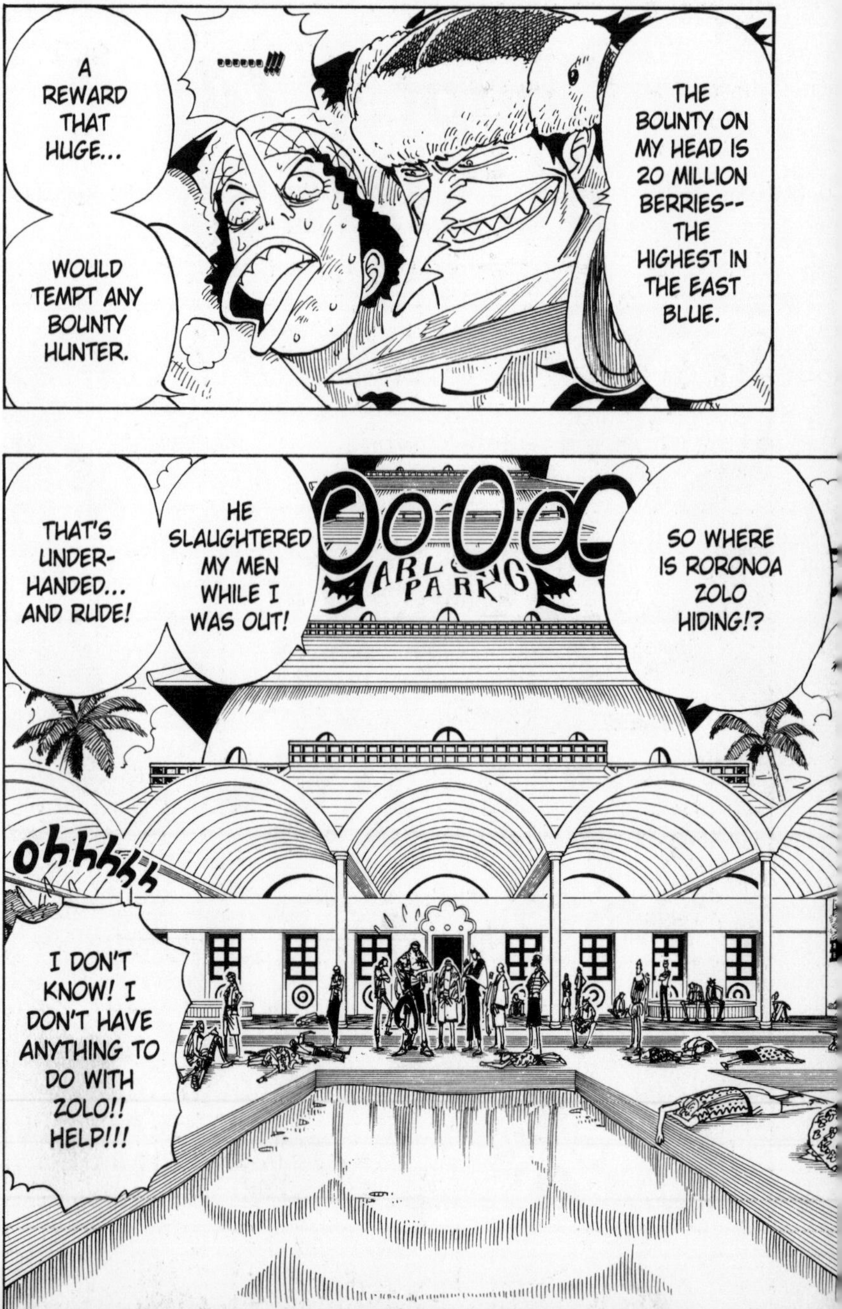
THE BOUNTY ON MY HEAD IS 20 MILLION BERRIES--THE HIGHEST IN THE EAST BLUE.
......!!!
A REWARD THAT HUGE...
WOULD TEMPT ANY BOUNTY HUNTER.
SO WHERE IS RORONOA ZOLO HIDING!?
HE SLAUGHTERED MY MEN WHILE I WAS OUT!
THAT'S UNDER-HANDED... AND RUDE!
ARLONG PARK
ohhhhh
I DON'T KNOW! I DON'T HAVE ANYTHING TO DO WITH ZOLO!! HELP!!!

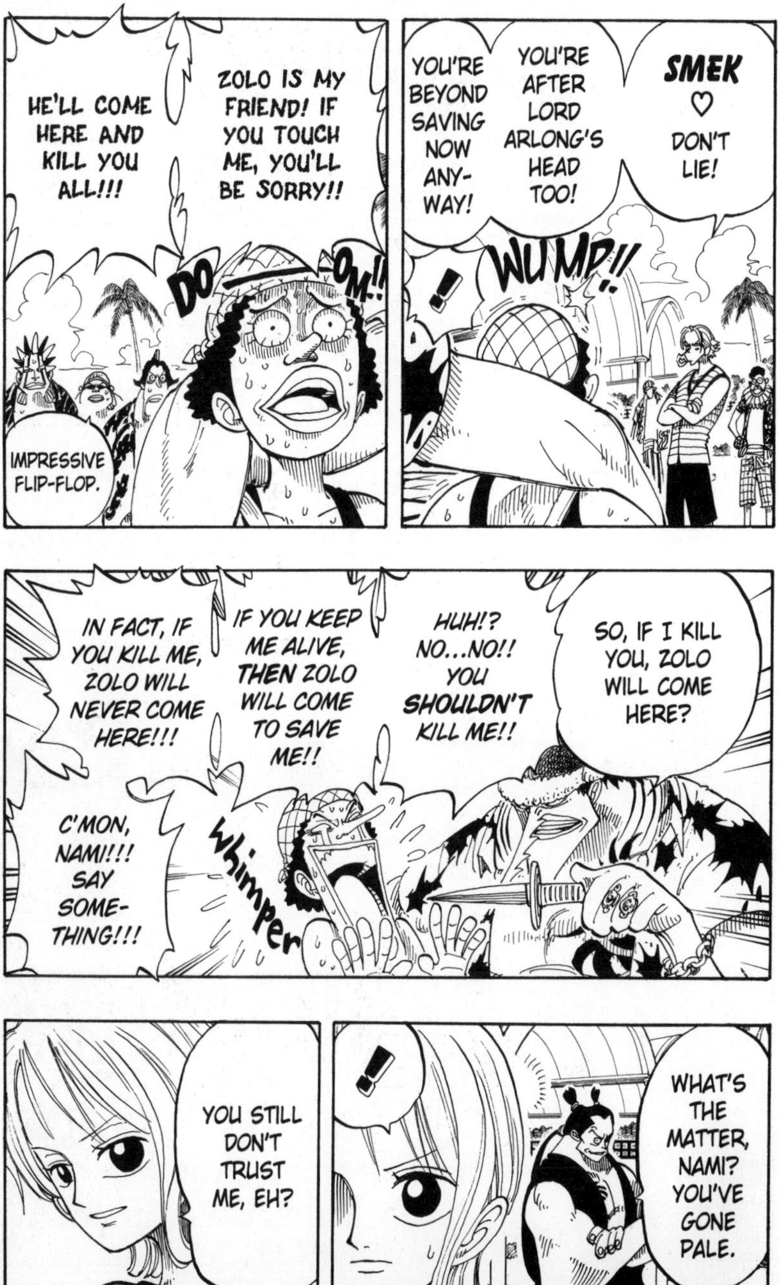
SMEK ♡ DON'T LIE!
YOU'RE AFTER LORD ARLONG'S HEAD TOO!
YOU'RE BEYOND SAVING NOW ANY-WAY!
WUMP!!
!
ZOLO IS MY FRIEND! IF YOU TOUCH ME, YOU'LL BE SORRY!!
HE'LL COME HERE AND KILL YOU ALL!!!
DO—OM!!
IMPRESSIVE FLIP-FLOP.
SO, IF I KILL YOU, ZOLO WILL COME HERE?
HUH!? NO...NO!! YOU SHOULDN'T KILL ME!!
IF YOU KEEP ME ALIVE, THEN ZOLO WILL COME TO SAVE ME!!
IN FACT, IF YOU KILL ME, ZOLO WILL NEVER COME HERE!!!
whimper
C'MON, NAMI!!!! SAY SOME-THING!!!
!
WHAT'S THE MATTER, NAMI? YOU'VE GONE PALE.
YOU STILL DON'T TRUST ME, EH?

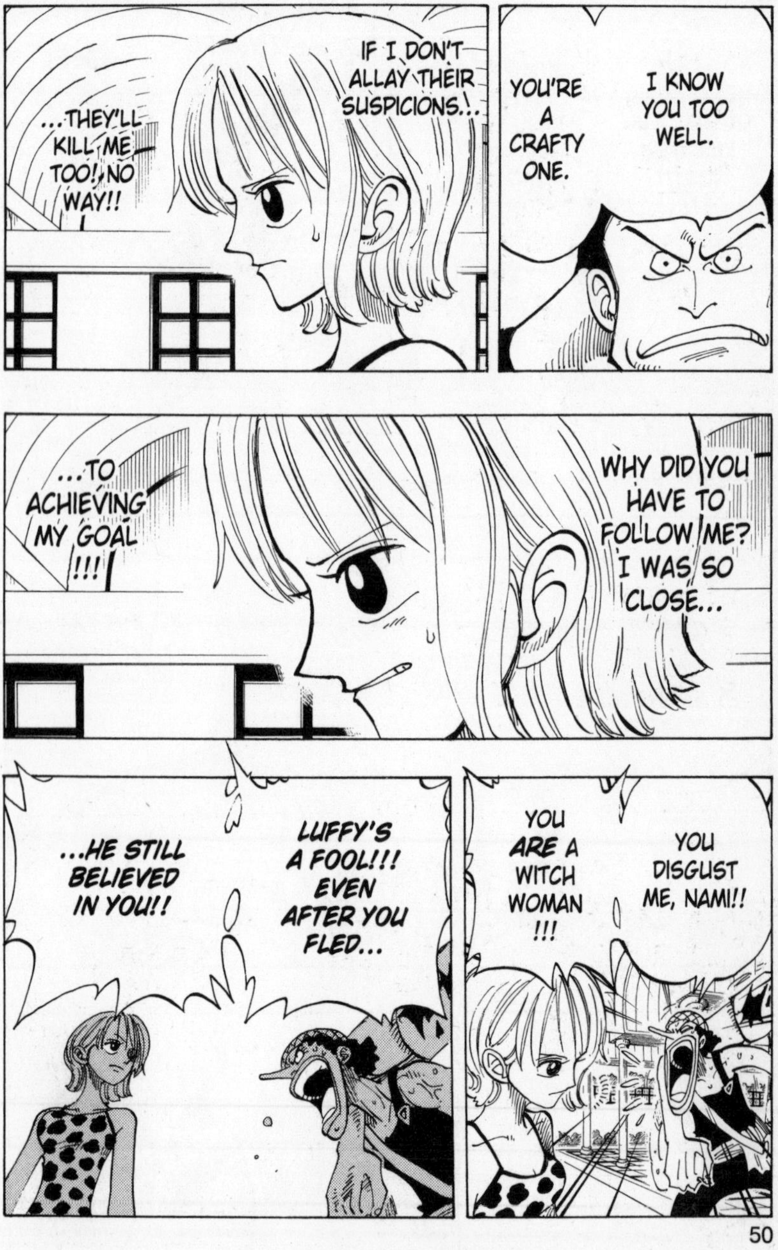
I KNOW YOU TOO WELL.
YOU'RE A CRAFTY ONE.
IF I DON'T ALLAY THEIR SUSPICIONS...
...THEY'LL KILL ME TOO! NO WAY!!
WHY DID YOU HAVE TO FOLLOW ME? I WAS SO CLOSE...
...TO ACHIEVING MY GOAL!!!
YOU DISGUST ME, NAMI!!
YOU ARE A WITCH WOMAN!!!
LUFFY'S A FOOL!!! EVEN AFTER YOU FLED...
...HE STILL BELIEVED IN YOU!!

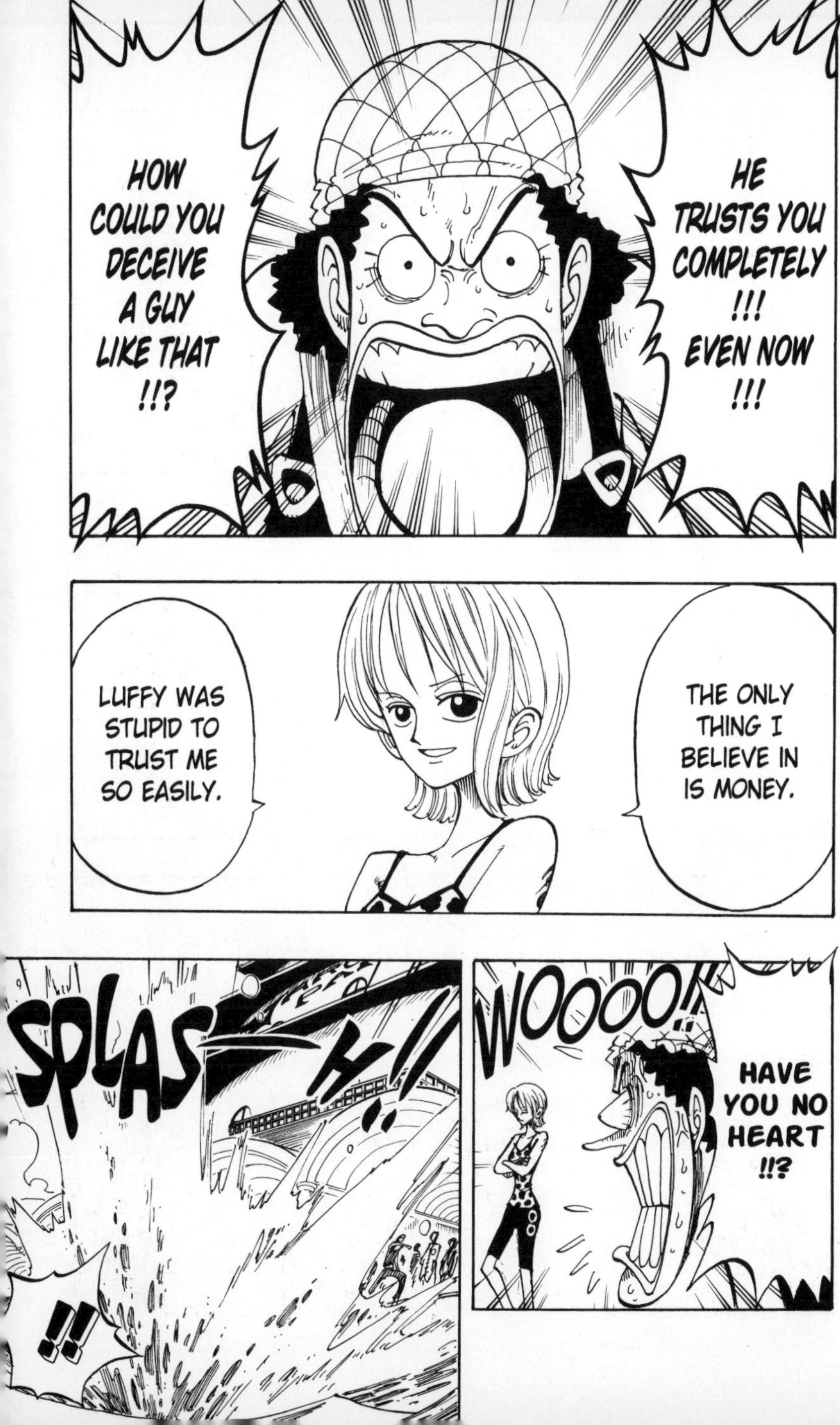
HE TRUSTS YOU COMPLETELY!!! EVEN NOW!!!
HOW COULD YOU DECEIVE A GUY LIKE THAT!!?
THE ONLY THING I BELIEVE IN IS MONEY.
LUFFY WAS STUPID TO TRUST ME SO EASILY.
WOOOO!!
HAVE YOU NO HEART!!?
SPLASH!!
!!

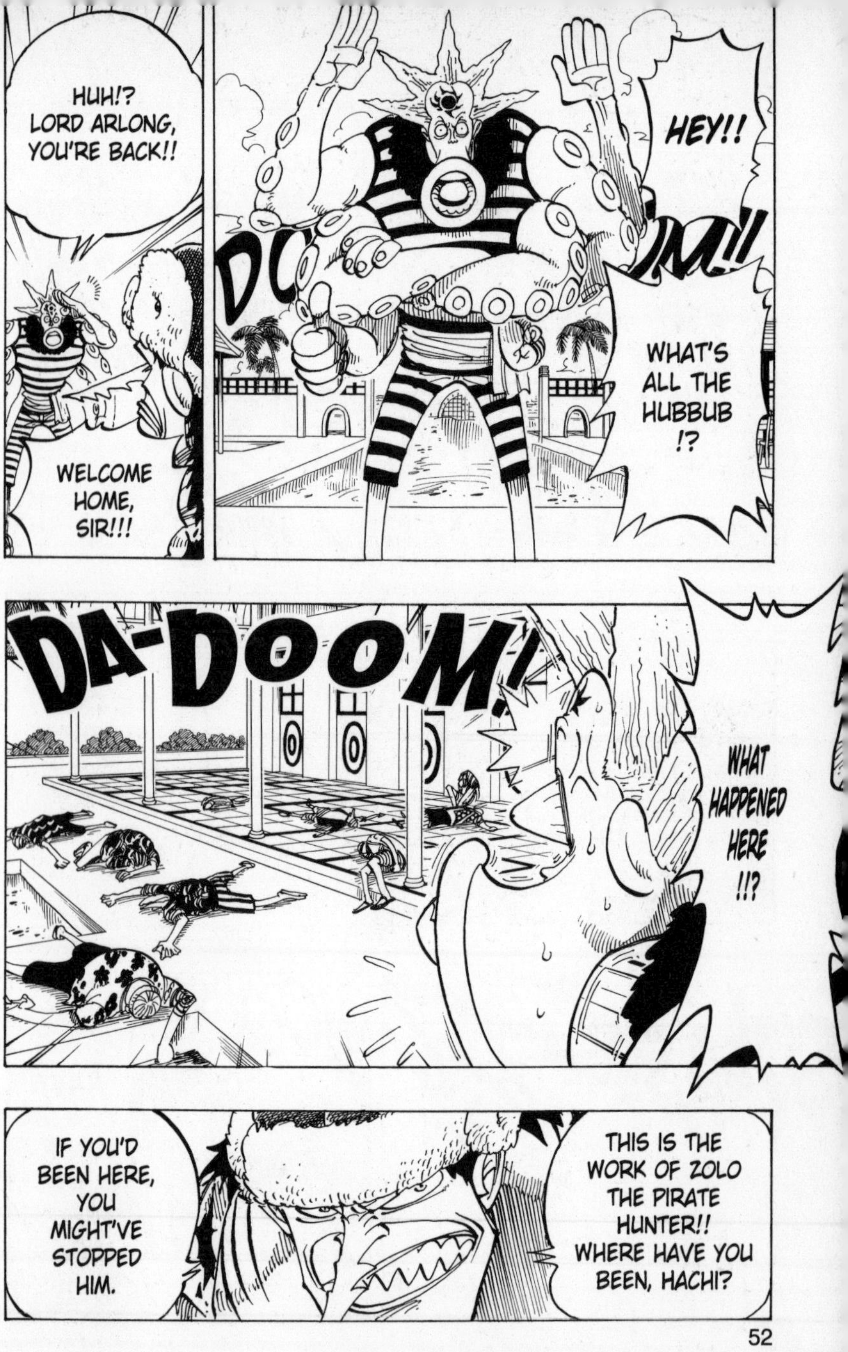

HEY!!
WHAT'S ALL THE HUBBUB !?
HUH!? LORD ARLONG, YOU'RE BACK!!
WELCOME HOME, SIR!!!
DA-DOOM!
WHAT HAPPENED HERE !!?
THIS IS THE WORK OF ZOLO THE PIRATE HUNTER!! WHERE HAVE YOU BEEN, HACHI?
IF YOU'D BEEN HERE, YOU MIGHT'VE STOPPED HIM.

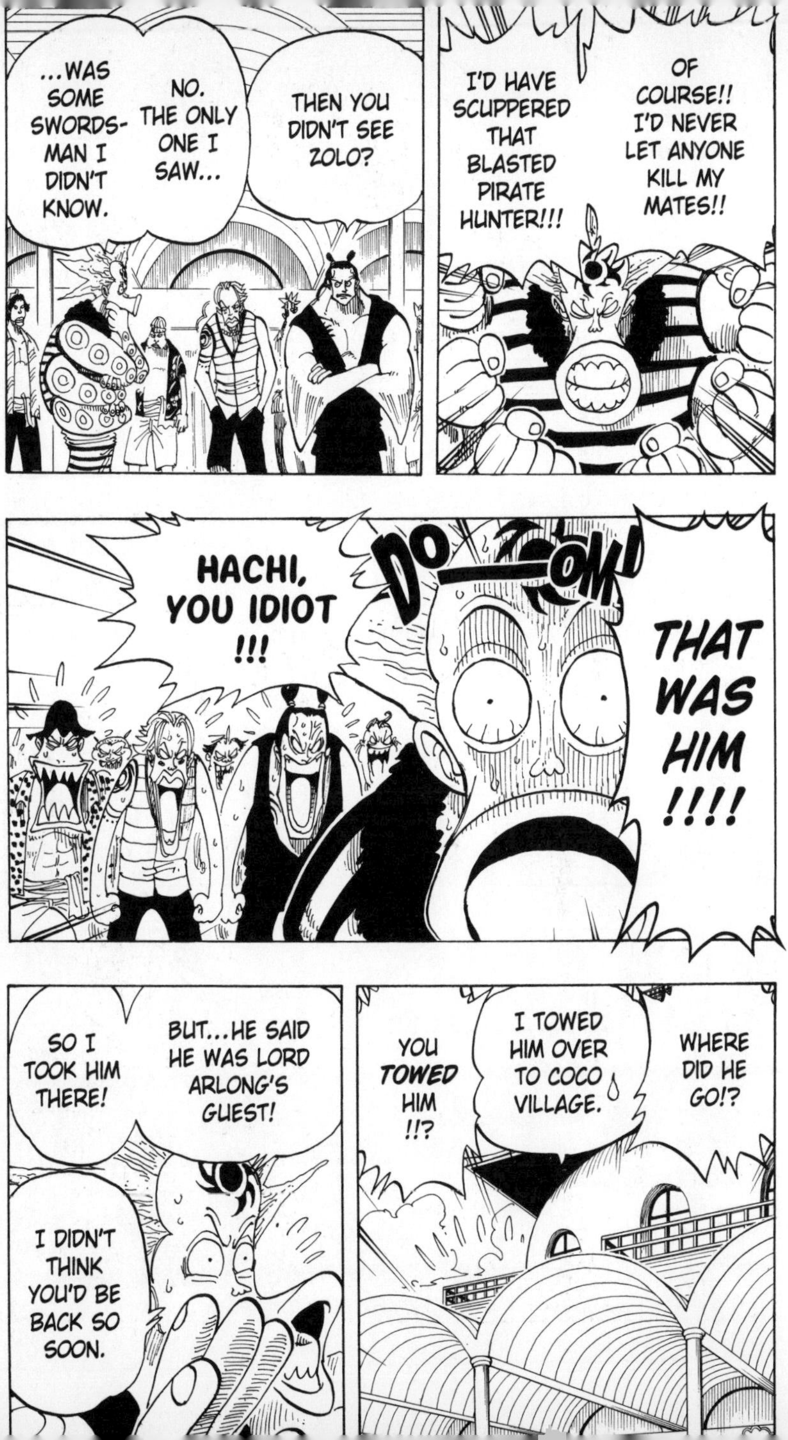
OF COURSE!! I'D NEVER LET ANYONE KILL MY MATES!!
I'D HAVE SCUPPERED THAT BLASTED PIRATE HUNTER!!!
THEN YOU DIDN'T SEE ZOLO?
NO. THE ONLY ONE I SAW...
...WAS SOME SWORDS-MAN I DIDN'T KNOW.
DO—OM!
THAT WAS HIM!!!!
HACHI, YOU IDIOT!!!
WHERE DID HE GO!?
I TOWED HIM OVER TO COCO VILLAGE.
YOU TOWED HIM!!?
BUT...HE SAID HE WAS LORD ARLONG'S GUEST!
SO I TOOK HIM THERE!
I DIDN'T THINK YOU'D BE BACK SO SOON.

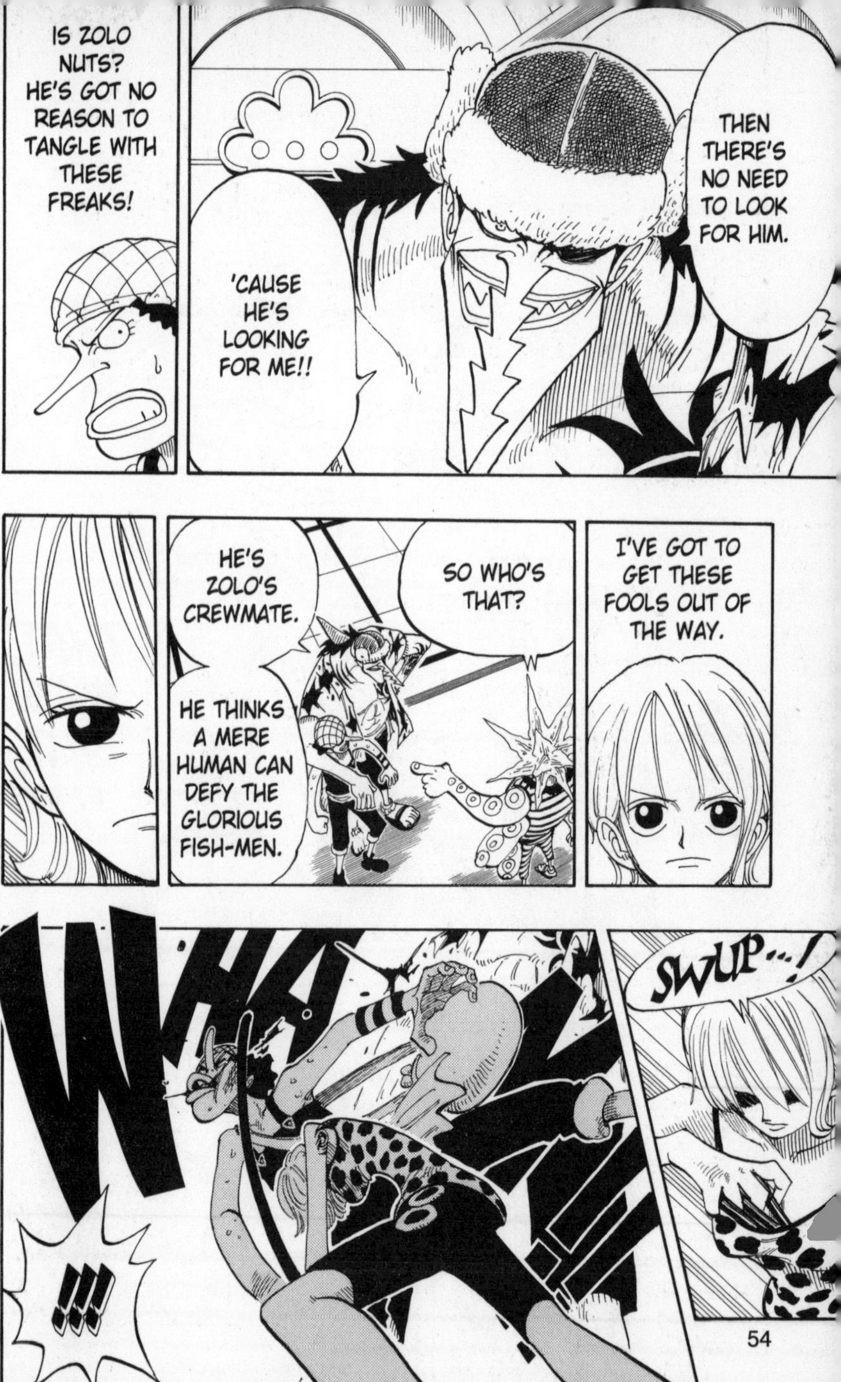
THEN THERE'S NO NEED TO LOOK FOR HIM.
'CAUSE HE'S LOOKING FOR ME!!
IS ZOLO NUTS? HE'S GOT NO REASON TO TANGLE WITH THESE FREAKS!
I'VE GOT TO GET THESE FOOLS OUT OF THE WAY.
SO WHO'S THAT?
HE'S ZOLO'S CREWMATE.
HE THINKS A MERE HUMAN CAN DEFY THE GLORIOUS FISH-MEN.
SWUP...!
!!!

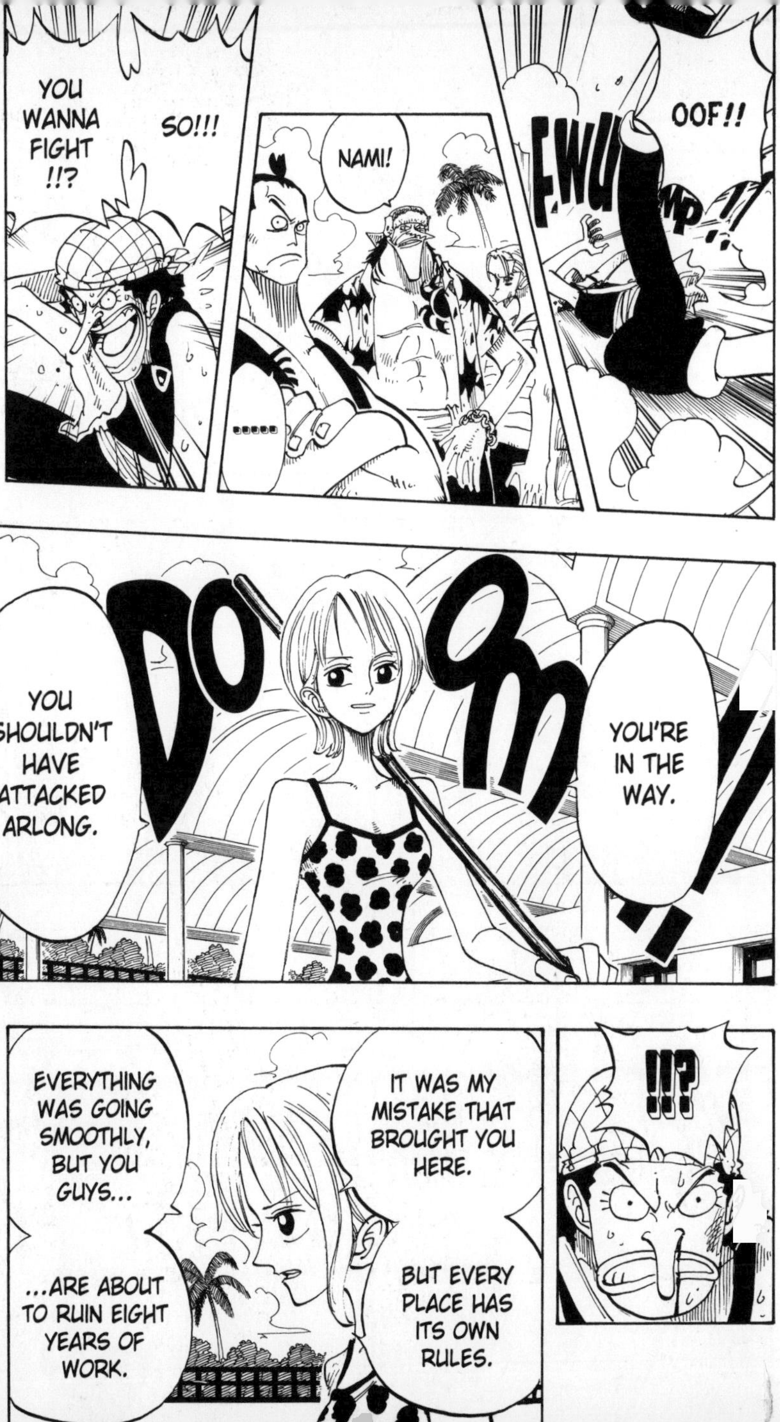

OOF!!
F.WUMP!!
NAMI!
SO!!!
YOU WANNA FIGHT !!?
YOU'RE IN THE WAY.
DOOM!!
YOU SHOULDN'T HAVE ATTACKED ARLONG.
!!?
IT WAS MY MISTAKE THAT BROUGHT YOU HERE.
BUT EVERY PLACE HAS ITS OWN RULES.
EVERYTHING WAS GOING SMOOTHLY, BUT YOU GUYS...
...ARE ABOUT TO RUIN EIGHT YEARS OF WORK.

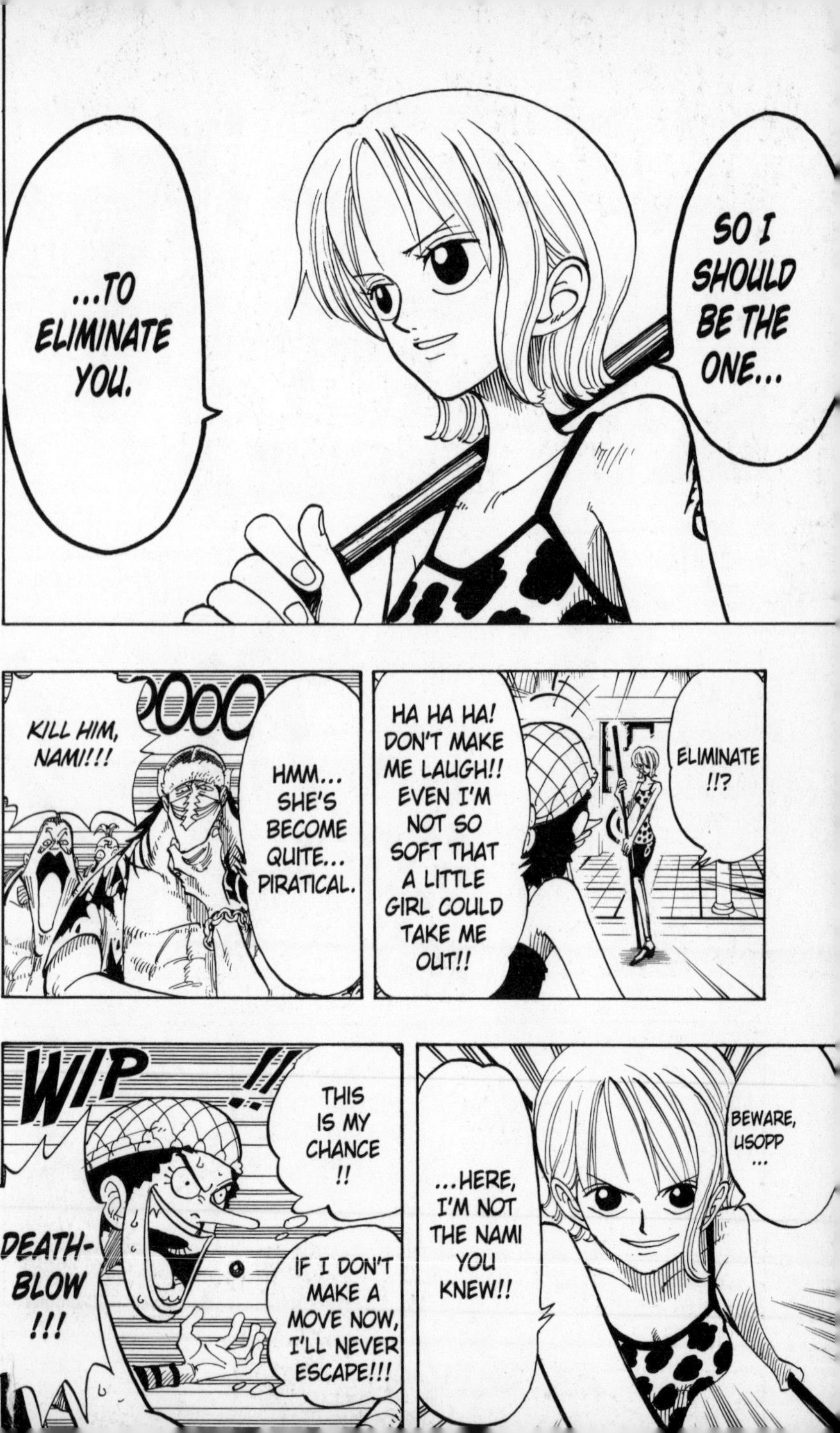
SO I SHOULD BE THE ONE...
...TO ELIMINATE YOU.
ELIMINATE!!?
HA HA HA! DON'T MAKE ME LAUGH!! EVEN I'M NOT SO SOFT THAT A LITTLE GIRL COULD TAKE ME OUT!!
HMM... SHE'S BECOME QUITE... PIRATICAL.
KILL HIM, NAMI!!!
BEWARE, USOPP ...
...HERE, I'M NOT THE NAMI YOU KNEW!!
WIP!!
THIS IS MY CHANCE!!
IF I DON'T MAKE A MOVE NOW, I'LL NEVER ESCAPE!!!
DEATH-BLOW!!!

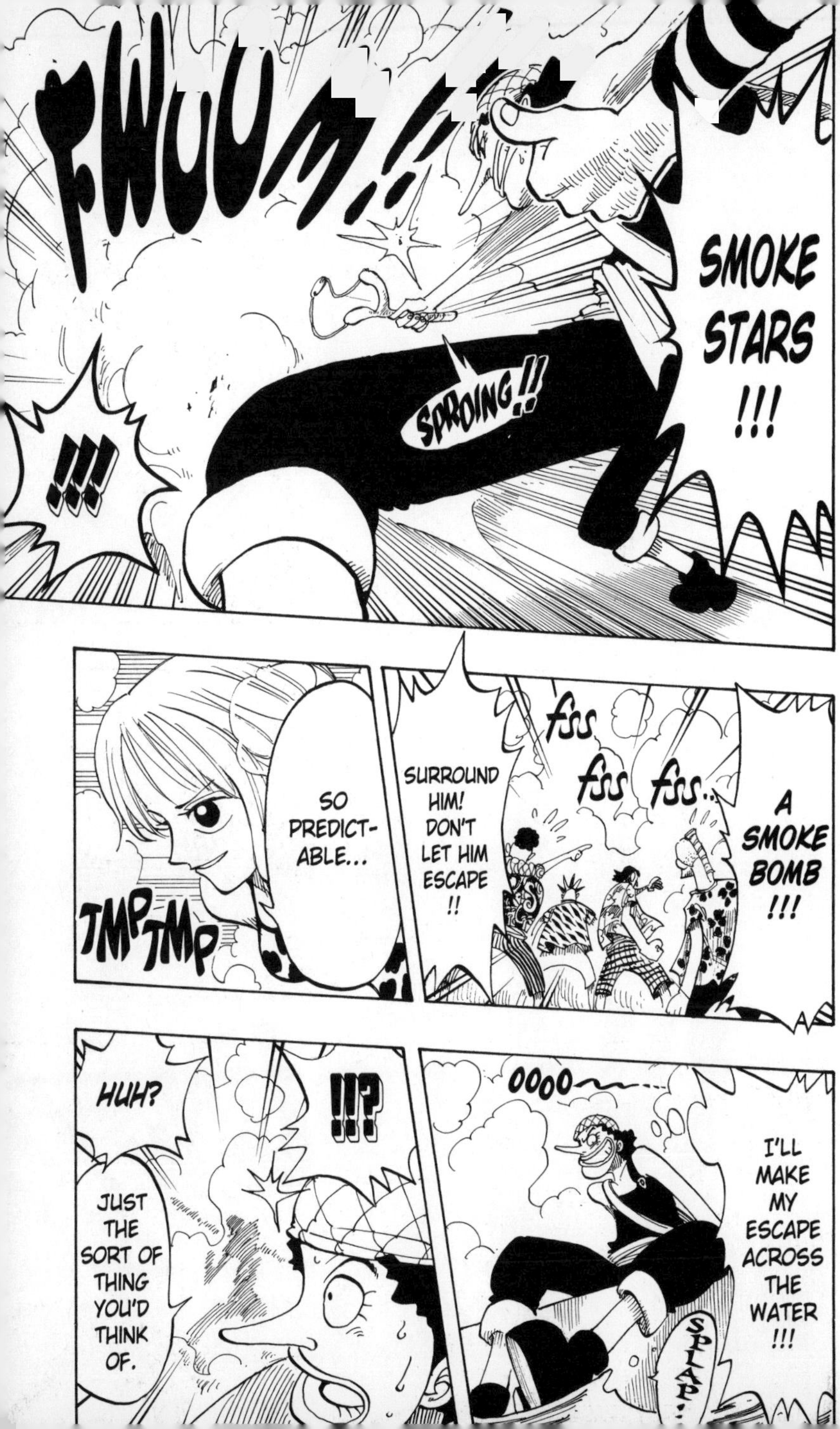
FWOOM!!
SMOKE STARS!!!
SPROING!!
!!!!
A SMOKE BOMB!!!
fss fss fss..
SURROUND HIM! DON'T LET HIM ESCAPE!!
SO PREDICT-ABLE...
TMP TMP
OOOO~
I'LL MAKE MY ESCAPE ACROSS THE WATER!!!
SPLAP!!
!!?
HUH?
JUST THE SORT OF THING YOU'D THINK OF.

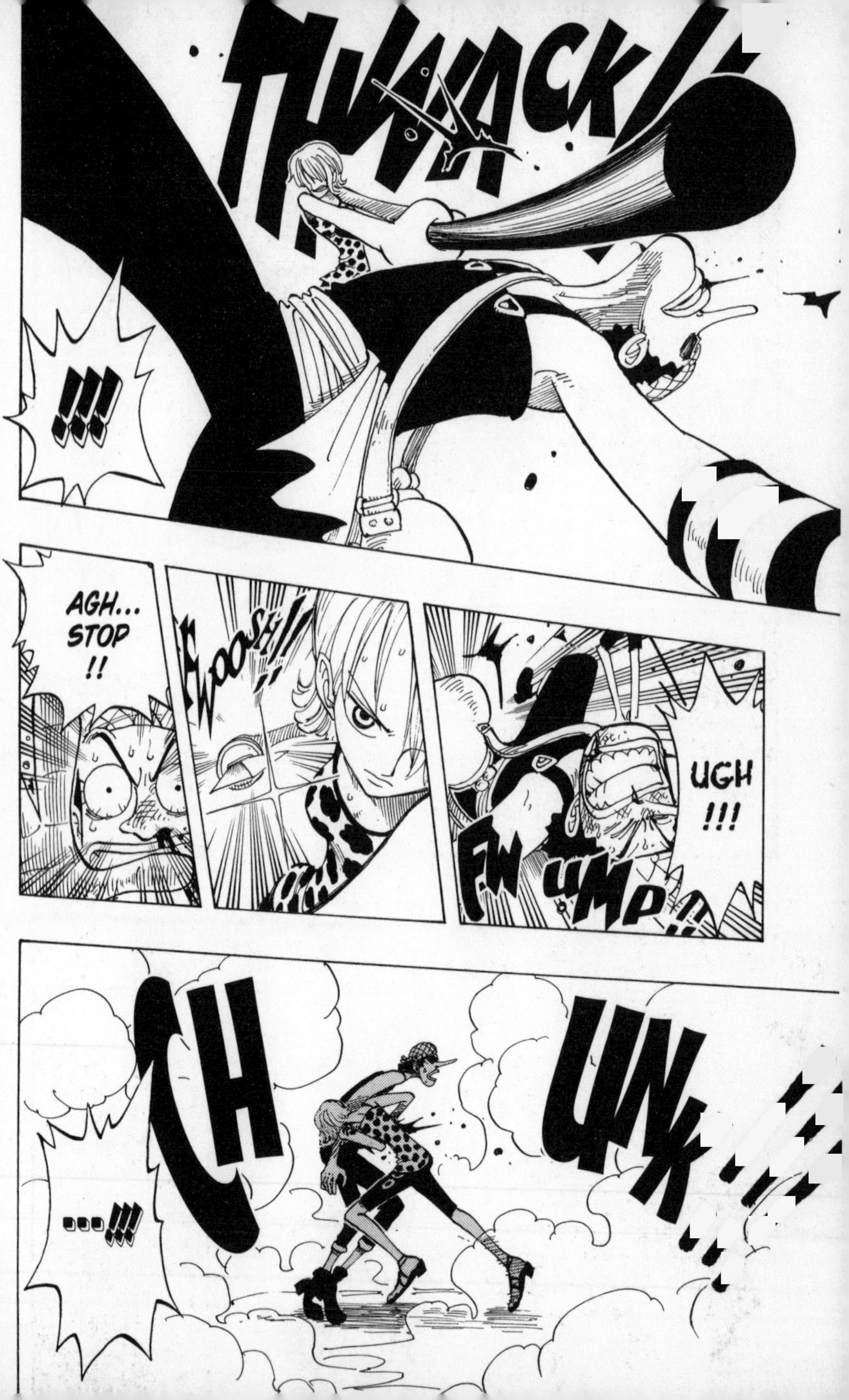
THWACK!!
!!!
UGH !!!
FWUMP!!
FWOOSH!!
AGH... STOP !!
CHUNK!!!
...!!!

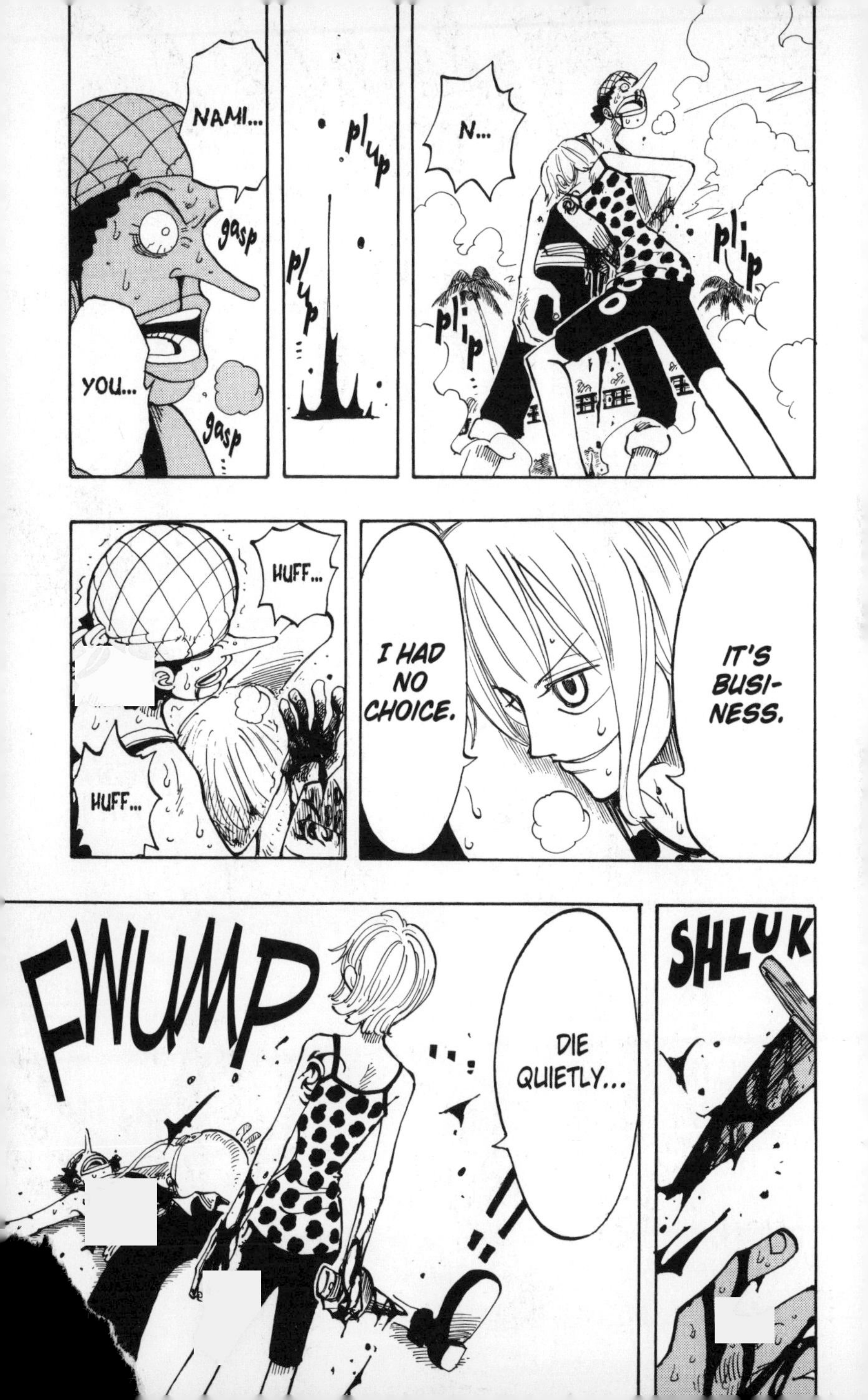
N...
plip
plip
plup
plup
NAMI...
gasp
YOU...
gasp
IT'S BUSI-NESS.
I HAD NO CHOICE.
HUFF...
HUFF...
SHLUK
DIE QUIETLY...
FWUMP

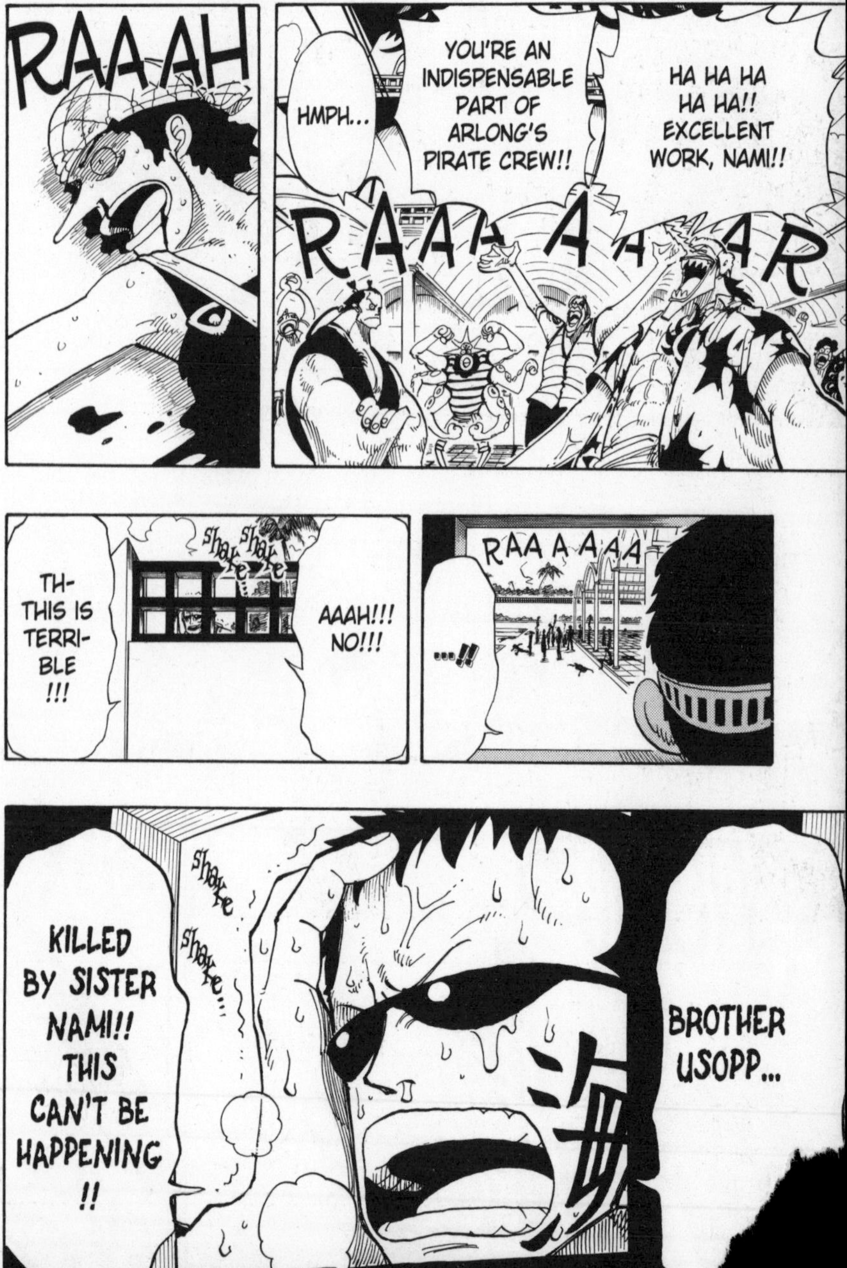
HA HA HA HA HA!! EXCELLENT WORK, NAMI!!
YOU'RE AN INDISPENSABLE PART OF ARLONG'S PIRATE CREW!!
HMPH...
RAAAAAAR
RAAAH
RAA A A AA
...!!
AAAH!!! NO!!!
shake shake
TH- THIS IS TERRI- BLE !!!
BROTHER USOPP...
shake shake...
KILLED BY SISTER NAMI!! THIS CAN'T BE HAPPENING !!

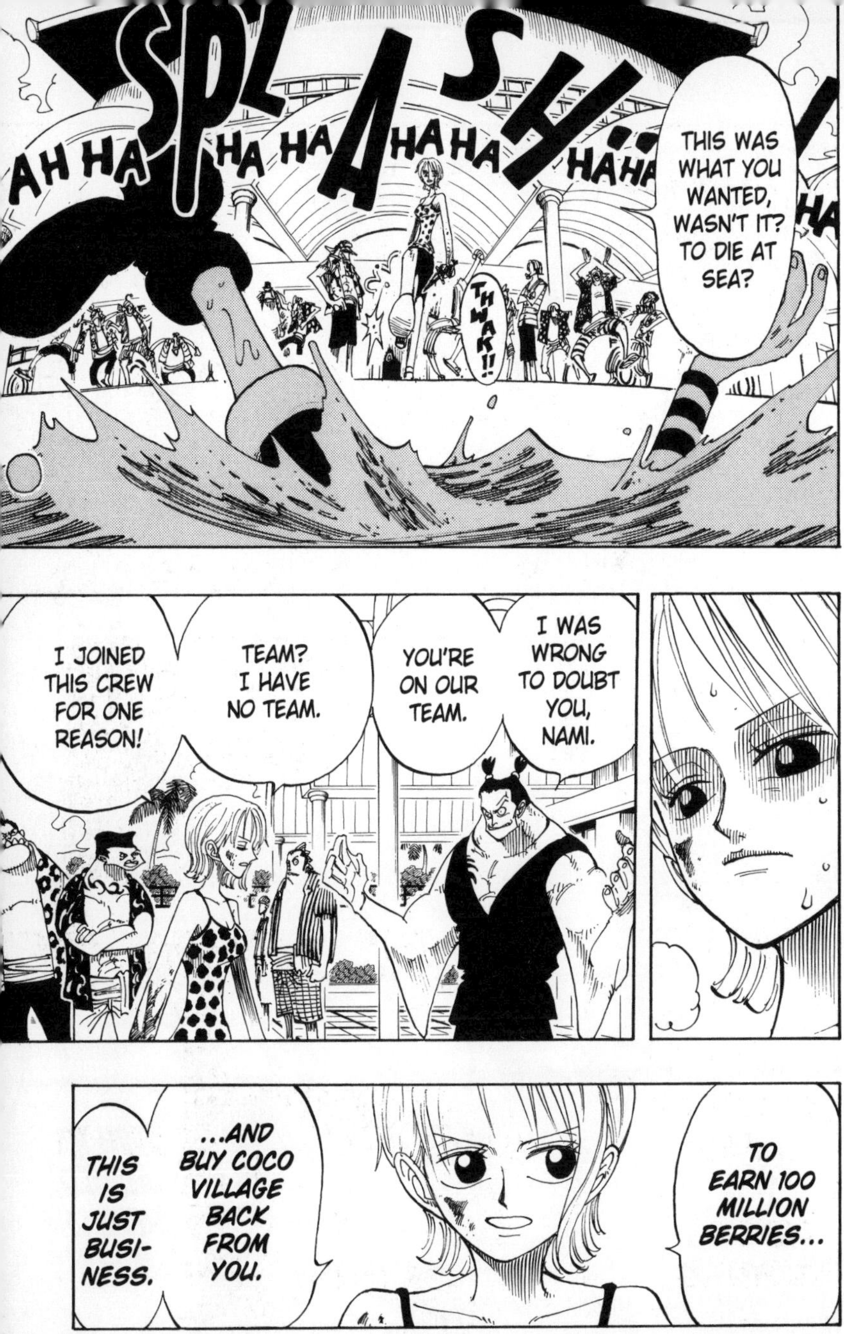
THIS WAS WHAT YOU WANTED, WASN'T IT? TO DIE AT SEA?
SPLASH...!
AH HA HA HA HA HA HA HA HA
THWAK!!
I WAS WRONG TO DOUBT YOU, NAMI.
YOU'RE ON OUR TEAM.
TEAM? I HAVE NO TEAM.
I JOINED THIS CREW FOR ONE REASON!
TO EARN 100 MILLION BERRIES...
...AND BUY COCO VILLAGE BACK FROM YOU.
THIS IS JUST BUSI-NESS.

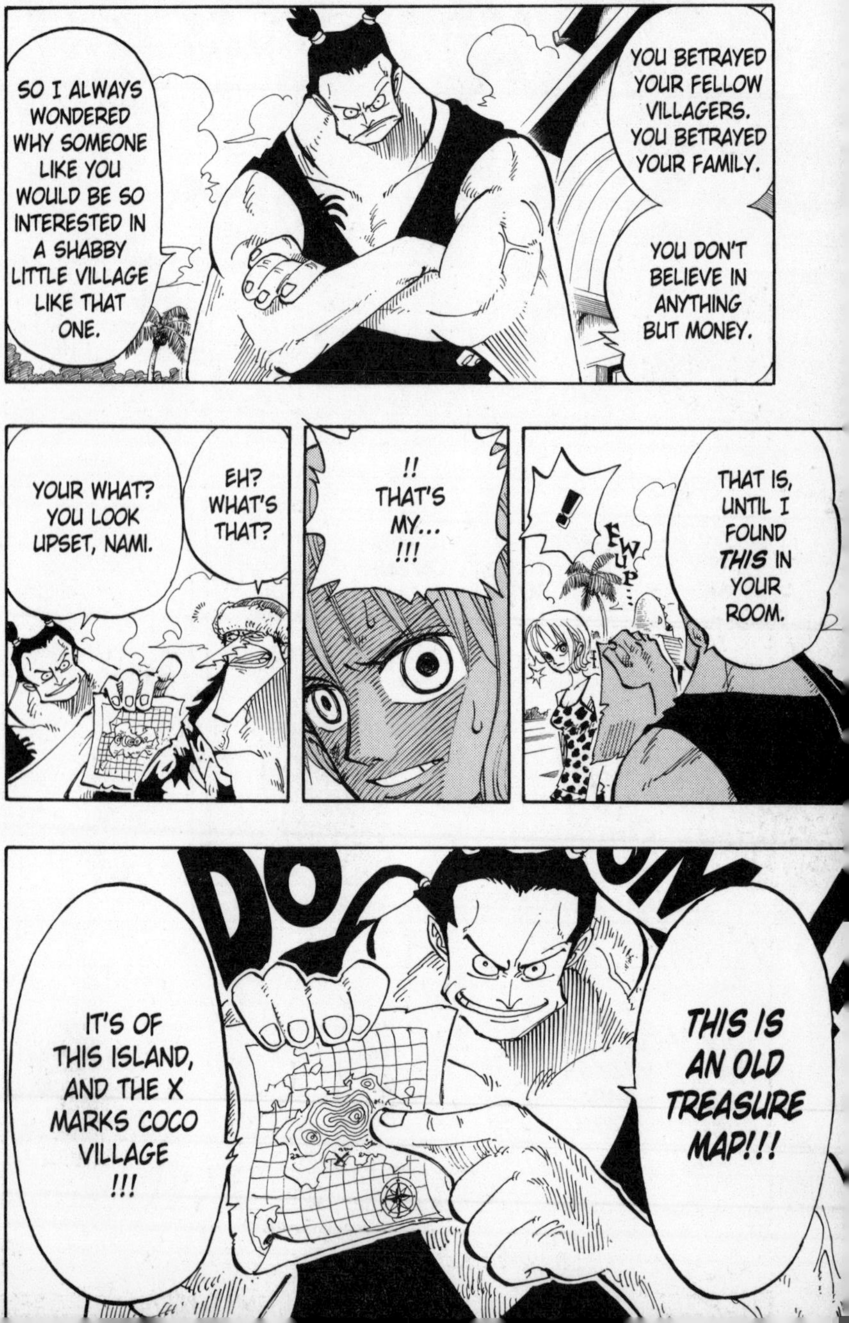

YOU BETRAYED YOUR FELLOW VILLAGERS. YOU BETRAYED YOUR FAMILY.
YOU DON'T BELIEVE IN ANYTHING BUT MONEY.
SO I ALWAYS WONDERED WHY SOMEONE LIKE YOU WOULD BE SO INTERESTED IN A SHABBY LITTLE VILLAGE LIKE THAT ONE.
THAT IS, UNTIL I FOUND *THIS* IN YOUR ROOM.
FWUP...
!
!! THAT'S MY... !!!
EH? WHAT'S THAT?
YOUR WHAT? YOU LOOK UPSET, NAMI.
THIS IS AN OLD TREASURE MAP!!!
IT'S OF THIS ISLAND, AND THE X MARKS COCO VILLAGE !!!

READ THIS WAY

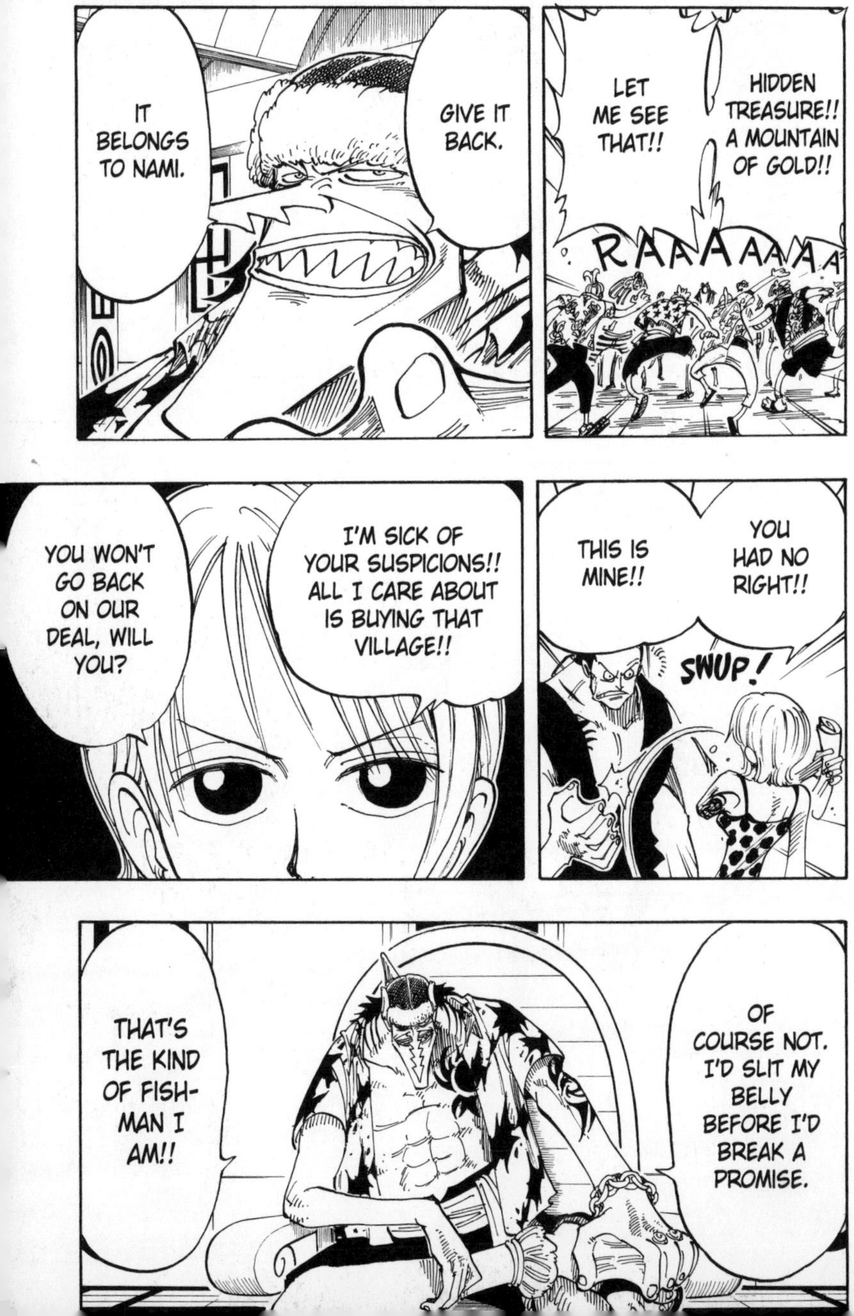

HIDDEN TREASURE!! A MOUNTAIN OF GOLD!!
LET ME SEE THAT!!
RAAAAAAA
GIVE IT BACK.
IT BELONGS TO NAMI.
YOU HAD NO RIGHT!!
THIS IS MINE!!
SWUP!
I'M SICK OF YOUR SUSPICIONS!! ALL I CARE ABOUT IS BUYING THAT VILLAGE!!
YOU WON'T GO BACK ON OUR DEAL, WILL YOU?
OF COURSE NOT. I'D SLIT MY BELLY BEFORE I'D BREAK A PROMISE.
THAT'S THE KIND OF FISH-MAN I AM!!

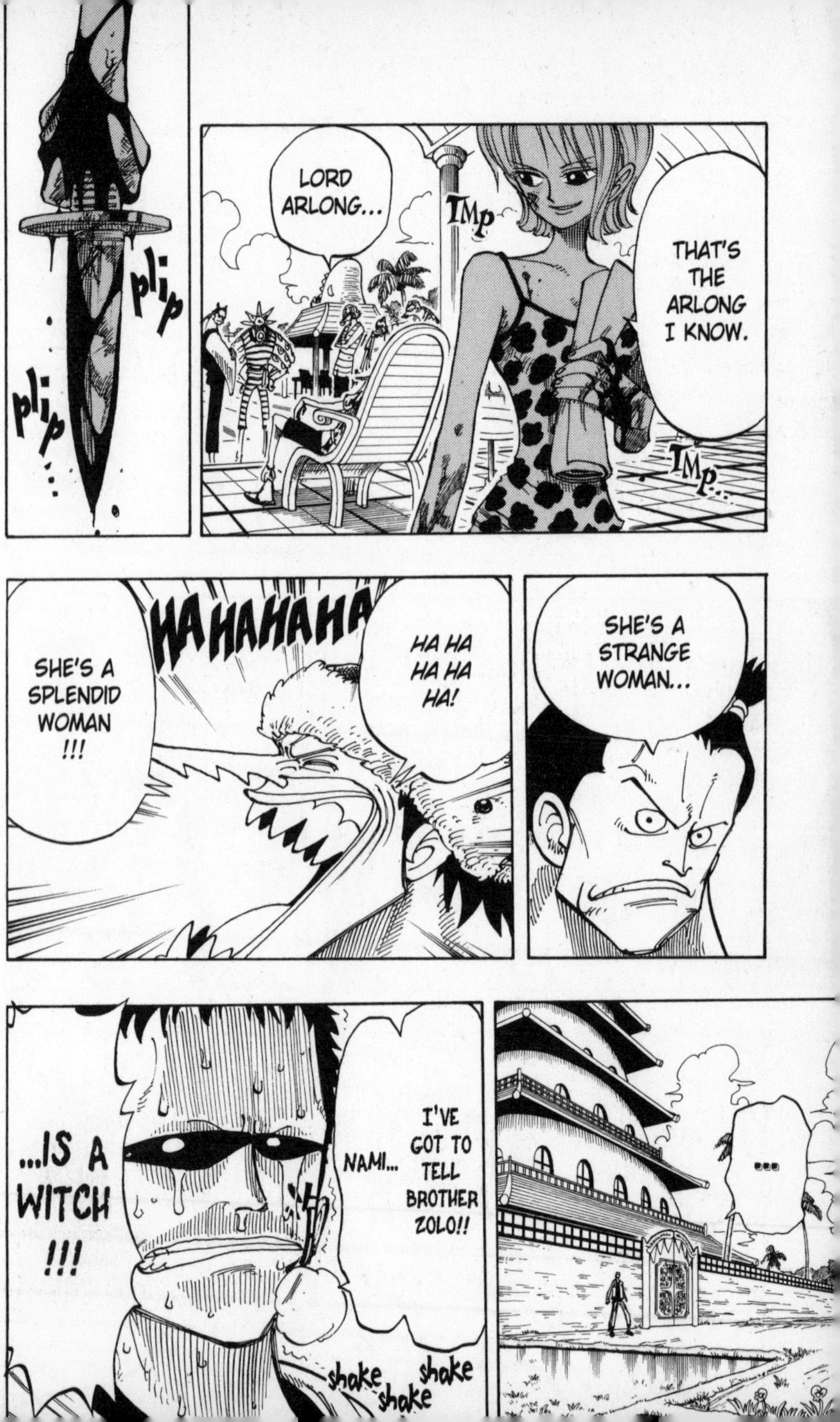

THAT'S THE ARLONG I KNOW.
TMP
LORD ARLONG...
TMP...
plip
plip...
SHE'S A STRANGE WOMAN...
HA HA HA HA HA!
HAHAHAHA
SHE'S A SPLENDID WOMAN !!!
...
I'VE GOT TO TELL BROTHER ZOLO!!
NAMI...
...IS A WITCH !!!
shake
shake
shake

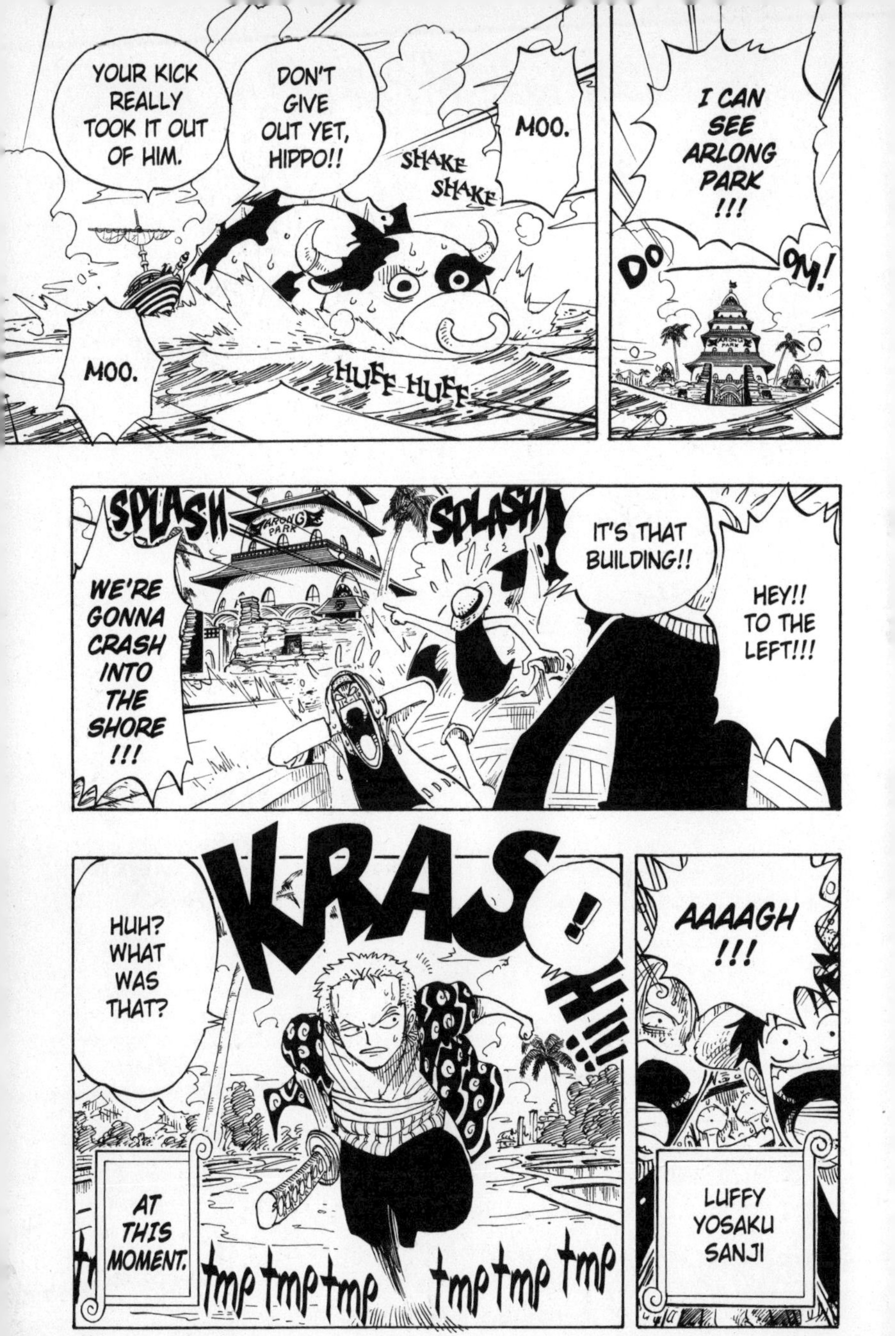
I CAN SEE ARLONG PARK!!!
DOOM!
MOO.
SHAKE SHAKE
DON'T GIVE OUT YET, HIPPO!!
YOUR KICK REALLY TOOK IT OUT OF HIM.
HUFF HUFF
MOO.
HEY!! TO THE LEFT!!!
IT'S THAT BUILDING!!
SPLASH
SPLASH
ARLONG PARK
WE'RE GONNA CRASH INTO THE SHORE!!!
AAAAGH!!!
LUFFY YOSAKU SANJI
KRASH!!!
HUH? WHAT WAS THAT?
AT THIS MOMENT.
tmp tmp tmp tmp tmp tmp tmp

QUESTION CORNER
chou chou
ビー
エス
エス

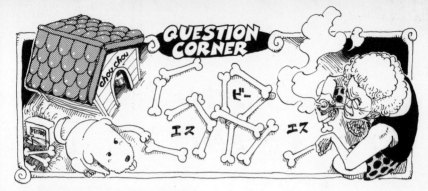

Q: **That's the kind of Sanji I like.**

A: What kind?

Q: Oda Sensei!! It's terrible!! My friend has caught the dreaded "I'll Die without a Snack" disease. What will cure it!? Hurry or he'll die!!

A: Don't panic!! Get a firm grip on yourself!! It'll be okay!! Keep your cool!! Calm down!! Good. Next question?

Q: How many fat-fats is Alvida's fatness?
Whizzzzz. Crack! Agh!

A: Oh please, get outta here.

Q: What do you call the pistols used in **One Piece**? They don't look like matchlocks.

A: They are flintlocks. Flint is a rock that makes a spark when it strikes metal. Think of it as one step above a matchlock.

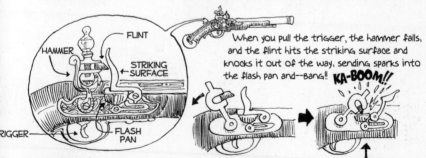

FLINT
HAMMER
STRIKING SURFACE
RIGGER
FLASH PAN
When you pull the trigger, the hammer falls, and the flint hits the striking surface and knocks it out of the way, sending sparks into the flash pan and--Bang!!
KA-BOOM!!

A flintlock had to be reloaded after every shot, so pirates sometimes carried 5 or 6 of them. However, in the world of **One Piece** some have been modified to fire repeatedly. Scary, huh?

Sparks ignite the gunpowder, and the bullet shoots off with a bang.

Chapter 75: OF MAPS AND FISH-MEN

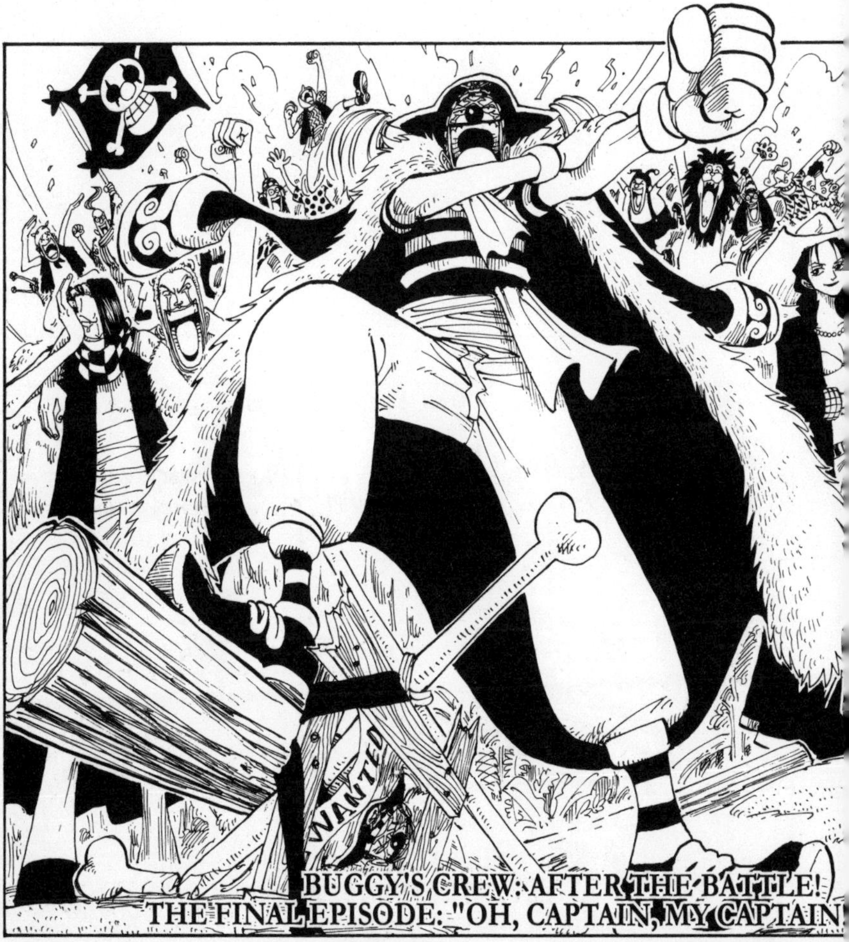
WANTED
BUGGY'S CREW: AFTER THE BATTLE!
THE FINAL EPISODE: "OH, CAPTAIN, MY CAPTAIN

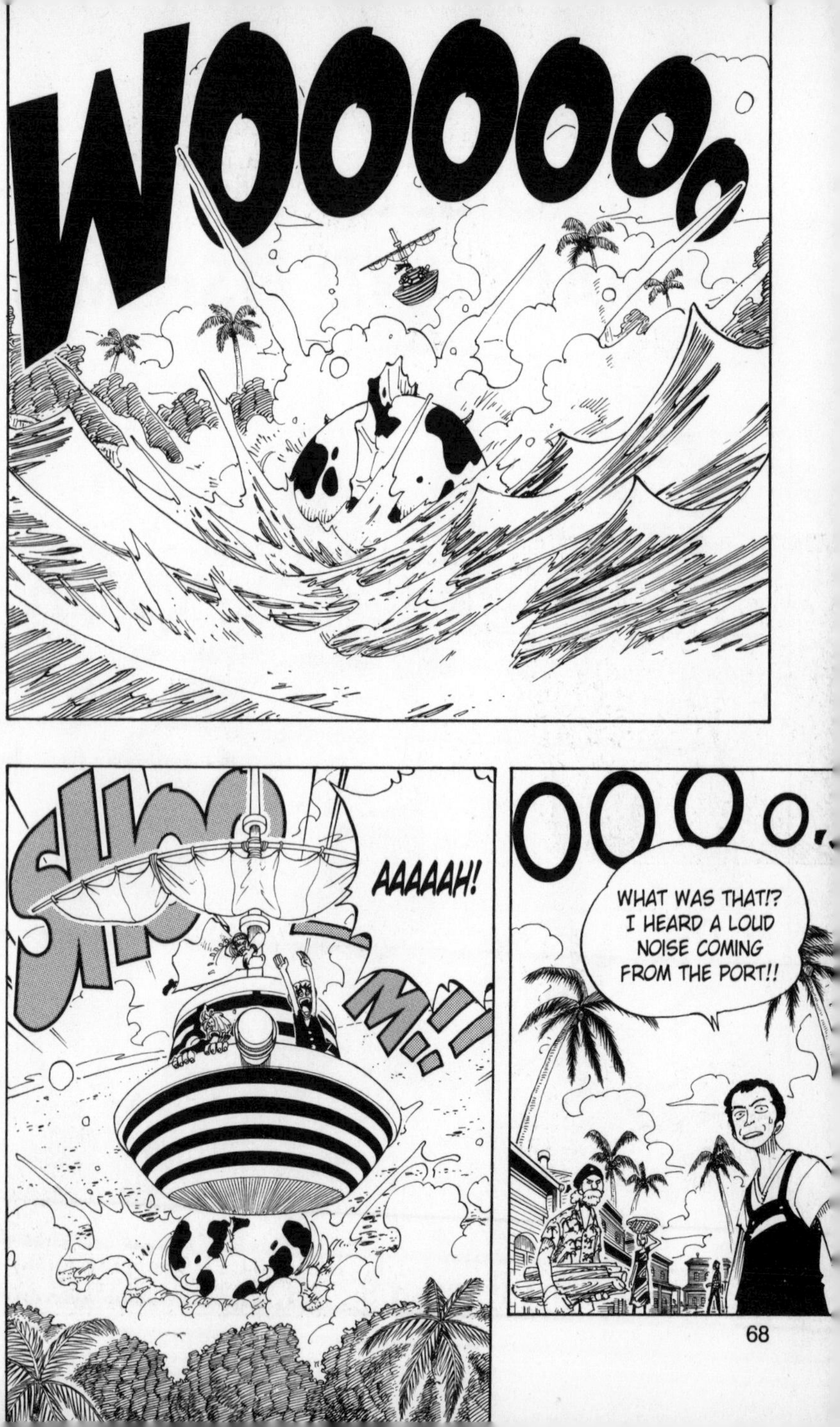
WOOOOOO
OOOO..
WHAT WAS THAT!? I HEARD A LOUD NOISE COMING FROM THE PORT!!
SHOOM!!
AAAAAH!

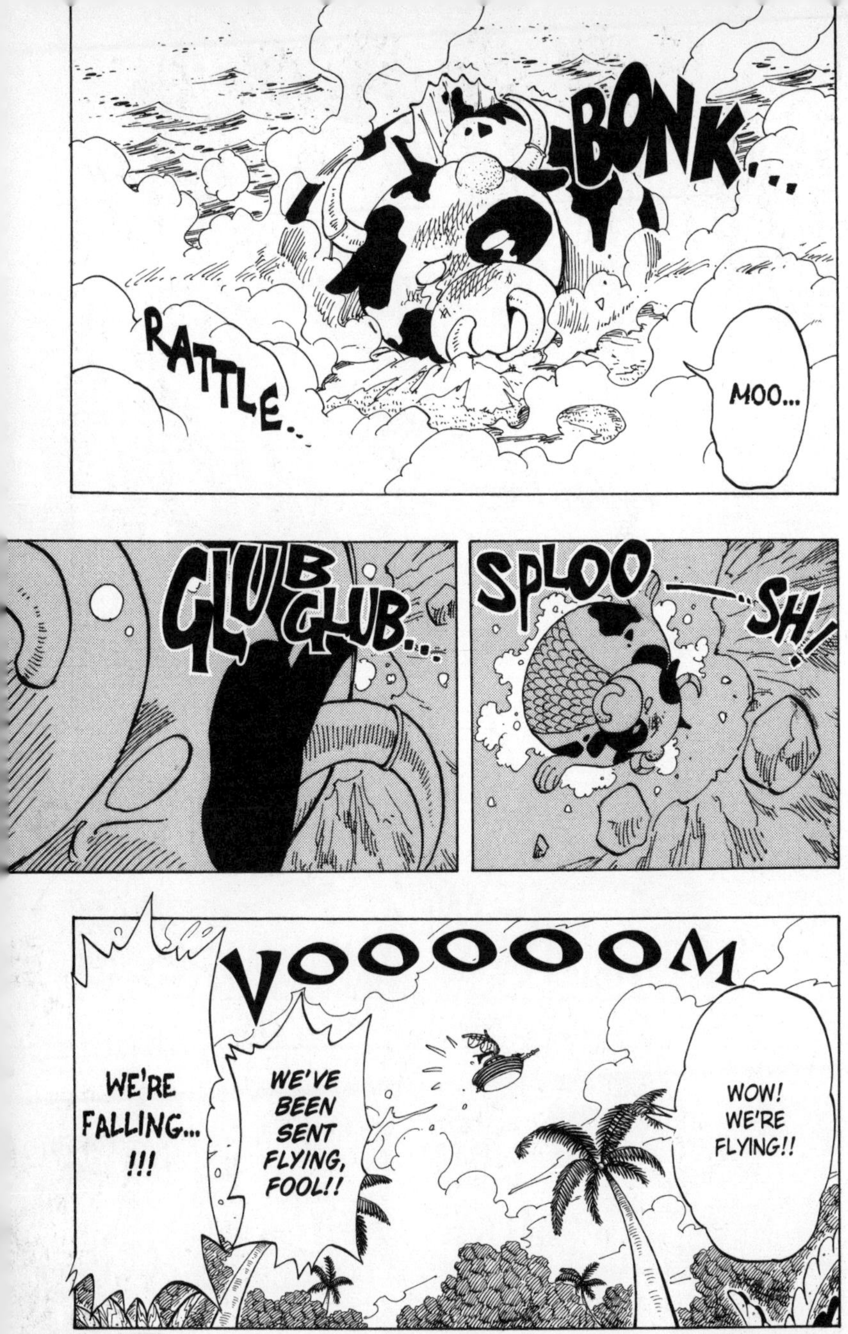
BONK...
MOO...
RATTLE...
SPLOO---SH!
GLUB GLUB...
VOOOOOM
WOW! WE'RE FLYING!!
WE'VE BEEN SENT FLYING, FOOL!!
WE'RE FALLING... !!!

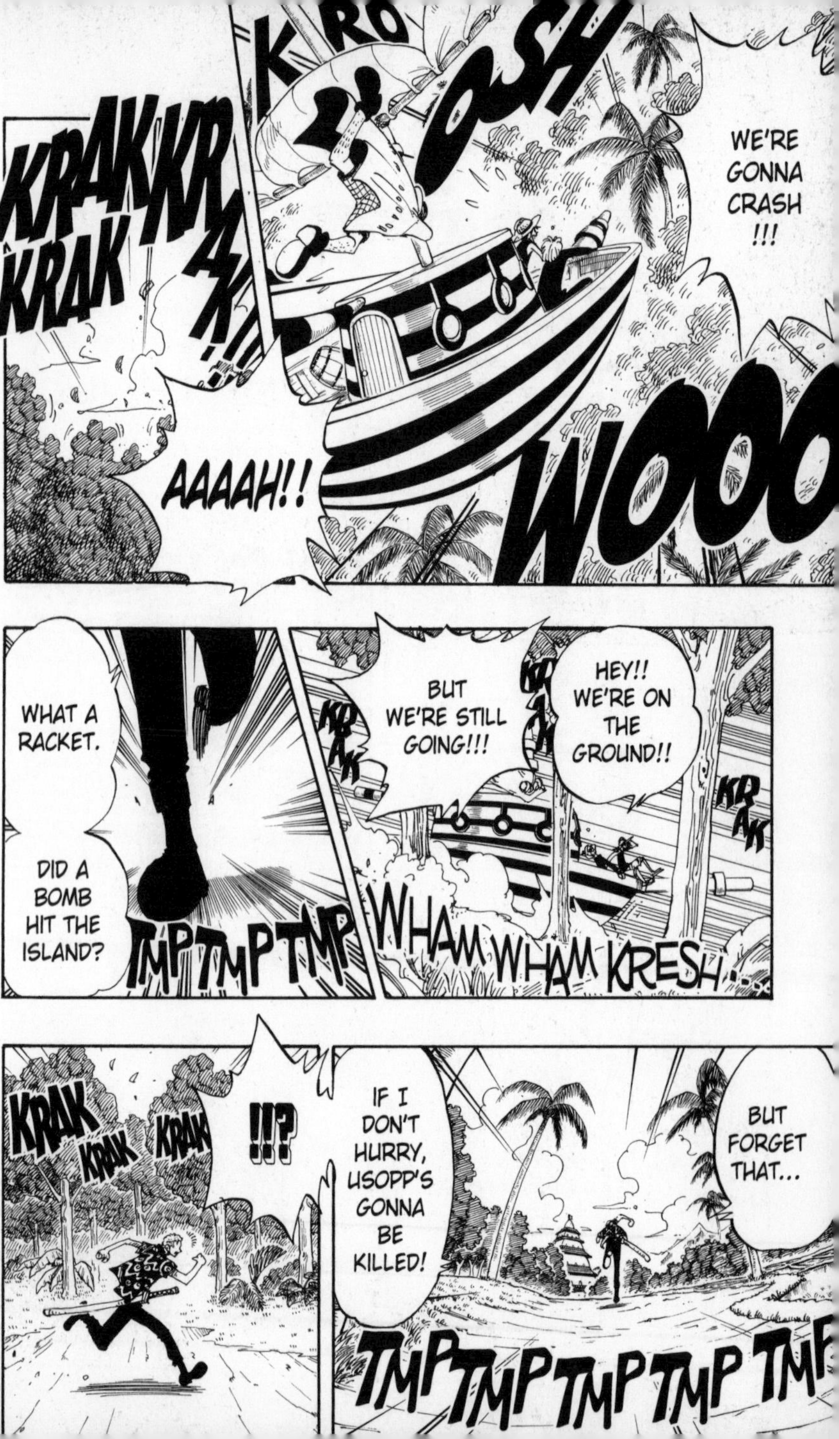
WE'RE GONNA CRASH!!!
KROOSH
KRAKKRAK KRAK KRAK!!
AAAAH!!
WOOO
HEY!! WE'RE ON THE GROUND!!
BUT WE'RE STILL GOING!!!
KRAK
KRAK
KRAK
WHAM WHAM KRESH...
WHAT A RACKET.
DID A BOMB HIT THE ISLAND?
TMP TMP TMP
BUT FORGET THAT...
IF I DON'T HURRY, USOPP'S GONNA BE KILLED!
TMP TMP TMP TMP TMP
!!?
KRAK KRAK KRAK

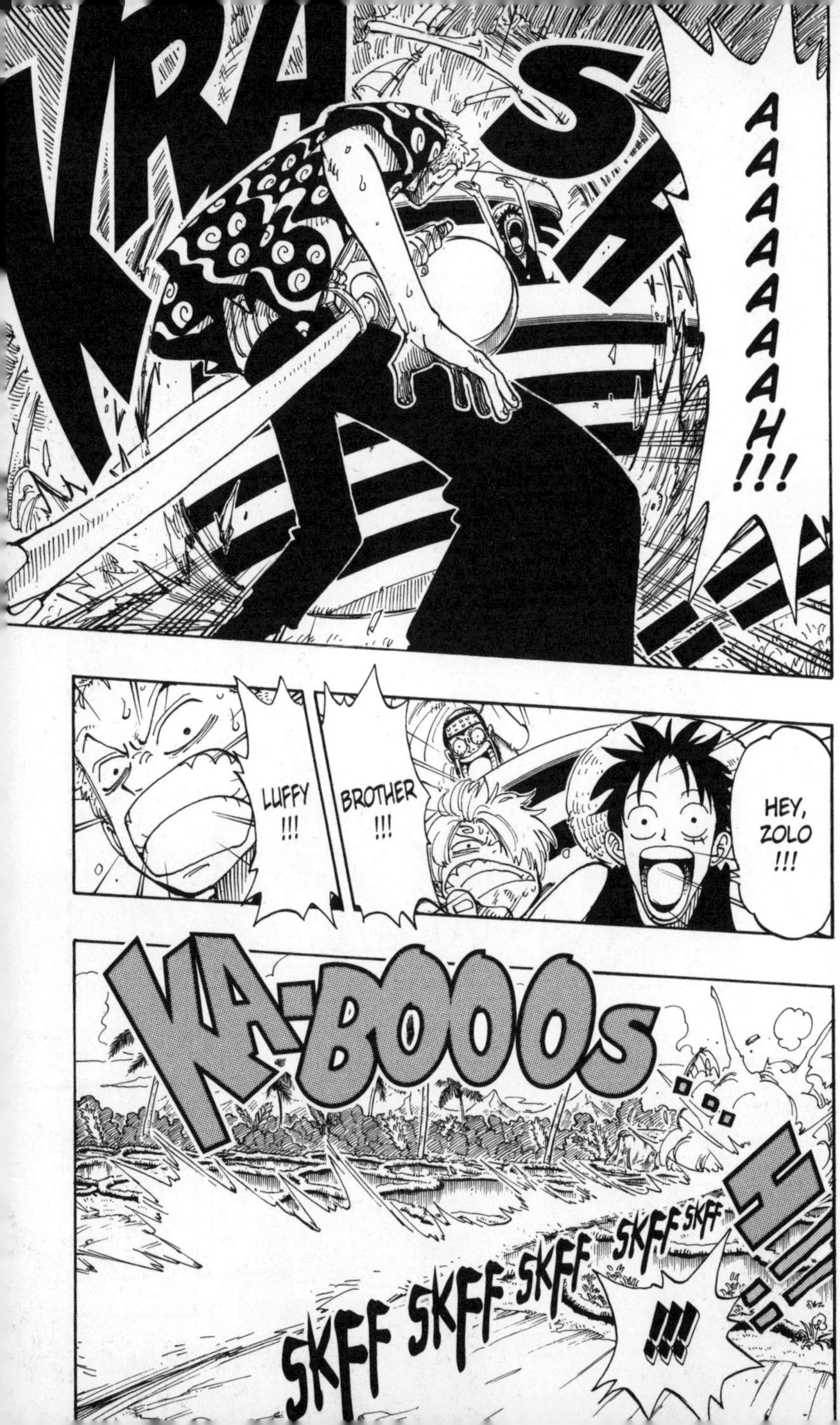
AAAAAAAH!!!
KRASH
HEY, ZOLO!!!
BROTHER!!!
LUFFY!!!
KA-BOOOS...H!!
!!!
SKFF SKFF SKFF SKFF SKFF SKFF

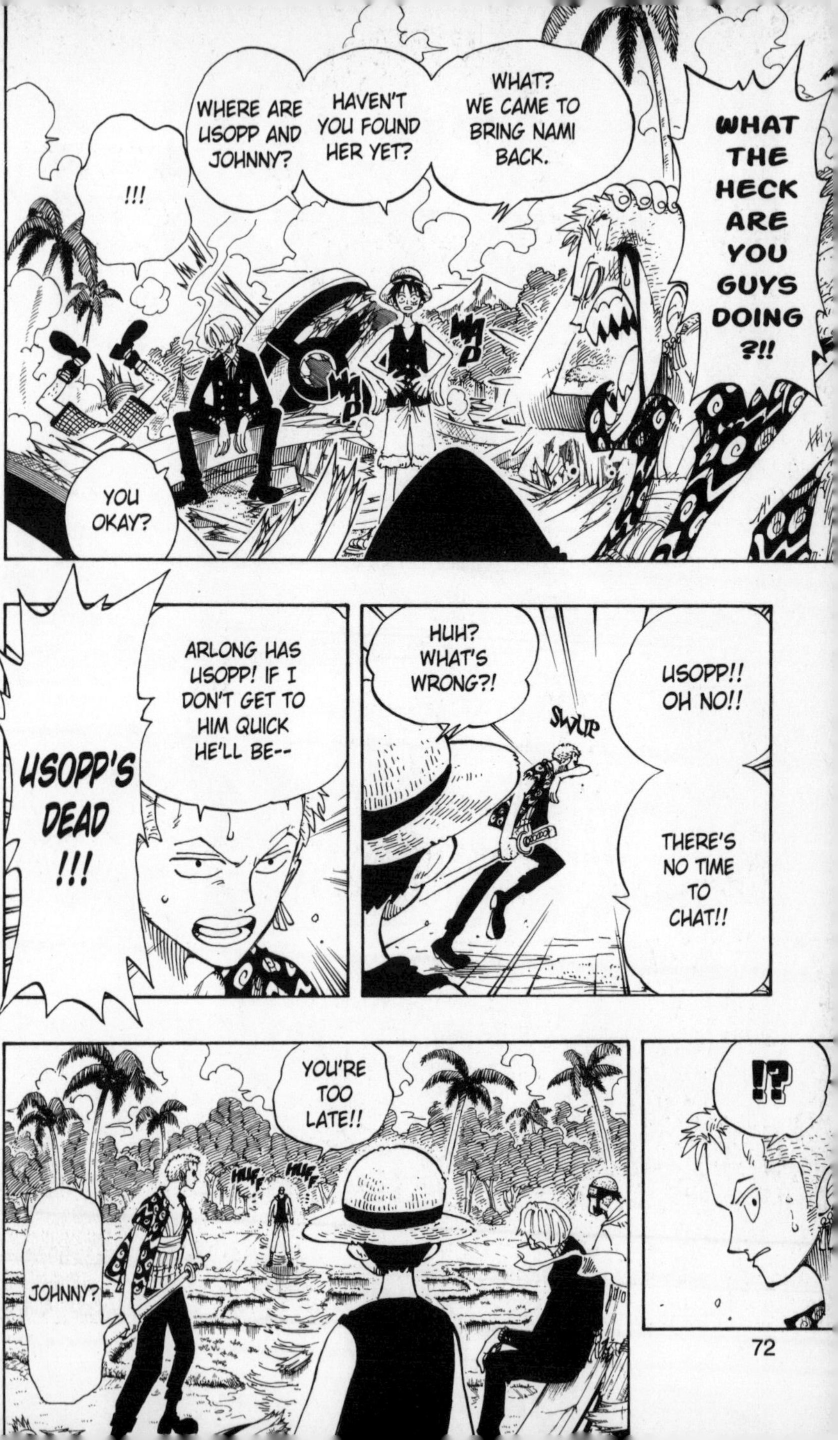
WHAT THE HECK ARE YOU GUYS DOING?!!
WHAT? WE CAME TO BRING NAMI BACK.
HAVEN'T YOU FOUND HER YET?
WHERE ARE USOPP AND JOHNNY?
!!!
WAP
WAP
YOU OKAY?
USOPP!! OH NO!!
THERE'S NO TIME TO CHAT!!
HUH? WHAT'S WRONG?!
SWUP
ARLONG HAS USOPP! IF I DON'T GET TO HIM QUICK HE'LL BE--
USOPP'S DEAD!!!
!?
YOU'RE TOO LATE!!
HUFF
HUFF
JOHNNY?

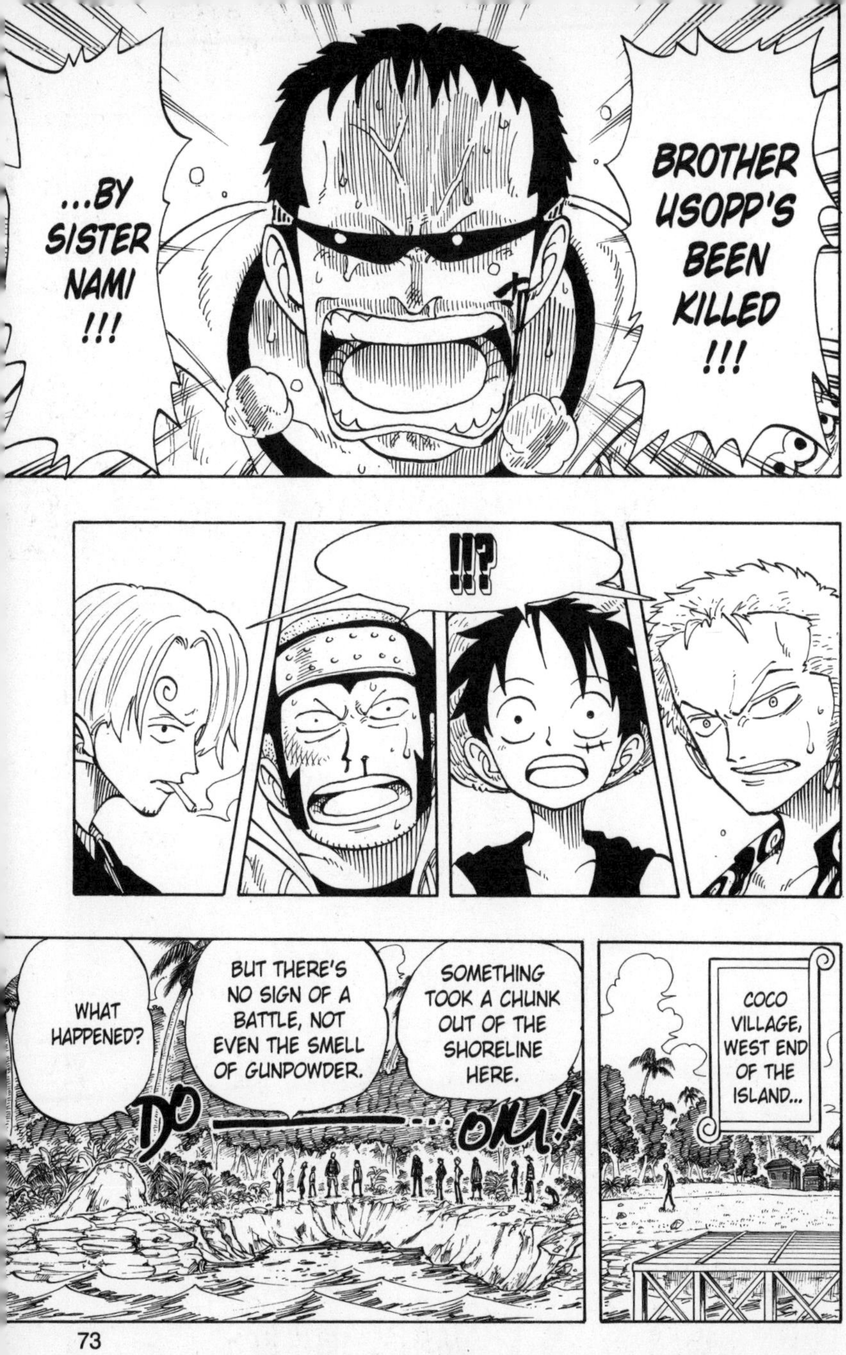
BROTHER USOPP'S BEEN KILLED!!!
...BY SISTER NAMI!!!
!!?
COCO VILLAGE, WEST END OF THE ISLAND...
SOMETHING TOOK A CHUNK OUT OF THE SHORELINE HERE.
BUT THERE'S NO SIGN OF A BATTLE, NOT EVEN THE SMELL OF GUNPOWDER.
WHAT HAPPENED?
DO————OM!

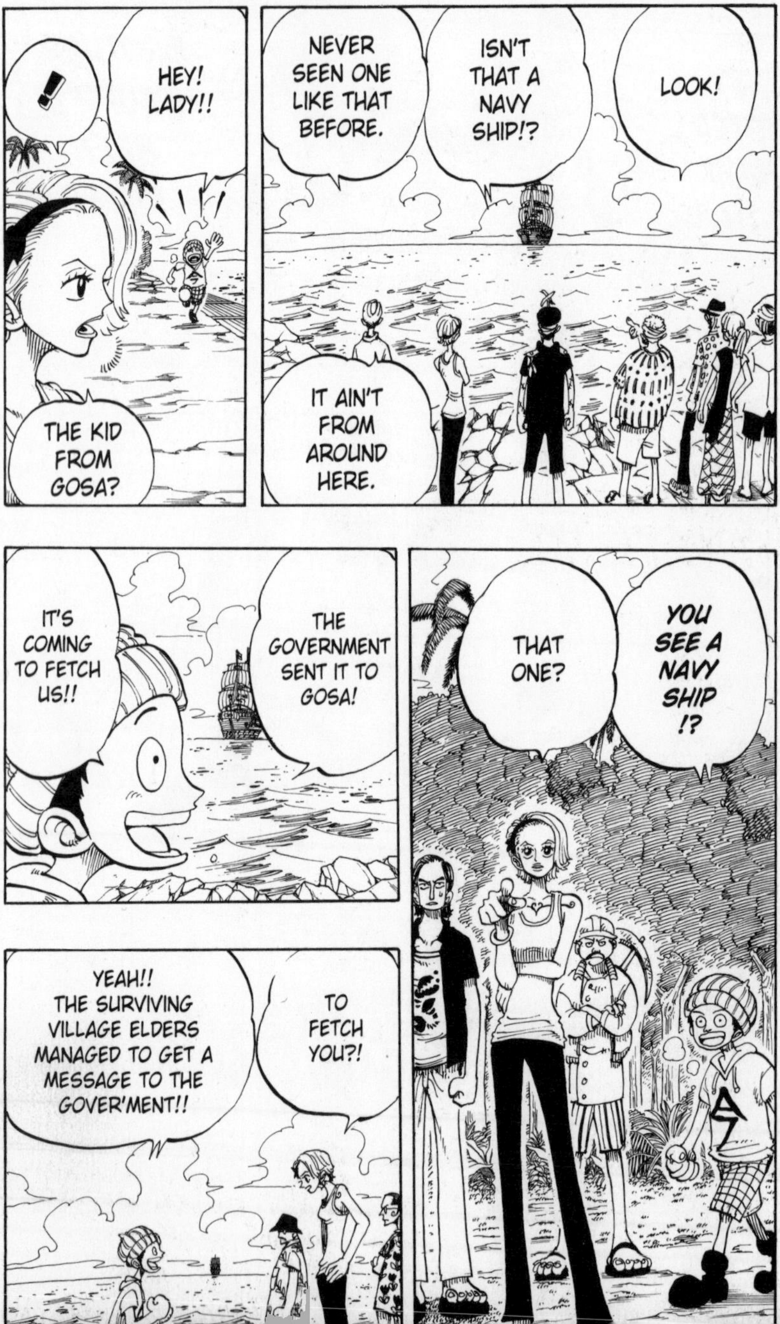
LOOK!
ISN'T THAT A NAVY SHIP!?
NEVER SEEN ONE LIKE THAT BEFORE.
IT AIN'T FROM AROUND HERE.
HEY! LADY!!
!
THE KID FROM GOSA?
YOU SEE A NAVY SHIP!?
THAT ONE?
THE GOVERNMENT SENT IT TO GOSA!
IT'S COMING TO FETCH US!!
TO FETCH YOU?!
YEAH!! THE SURVIVING VILLAGE ELDERS MANAGED TO GET A MESSAGE TO THE GOVER'MENT!!

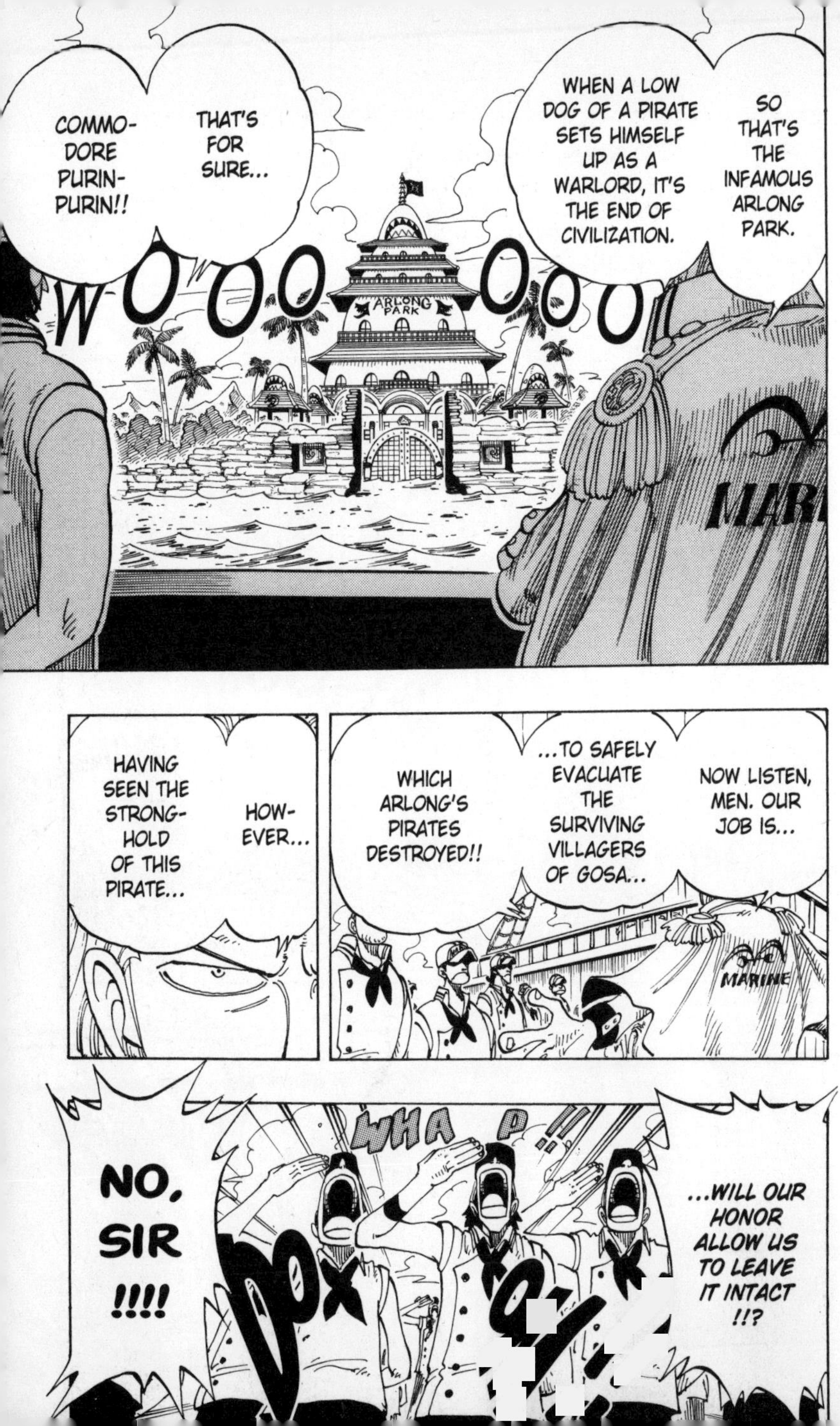
SO THAT'S THE INFAMOUS ARLONG PARK.
WHEN A LOW DOG OF A PIRATE SETS HIMSELF UP AS A WARLORD, IT'S THE END OF CIVILIZATION.
THAT'S FOR SURE...
COMMO-DORE PURIN-PURIN!!
WOOOOOOO
ARLONG PARK
NOW LISTEN, MEN. OUR JOB IS...
...TO SAFELY EVACUATE THE SURVIVING VILLAGERS OF GOSA...
WHICH ARLONG'S PIRATES DESTROYED!!
MARINE
HOW-EVER...
HAVING SEEN THE STRONG-HOLD OF THIS PIRATE...
...WILL OUR HONOR ALLOW US TO LEAVE IT INTACT !!?
WHA P!!!
NO, SIR !!!!

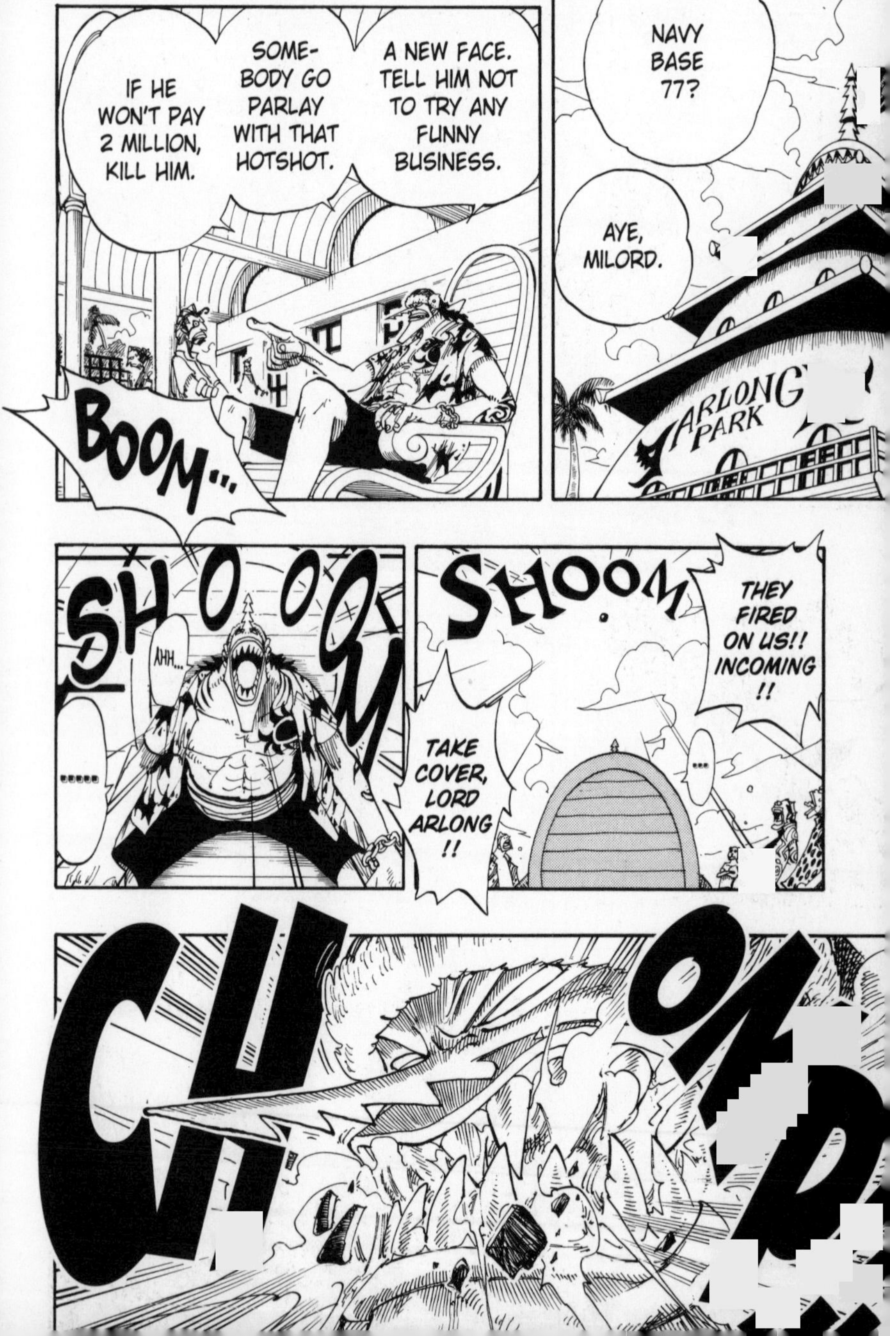
NAVY BASE 77?
AYE, MILORD.
A NEW FACE. TELL HIM NOT TO TRY ANY FUNNY BUSINESS.
SOME-BODY GO PARLAY WITH THAT HOTSHOT.
IF HE WON'T PAY 2 MILLION, KILL HIM.
BOOM...
SHOOM
THEY FIRED ON US!! INCOMING!!
...
TAKE COVER, LORD ARLONG!!
SHOOOM
AHH...
.....
ARLONG PARK

READ THIS WAY

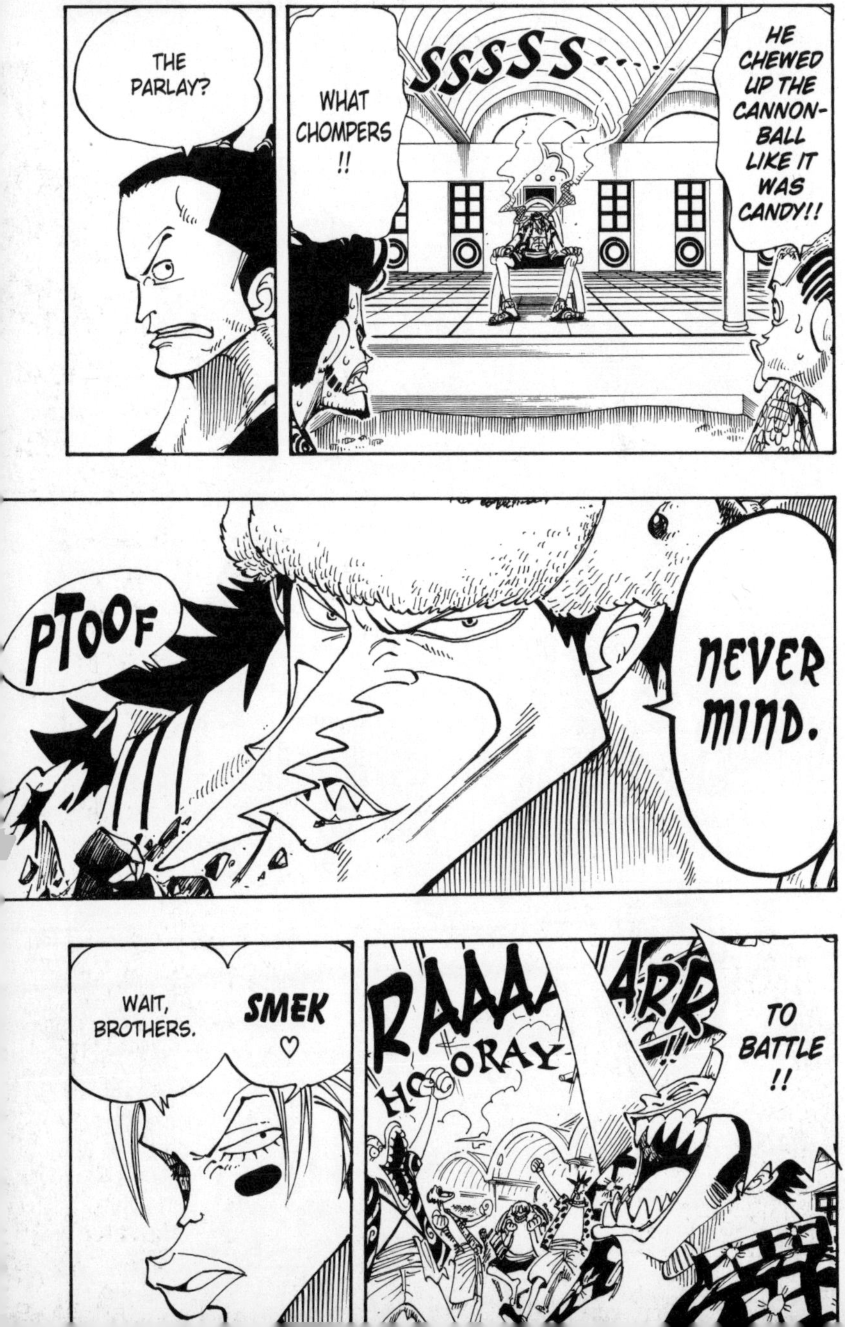
HE CHEWED UP THE CANNON-BALL LIKE IT WAS CANDY!!
SSSSS...
WHAT CHOMPERS!!
THE PARLAY?
NEVER MIND.
PTOOF
TO BATTLE!!
RAAAAARR!!
HOORAY
SMEK ♡
WAIT, BROTHERS.

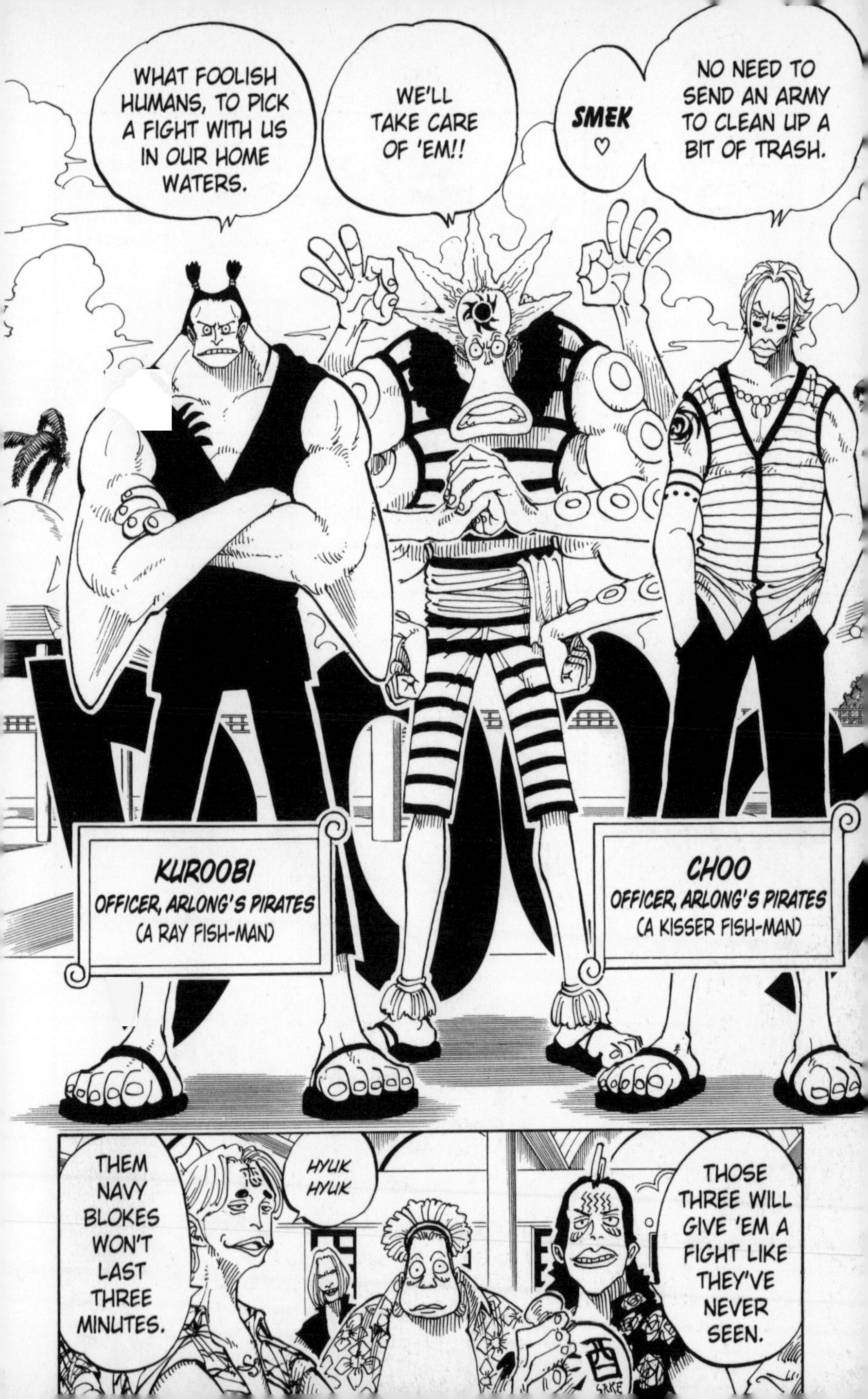
NO NEED TO SEND AN ARMY TO CLEAN UP A BIT OF TRASH.
SMEK ♡
WE'LL TAKE CARE OF 'EM!!
WHAT FOOLISH HUMANS, TO PICK A FIGHT WITH US IN OUR HOME WATERS.
CHOO
OFFICER, ARLONG'S PIRATES
(A KISSER FISH-MAN)
KUROOBI
OFFICER, ARLONG'S PIRATES
(A RAY FISH-MAN)
THOSE THREE WILL GIVE 'EM A FIGHT LIKE THEY'VE NEVER SEEN.
HYUK HYUK
THEM NAVY BLOKES WON'T LAST THREE MINUTES.

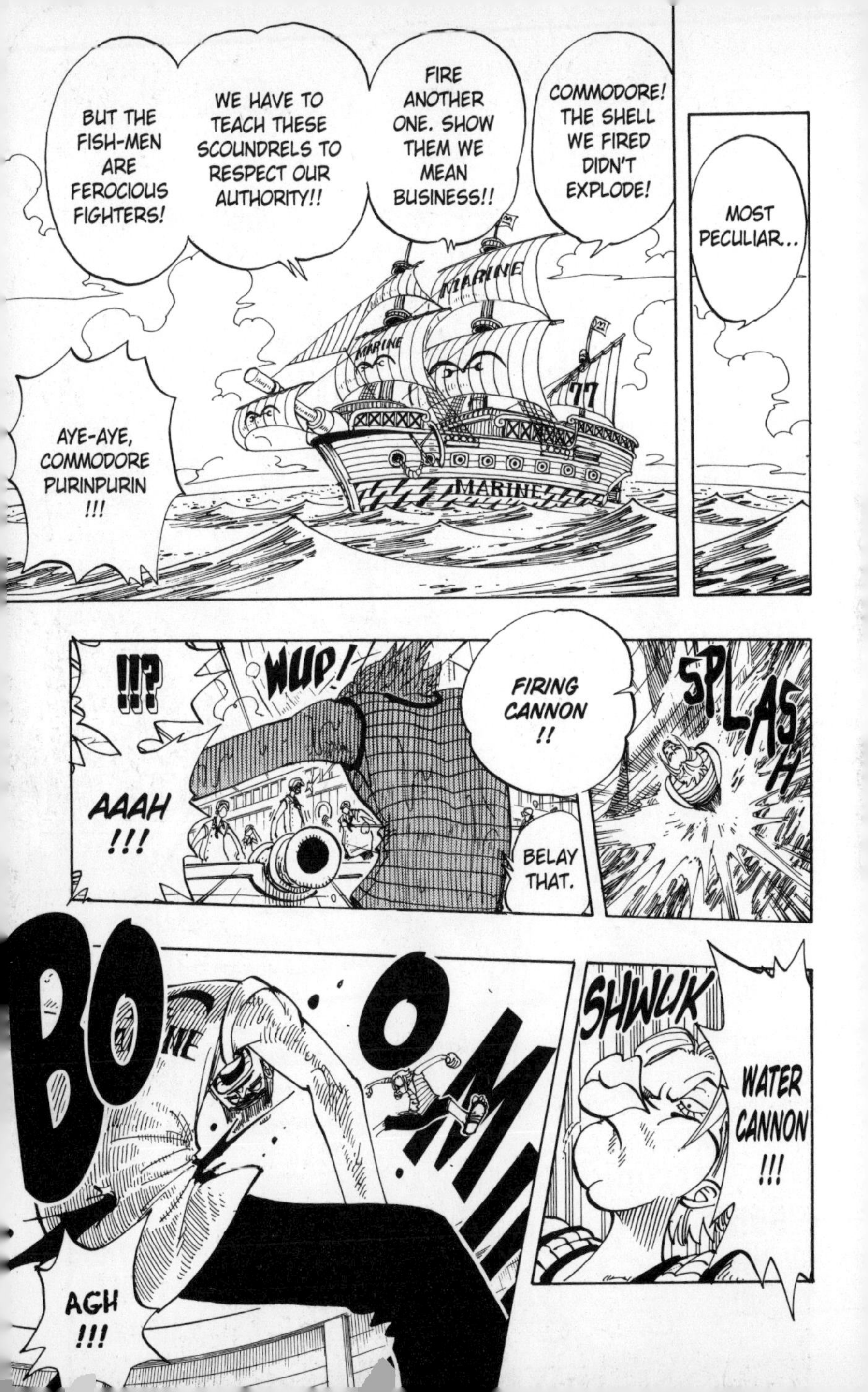
MOST PECULIAR...
COMMODORE! THE SHELL WE FIRED DIDN'T EXPLODE!
FIRE ANOTHER ONE. SHOW THEM WE MEAN BUSINESS!!
WE HAVE TO TEACH THESE SCOUNDRELS TO RESPECT OUR AUTHORITY!!
BUT THE FISH-MEN ARE FEROCIOUS FIGHTERS!
AYE-AYE, COMMODORE PURINPURIN !!!
SPLASH
FIRING CANNON !!
BELAY THAT.
WUP!
!!?
AAAH !!!
SHWUK
WATER CANNON !!!
BOOM
AGH !!!

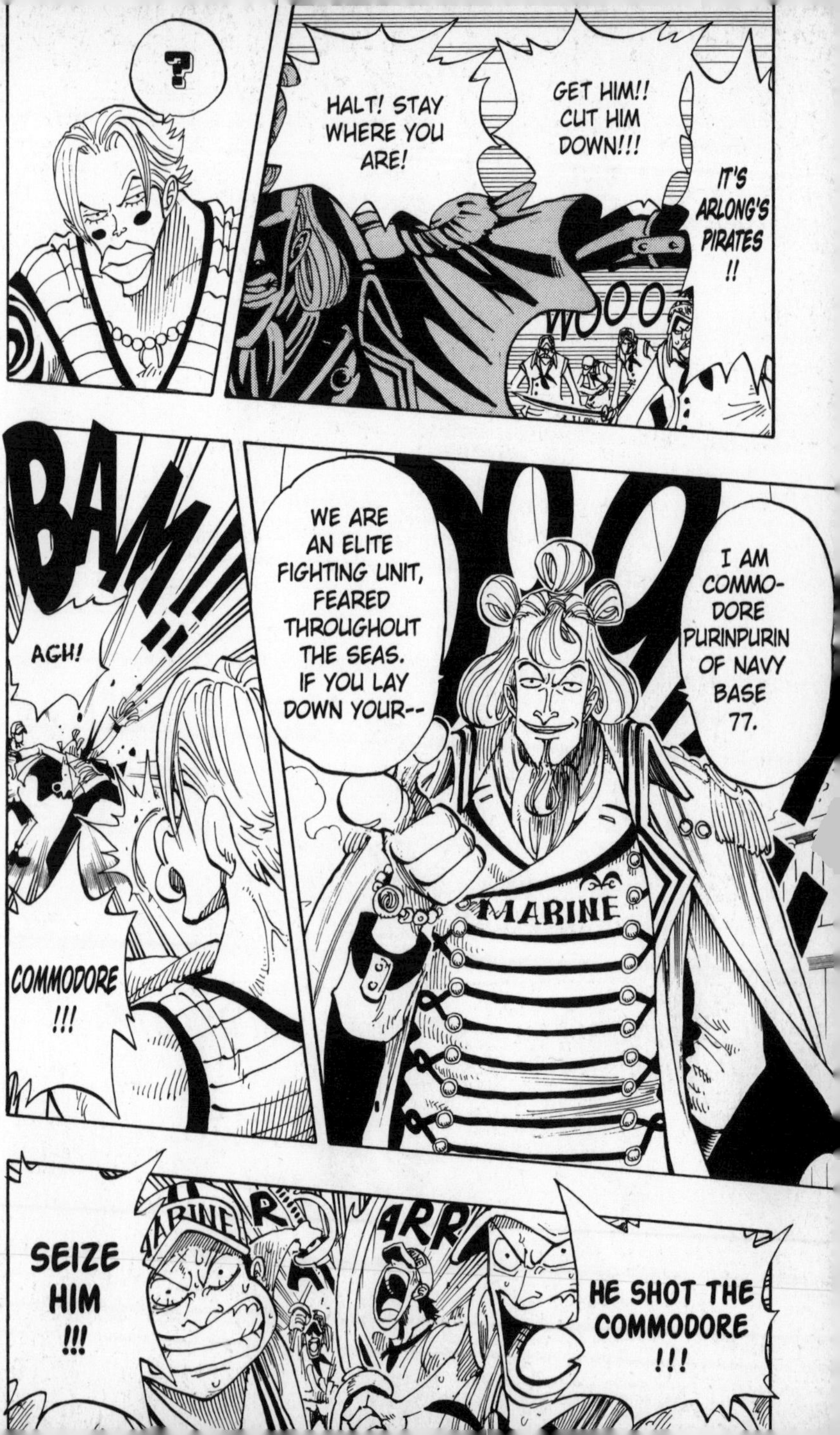
GET HIM!! CUT HIM DOWN!!!
IT'S ARLONG'S PIRATES!!
HALT! STAY WHERE YOU ARE!
WOOOO
?
I AM COMMODORE PURINPURIN OF NAVY BASE 77.
WE ARE AN ELITE FIGHTING UNIT, FEARED THROUGHOUT THE SEAS. IF YOU LAY DOWN YOUR--
MARINE
BAM!!
AGH!
COMMODORE!!!
HE SHOT THE COMMODORE!!!
ARR
R
SEIZE HIM!!!

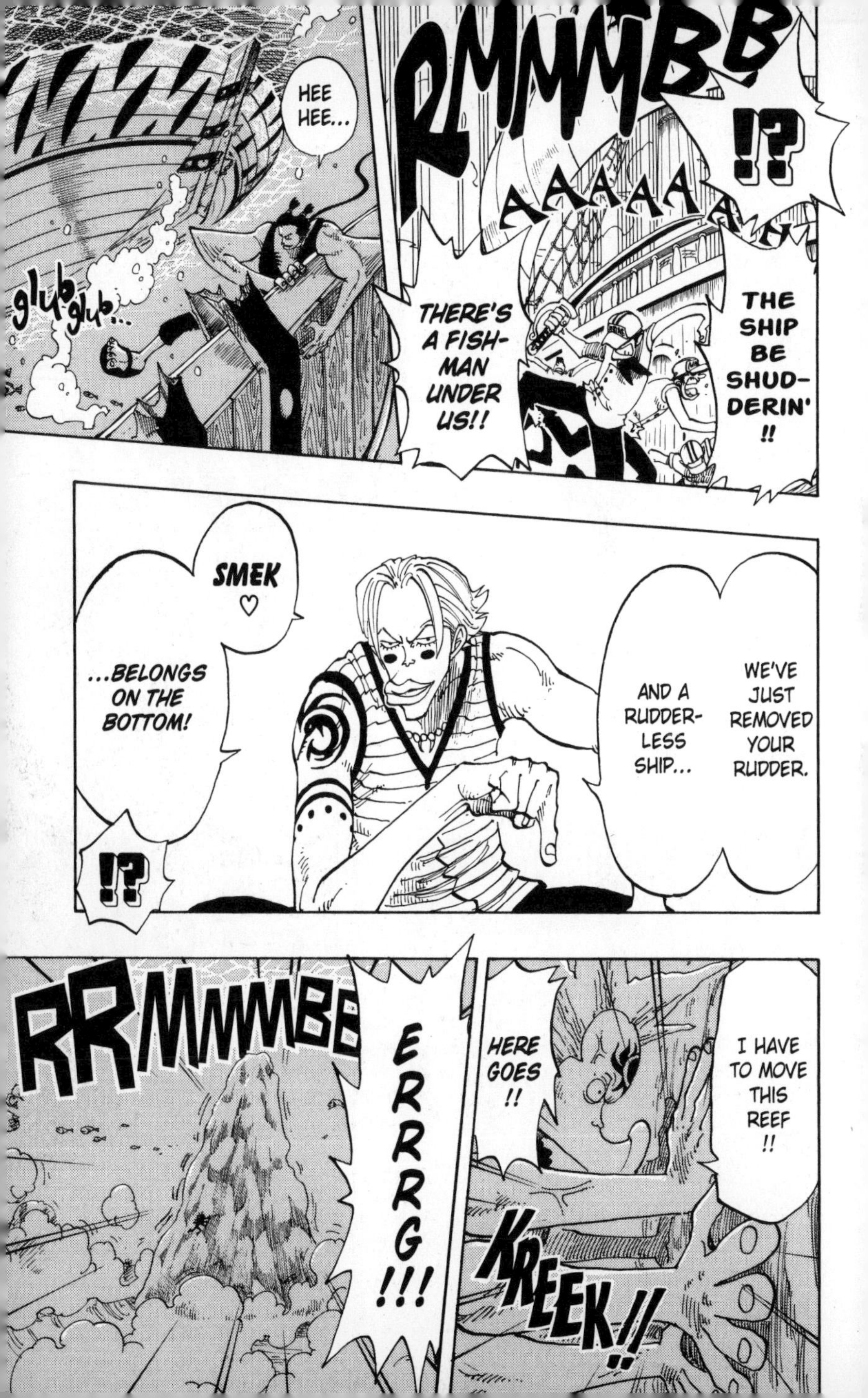
RMMMBB
!?
AAAAAH
THE SHIP BE SHUDDERIN'!!
THERE'S A FISH-MAN UNDER US!!
HEE HEE...
glub glub...
WE'VE JUST REMOVED YOUR RUDDER.
AND A RUDDERLESS SHIP...
...BELONGS ON THE BOTTOM!
SMEK ♡
!?
I HAVE TO MOVE THIS REEF!!
HERE GOES!!
KREEK!!
ERRRG!!!
RRMMMBB

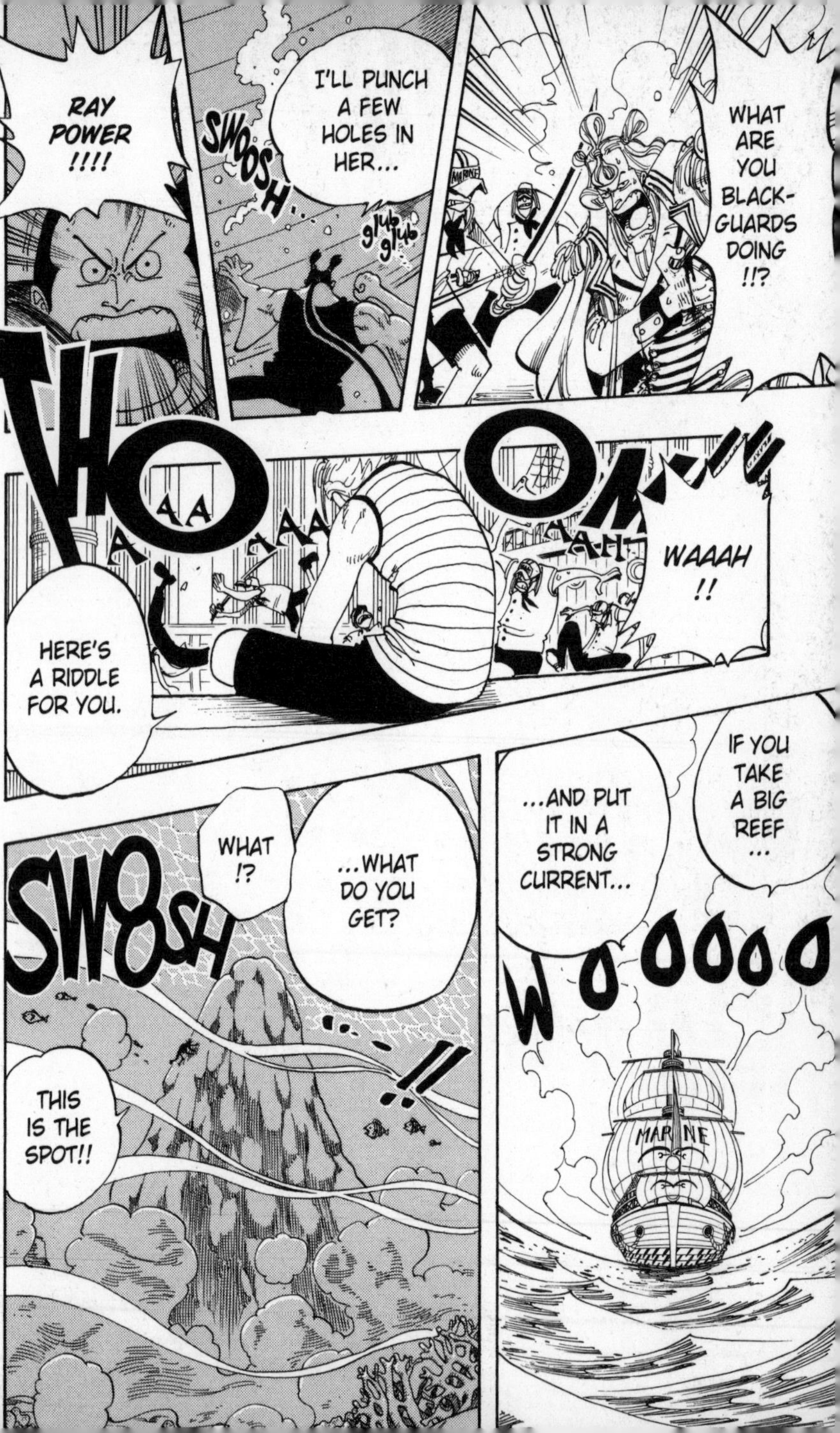
WHAT ARE YOU BLACK-GUARDS DOING !!?
I'LL PUNCH A FEW HOLES IN HER...
SWOOSH
glub glub
RAY POWER !!!!
THOOM
WAAAH !!
HERE'S A RIDDLE FOR YOU.
IF YOU TAKE A BIG REEF ...
...AND PUT IT IN A STRONG CURRENT...
WOOOOO
...WHAT DO YOU GET?
WHAT !?
SWOOSH
THIS IS THE SPOT!!

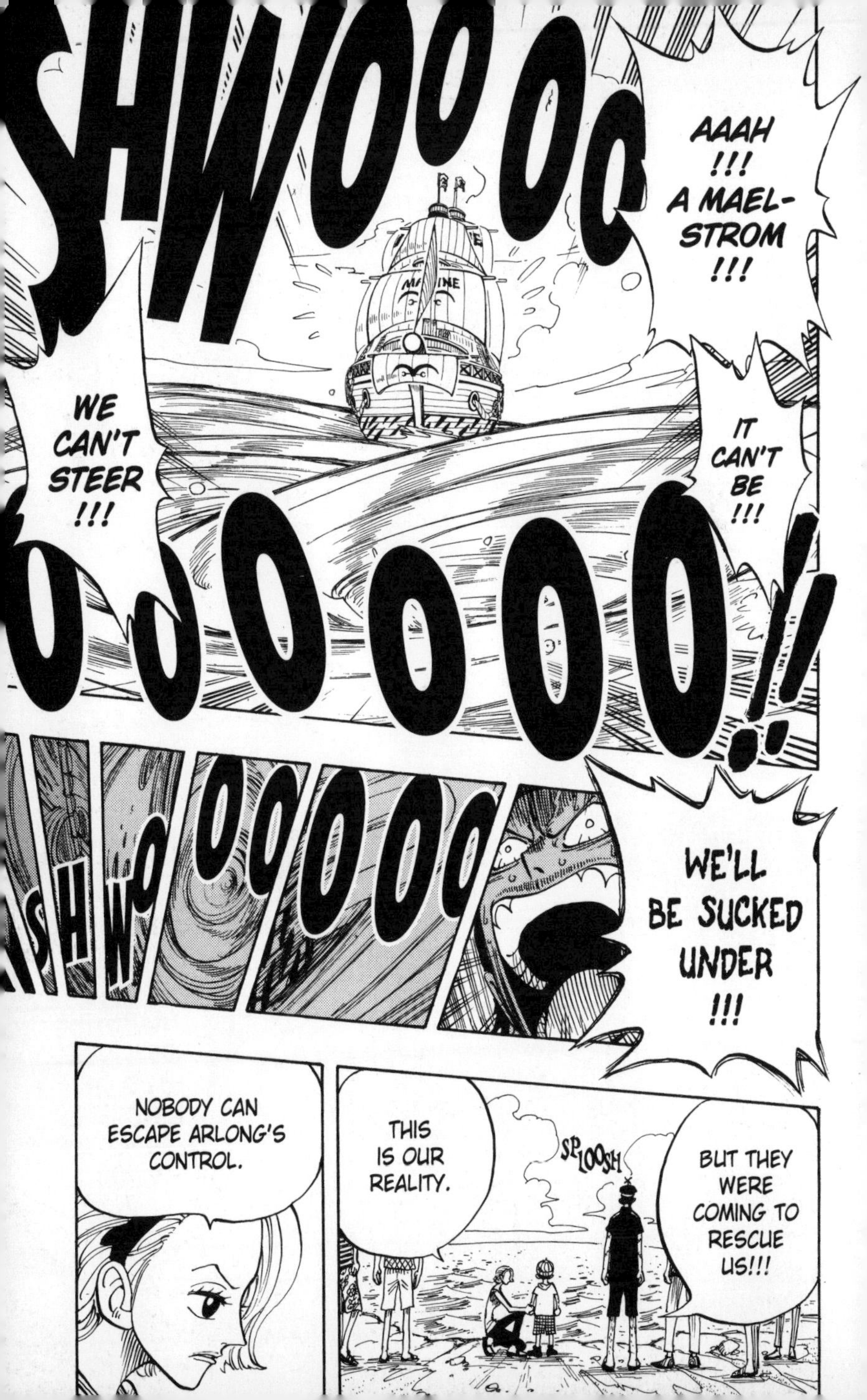
SHWOOOOOOOOOOO!!
AAAH!!! A MAEL-STROM!!!
IT CAN'T BE!!!
WE CAN'T STEER!!!
SHWOOOOOOO
WE'LL BE SUCKED UNDER!!!
BUT THEY WERE COMING TO RESCUE US!!!
SPLOOSH
THIS IS OUR REALITY.
NOBODY CAN ESCAPE ARLONG'S CONTROL.

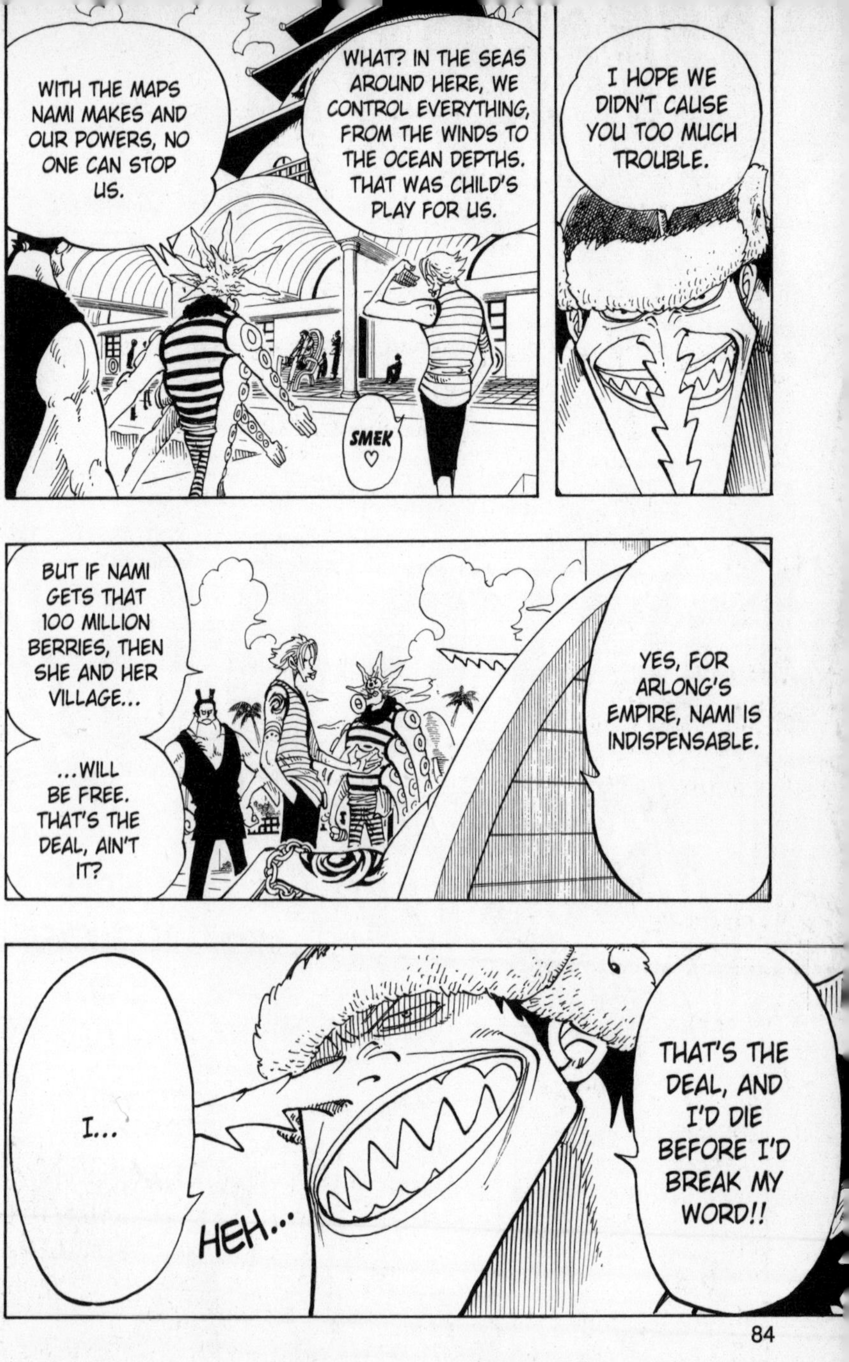
I HOPE WE DIDN'T CAUSE YOU TOO MUCH TROUBLE.
WHAT? IN THE SEAS AROUND HERE, WE CONTROL EVERYTHING, FROM THE WINDS TO THE OCEAN DEPTHS. THAT WAS CHILD'S PLAY FOR US.
WITH THE MAPS NAMI MAKES AND OUR POWERS, NO ONE CAN STOP US.
SMEK ♡
YES, FOR ARLONG'S EMPIRE, NAMI IS INDISPENSABLE.
BUT IF NAMI GETS THAT 100 MILLION BERRIES, THEN SHE AND HER VILLAGE...
...WILL BE FREE. THAT'S THE DEAL, AIN'T IT?
THAT'S THE DEAL, AND I'D DIE BEFORE I'D BREAK MY WORD!!
I...
HEH...

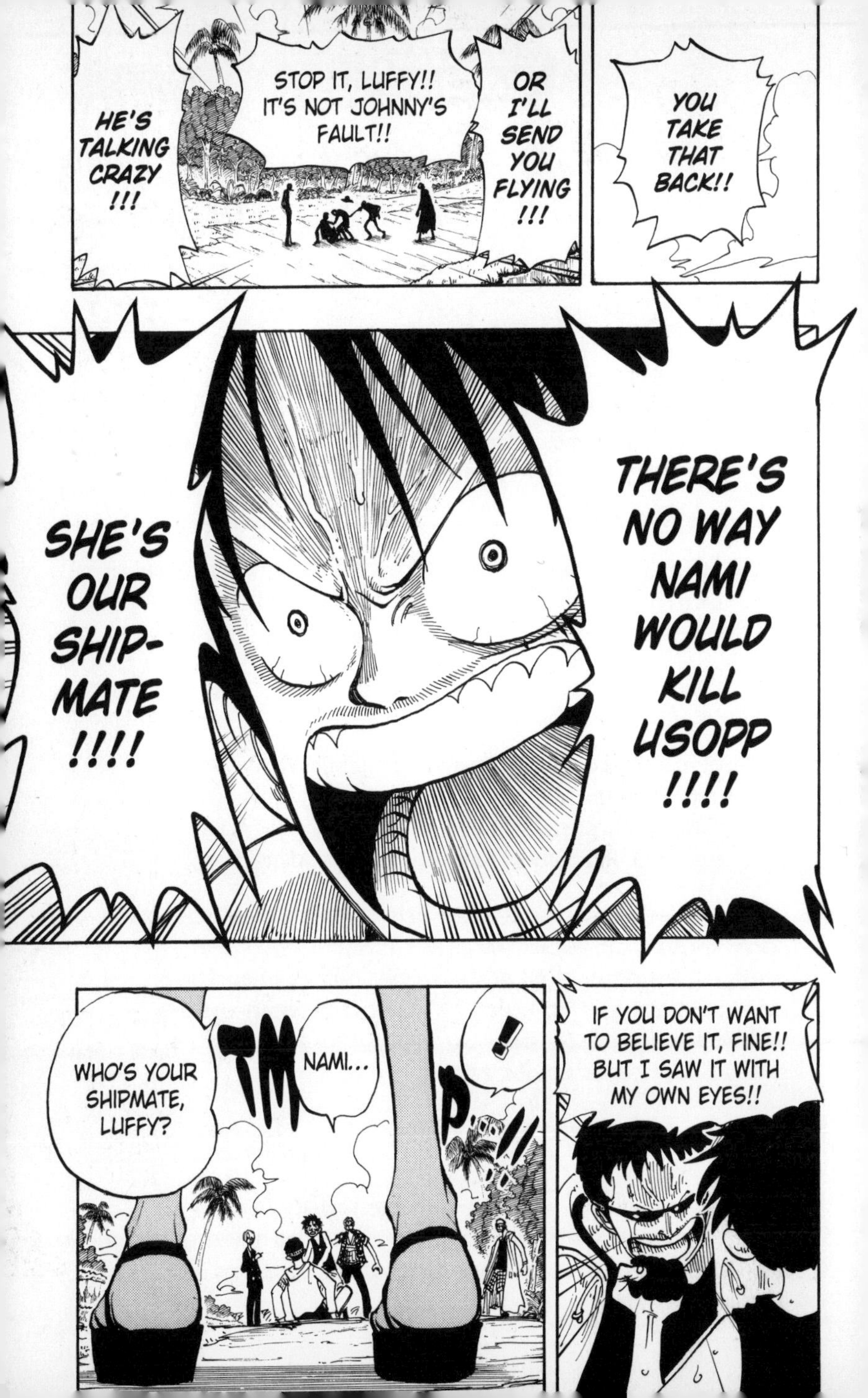
YOU TAKE THAT BACK!!
OR I'LL SEND YOU FLYING!!!
STOP IT, LUFFY!! IT'S NOT JOHNNY'S FAULT!!
HE'S TALKING CRAZY!!!
THERE'S NO WAY NAMI WOULD KILL USOPP!!!!
SHE'S OUR SHIP-MATE!!!!
IF YOU DON'T WANT TO BELIEVE IT, FINE!! BUT I SAW IT WITH MY OWN EYES!!
!
TMP
NAMI...
WHO'S YOUR SHIPMATE, LUFFY?

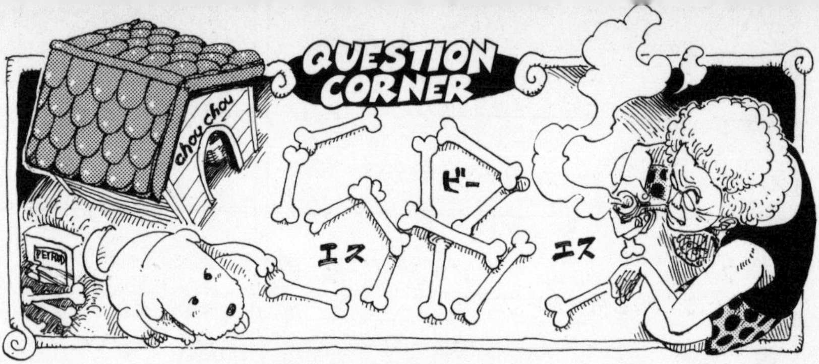
QUESTION CORNER
chou chou
PETRO
エス
ビー
エス

Q: Hey, Mr. Oda!! Sit down!! I know you want to see your own profile, but be careful!! You could break your neck! Value your life more!! And shame on you for having to be told by someone younger than yourself!! Repent!! Dismissed!!

A: You're right...I'm sorry.

Q: I tried that thing in your note of VOLUME 7 about trying to see your own face in profile with only one mirror, and I sprained my neck. The doctor asked me how it happened. I didn't know what to tell him.

A: Then you're one of **us**.

Q: Hello. I had this bottle of wine and I thought, "What country is this from?" I looked at the label and it said, "dry, full body." I was a little bit surprised, but also pleased. That's the origin of the name of Lt. Fullbody's name, isn't it? Don't deny it.

A: I won't, that's exactly it! I don't drink much alcohol so I don't know a lot about wine, but it seems that the depth of flavor is called body! Strong wines aged for a long time are said to have "full" body. Lighter wines are said to have "medium" or "light" body. And that's where Lt. Fullbody's name comes from!

Q: Where was Gin hiding that weapon?
Was it "down there" or what?

A: What?! Are you insinuating that the weapon was hidden between Gin's legs?! He wouldn't do a thing like that. Gin's fans are gonna be mad at you--and he's very popular.

Chapter 76: SLEEP

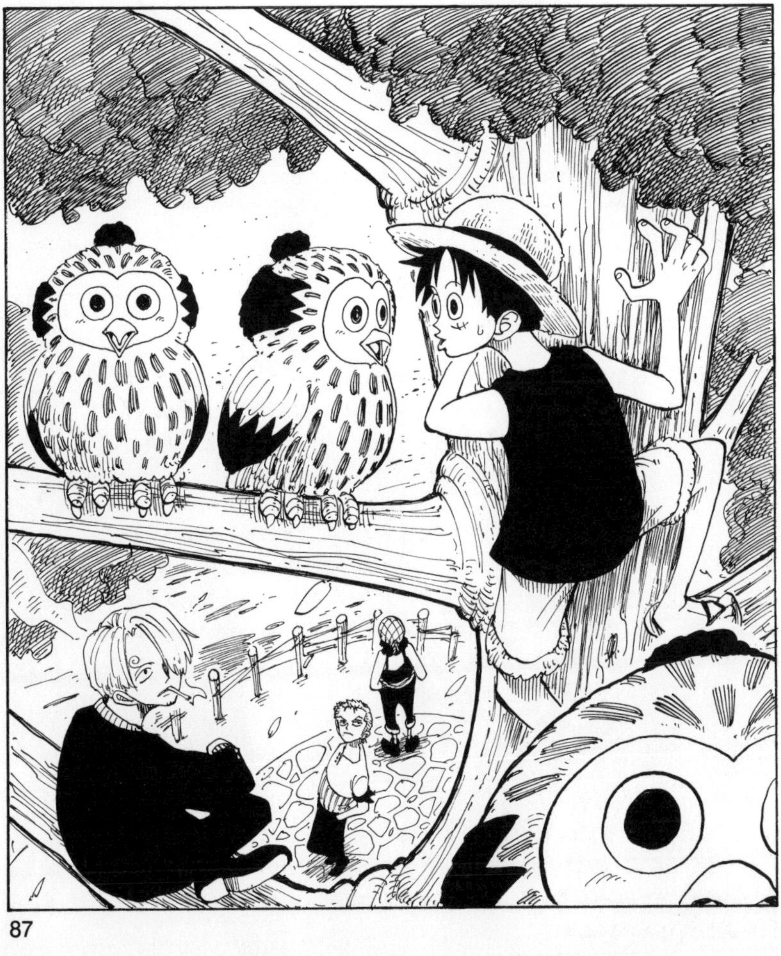

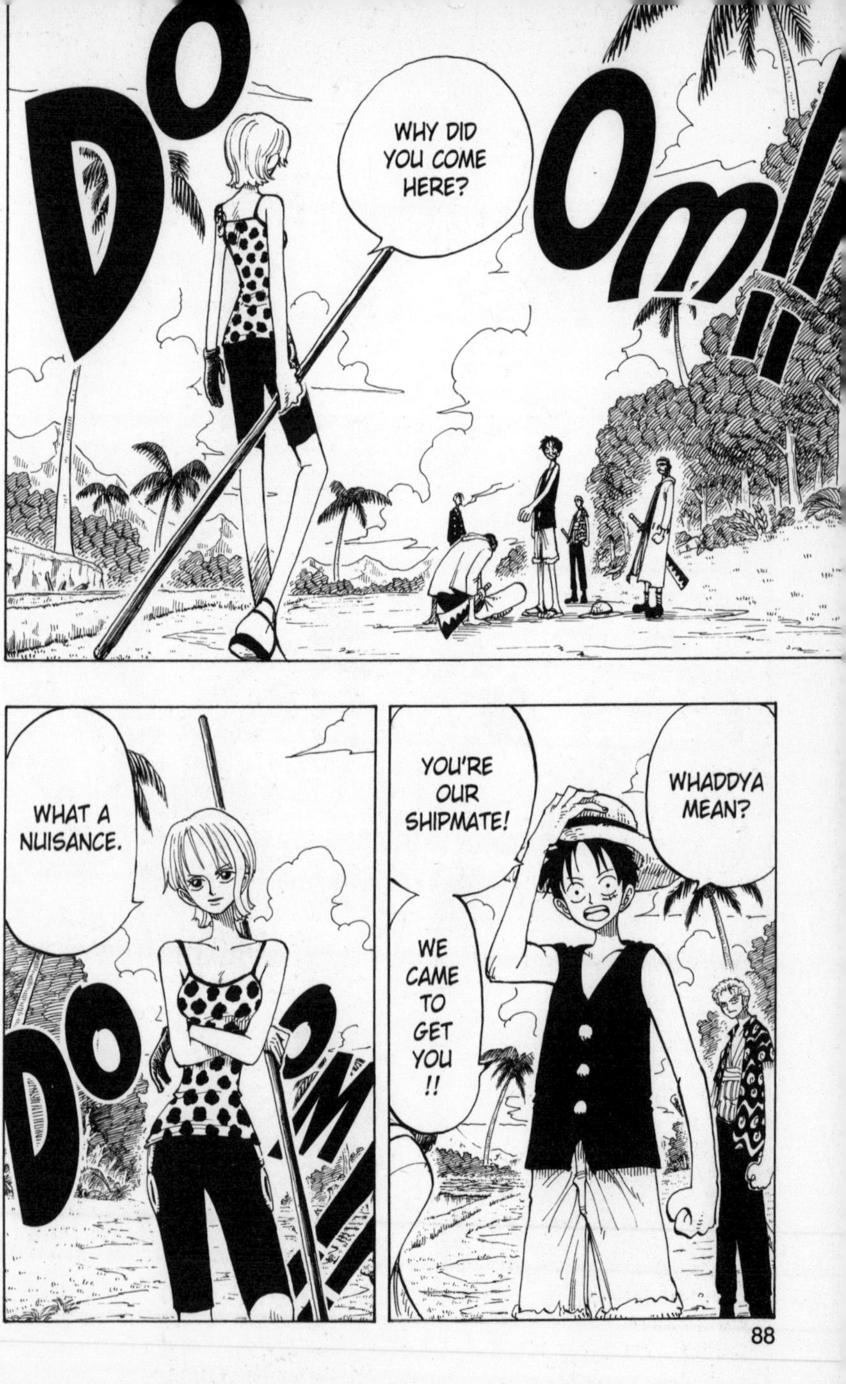
DOOM!!
WHY DID YOU COME HERE?
WHADDYA MEAN?
YOU'RE OUR SHIPMATE!
WE CAME TO GET YOU !!
WHAT A NUISANCE.
DOOM!!

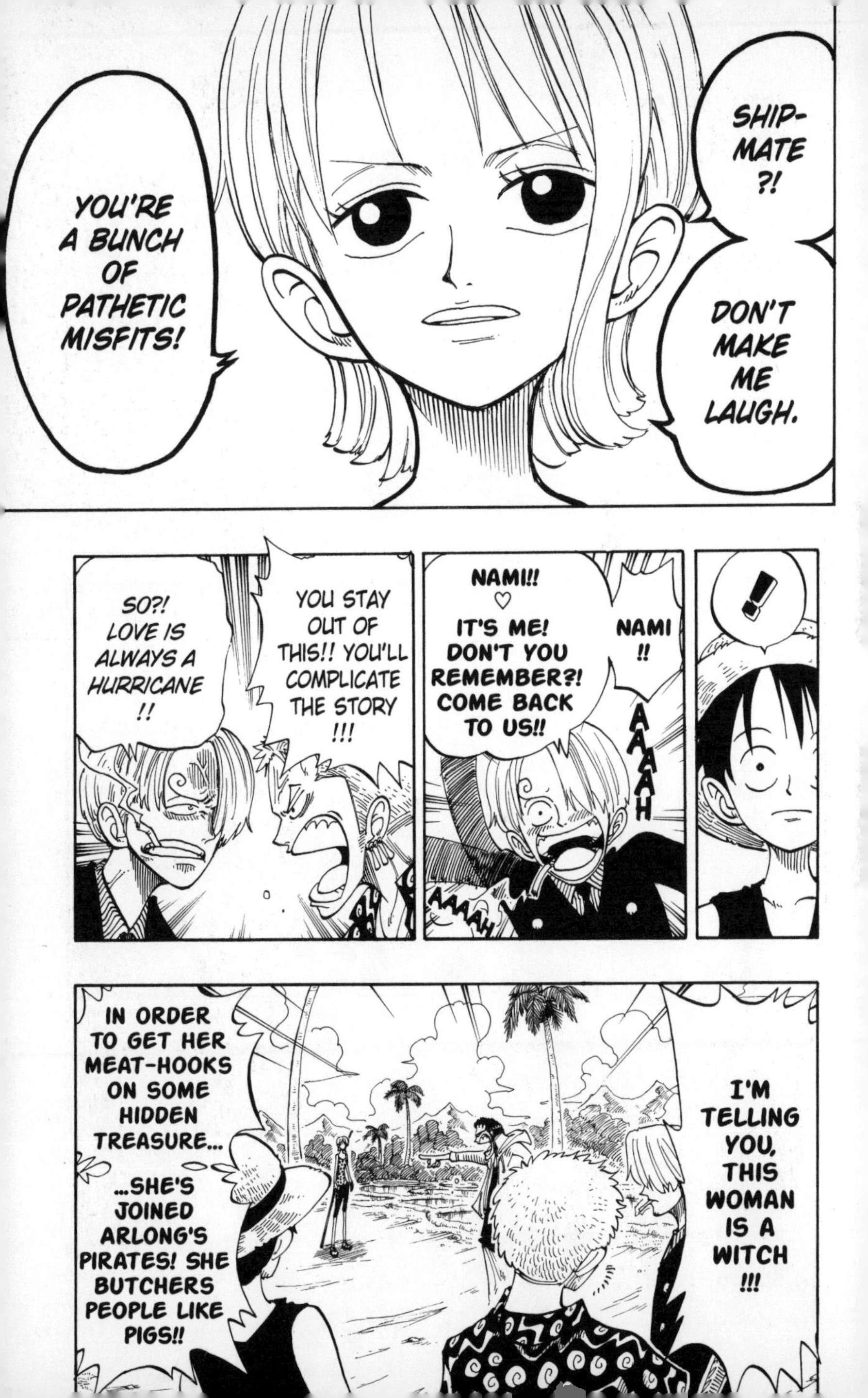
SHIP-MATE ?!
DON'T MAKE ME LAUGH.
YOU'RE A BUNCH OF PATHETIC MISFITS!
!
NAMI !!
NAMI!! ♡ IT'S ME! DON'T YOU REMEMBER?! COME BACK TO US!!
AAAAH
AAAAH
YOU STAY OUT OF THIS!! YOU'LL COMPLICATE THE STORY !!!
SO?! LOVE IS ALWAYS A HURRICANE !!
I'M TELLING YOU, THIS WOMAN IS A WITCH !!!
IN ORDER TO GET HER MEAT-HOOKS ON SOME HIDDEN TREASURE...
...SHE'S JOINED ARLONG'S PIRATES! SHE BUTCHERS PEOPLE LIKE PIGS!!

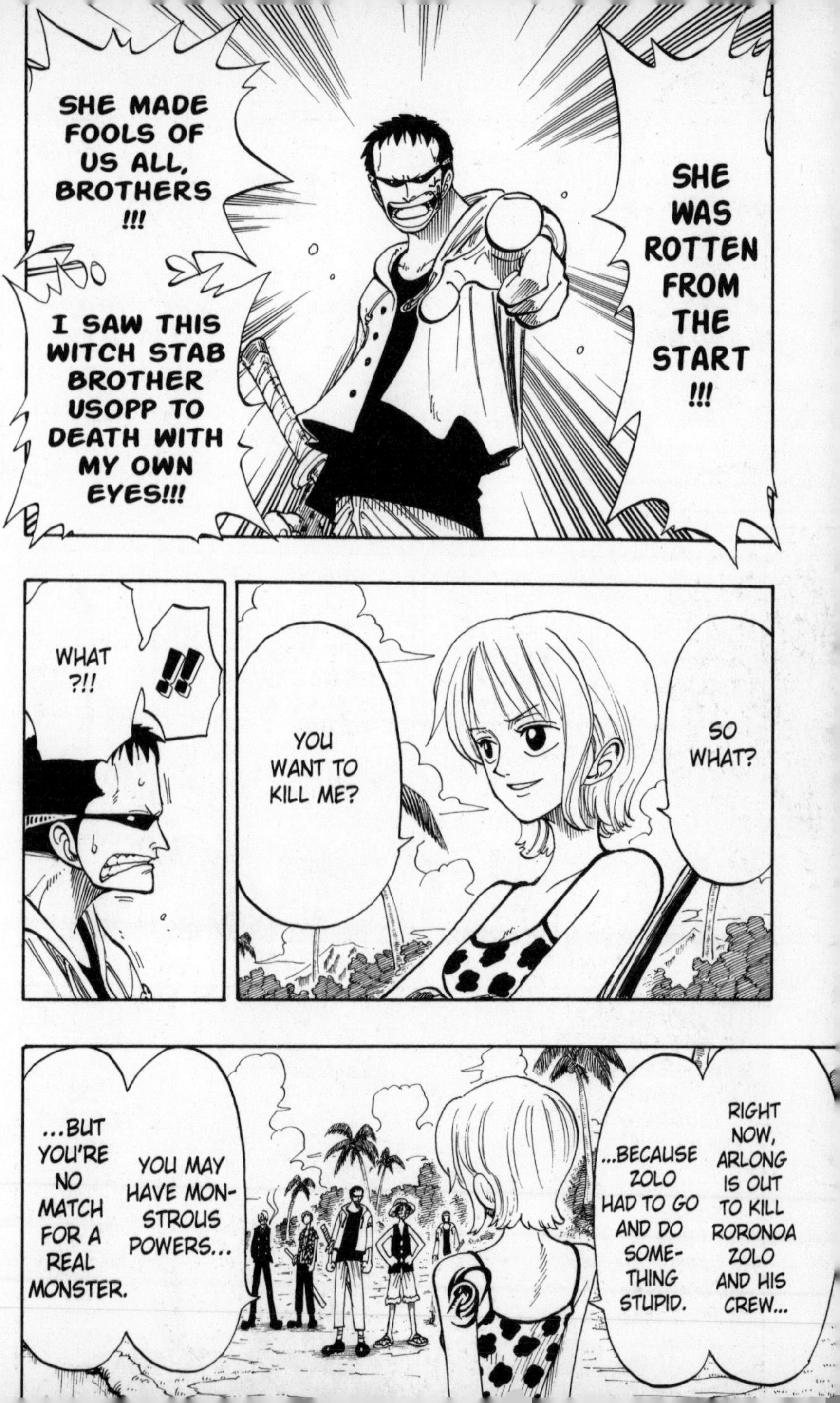
SHE WAS ROTTEN FROM THE START!!!
SHE MADE FOOLS OF US ALL, BROTHERS!!!
I SAW THIS WITCH STAB BROTHER USOPP TO DEATH WITH MY OWN EYES!!!
SO WHAT?
YOU WANT TO KILL ME?
!!
WHAT?!!
RIGHT NOW, ARLONG IS OUT TO KILL RORONOA ZOLO AND HIS CREW...
...BECAUSE ZOLO HAD TO GO AND DO SOME-THING STUPID.
YOU MAY HAVE MON-STROUS POWERS...
...BUT YOU'RE NO MATCH FOR A REAL MONSTER.

READ THIS WAY

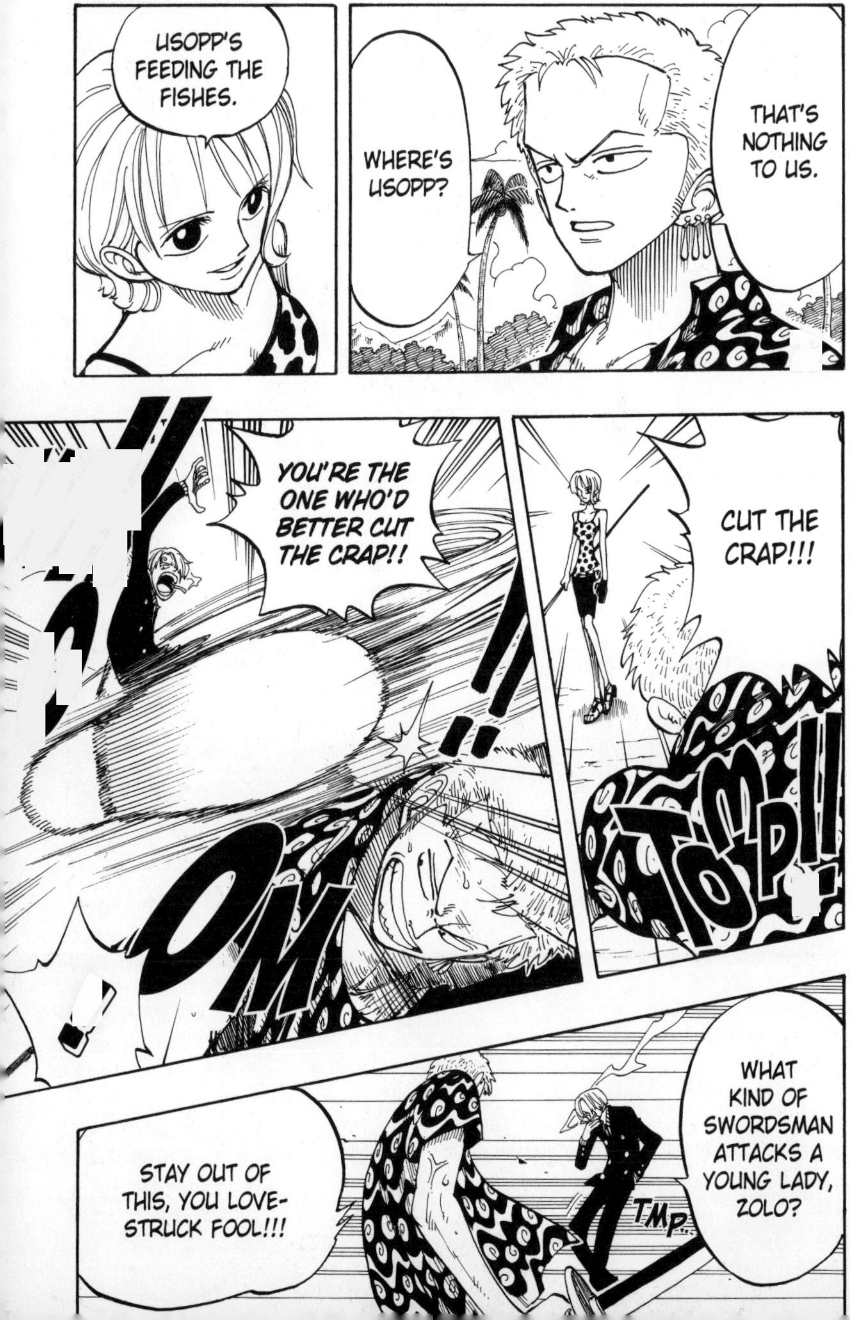
THAT'S NOTHING TO US.
WHERE'S USOPP?
USOPP'S FEEDING THE FISHES.
CUT THE CRAP!!!
TOMP!!
YOU'RE THE ONE WHO'D BETTER CUT THE CRAP!!
WHAT KIND OF SWORDSMAN ATTACKS A YOUNG LADY, ZOLO?
TMP...
STAY OUT OF THIS, YOU LOVE-STRUCK FOOL!!!

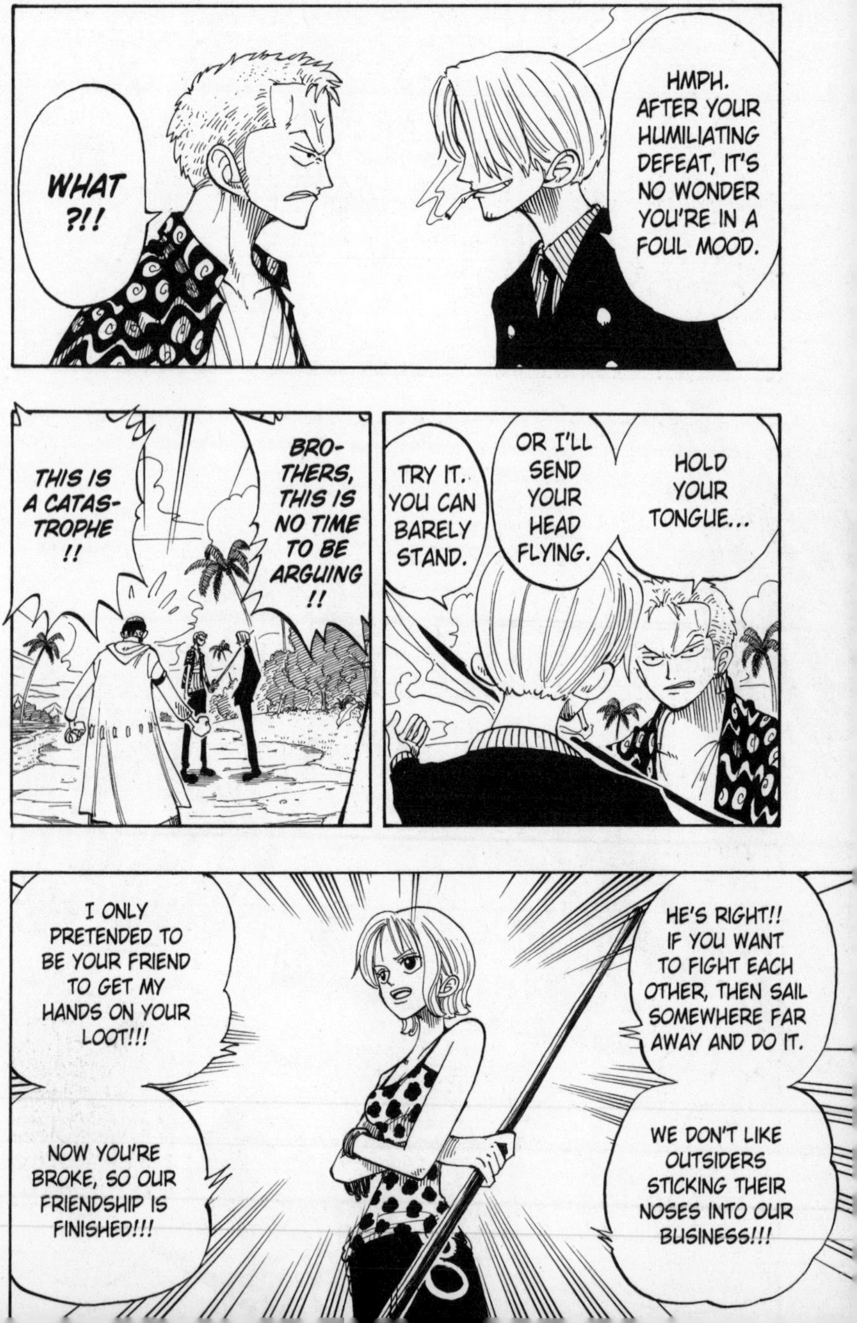
HMPH. AFTER YOUR HUMILIATING DEFEAT, IT'S NO WONDER YOU'RE IN A FOUL MOOD.
WHAT ?!!
HOLD YOUR TONGUE...
OR I'LL SEND YOUR HEAD FLYING.
TRY IT. YOU CAN BARELY STAND.
BROTHERS, THIS IS NO TIME TO BE ARGUING !!
THIS IS A CATASTROPHE !!
HE'S RIGHT!! IF YOU WANT TO FIGHT EACH OTHER, THEN SAIL SOMEWHERE FAR AWAY AND DO IT.
WE DON'T LIKE OUTSIDERS STICKING THEIR NOSES INTO OUR BUSINESS!!!
I ONLY PRETENDED TO BE YOUR FRIEND TO GET MY HANDS ON YOUR LOOT!!!
NOW YOU'RE BROKE, SO OUR FRIENDSHIP IS FINISHED!!!

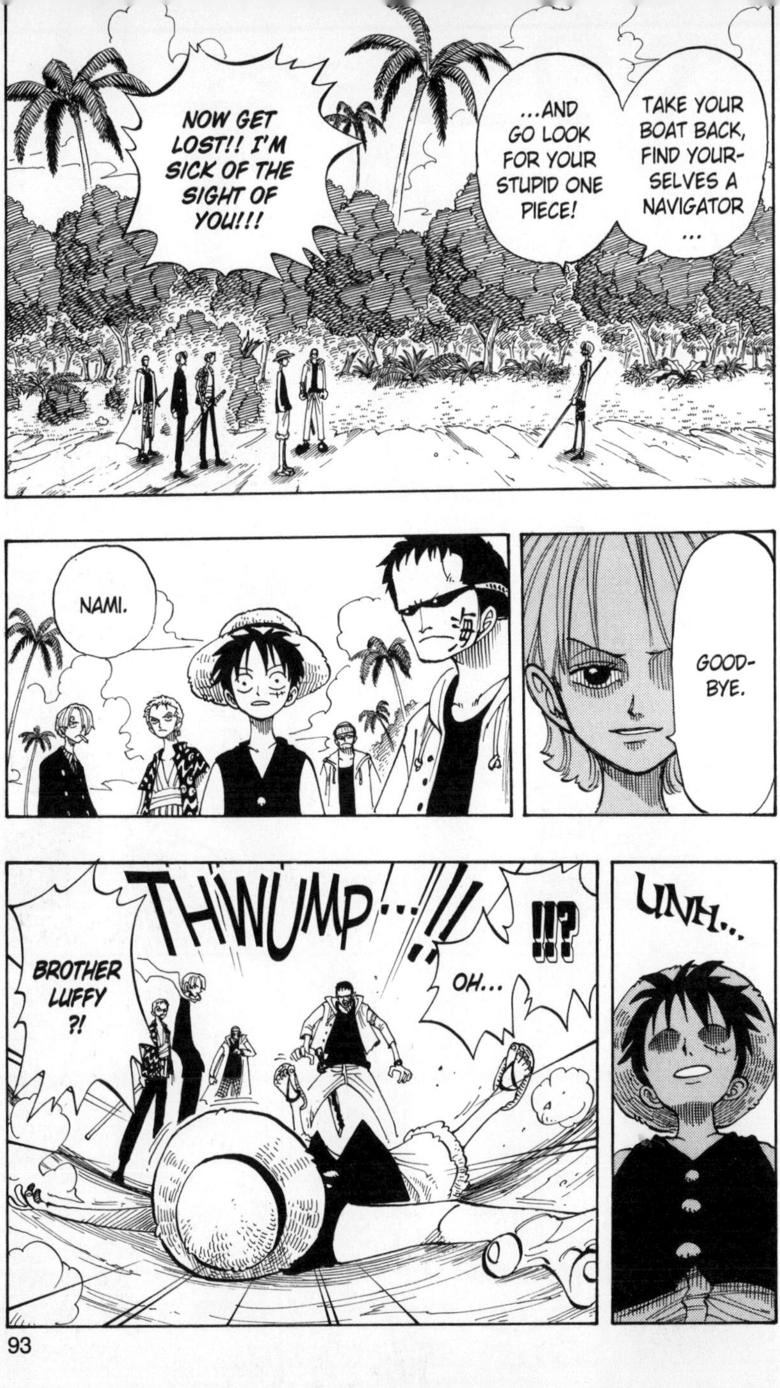
TAKE YOUR BOAT BACK, FIND YOURSELVES A NAVIGATOR ...
...AND GO LOOK FOR YOUR STUPID ONE PIECE!
NOW GET LOST!! I'M SICK OF THE SIGHT OF YOU!!!
GOOD-BYE.
NAMI.
UNH...
!!?
THWUMP...!!
OH...
BROTHER LUFFY ?!

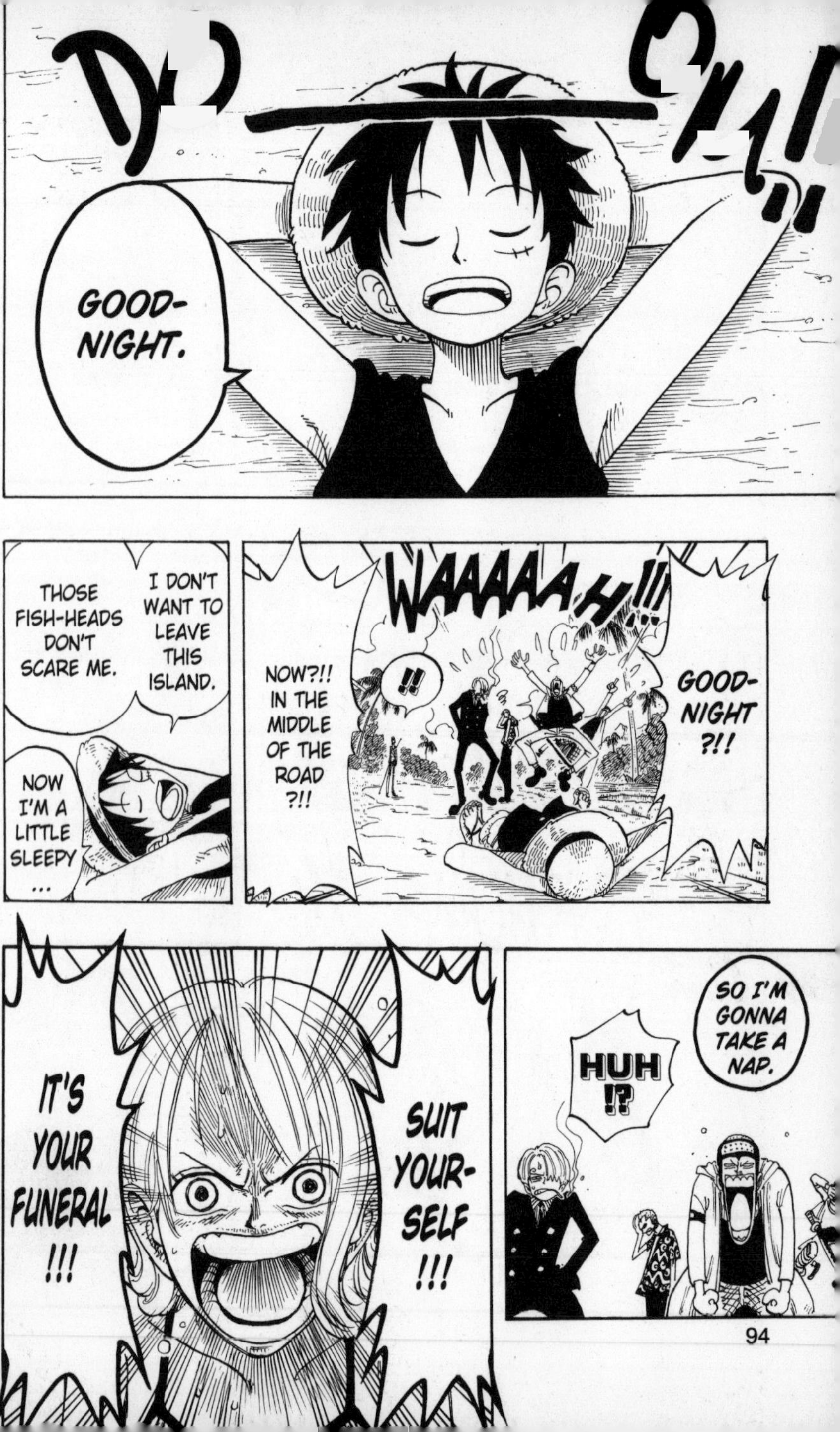
GOOD-NIGHT.
WAAAAAH!!!
GOOD-NIGHT ?!!
!!
NOW?!! IN THE MIDDLE OF THE ROAD ?!!
I DON'T WANT TO LEAVE THIS ISLAND.
THOSE FISH-HEADS DON'T SCARE ME.
NOW I'M A LITTLE SLEEPY ...
SO I'M GONNA TAKE A NAP.
HUH !?
SUIT YOUR-SELF !!!
IT'S YOUR FUNERAL !!!

READ THIS WAY

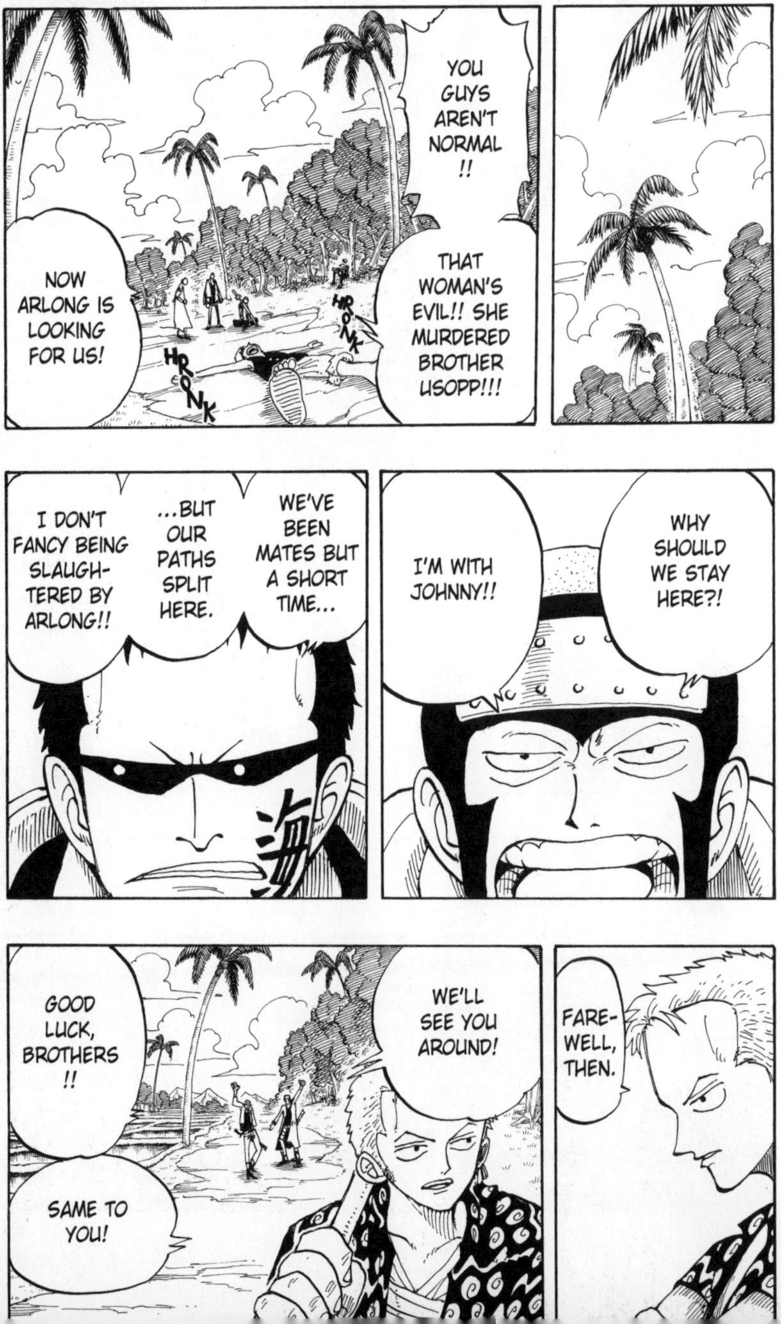
YOU GUYS AREN'T NORMAL!!
THAT WOMAN'S EVIL!! SHE MURDERED BROTHER USOPP!!!
HRONK
NOW ARLONG IS LOOKING FOR US!
HRONK
WHY SHOULD WE STAY HERE?!
I'M WITH JOHNNY!!
WE'VE BEEN MATES BUT A SHORT TIME...
...BUT OUR PATHS SPLIT HERE.
I DON'T FANCY BEING SLAUGH-TERED BY ARLONG!!
FARE-WELL, THEN.
WE'LL SEE YOU AROUND!
GOOD LUCK, BROTHERS!!
SAME TO YOU!

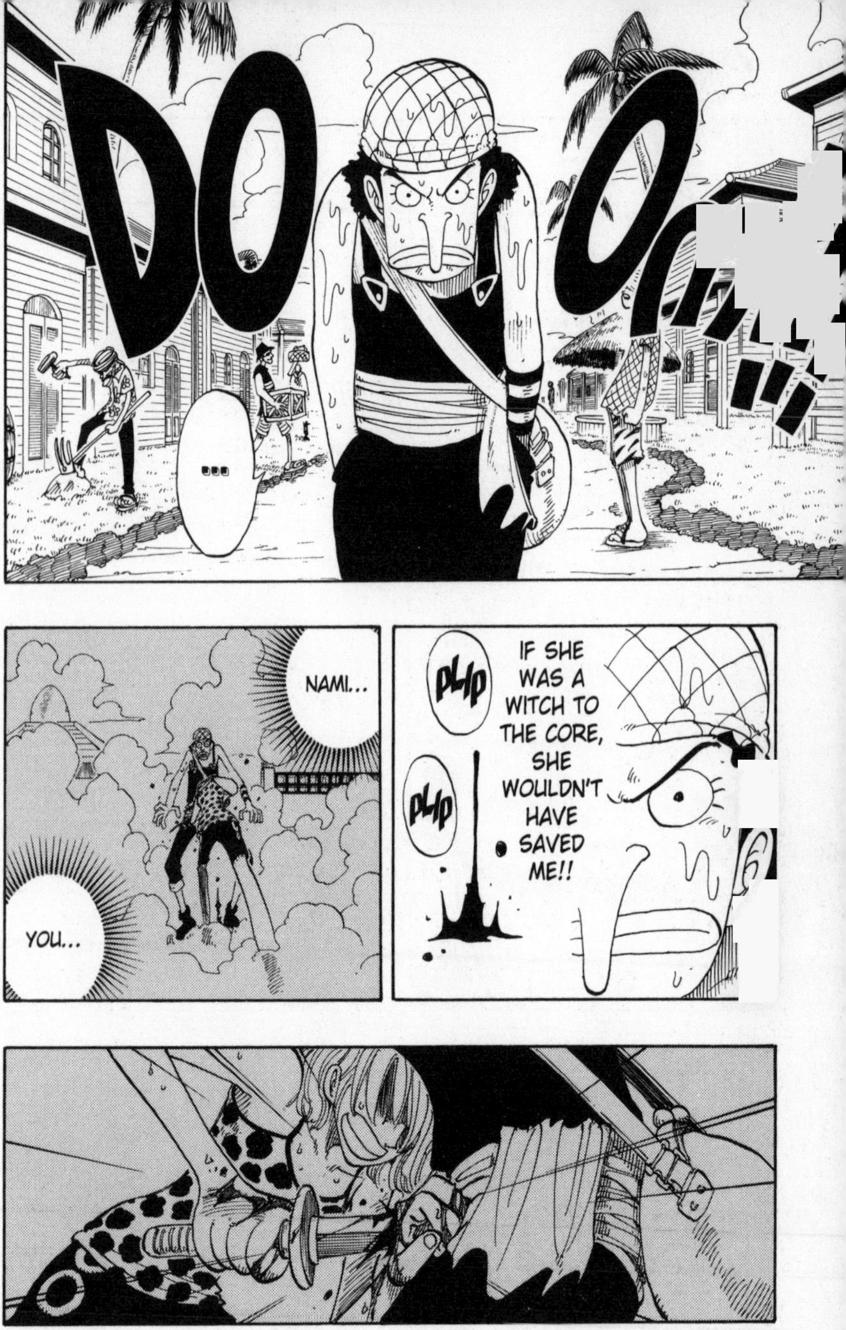
DOO
...
IF SHE WAS A WITCH TO THE CORE, SHE WOULDN'T HAVE SAVED ME!!
PLIP
PLIP
NAMI...
YOU...

READ THIS WAY

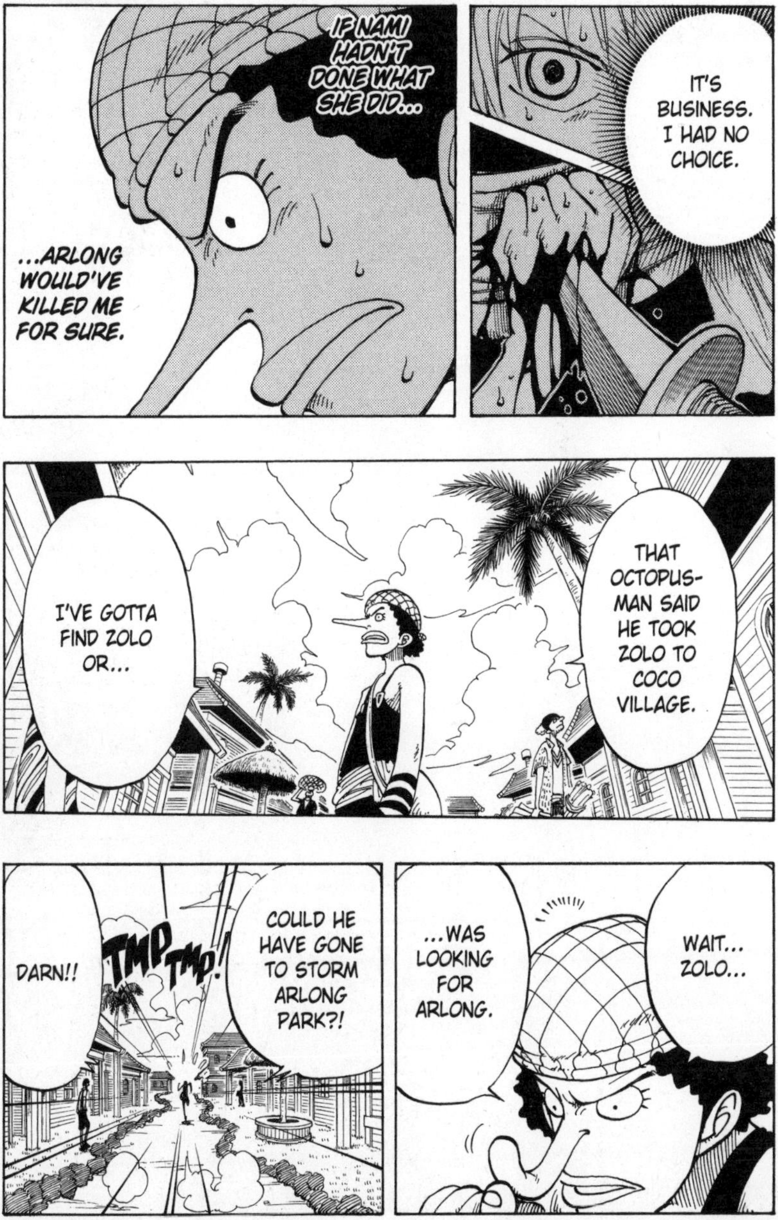
IT'S BUSINESS. I HAD NO CHOICE.
IF NAMI HADN'T DONE WHAT SHE DID...
...ARLONG WOULD'VE KILLED ME FOR SURE.
THAT OCTOPUS-MAN SAID HE TOOK ZOLO TO COCO VILLAGE.
I'VE GOTTA FIND ZOLO OR...
WAIT... ZOLO...
...WAS LOOKING FOR ARLONG.
COULD HE HAVE GONE TO STORM ARLONG PARK?!
TMP TMP!
DARN!!

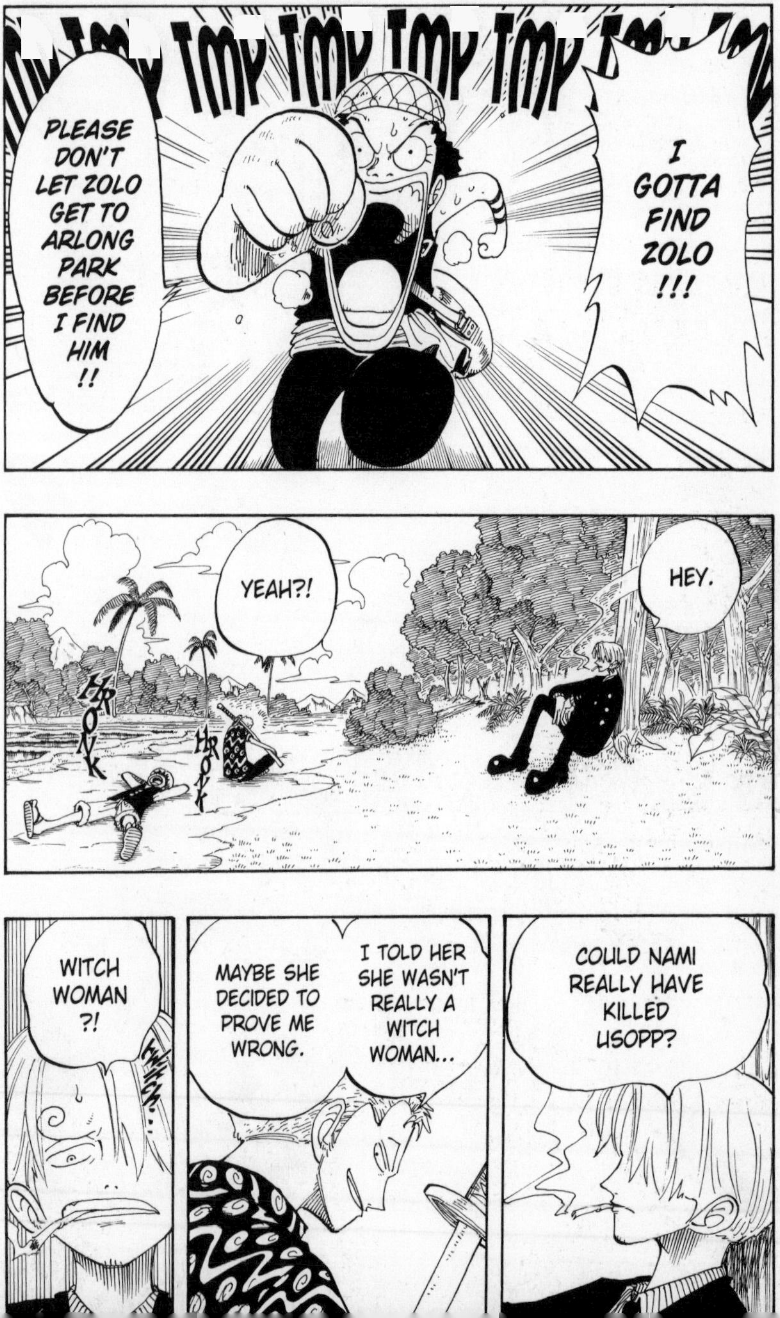
TMP TMP TMP TMP TMP TMP
I GOTTA FIND ZOLO !!!
PLEASE DON'T LET ZOLO GET TO ARLONG PARK BEFORE I FIND HIM !!
HEY.
YEAH?!
HRONK
HRONK
COULD NAMI REALLY HAVE KILLED USOPP?
I TOLD HER SHE WASN'T REALLY A WITCH WOMAN...
MAYBE SHE DECIDED TO PROVE ME WRONG.
WITCH WOMAN ?!
TWITCH...

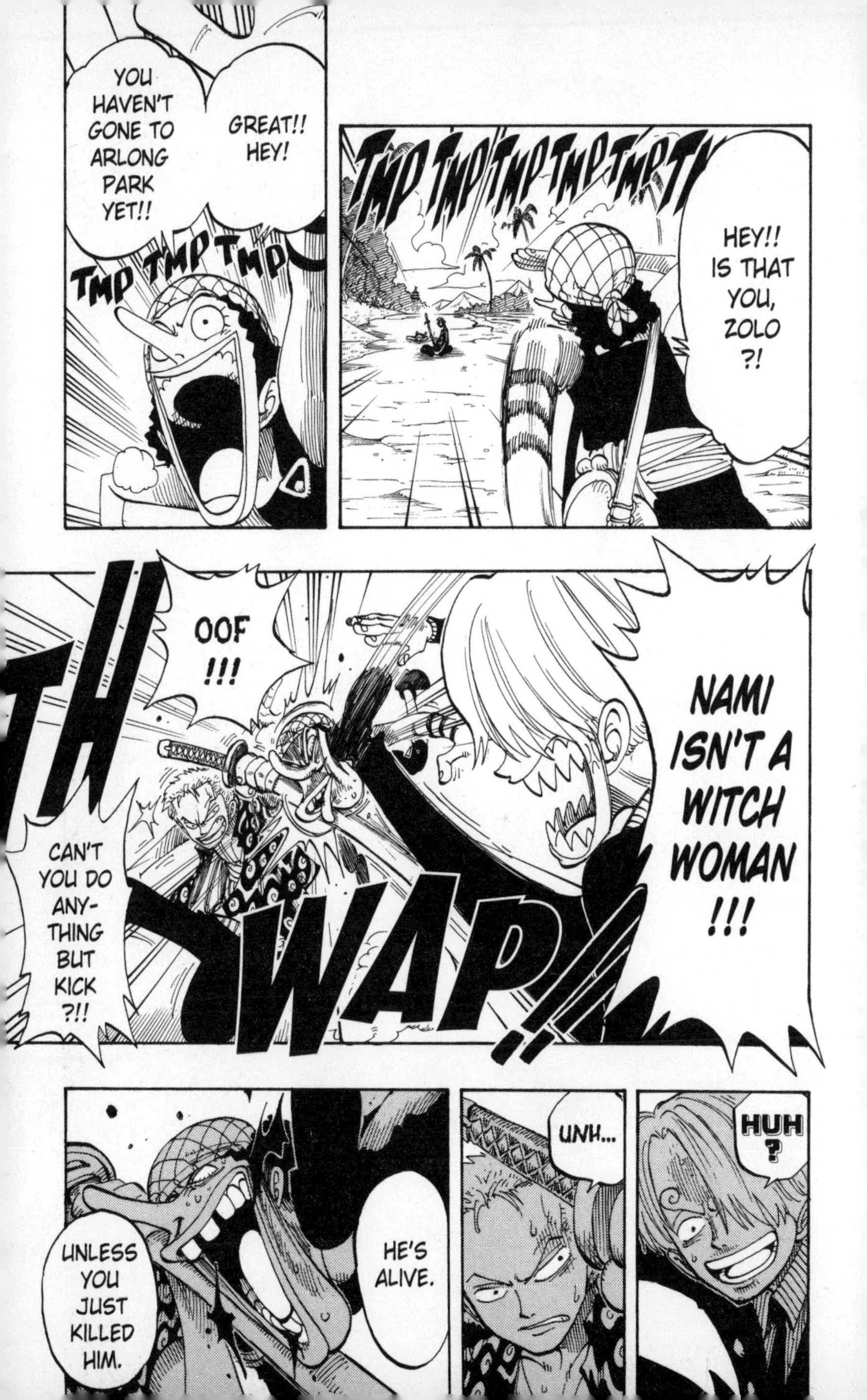
TMP TMP TMP TMP TMP!
HEY!! IS THAT YOU, ZOLO ?!
GREAT!! HEY!
YOU HAVEN'T GONE TO ARLONG PARK YET!!
TMP TMP TMP TMP
NAMI ISN'T A WITCH WOMAN !!!
OOF !!!
TH
CAN'T YOU DO ANY-THING BUT KICK ?!!
WAP!!
HUH ?
UNH...
HE'S ALIVE.
UNLESS YOU JUST KILLED HIM.

WHAM...

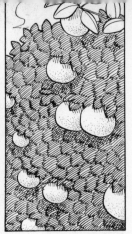

KLANK!!
KRASH!!

KLANK!!

HUH?

WRECKING THE HOUSE AGAIN, NAMI?

WHAT'S WRONG?

OH NO.

KREEK...

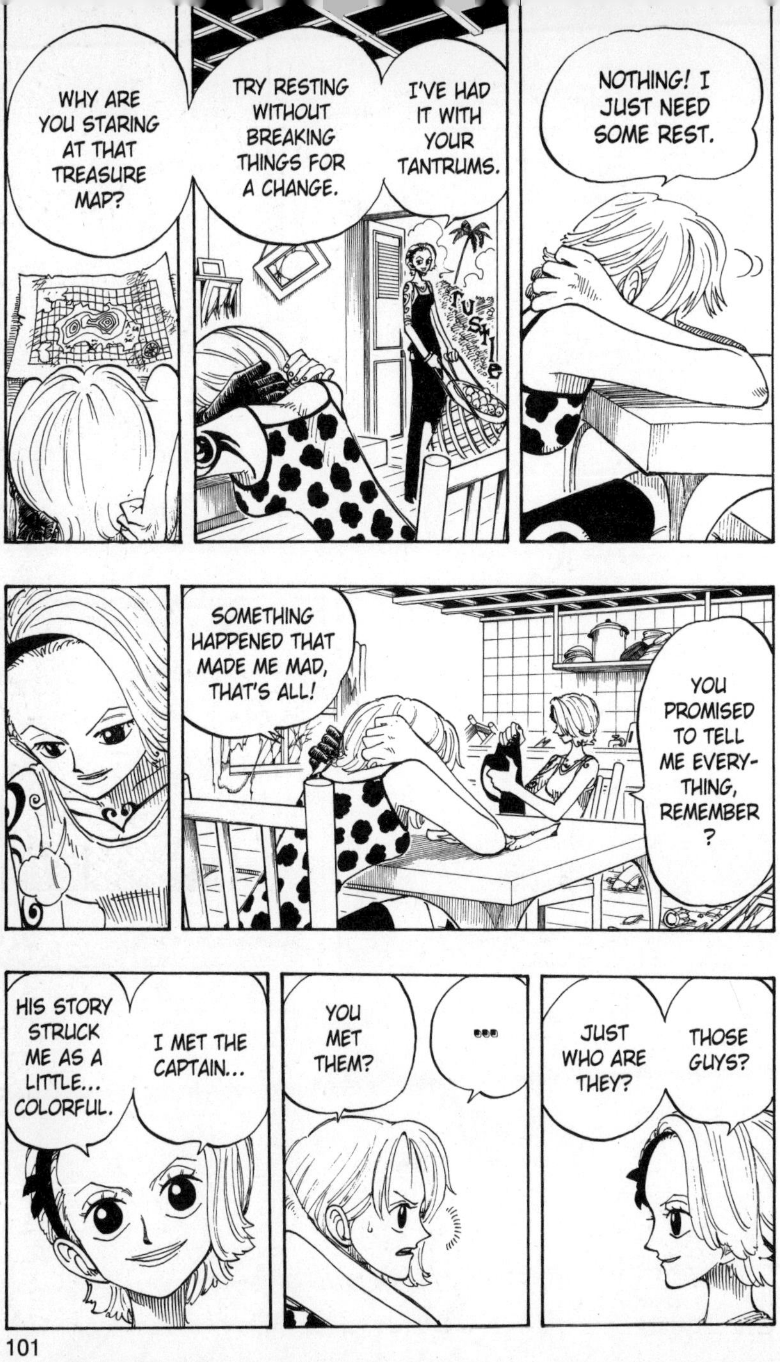
NOTHING! I JUST NEED SOME REST.
I'VE HAD IT WITH YOUR TANTRUMS.
TRY RESTING WITHOUT BREAKING THINGS FOR A CHANGE.
RUSTLE
WHY ARE YOU STARING AT THAT TREASURE MAP?
YOU PROMISED TO TELL ME EVERY-THING, REMEMBER?
SOMETHING HAPPENED THAT MADE ME MAD, THAT'S ALL!
THOSE GUYS?
JUST WHO ARE THEY?
...
YOU MET THEM?
I MET THE CAPTAIN...
HIS STORY STRUCK ME AS A LITTLE... COLORFUL.

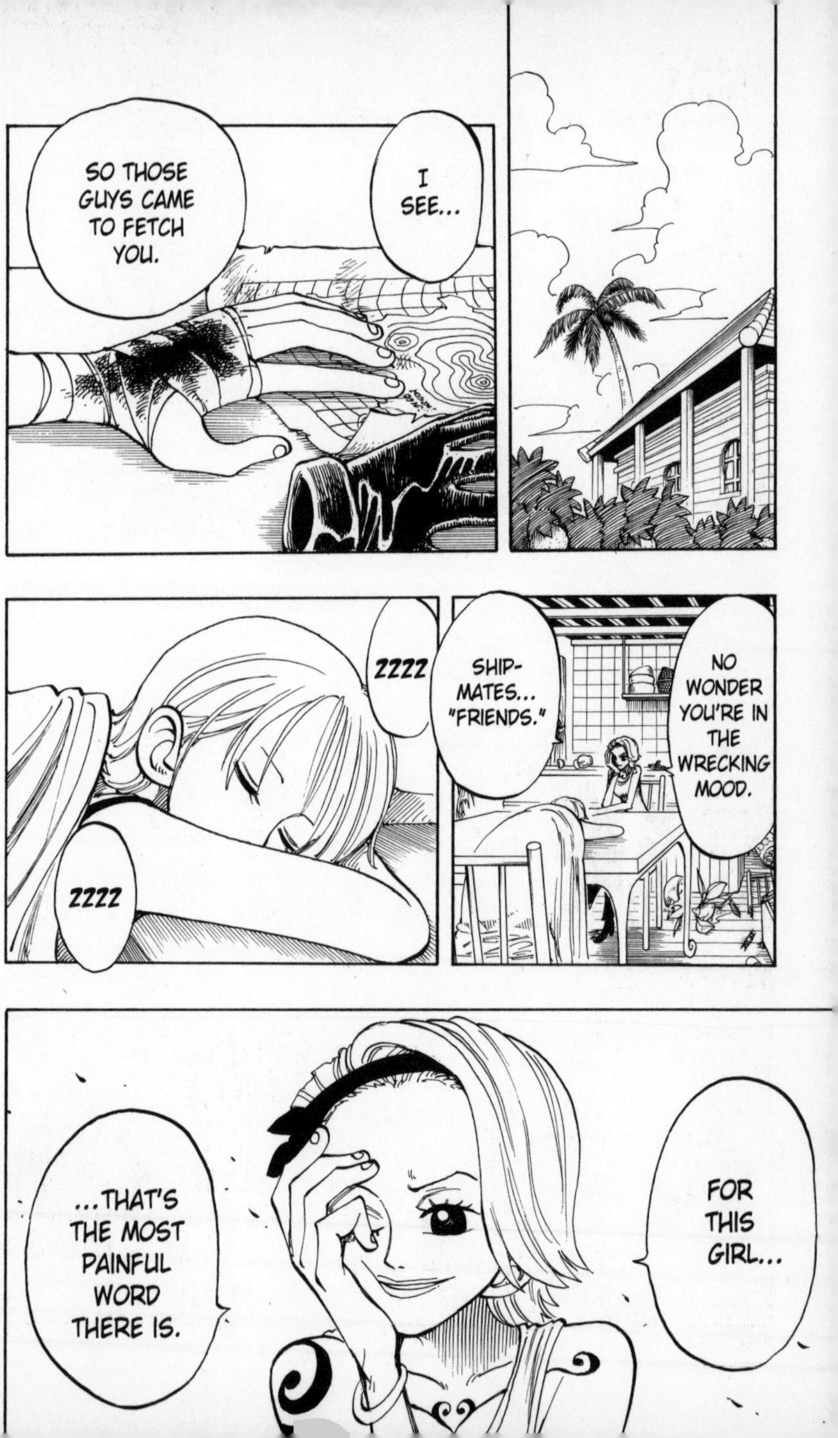
I SEE...
SO THOSE GUYS CAME TO FETCH YOU.
NO WONDER YOU'RE IN THE WRECKING MOOD.
SHIP-MATES... "FRIENDS."
ZZZZ
ZZZZ
FOR THIS GIRL...
...THAT'S THE MOST PAINFUL WORD THERE IS.

READ THIS WAY

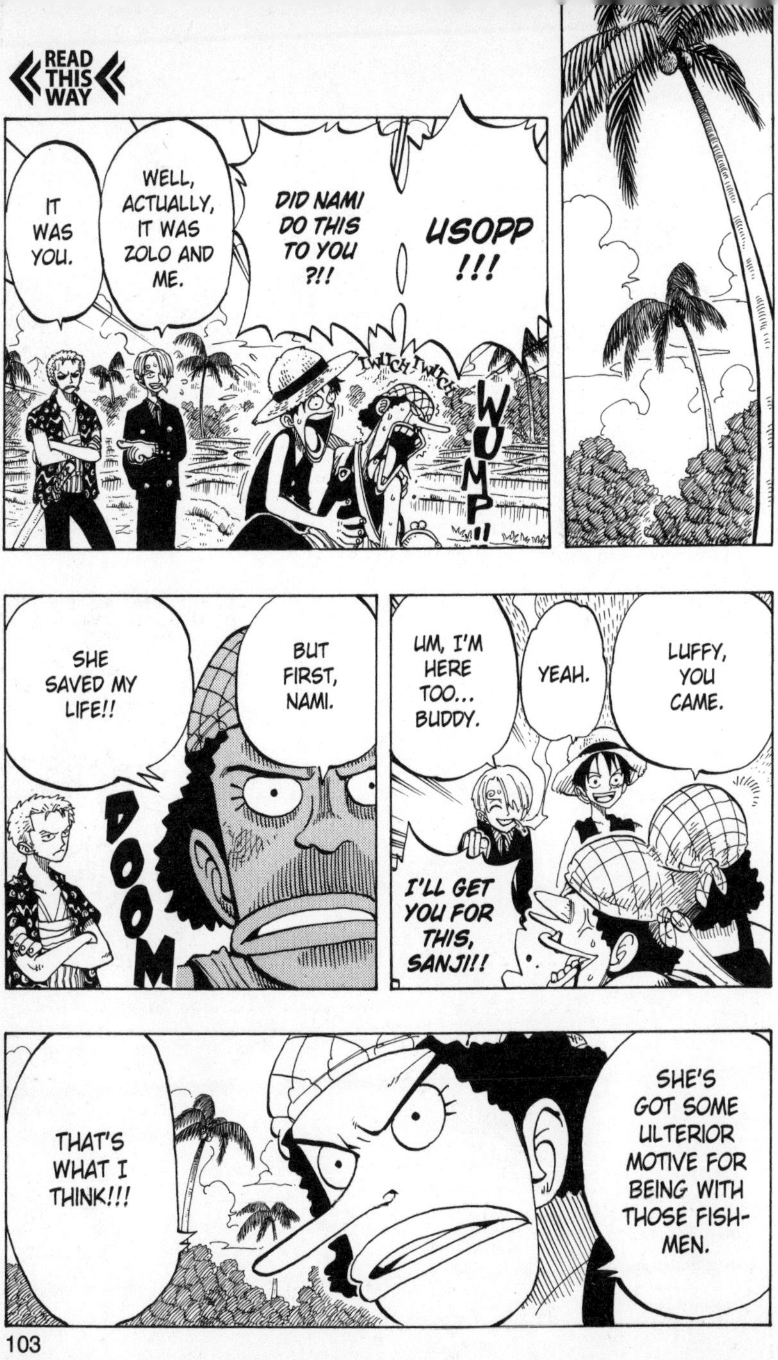
USOPP !!!
WUMP!!
TWITCH TWITCH
DID NAMI DO THIS TO YOU ?!!
WELL, ACTUALLY, IT WAS ZOLO AND ME.
IT WAS YOU.
LUFFY, YOU CAME.
YEAH.
UM, I'M HERE TOO... BUDDY.
I'LL GET YOU FOR THIS, SANJI!!
BUT FIRST, NAMI.
SHE SAVED MY LIFE!!
DOOM
SHE'S GOT SOME ULTERIOR MOTIVE FOR BEING WITH THOSE FISH-MEN.
THAT'S WHAT I THINK!!!

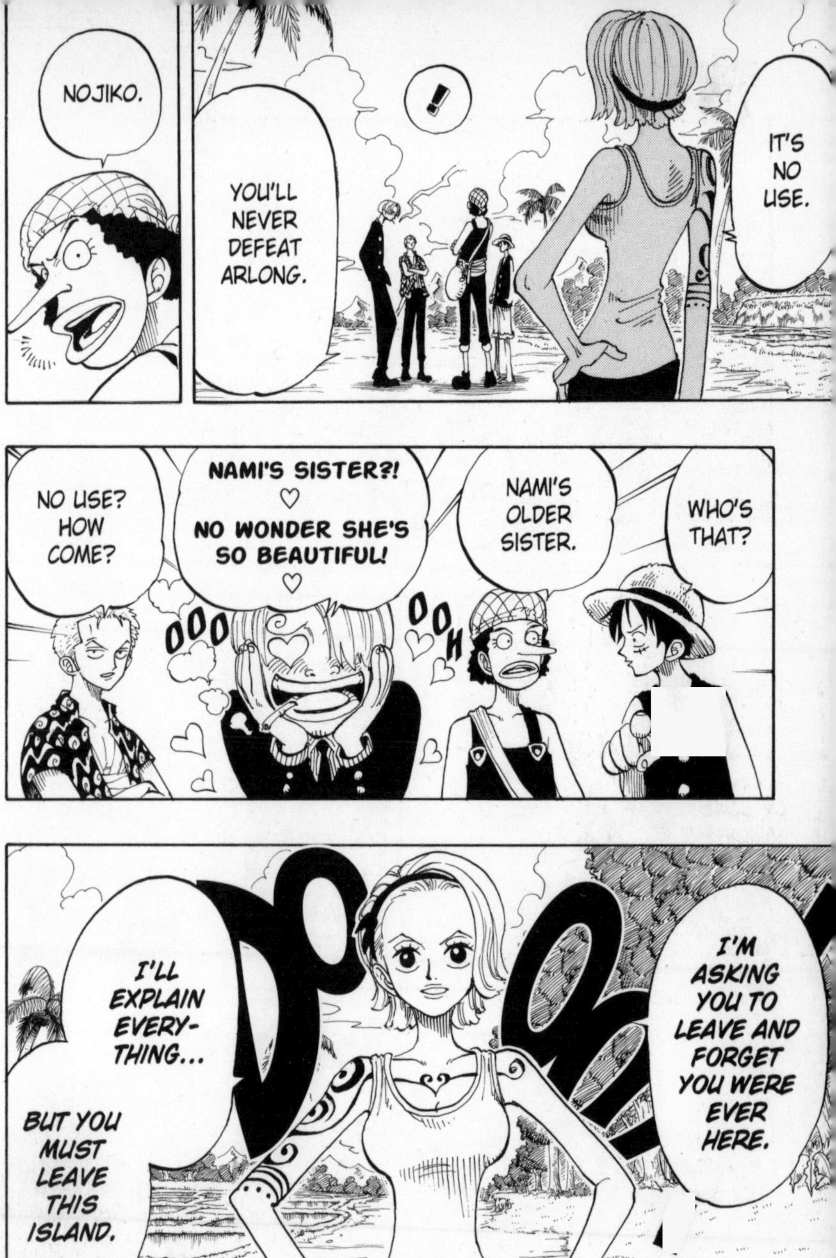
IT'S NO USE.
!
YOU'LL NEVER DEFEAT ARLONG.
NOJIKO.
WHO'S THAT?
NAMI'S OLDER SISTER.
NAMI'S SISTER?! ♡ NO WONDER SHE'S SO BEAUTIFUL! ♡
OOH
OOO
NO USE? HOW COME?
I'M ASKING YOU TO LEAVE AND FORGET YOU WERE EVER HERE.
I'LL EXPLAIN EVERYTHING...
BUT YOU MUST LEAVE THIS ISLAND.

READ THIS WAY

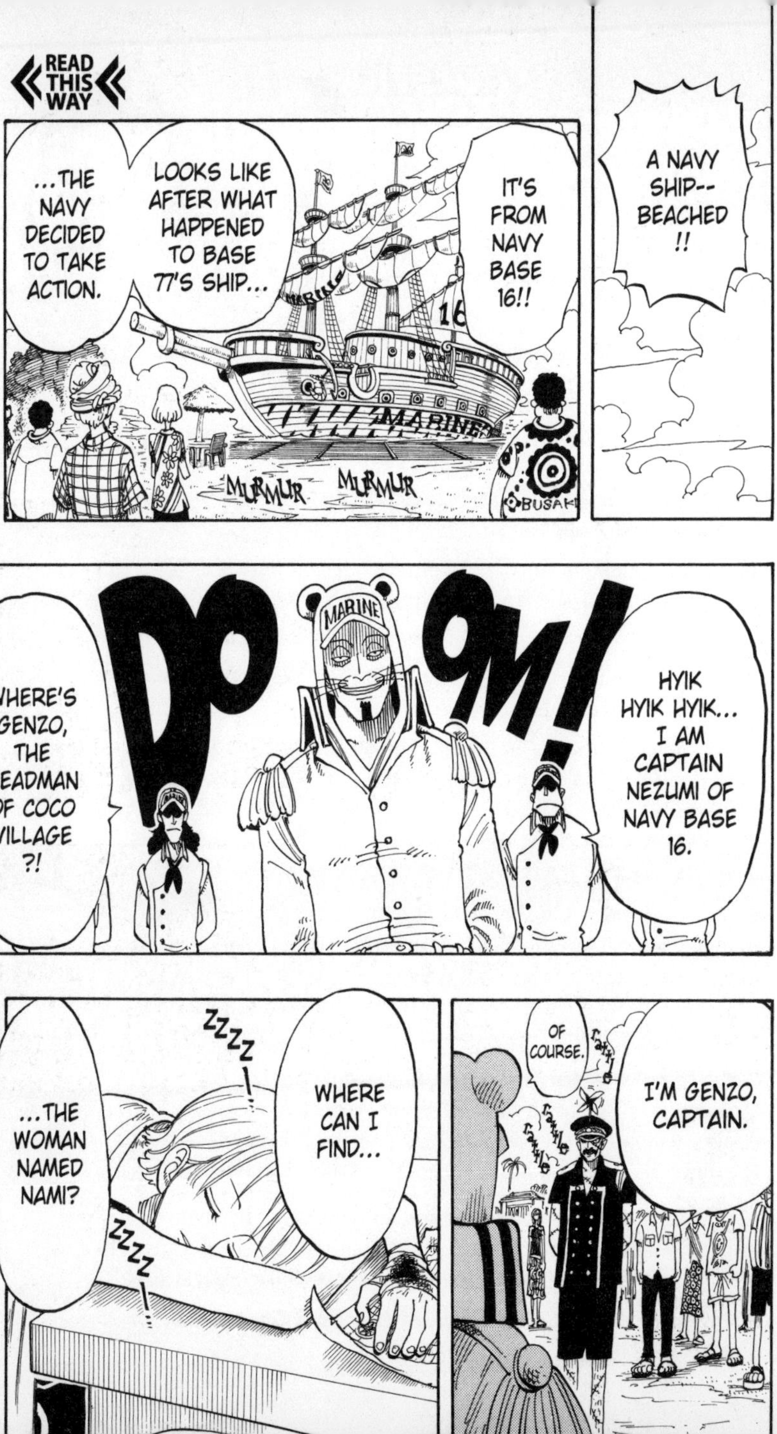
A NAVY SHIP-- BEACHED!!
IT'S FROM NAVY BASE 16!!
LOOKS LIKE AFTER WHAT HAPPENED TO BASE 77'S SHIP...
...THE NAVY DECIDED TO TAKE ACTION.
MURMUR
MURMUR
DOOM!
HYIK HYIK HYIK... I AM CAPTAIN NEZUMI OF NAVY BASE 16.
WHERE'S GENZO, THE HEADMAN OF COCO VILLAGE?!
I'M GENZO, CAPTAIN.
OF COURSE.
WHERE CAN I FIND...
...THE WOMAN NAMED NAMI?
ZZZZ
ZZZZ

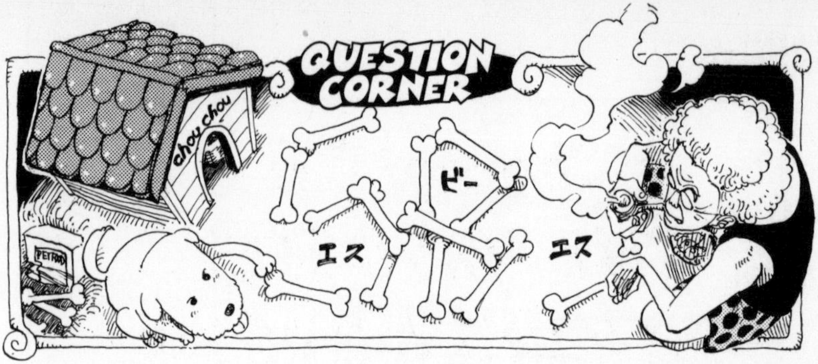
QUESTION CORNER
chou chou
PETFOOD
エス
ビー
エス

Q: Hey, you!! Nami-lover from Volume 7!! Wanna fight?! I definitely love Nami more than you do! (x100) But I like you too! Am I crazy? Let's be friends.

A: You sound confused. Nami-lover from Volume 7, be his friend, okay?

Q: In the SBS Question Corner in Volume 7, it said that Sanji is 19, but my friend and I discussed it and we think that's a lie. How old is he really?

A: I'm sorry if you think it's a lie, but it's true. True, I tell you!!

Q: Why did "Red-Shoes" Zeff" eat his right foot? Wouldn't it have been smarter to eat his left foot?

A: Bzzz. That's wrong, actually. The plant foot is the foundation of a strong kick. How could you kick a ball with your right foot if you had no left foot to stand on? You couldn't! Ask a friend who plays soccer. A good hard kick depends on the foot that supports your weight!!

Q: Stand at attention, Oda Sensei! Put your pen down! STOP writing manga! I have a question. My older brother and I take turns buying **One Piece** graphic novels, but we've ended up with two copies of Volume 5. What should we do? You are permitted to pick up your pen if you were listening.

A: Let's see...Why don't you buy five more copies of Volume 5? Then the fact that you bought two copies will seem like no big deal and you'll just laugh it off! Can I pick up my pen now?

Q: Luffy needs a musician for his crew, so why hasn't he come to my house? Is it because I don't live near the ocean? Or is it because I'm actually an alien from outer space? Or is it because my feet stink?

A: It's the feet. Well, that's it for the SBS Question Corner--until the next volume!!

Chapter 77:
THE FIRST STEP TOWARD A DREAM

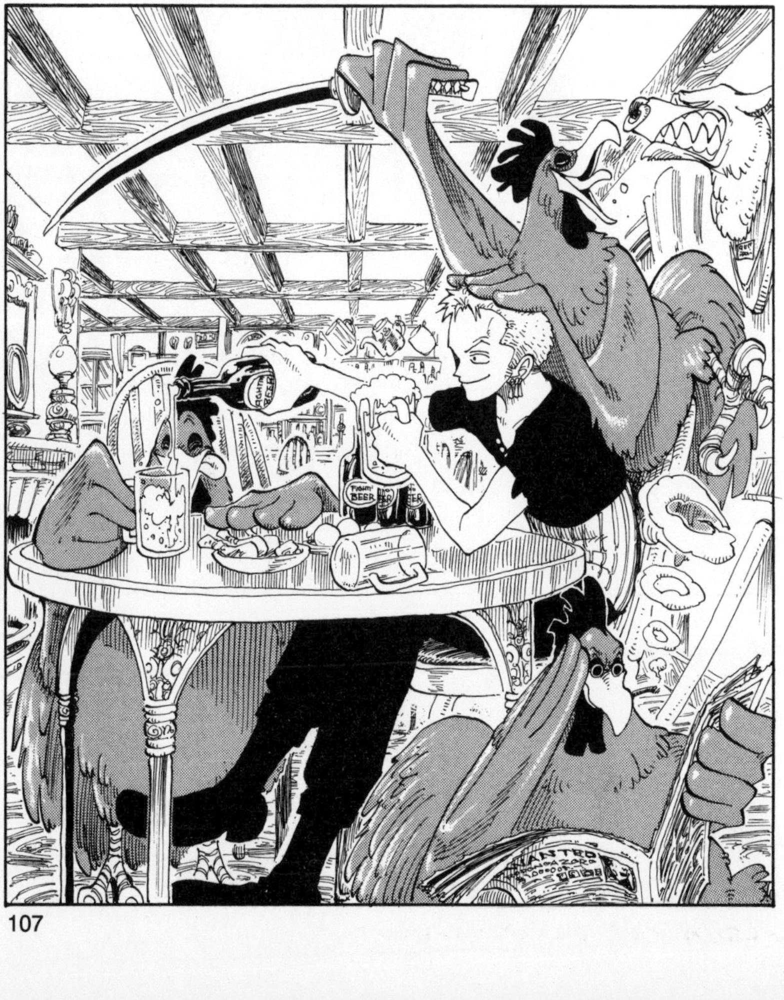
FIGHT! BEER

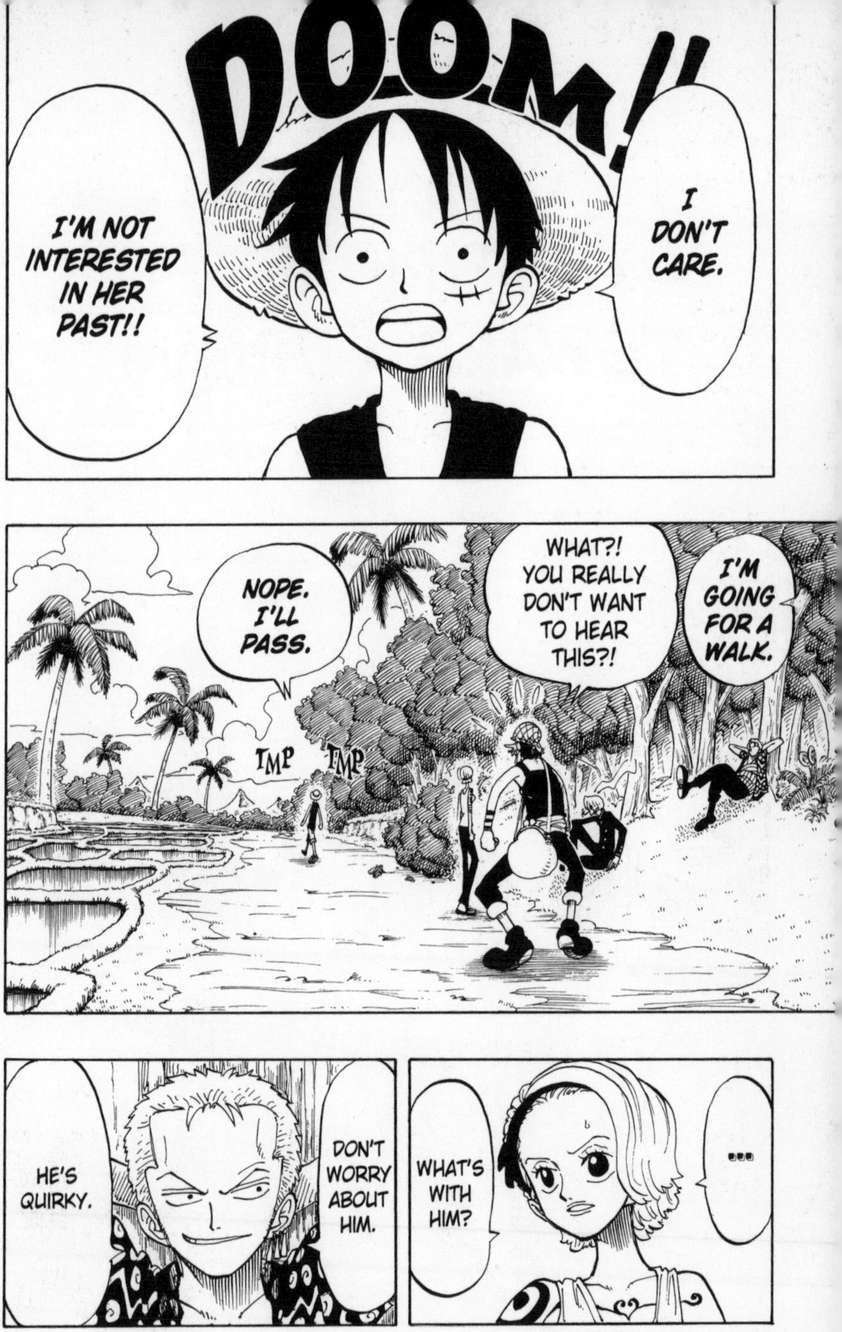
DOOM!!
I DON'T CARE.
I'M NOT INTERESTED IN HER PAST!!
I'M GOING FOR A WALK.
WHAT?! YOU REALLY DON'T WANT TO HEAR THIS?!
NOPE. I'LL PASS.
TMP TMP
...
WHAT'S WITH HIM?
DON'T WORRY ABOUT HIM.
HE'S QUIRKY.

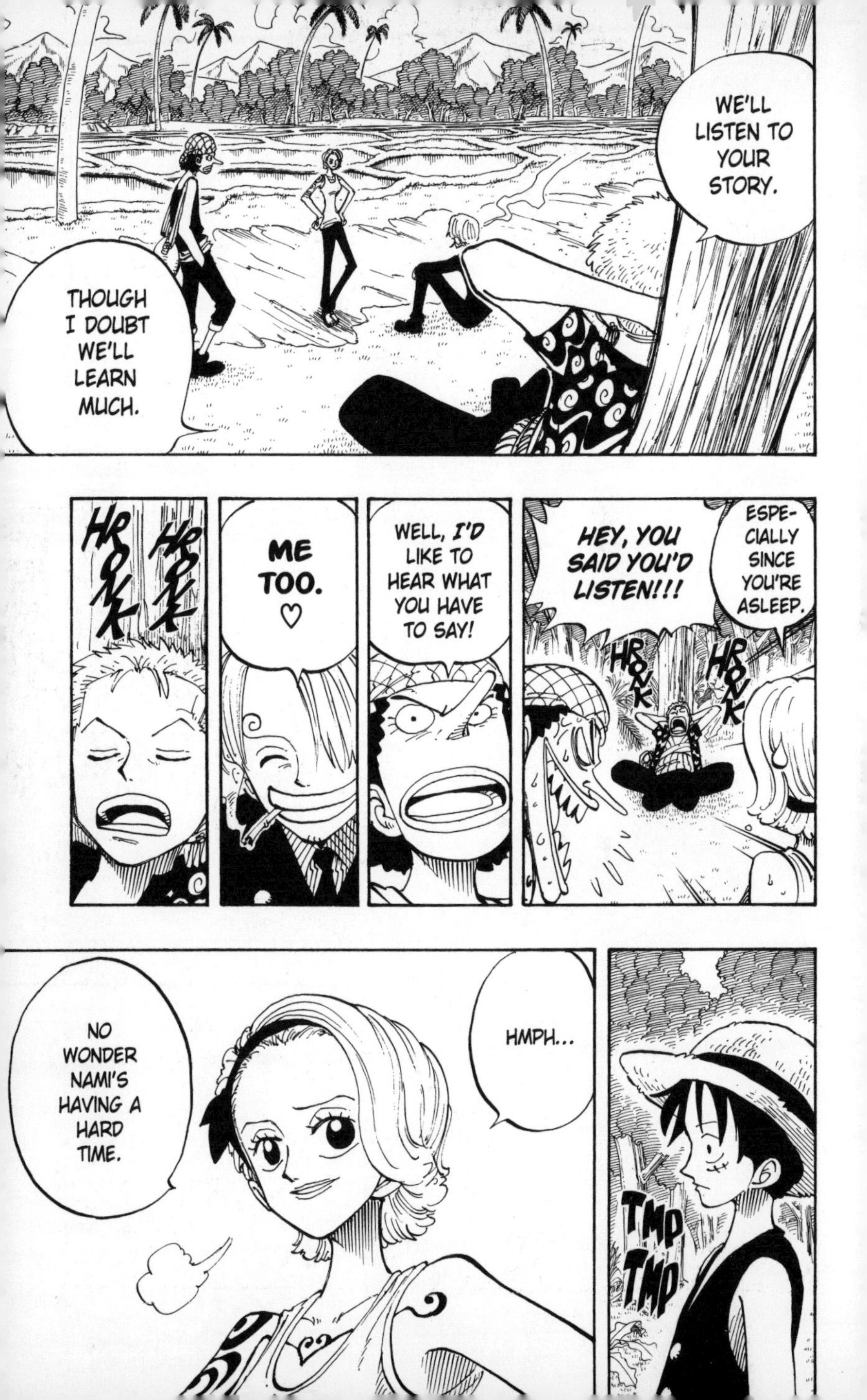

WE'LL LISTEN TO YOUR STORY.
THOUGH I DOUBT WE'LL LEARN MUCH.
ESPE-CIALLY SINCE YOU'RE ASLEEP.
HEY, YOU SAID YOU'D LISTEN!!!
HRONK
HRONK
WELL, I'D LIKE TO HEAR WHAT YOU HAVE TO SAY!
ME TOO. ♡
HRONK
HRONK
TMP TMP
HMPH...
NO WONDER NAMI'S HAVING A HARD TIME.

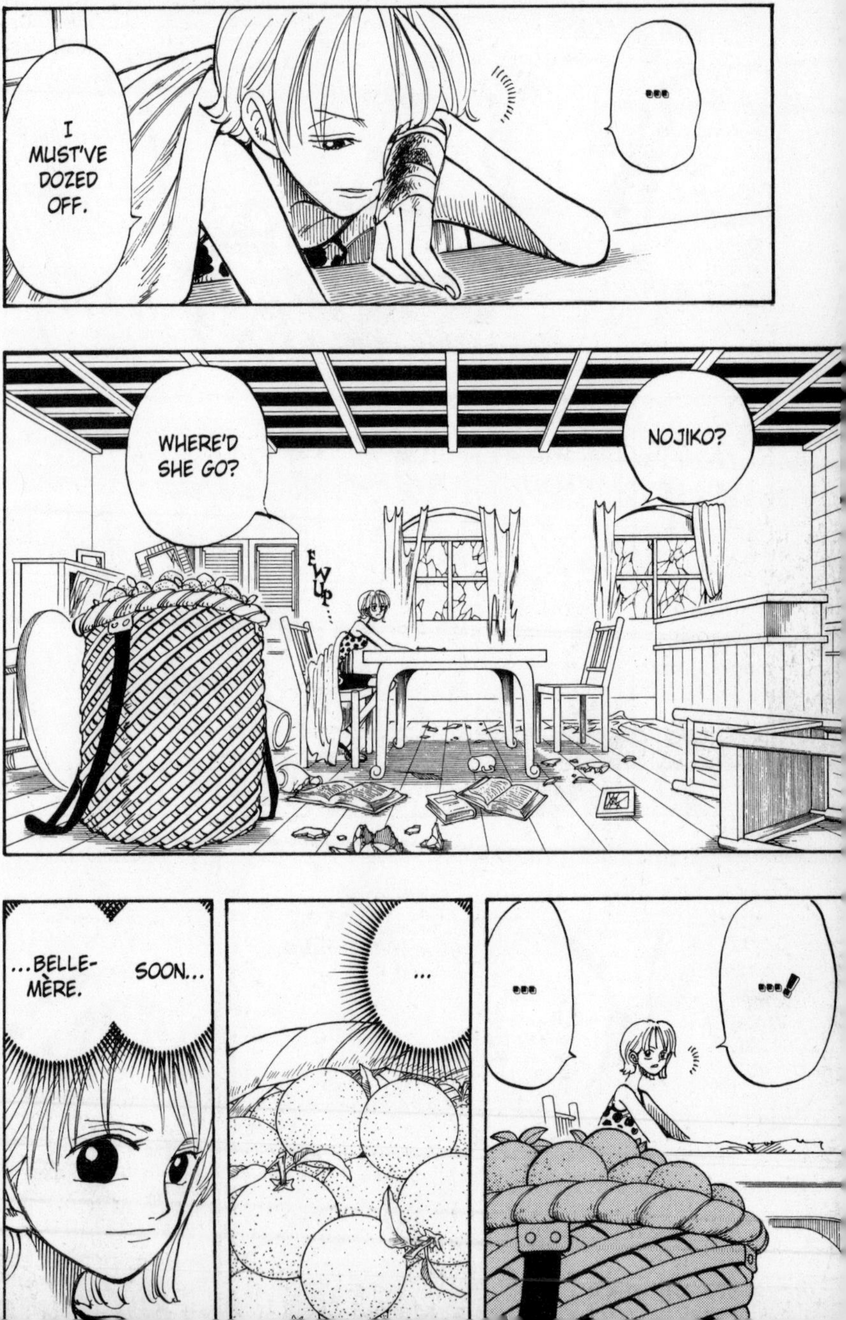
...
I MUST'VE DOZED OFF.
NOJIKO?
WHERE'D SHE GO?
...!
...
...
SOON...
...BELLE-MÈRE.

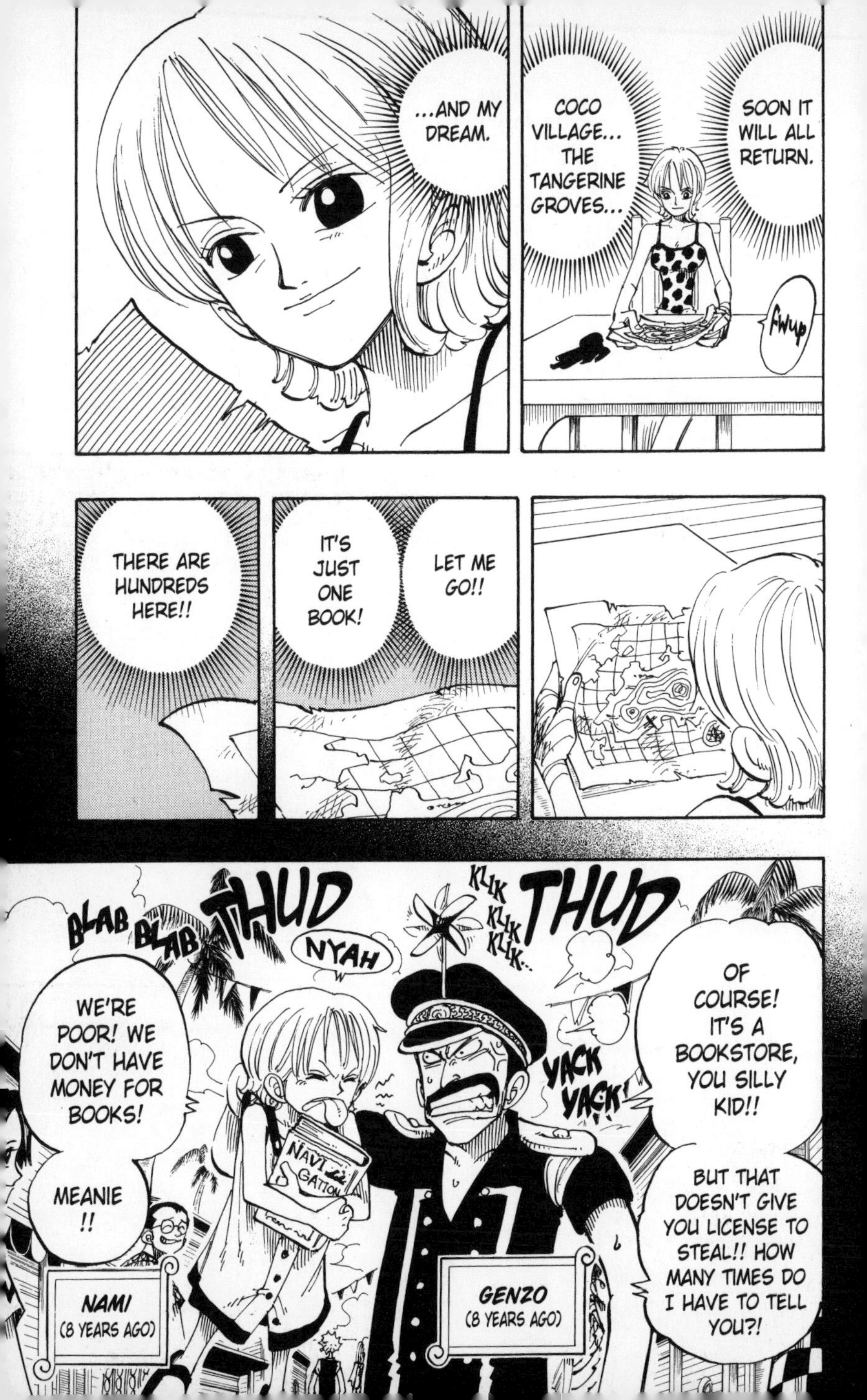

SOON IT WILL ALL RETURN.
COCO VILLAGE... THE TANGERINE GROVES...
fwup
...AND MY DREAM.
LET ME GO!!
IT'S JUST ONE BOOK!
THERE ARE HUNDREDS HERE!!
THUD
KLIK KLIK KLIK...
OF COURSE! IT'S A BOOKSTORE, YOU SILLY KID!!
YACK YACK!
BUT THAT DOESN'T GIVE YOU LICENSE TO STEAL!! HOW MANY TIMES DO I HAVE TO TELL YOU?!
GENZO (8 YEARS AGO)
NYAH
THUD
BLAB BLAB
WE'RE POOR! WE DON'T HAVE MONEY FOR BOOKS!
MEANIE !!
NAVI GATION
NAMI (8 YEARS AGO)

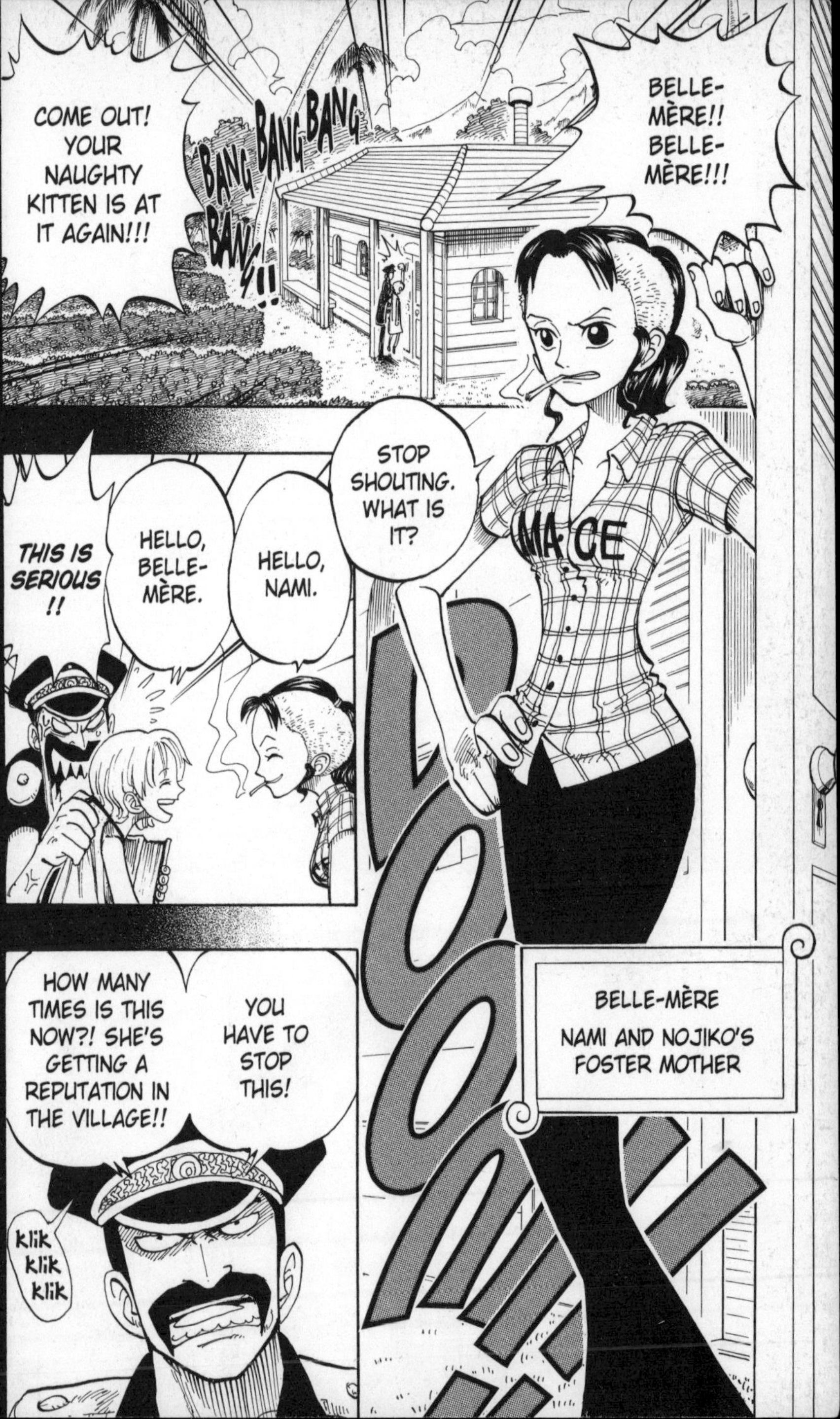
BELLE-MÈRE!! BELLE-MÈRE!!!
BANG BANG BANG BANG!!
COME OUT! YOUR NAUGHTY KITTEN IS AT IT AGAIN!!!
STOP SHOUTING. WHAT IS IT?
MA CE
BELLE-MÈRE
NAMI AND NOJIKO'S FOSTER MOTHER
HELLO, NAMI.
HELLO, BELLE-MÈRE.
THIS IS SERIOUS!!
YOU HAVE TO STOP THIS!
HOW MANY TIMES IS THIS NOW?! SHE'S GETTING A REPUTATION IN THE VILLAGE!!
klik klik klik

READ THIS WAY

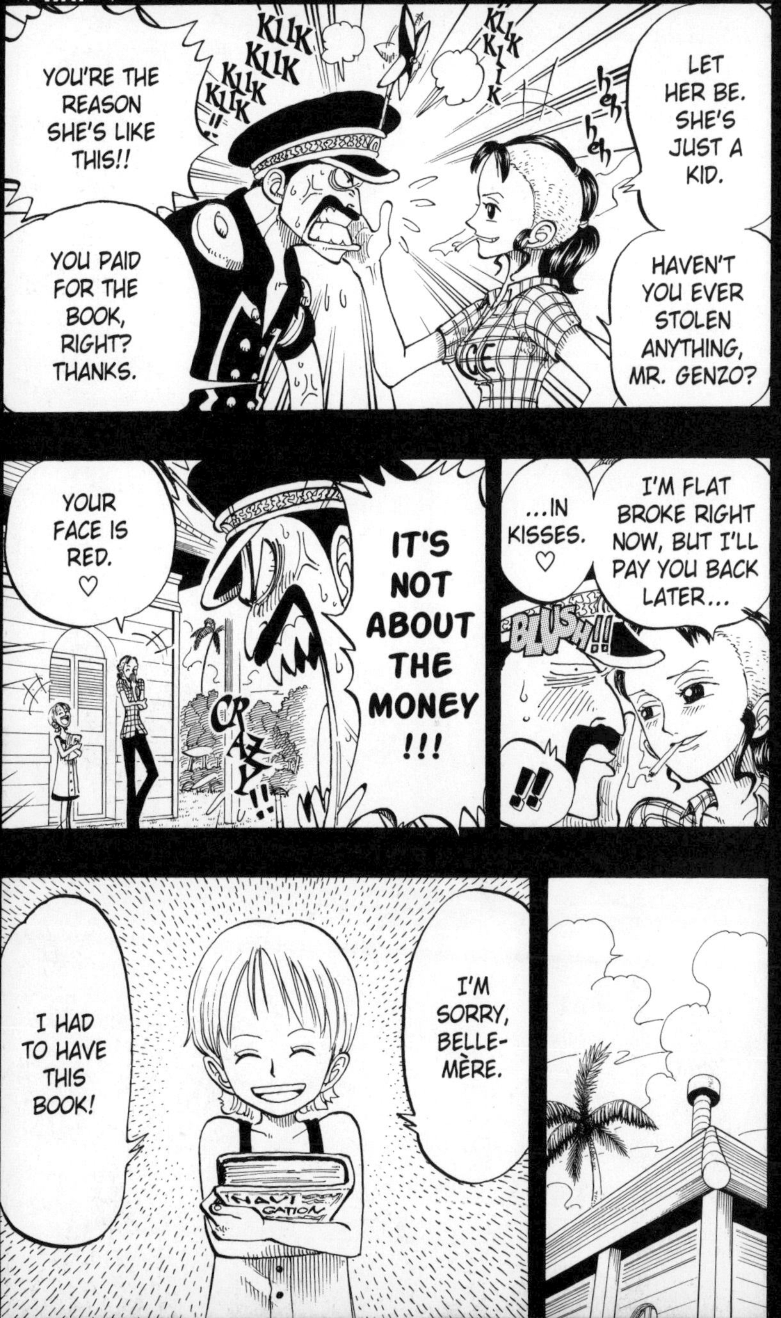
LET HER BE. SHE'S JUST A KID.
heh heh
KLIK KLIK KLIK KLIK
KLIK KLIK
!!
YOU'RE THE REASON SHE'S LIKE THIS!!
HAVEN'T YOU EVER STOLEN ANYTHING, MR. GENZO?
YOU PAID FOR THE BOOK, RIGHT? THANKS.
I'M FLAT BROKE RIGHT NOW, BUT I'LL PAY YOU BACK LATER...
...IN KISSES. ♡
BLUSH!!
!!
IT'S NOT ABOUT THE MONEY!!!
CRAZY!!
YOUR FACE IS RED. ♡
I'M SORRY, BELLE-MÈRE.
I HAD TO HAVE THIS BOOK!
NAVIGATION

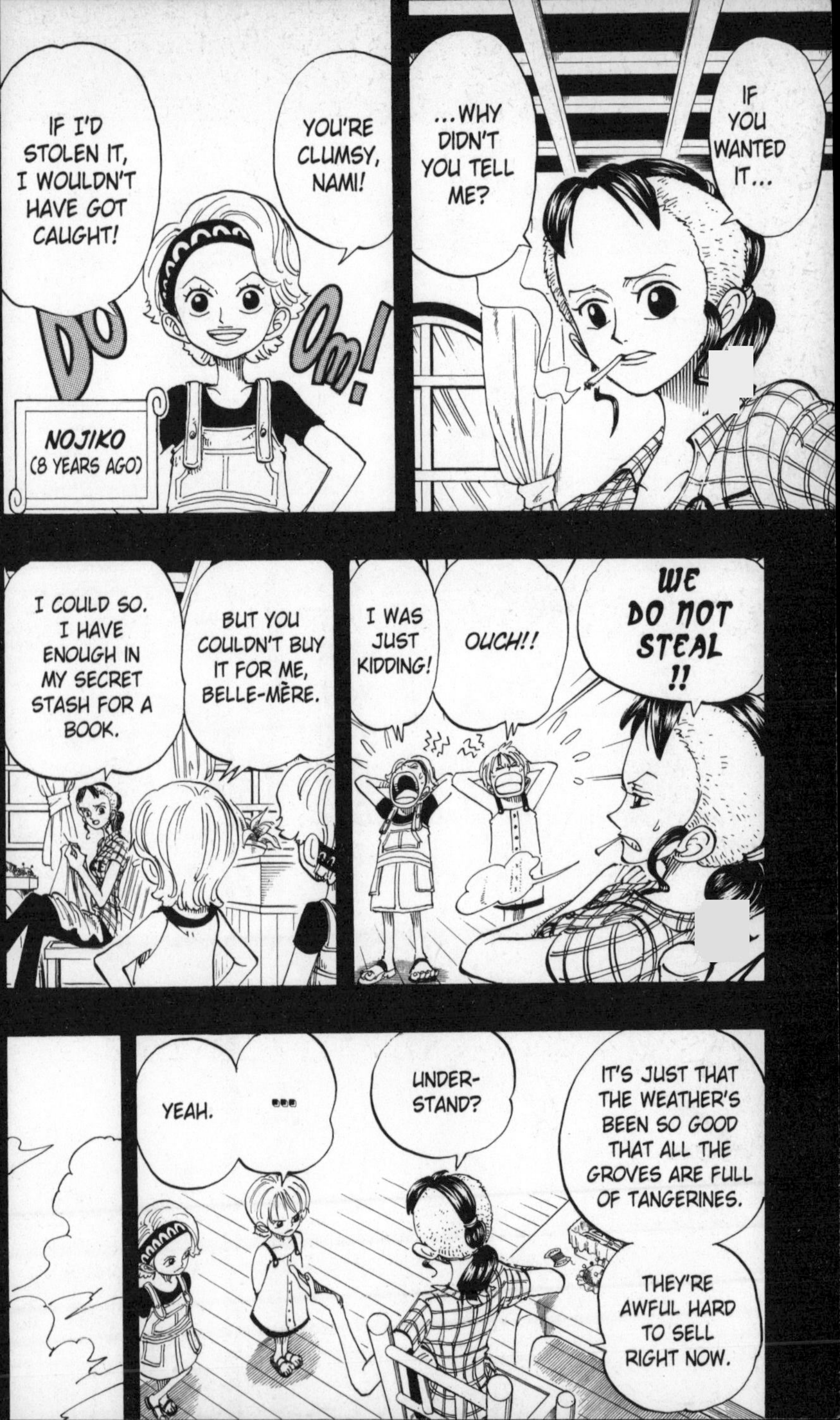
IF YOU WANTED IT...
...WHY DIDN'T YOU TELL ME?
YOU'RE CLUMSY, NAMI!
IF I'D STOLEN IT, I WOULDN'T HAVE GOT CAUGHT!
DOOM!
NOJIKO (8 YEARS AGO)
WE DO NOT STEAL!!
OUCH!!
I WAS JUST KIDDING!
BUT YOU COULDN'T BUY IT FOR ME, BELLE-MÈRE.
I COULD SO. I HAVE ENOUGH IN MY SECRET STASH FOR A BOOK.
IT'S JUST THAT THE WEATHER'S BEEN SO GOOD THAT ALL THE GROVES ARE FULL OF TANGERINES.
THEY'RE AWFUL HARD TO SELL RIGHT NOW.
UNDER-STAND?
...
YEAH.

READ THIS WAY

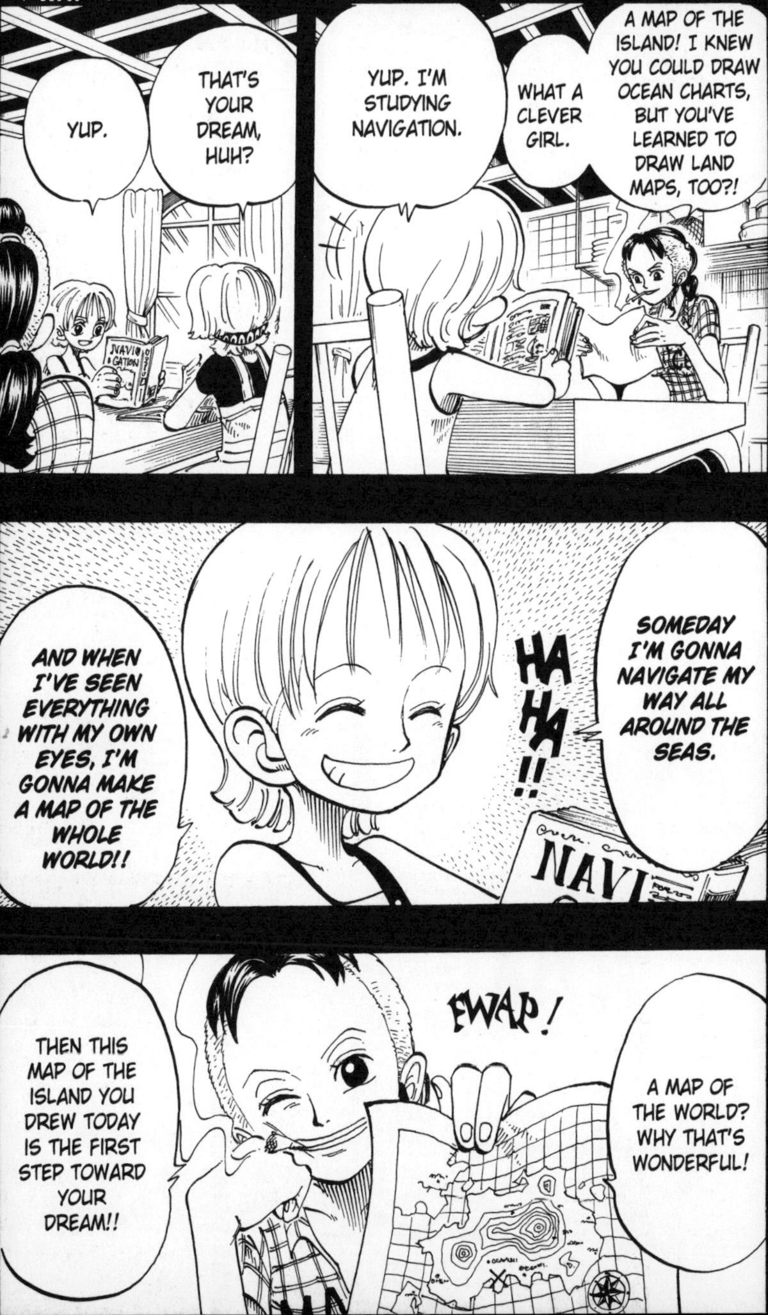
A MAP OF THE ISLAND! I KNEW YOU COULD DRAW OCEAN CHARTS, BUT YOU'VE LEARNED TO DRAW LAND MAPS, TOO?!
WHAT A CLEVER GIRL.
YUP. I'M STUDYING NAVIGATION.
THAT'S YOUR DREAM, HUH?
YUP.
NAVI GATION
SOMEDAY I'M GONNA NAVIGATE MY WAY ALL AROUND THE SEAS.
HA HA!!
AND WHEN I'VE SEEN EVERYTHING WITH MY OWN EYES, I'M GONNA MAKE A MAP OF THE WHOLE WORLD!!
NAVI
A MAP OF THE WORLD? WHY THAT'S WONDERFUL!
FWAP!
THEN THIS MAP OF THE ISLAND YOU DREW TODAY IS THE FIRST STEP TOWARD YOUR DREAM!!

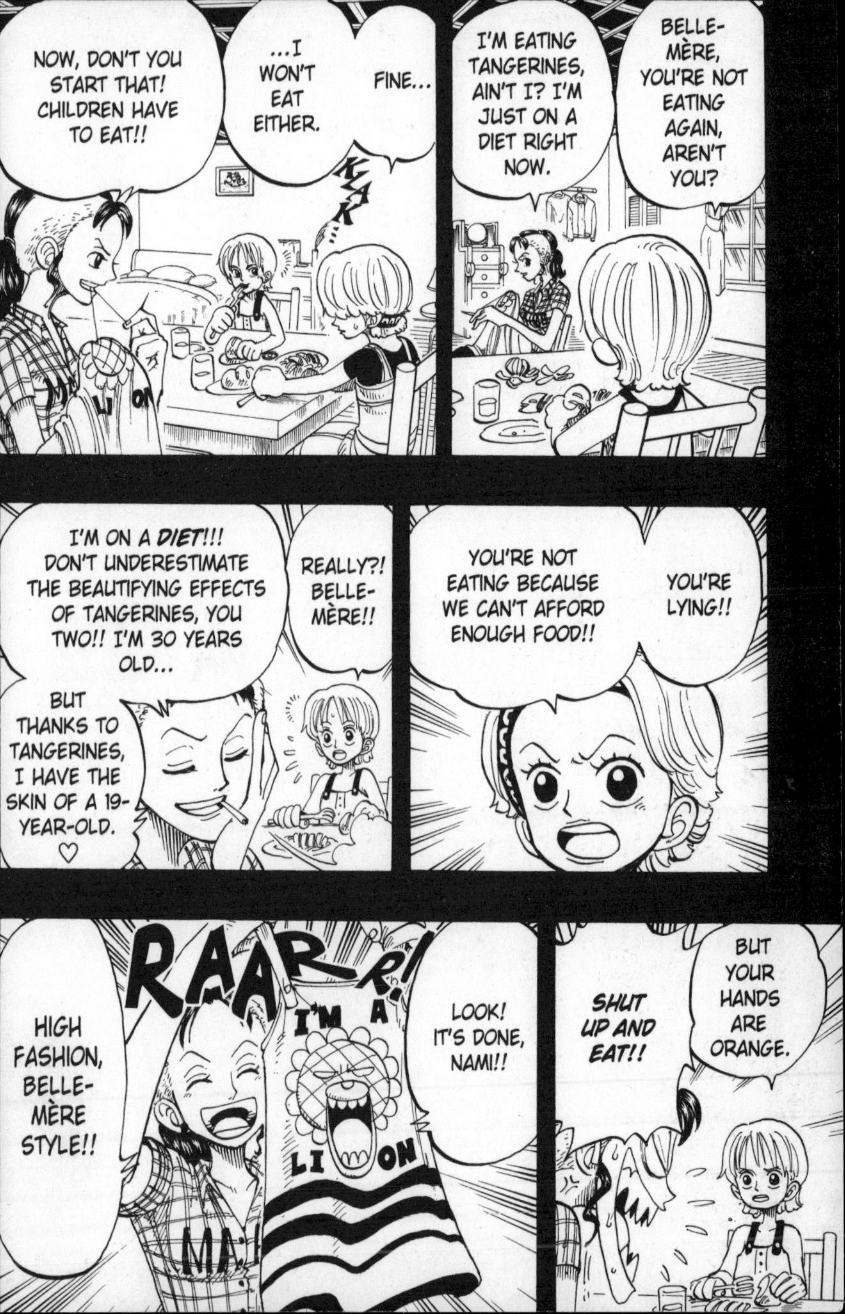
BELLE-MÈRE, YOU'RE NOT EATING AGAIN, AREN'T YOU?
I'M EATING TANGERINES, AIN'T I? I'M JUST ON A DIET RIGHT NOW.
FINE...
...I WON'T EAT EITHER.
KLAK...
NOW, DON'T YOU START THAT! CHILDREN HAVE TO EAT!!
YOU'RE LYING!!
YOU'RE NOT EATING BECAUSE WE CAN'T AFFORD ENOUGH FOOD!!
REALLY?! BELLE-MÈRE!!
I'M ON A *DIET*!!! DON'T UNDERESTIMATE THE BEAUTIFYING EFFECTS OF TANGERINES, YOU TWO!! I'M 30 YEARS OLD...
BUT THANKS TO TANGERINES, I HAVE THE SKIN OF A 19-YEAR-OLD. ♡
BUT YOUR HANDS ARE ORANGE.
SHUT UP AND EAT!!
LOOK! IT'S DONE, NAMI!!
RAAR-R!
I'M A
LI ON
HIGH FASHION, BELLE-MÈRE STYLE!!

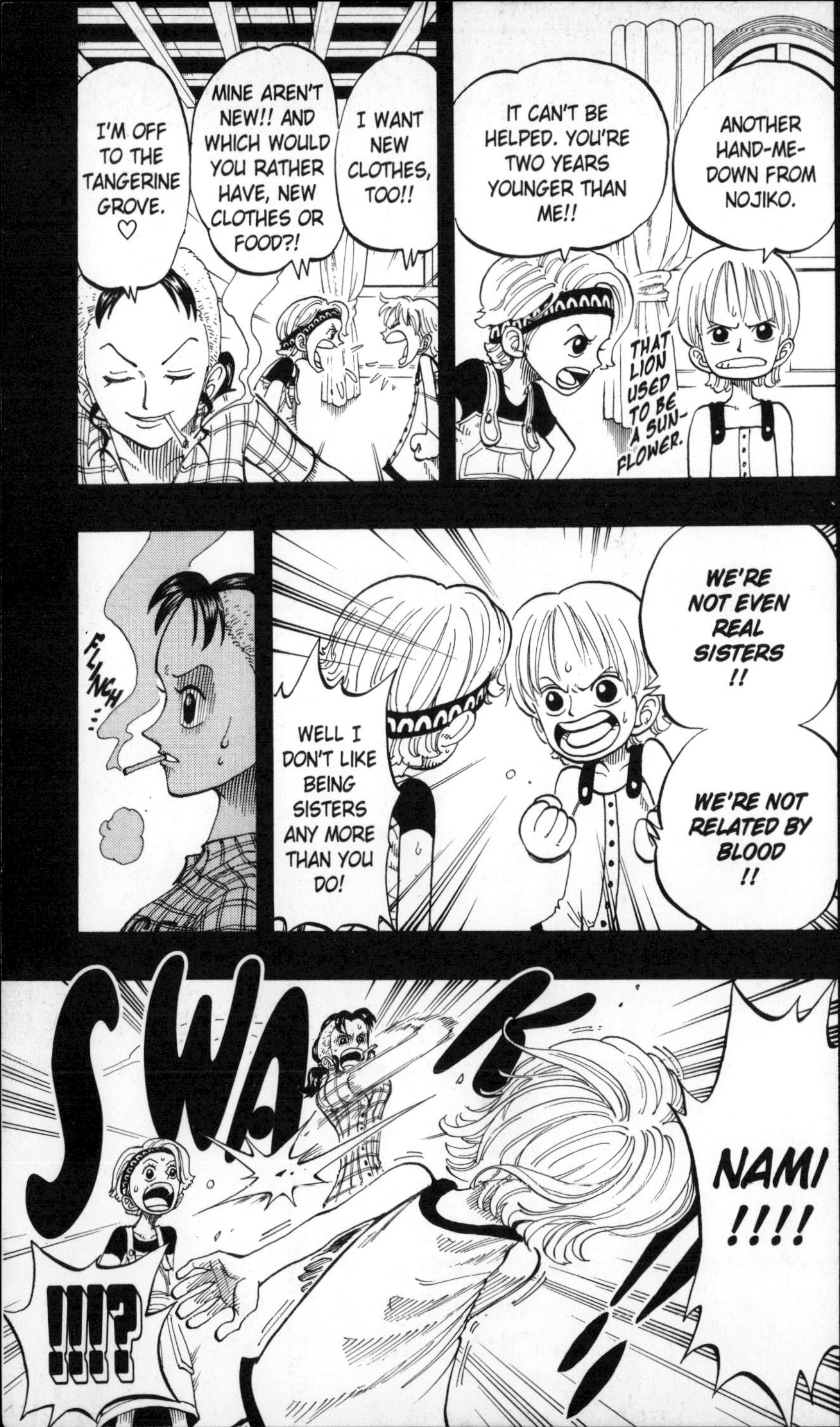
ANOTHER HAND-ME-DOWN FROM NOJIKO.
IT CAN'T BE HELPED. YOU'RE TWO YEARS YOUNGER THAN ME!!
THAT LION USED TO BE A SUN-FLOWER.
I WANT NEW CLOTHES, TOO!!
MINE AREN'T NEW!! AND WHICH WOULD YOU RATHER HAVE, NEW CLOTHES OR FOOD?!
I'M OFF TO THE TANGERINE GROVE. ♡
WE'RE NOT EVEN REAL SISTERS !!
WE'RE NOT RELATED BY BLOOD !!
WELL I DON'T LIKE BEING SISTERS ANY MORE THAN YOU DO!
FLINCH
SWAK
NAMI !!!!
!!!?

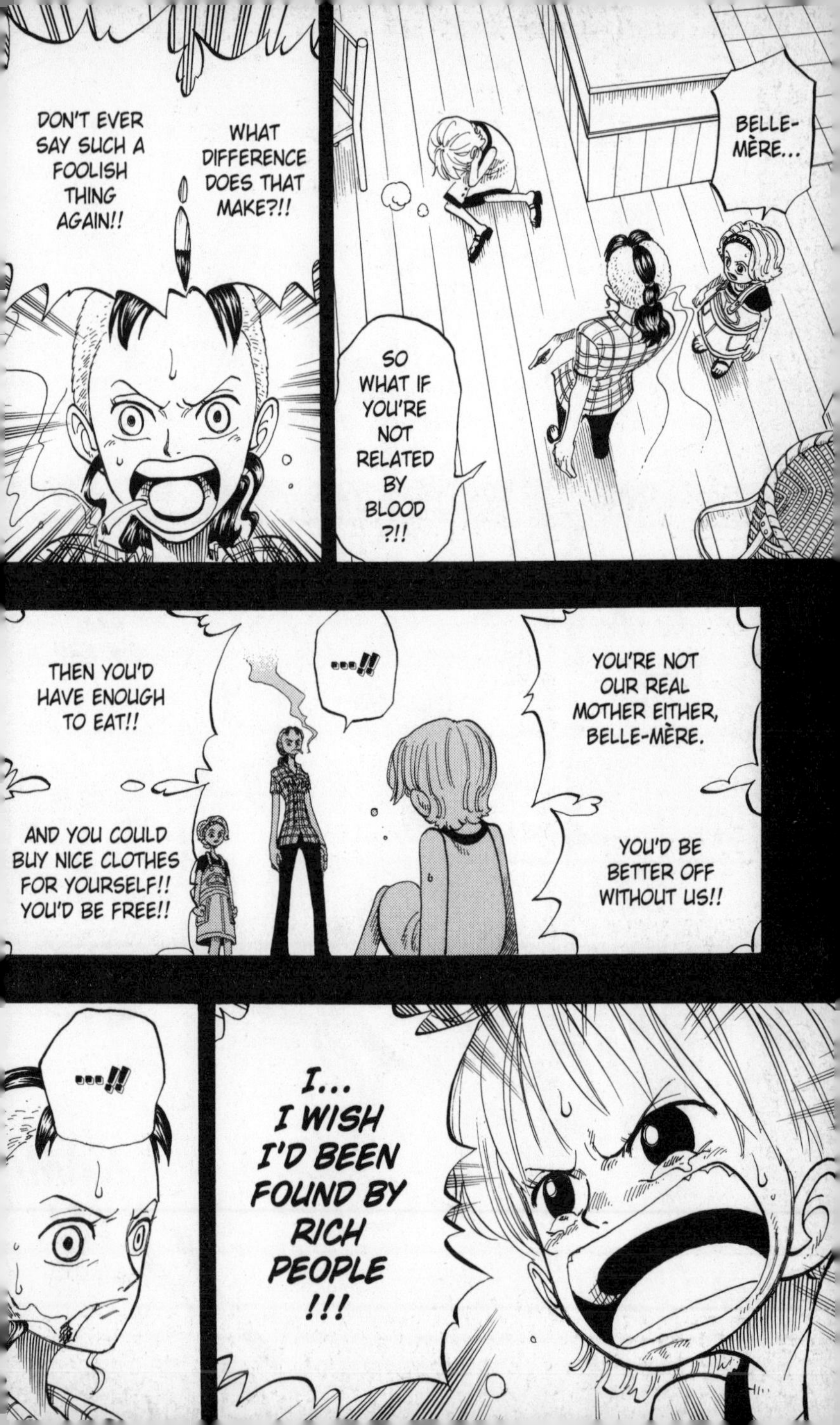
BELLE-MÈRE...
SO WHAT IF YOU'RE NOT RELATED BY BLOOD?!!
WHAT DIFFERENCE DOES THAT MAKE?!!
DON'T EVER SAY SUCH A FOOLISH THING AGAIN!!
YOU'RE NOT OUR REAL MOTHER EITHER, BELLE-MÈRE.
YOU'D BE BETTER OFF WITHOUT US!!
...!!
THEN YOU'D HAVE ENOUGH TO EAT!!
AND YOU COULD BUY NICE CLOTHES FOR YOURSELF!! YOU'D BE FREE!!
I... I WISH I'D BEEN FOUND BY RICH PEOPLE!!!
...!!

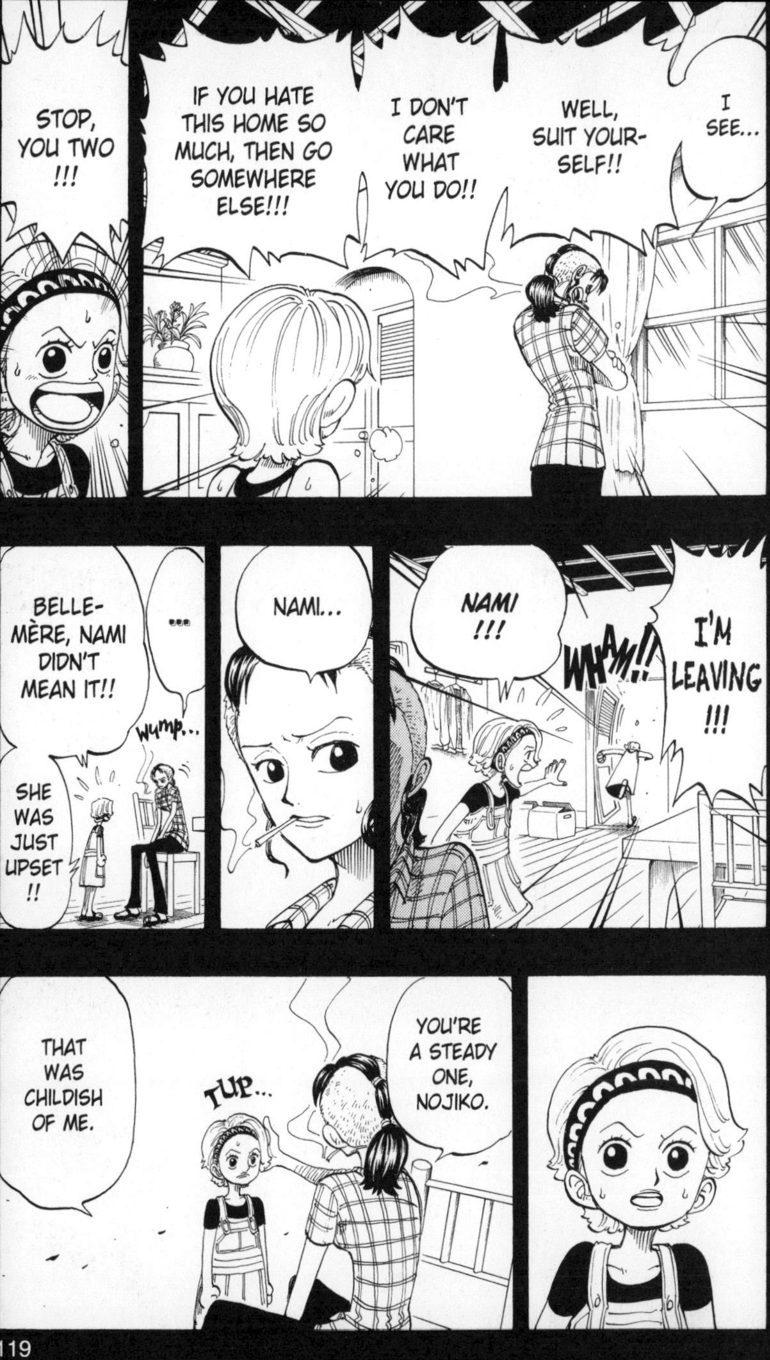
I SEE...
WELL, SUIT YOURSELF!!
I DON'T CARE WHAT YOU DO!!
IF YOU HATE THIS HOME SO MUCH, THEN GO SOMEWHERE ELSE!!!
STOP, YOU TWO!!!
I'M LEAVING!!!
WHAM!!
NAMI!!!
NAMI...
...
wump...
BELLE-MÈRE, NAMI DIDN'T MEAN IT!!
SHE WAS JUST UPSET!!
YOU'RE A STEADY ONE, NOJIKO.
TUP...
THAT WAS CHILDISH OF ME.

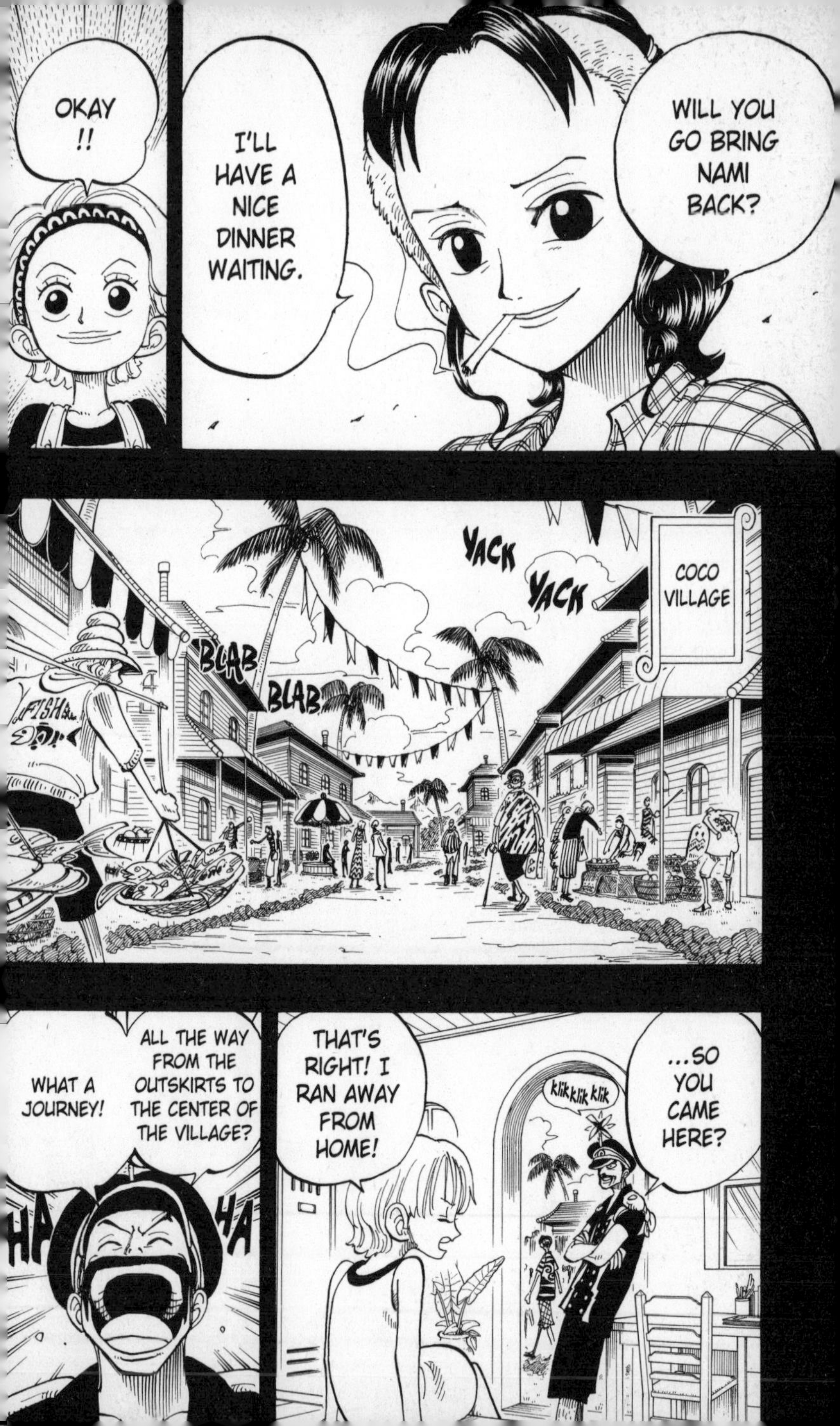
WILL YOU GO BRING NAMI BACK?
I'LL HAVE A NICE DINNER WAITING.
OKAY !!
COCO VILLAGE
YACK YACK
BLAB BLAB
...SO YOU CAME HERE?
klik klik klik
THAT'S RIGHT! I RAN AWAY FROM HOME!
ALL THE WAY FROM THE OUTSKIRTS TO THE CENTER OF THE VILLAGE?
WHAT A JOURNEY!
HA HA

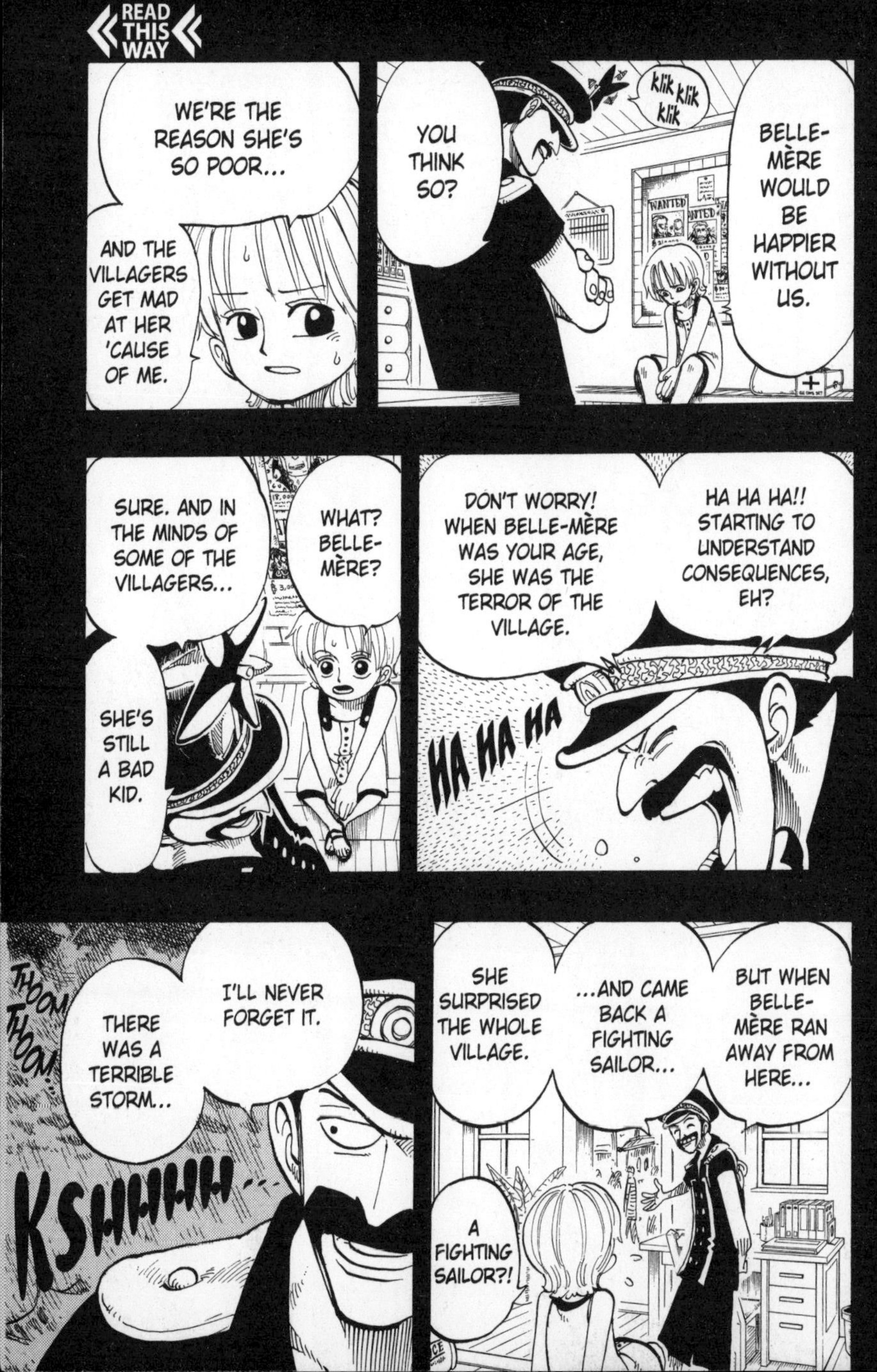
READ THIS WAY
klik klik klik
BELLE-MÈRE WOULD BE HAPPIER WITHOUT US.
YOU THINK SO?
WE'RE THE REASON SHE'S SO POOR...
AND THE VILLAGERS GET MAD AT HER 'CAUSE OF ME.
HA HA HA!! STARTING TO UNDERSTAND CONSEQUENCES, EH?
DON'T WORRY! WHEN BELLE-MÈRE WAS YOUR AGE, SHE WAS THE TERROR OF THE VILLAGE.
HA HA HA
WHAT? BELLE-MÈRE?
SURE. AND IN THE MINDS OF SOME OF THE VILLAGERS...
SHE'S STILL A BAD KID.
BUT WHEN BELLE-MÈRE RAN AWAY FROM HERE...
...AND CAME BACK A FIGHTING SAILOR...
SHE SURPRISED THE WHOLE VILLAGE.
A FIGHTING SAILOR?!
I'LL NEVER FORGET IT.
THERE WAS A TERRIBLE STORM...
THOOM THOOM
KSHHHH...

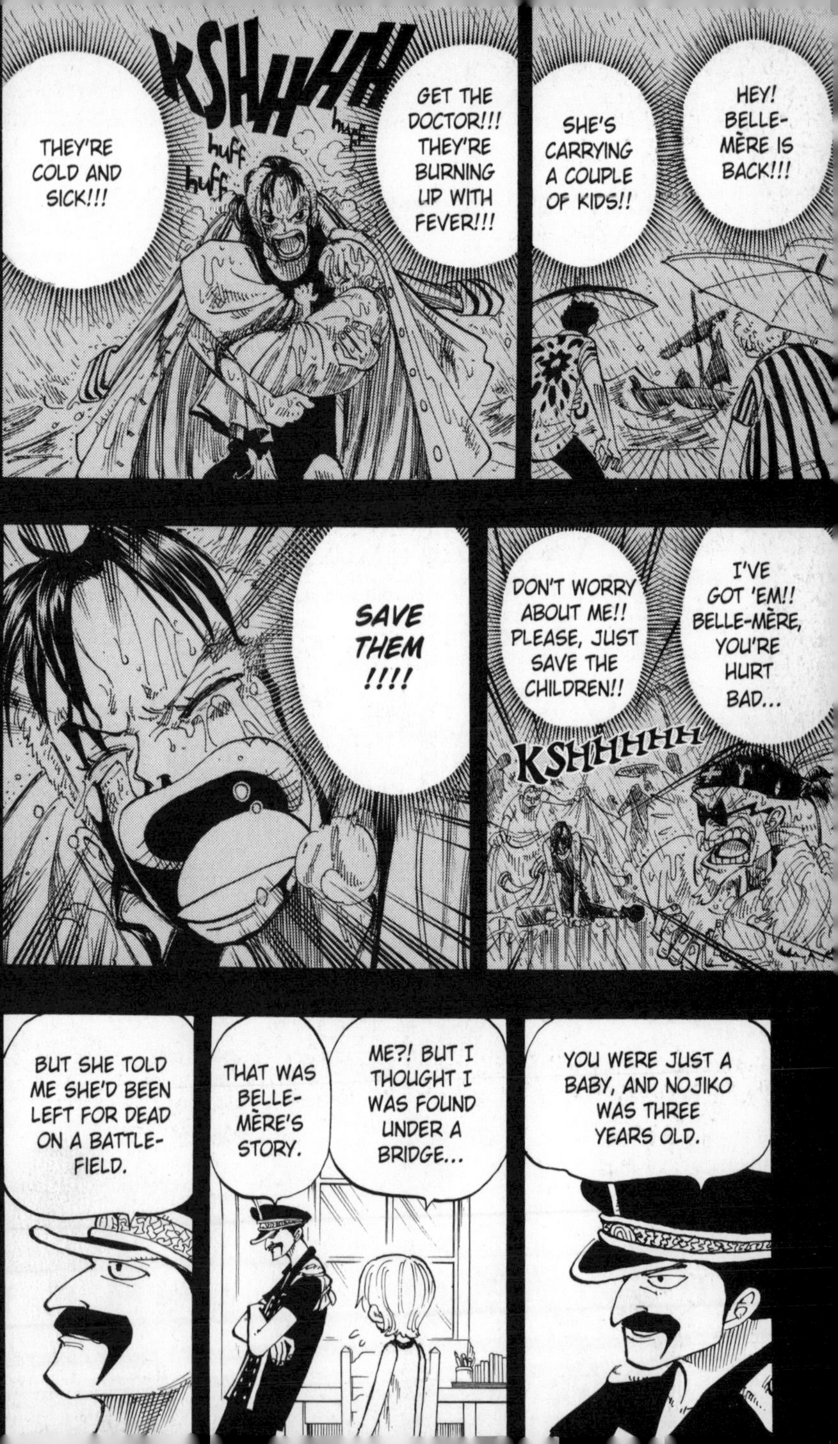
HEY! BELLE-MÈRE IS BACK!!!
SHE'S CARRYING A COUPLE OF KIDS!!
GET THE DOCTOR!!! THEY'RE BURNING UP WITH FEVER!!!
KSHHHH
huff huff huff
THEY'RE COLD AND SICK!!!
I'VE GOT 'EM!! BELLE-MÈRE, YOU'RE HURT BAD...
DON'T WORRY ABOUT ME!! PLEASE, JUST SAVE THE CHILDREN!!
KSHHHHHH
SAVE THEM !!!!
YOU WERE JUST A BABY, AND NOJIKO WAS THREE YEARS OLD.
ME?! BUT I THOUGHT I WAS FOUND UNDER A BRIDGE...
THAT WAS BELLE-MÈRE'S STORY.
BUT SHE TOLD ME SHE'D BEEN LEFT FOR DEAD ON A BATTLE-FIELD.

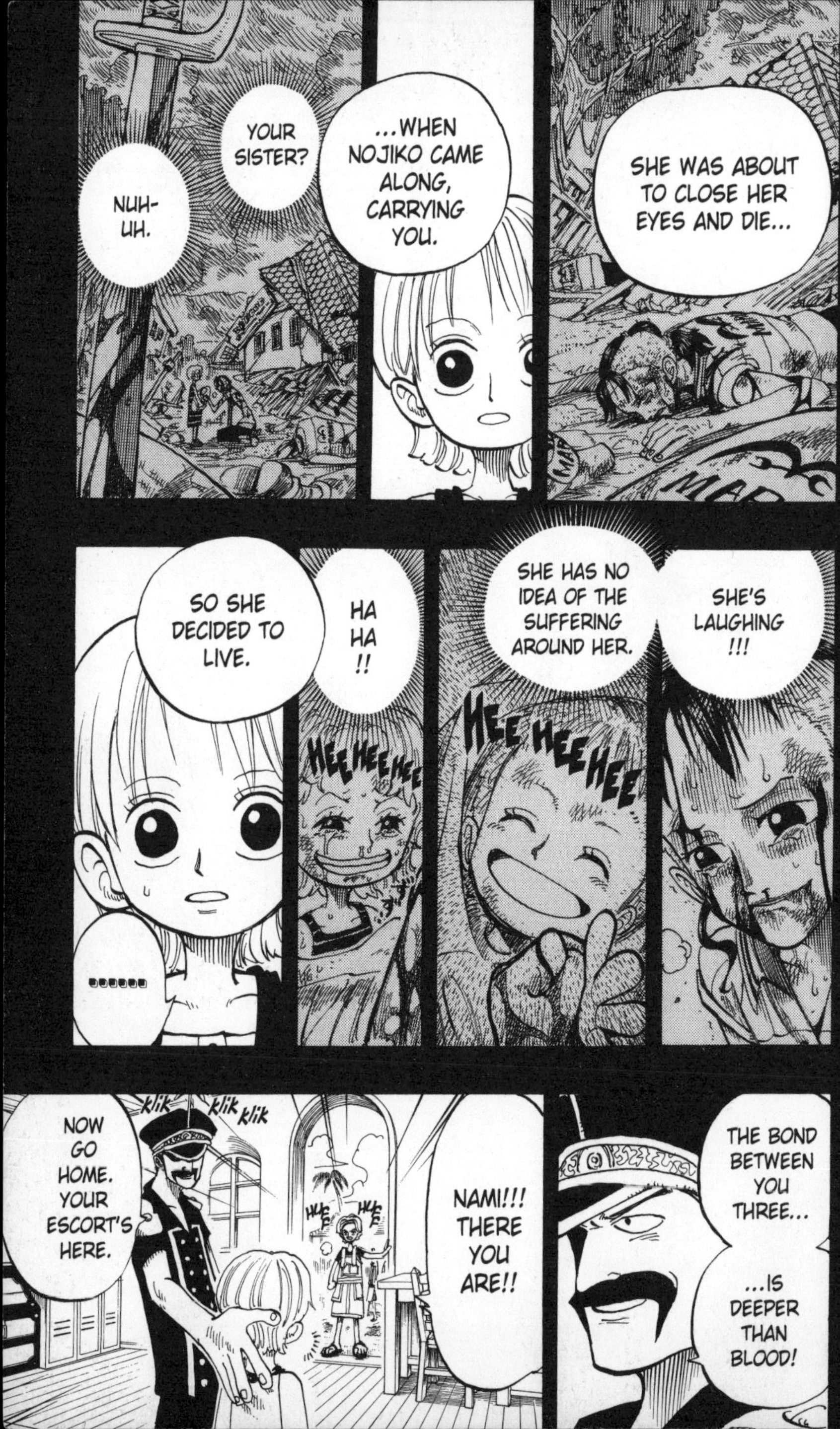
SHE WAS ABOUT TO CLOSE HER EYES AND DIE...
...WHEN NOJIKO CAME ALONG, CARRYING YOU.
YOUR SISTER?
NUH-UH.
SHE'S LAUGHING!!!
SHE HAS NO IDEA OF THE SUFFERING AROUND HER.
HEE HEE HEE HEE
HA HA!!
HEE HEE HEE HEE
SO SHE DECIDED TO LIVE.
......
THE BOND BETWEEN YOU THREE...
...IS DEEPER THAN BLOOD!
NAMI!!! THERE YOU ARE!!
klik klik klik
HUF HUF
NOW GO HOME. YOUR ESCORT'S HERE.

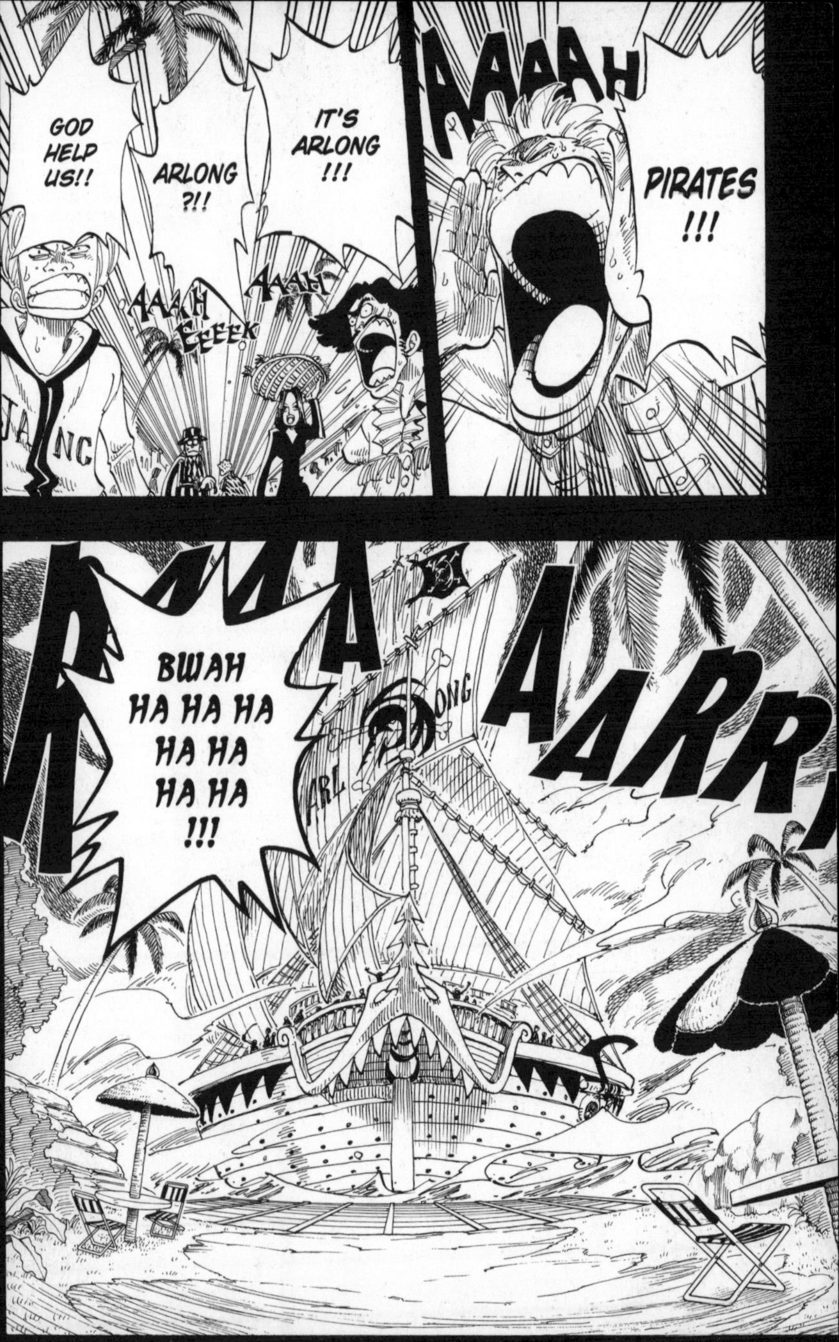
AAAAH
PIRATES !!!
IT'S ARLONG !!!
AAAH
ARLONG ?!!
AAAH
EEEEK
GOD HELP US!!
AARR
BWAH HA HA HA HA HA HA HA !!!

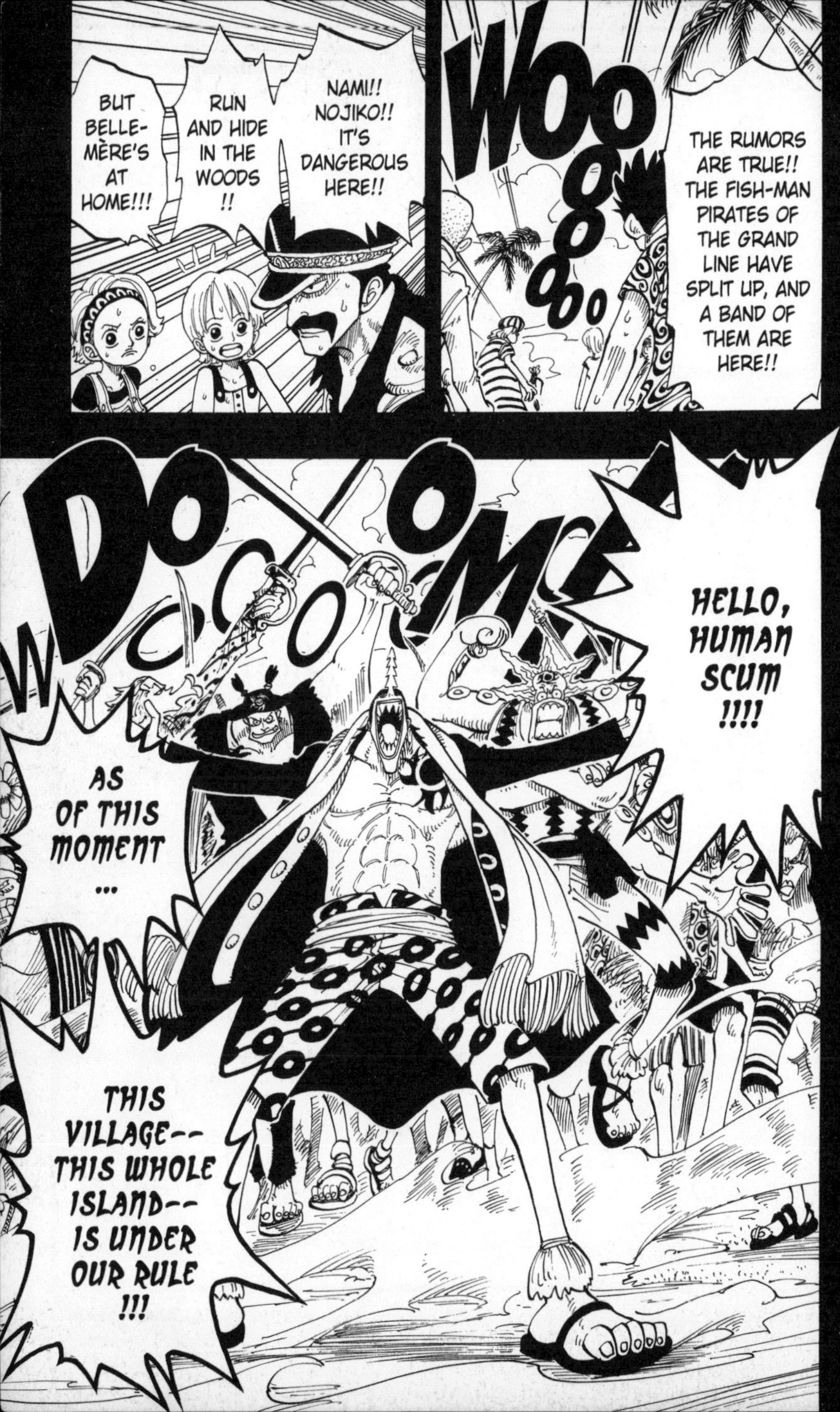
WOOOOOO
THE RUMORS ARE TRUE!! THE FISH-MAN PIRATES OF THE GRAND LINE HAVE SPLIT UP, AND A BAND OF THEM ARE HERE!!
NAMI!! NOJIKO!! IT'S DANGEROUS HERE!!
RUN AND HIDE IN THE WOODS !!
BUT BELLE-MÈRE'S AT HOME!!!
DOOOM
WOOOM
HELLO, HUMAN SCUM !!!!
AS OF THIS MOMENT ...
THIS VILLAGE-- THIS WHOLE ISLAND-- IS UNDER OUR RULE !!!

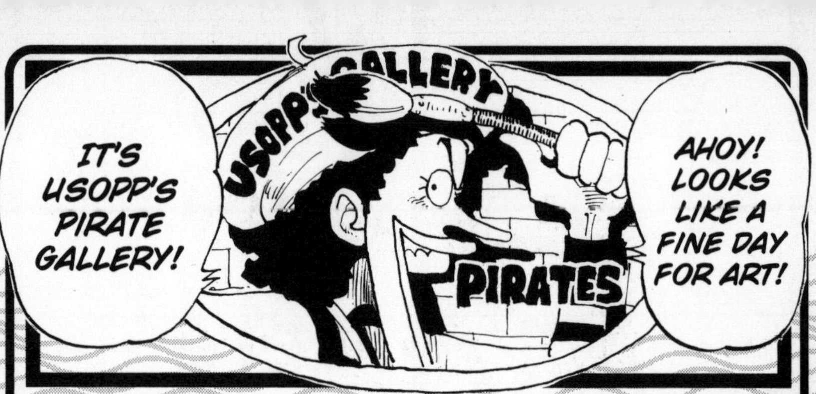
USOPP'S GALLERY PIRATES
AHOY! LOOKS LIKE A FINE DAY FOR ART!
IT'S USOPP'S PIRATE GALLERY!

ONE PIECE HEARTTHROB, SANJI.

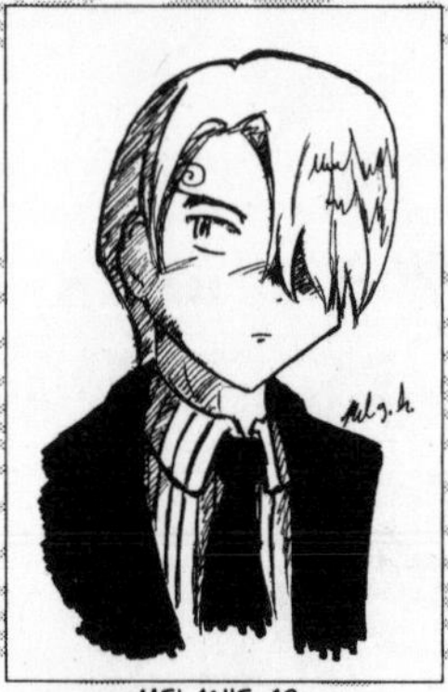

MELANIE, 18

ARRRR!

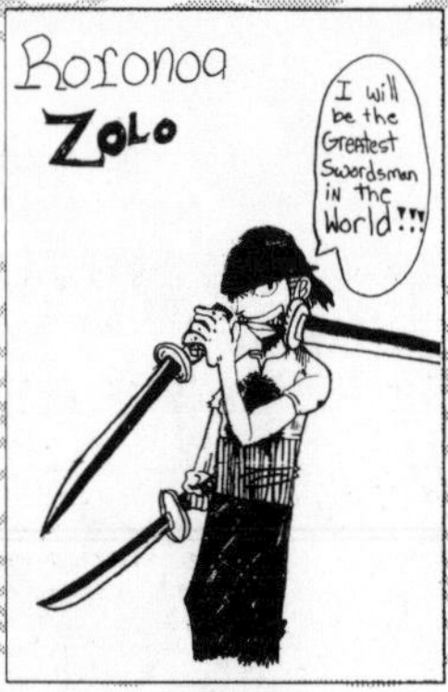
Roronoa
ZOLO
I will be the Greatest Swordsman in the World!!!

ANDY, 14

THE WORLD'S BEST NAVIGATOR.

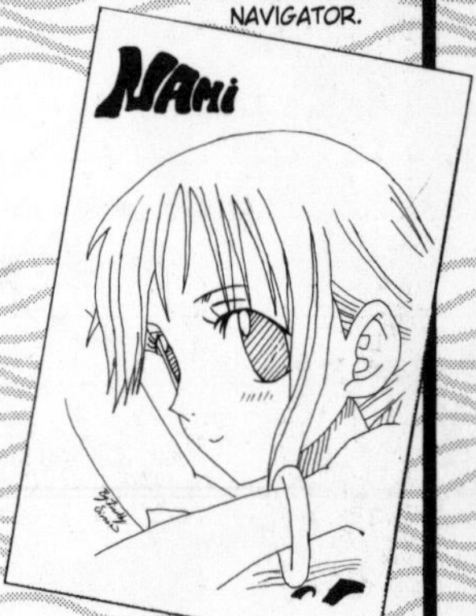
NAMI

TIMOTHY, 23

WHO'S THE TOUGHEST PIRATE HERE?

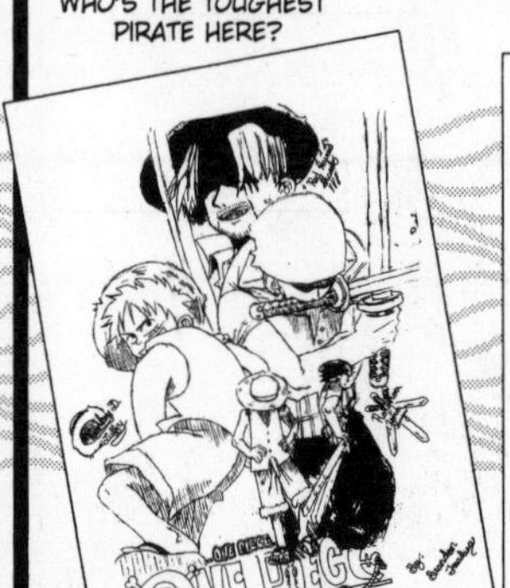
ONE PIECE

BRANDON, 13

UH-OH! IT'S MOMOO!

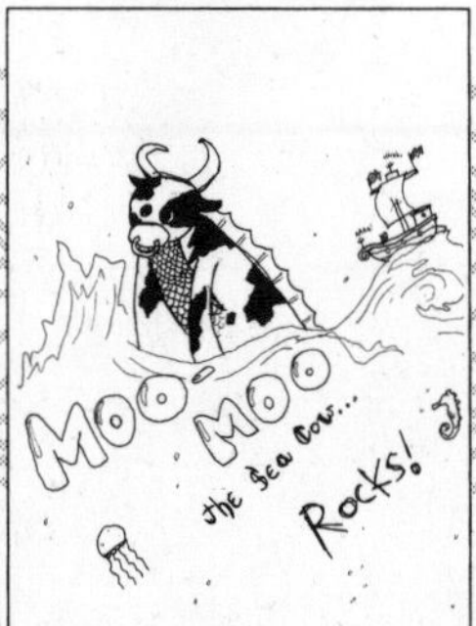
MOO MOO
the Sea Cow...
Rocks!

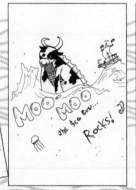

CLAVE, 13

HERE'S WINKING AT YOU.

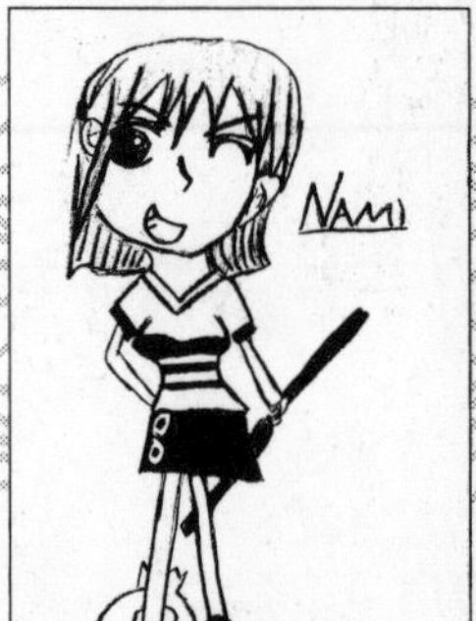
NAMI

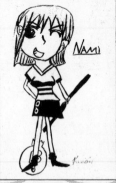

RACHEL, 13

SUBMIT YOUR FAN ART TO:
SHONEN JUMP C/O VIZ MEDIA, LLC P.O. BOX 77010, SAN FRANCISCO, CA, 94107
REMEMBER TO INCLUDE YOUR NAME AND AGE!!

USOPP'S COMMENTS WERE TRANSMITTED THROUGH THE U.S. SHONEN JUMP TEAM—*EDITOR*

Chapter 78:
Belle-Mère

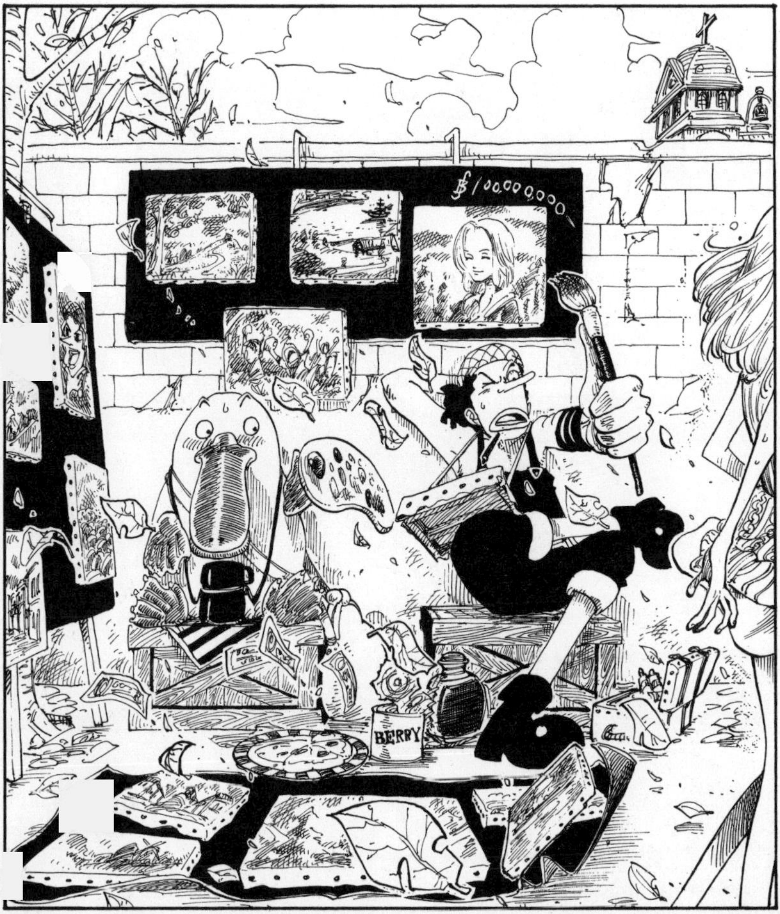

BERRY

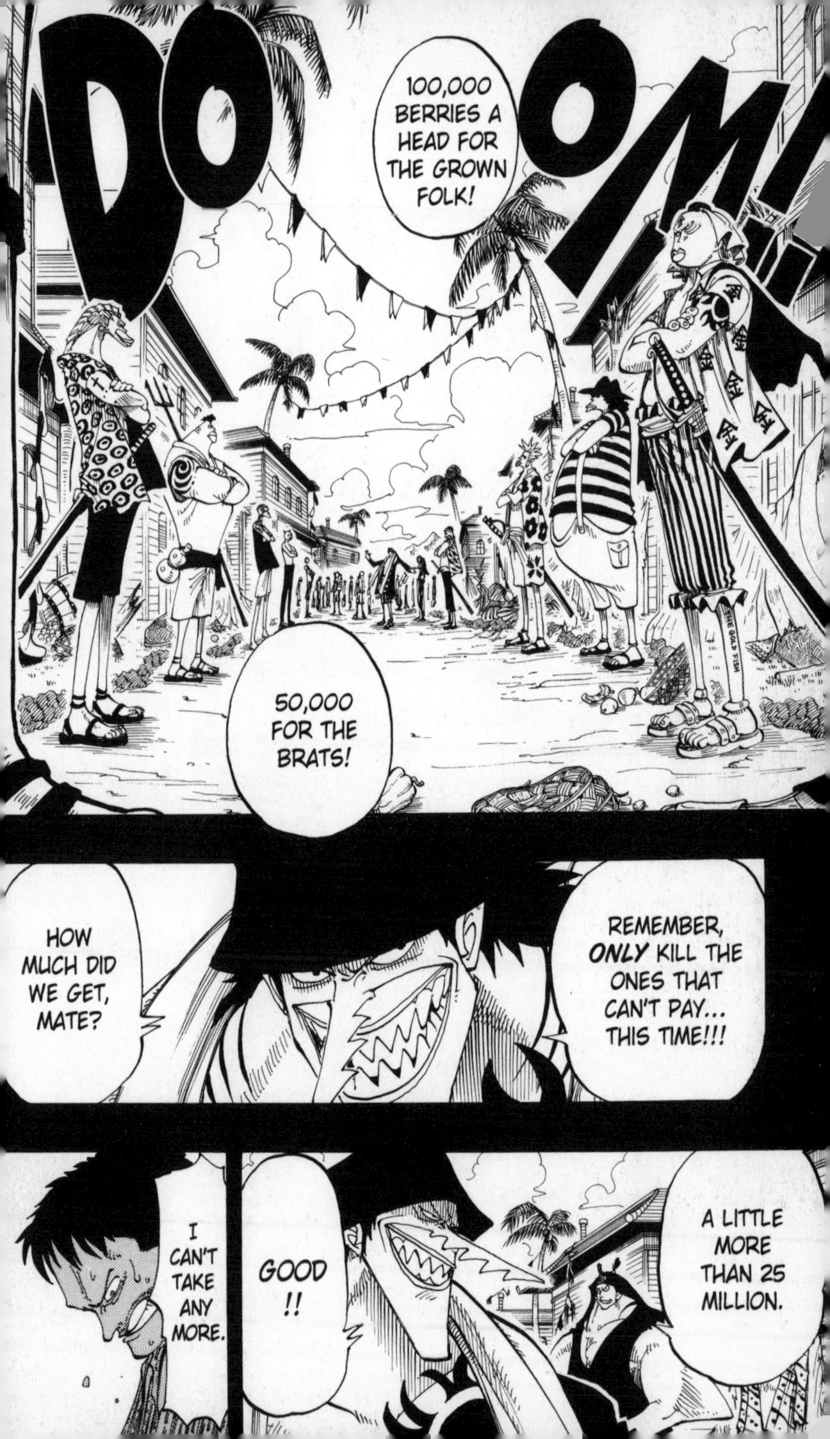
DOOM!!
100,000 BERRIES A HEAD FOR THE GROWN FOLK!
50,000 FOR THE BRATS!
REMEMBER, ONLY KILL THE ONES THAT CAN'T PAY... THIS TIME!!!
HOW MUCH DID WE GET, MATE?
A LITTLE MORE THAN 25 MILLION.
GOOD !!
I CAN'T TAKE ANY MORE.

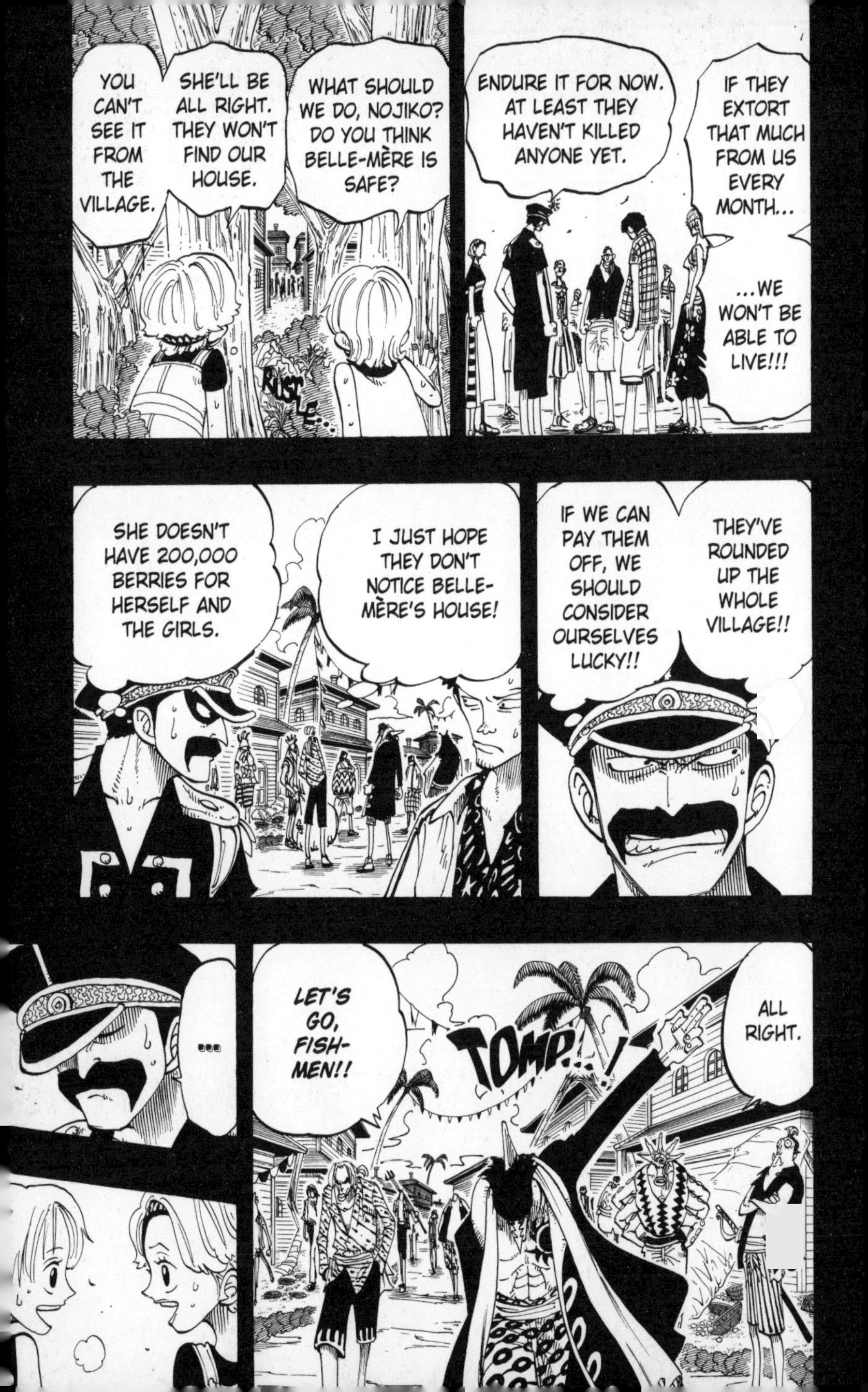
IF THEY EXTORT THAT MUCH FROM US EVERY MONTH...
...WE WON'T BE ABLE TO LIVE!!!
ENDURE IT FOR NOW. AT LEAST THEY HAVEN'T KILLED ANYONE YET.
WHAT SHOULD WE DO, NOJIKO? DO YOU THINK BELLE-MÈRE IS SAFE?
SHE'LL BE ALL RIGHT. THEY WON'T FIND OUR HOUSE.
YOU CAN'T SEE IT FROM THE VILLAGE.
RUSTLE...
THEY'VE ROUNDED UP THE WHOLE VILLAGE!!
IF WE CAN PAY THEM OFF, WE SHOULD CONSIDER OURSELVES LUCKY!!
I JUST HOPE THEY DON'T NOTICE BELLE-MÈRE'S HOUSE!
SHE DOESN'T HAVE 200,000 BERRIES FOR HERSELF AND THE GIRLS.
ALL RIGHT.
TOMP...!
LET'S GO, FISH-MEN!!
...

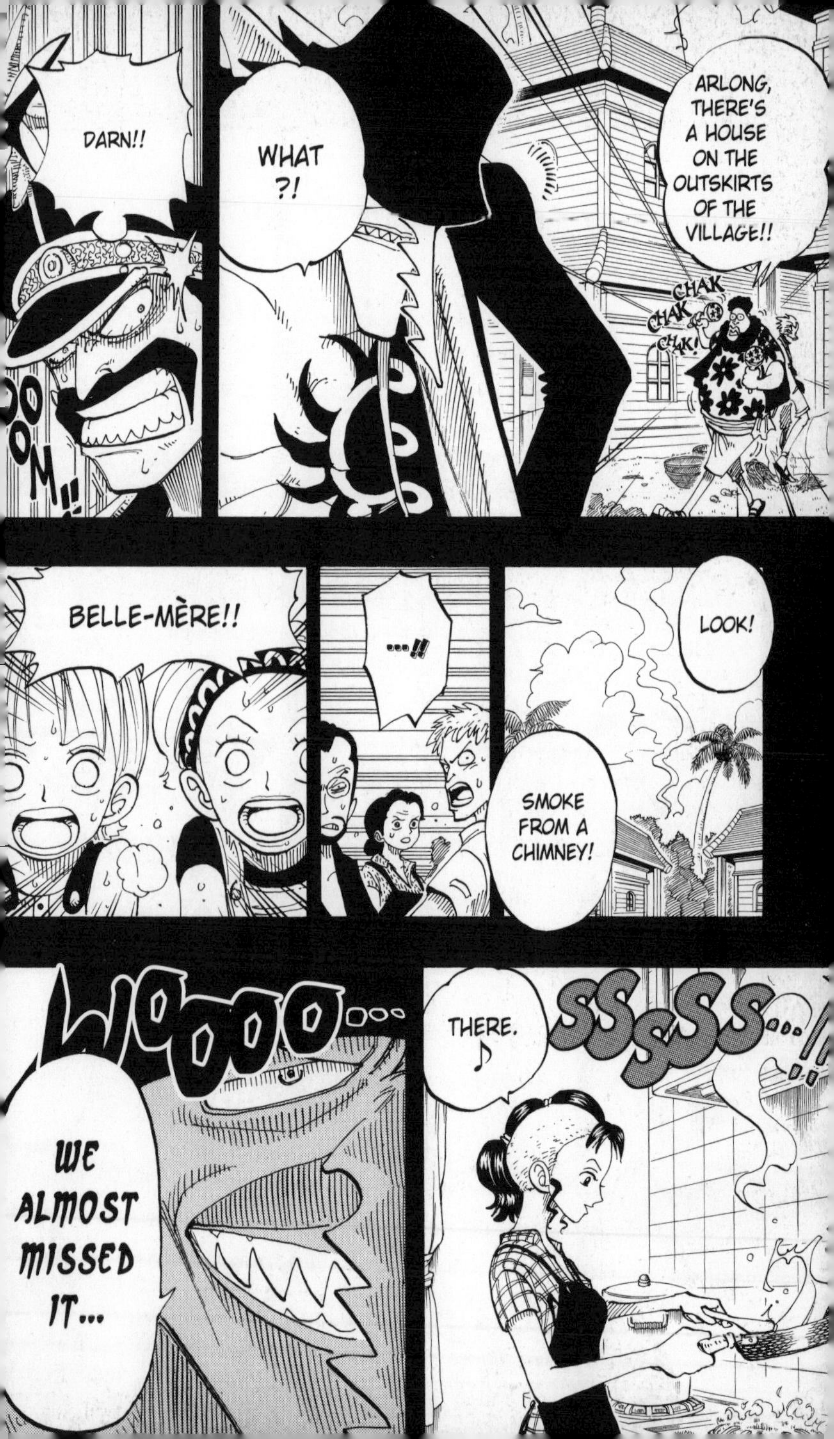

ARLONG, THERE'S A HOUSE ON THE OUTSKIRTS OF THE VILLAGE!!
CHAK CHAK CHAK!
WHAT ?!
DARN!!
LOOK!
SMOKE FROM A CHIMNEY!
...!!
BELLE-MÈRE!!
THERE. ♪
SSSSS...!!
WOOOO...
WE ALMOST MISSED IT...

READ THIS WAY

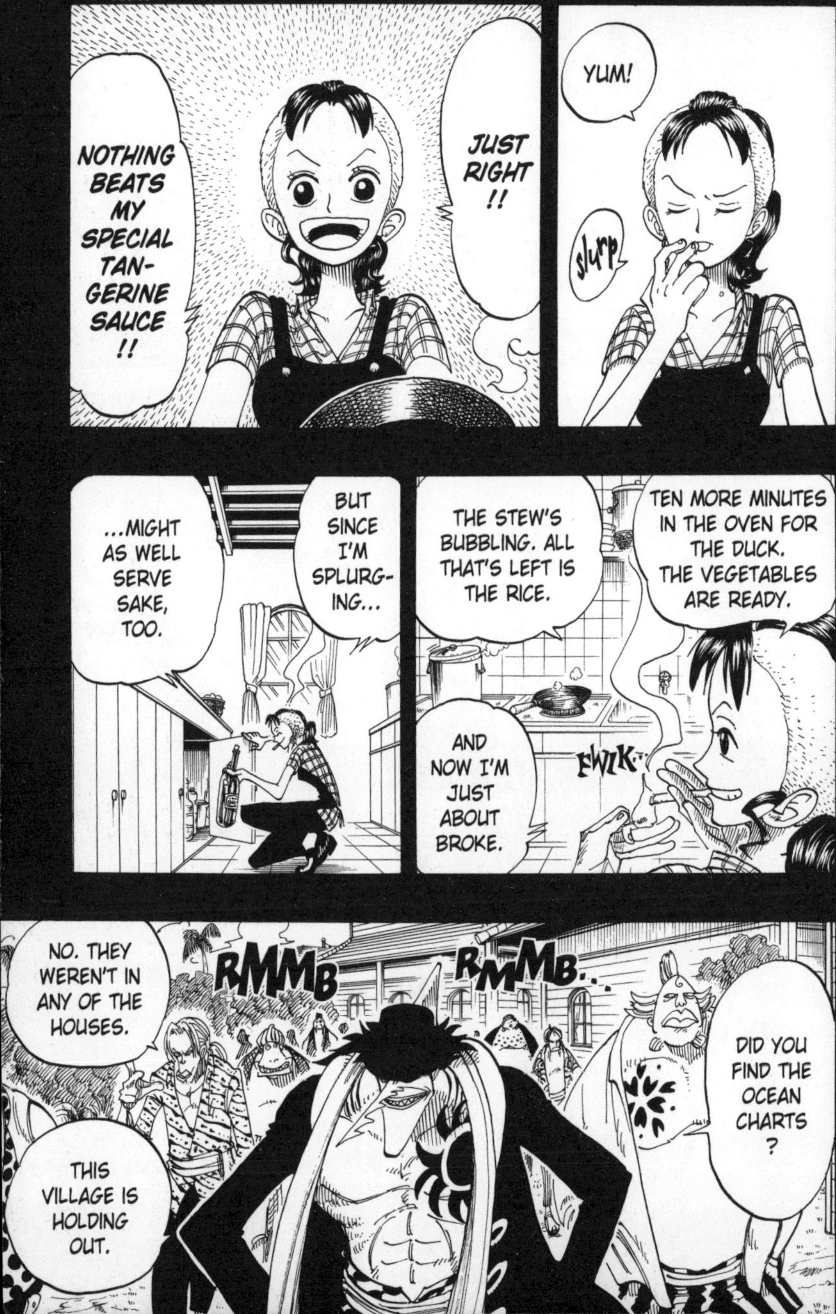
YUM!
slurp
JUST RIGHT!!
NOTHING BEATS MY SPECIAL TAN-GERINE SAUCE!!
TEN MORE MINUTES IN THE OVEN FOR THE DUCK. THE VEGETABLES ARE READY.
THE STEW'S BUBBLING. ALL THAT'S LEFT IS THE RICE.
FWIK..
AND NOW I'M JUST ABOUT BROKE.
BUT SINCE I'M SPLURG-ING...
...MIGHT AS WELL SERVE SAKE, TOO.
DID YOU FIND THE OCEAN CHARTS?
RMMB...
RMMB
NO. THEY WEREN'T IN ANY OF THE HOUSES.
THIS VILLAGE IS HOLDING OUT.

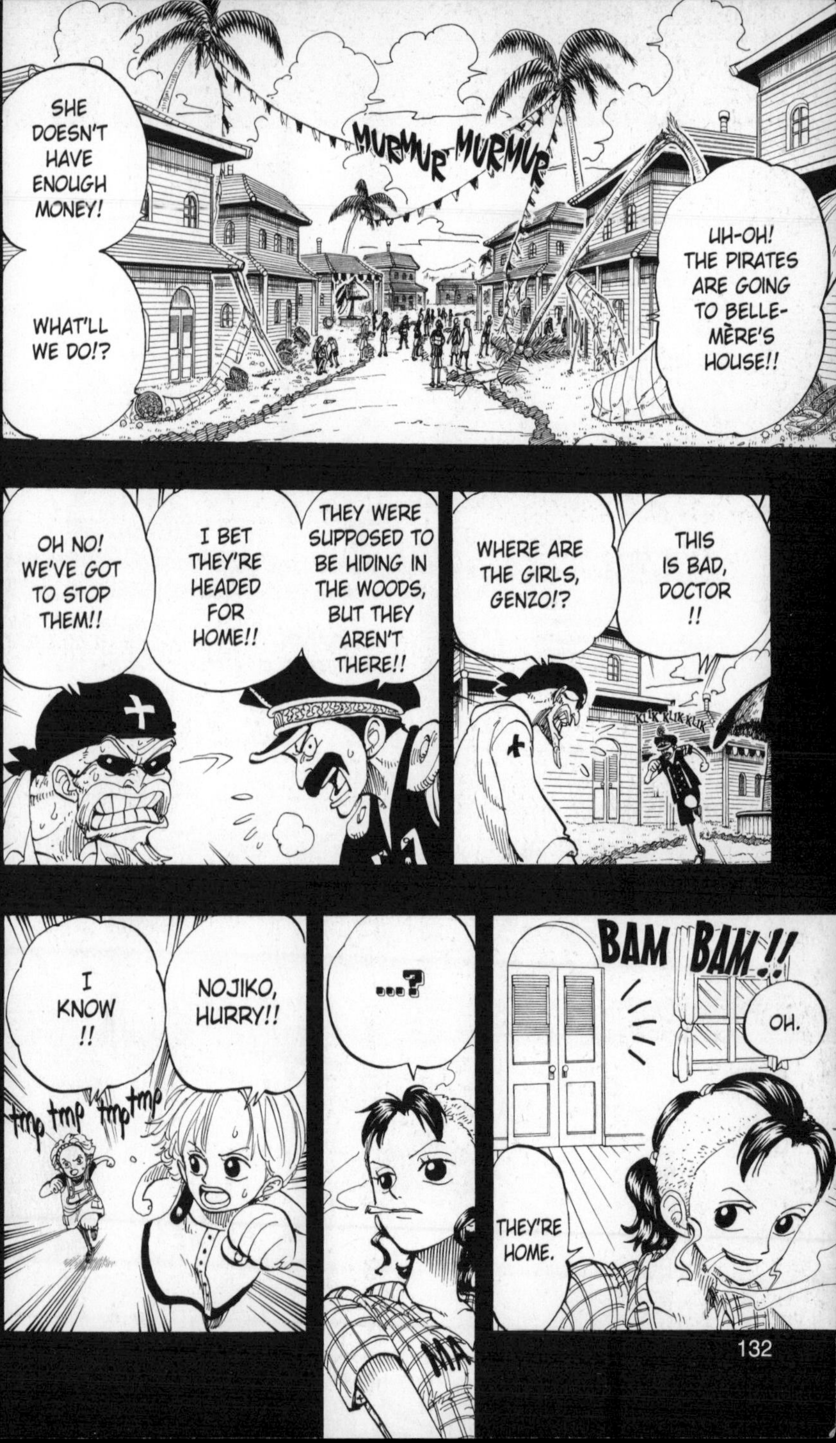
UH-OH! THE PIRATES ARE GOING TO BELLE-MÈRE'S HOUSE!!
MURMUR MURMUR
SHE DOESN'T HAVE ENOUGH MONEY!
WHAT'LL WE DO!?
THIS IS BAD, DOCTOR !!
WHERE ARE THE GIRLS, GENZO!?
KLIK KLIK KLIK
THEY WERE SUPPOSED TO BE HIDING IN THE WOODS, BUT THEY AREN'T THERE!!
I BET THEY'RE HEADED FOR HOME!!
OH NO! WE'VE GOT TO STOP THEM!!
BAM BAM!!
OH.
THEY'RE HOME.
...?
NOJIKO, HURRY!!
I KNOW !!
tmp tmp tmp tmp

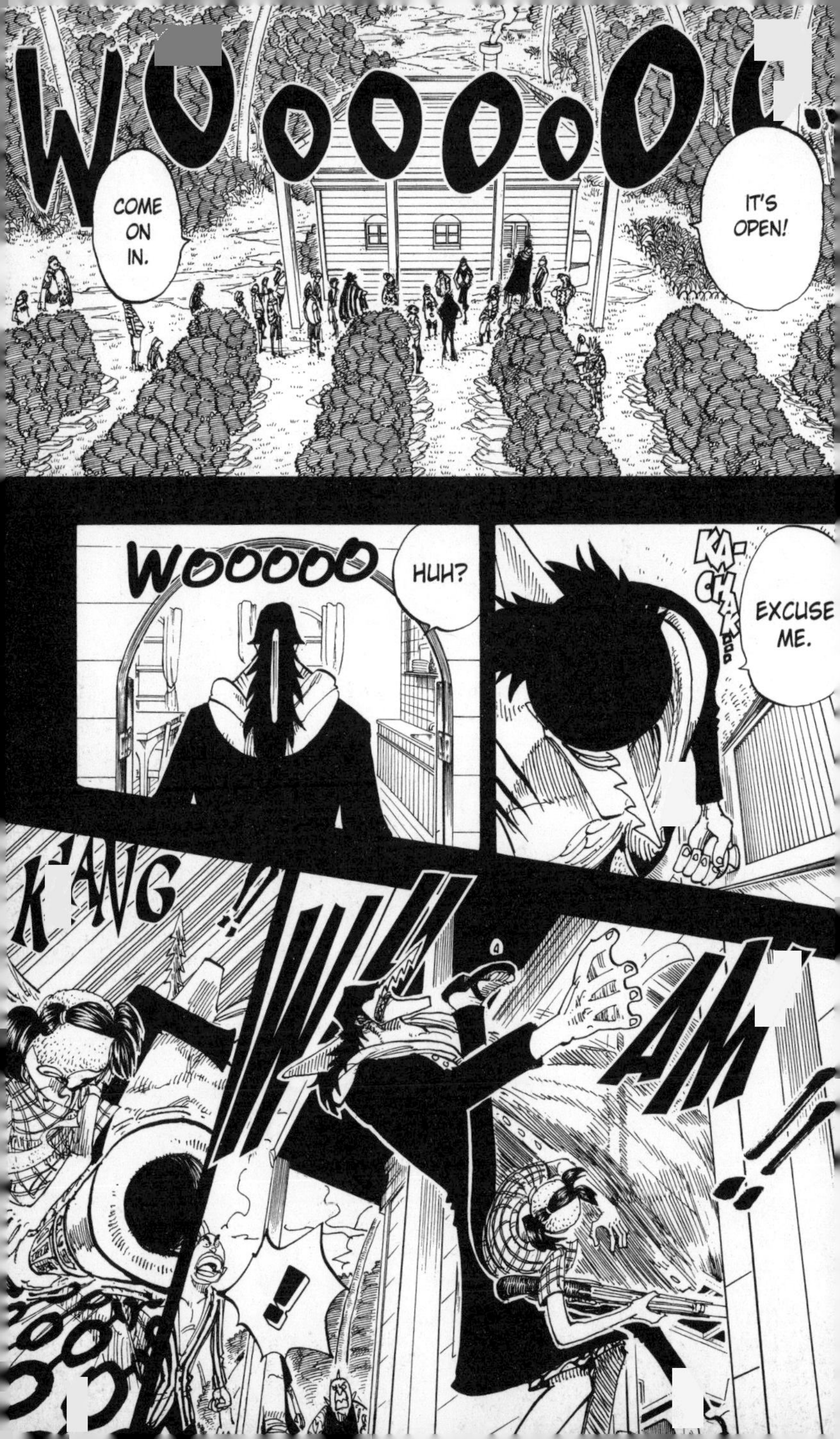
IT'S OPEN!
COME ON IN.
KA-CHAK...
EXCUSE ME.
HUH?
WOOOOO
ANG
!!
!
!!

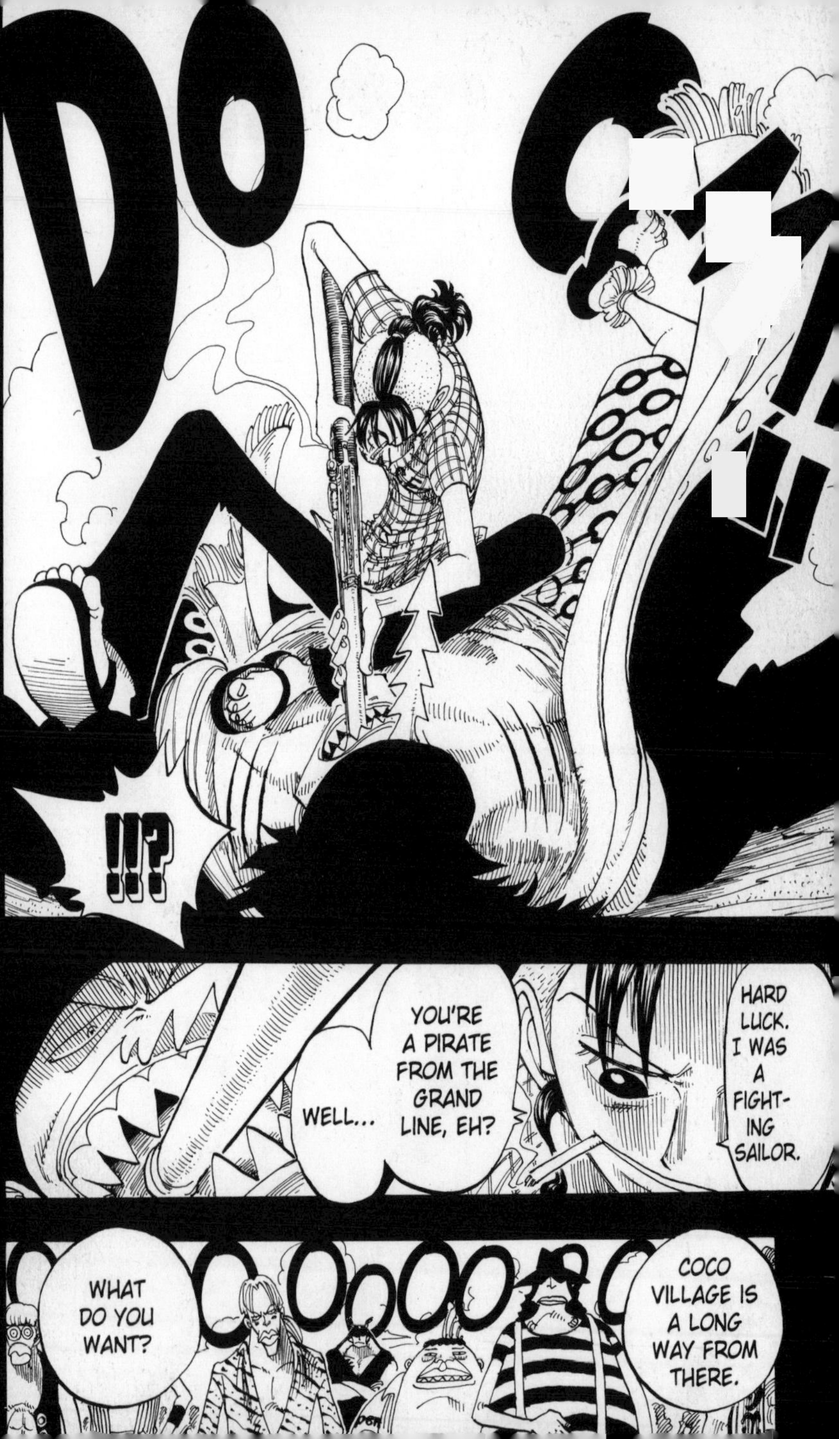
DO
!!?
HARD LUCK. I WAS A FIGHTING SAILOR.
YOU'RE A PIRATE FROM THE GRAND LINE, EH?
WELL...
COCO VILLAGE IS A LONG WAY FROM THERE.
WHAT DO YOU WANT?

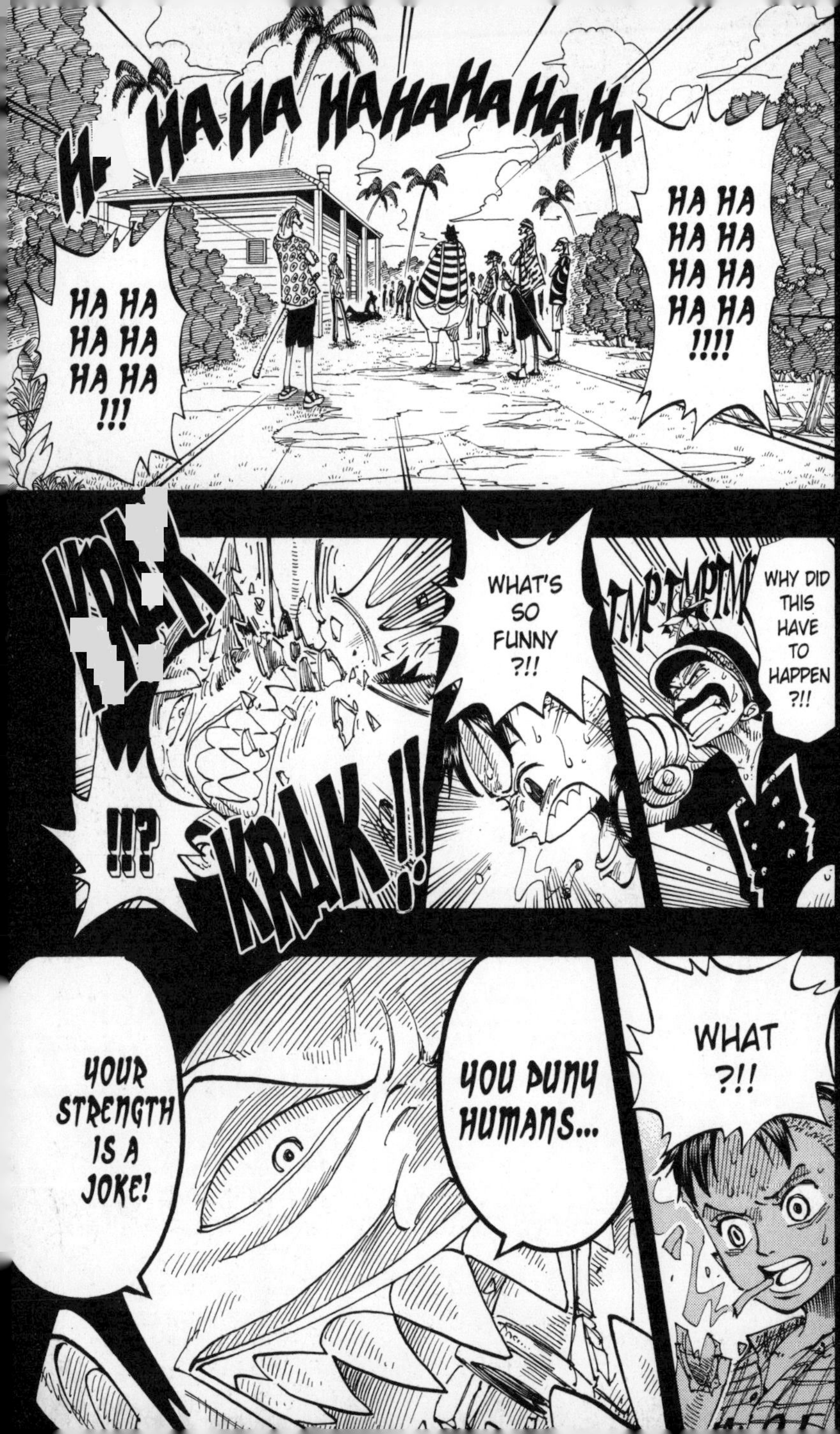
HA HA HA HA HA HA HA HA !!!!
HA HA HAHAHAHAHAHA
HA HA HA HA HA HA !!!
WHY DID THIS HAVE TO HAPPEN ?!!
TMPTMPTMP
WHAT'S SO FUNNY ?!!
!!?
KRAK!!
WHAT ?!!
YOU PUNY HUMANS...
YOUR STRENGTH IS A JOKE!

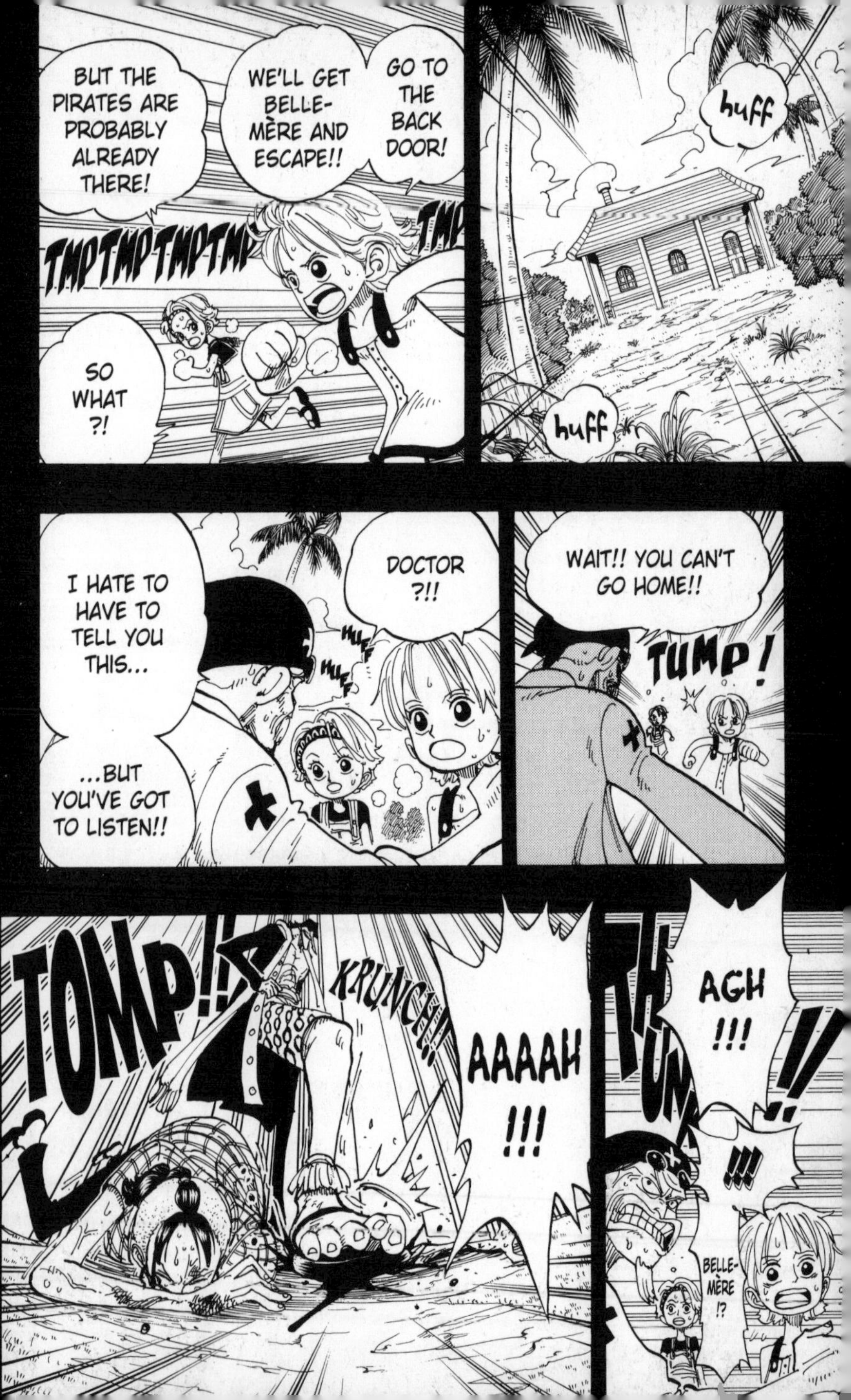
huff
huff
GO TO THE BACK DOOR!
WE'LL GET BELLE-MÈRE AND ESCAPE!!
TMP
BUT THE PIRATES ARE PROBABLY ALREADY THERE!
TMPTMPTMPTMP
SO WHAT ?!
WAIT!! YOU CAN'T GO HOME!!
TUMP!
DOCTOR ?!!
HUFF
HUFF
I HATE TO HAVE TO TELL YOU THIS...
...BUT YOU'VE GOT TO LISTEN!!
AGH !!!
THUNK !!!
BELLE-MÈRE !?
!!
TOMP!!
KRUNCH!!
AAAAH !!!

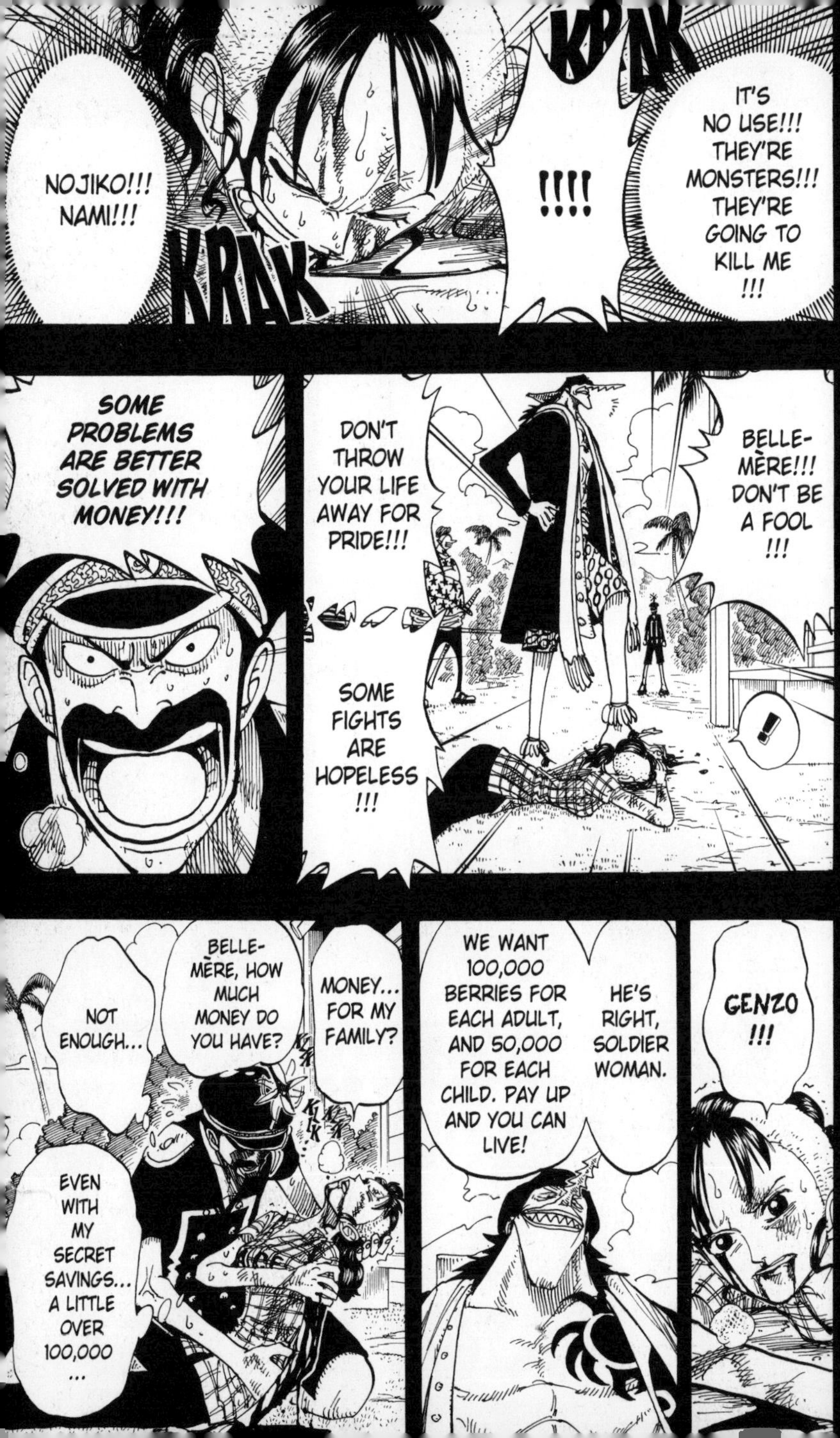
KRAK
IT'S NO USE!!! THEY'RE MONSTERS!!! THEY'RE GOING TO KILL ME!!!
!!!!
NOJIKO!!! NAMI!!!
KRAK
BELLE-MÈRE!!! DON'T BE A FOOL!!!
DON'T THROW YOUR LIFE AWAY FOR PRIDE!!!
!
SOME FIGHTS ARE HOPELESS!!!
SOME PROBLEMS ARE BETTER SOLVED WITH MONEY!!!
GENZO!!!
HE'S RIGHT, SOLDIER WOMAN.
WE WANT 100,000 BERRIES FOR EACH ADULT, AND 50,000 FOR EACH CHILD. PAY UP AND YOU CAN LIVE!
MONEY... FOR MY FAMILY?
BELLE-MÈRE, HOW MUCH MONEY DO YOU HAVE?
NOT ENOUGH...
EVEN WITH MY SECRET SAVINGS... A LITTLE OVER 100,000...

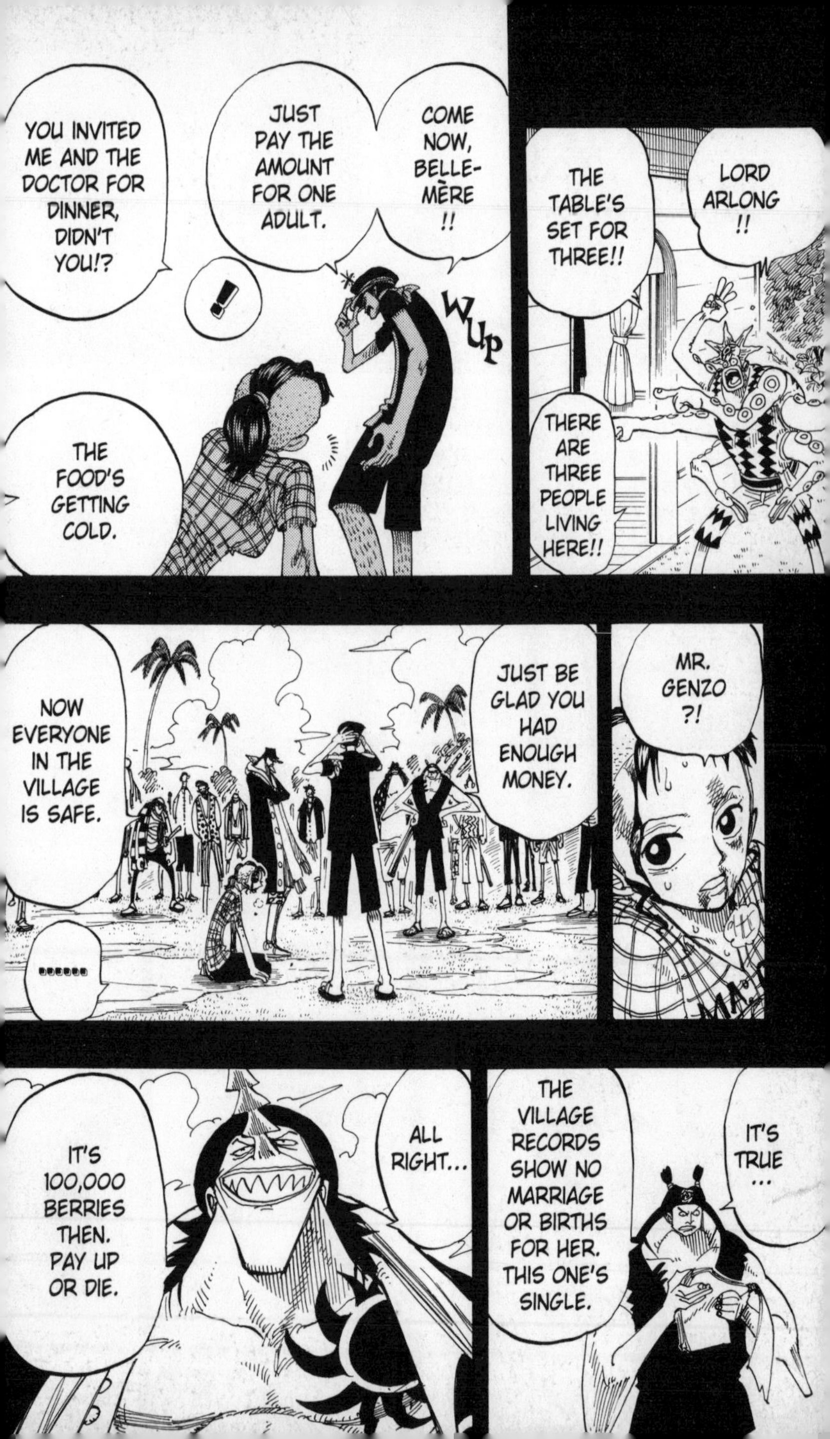
LORD ARLONG !!
THE TABLE'S SET FOR THREE!!
THERE ARE THREE PEOPLE LIVING HERE!!
COME NOW, BELLE-MÈRE !!
JUST PAY THE AMOUNT FOR ONE ADULT.
!
YOU INVITED ME AND THE DOCTOR FOR DINNER, DIDN'T YOU!?
WUP
THE FOOD'S GETTING COLD.
MR. GENZO ?!
JUST BE GLAD YOU HAD ENOUGH MONEY.
NOW EVERYONE IN THE VILLAGE IS SAFE.
......
IT'S TRUE ...
THE VILLAGE RECORDS SHOW NO MARRIAGE OR BIRTHS FOR HER. THIS ONE'S SINGLE.
ALL RIGHT...
IT'S 100,000 BERRIES THEN. PAY UP OR DIE.

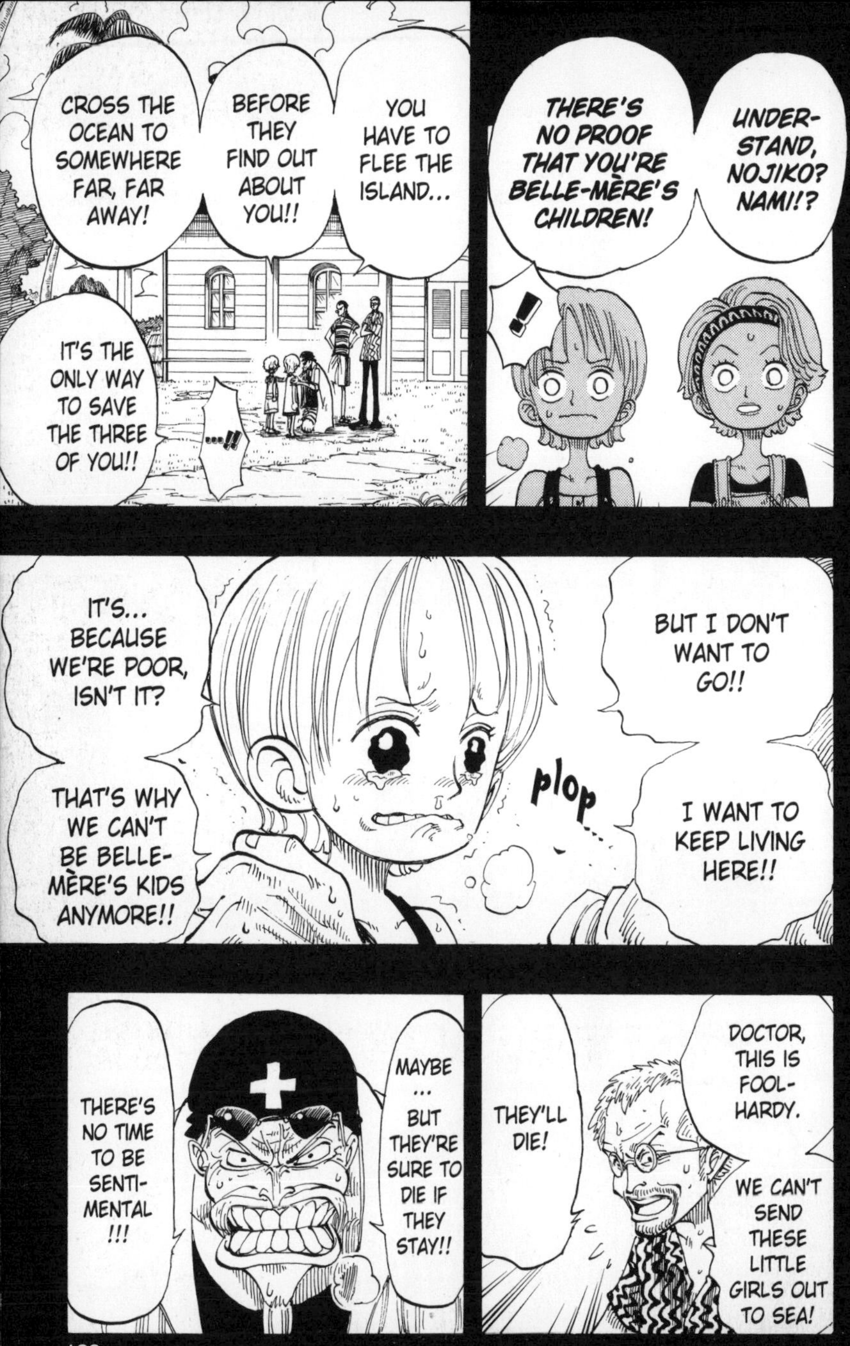
UNDERSTAND, NOJIKO? NAMI!?
THERE'S NO PROOF THAT YOU'RE BELLE-MÈRE'S CHILDREN!
!
YOU HAVE TO FLEE THE ISLAND...
BEFORE THEY FIND OUT ABOUT YOU!!
CROSS THE OCEAN TO SOMEWHERE FAR, FAR AWAY!
...!!
IT'S THE ONLY WAY TO SAVE THE THREE OF YOU!!
BUT I DON'T WANT TO GO!!
I WANT TO KEEP LIVING HERE!!
plop...
IT'S... BECAUSE WE'RE POOR, ISN'T IT?
THAT'S WHY WE CAN'T BE BELLE-MÈRE'S KIDS ANYMORE!!
DOCTOR, THIS IS FOOLHARDY.
WE CAN'T SEND THESE LITTLE GIRLS OUT TO SEA!
THEY'LL DIE!
MAYBE ... BUT THEY'RE SURE TO DIE IF THEY STAY!!
THERE'S NO TIME TO BE SENTIMENTAL!!!

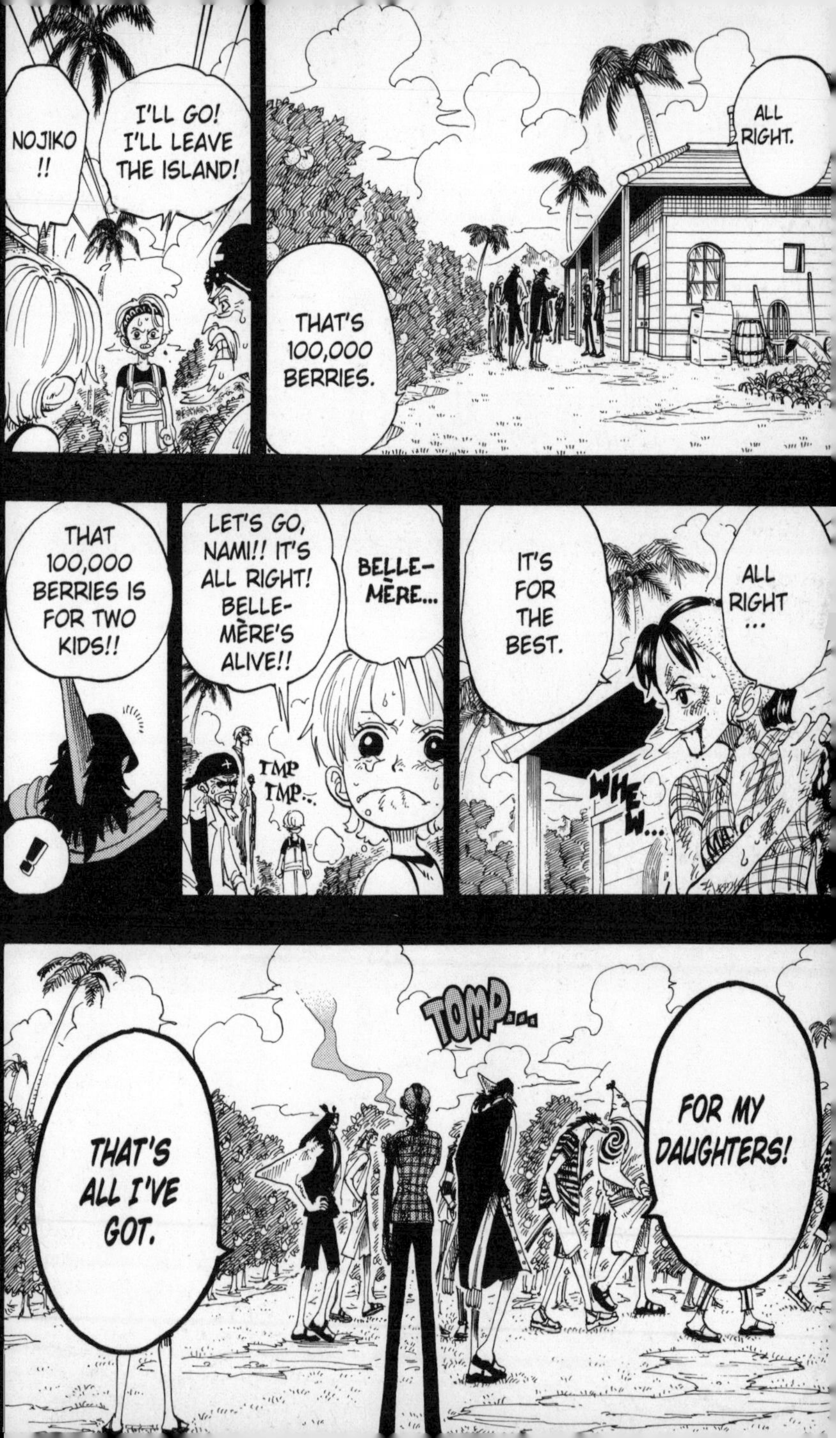
ALL RIGHT.
THAT'S 100,000 BERRIES.
I'LL GO! I'LL LEAVE THE ISLAND!
NOJIKO !!
ALL RIGHT ...
IT'S FOR THE BEST.
WHEW...
BELLE-MÈRE...
LET'S GO, NAMI!! IT'S ALL RIGHT! BELLE-MÈRE'S ALIVE!!
TMP TMP...
THAT 100,000 BERRIES IS FOR TWO KIDS!!
!
FOR MY DAUGHTERS!
TOMP...
THAT'S ALL I'VE GOT.

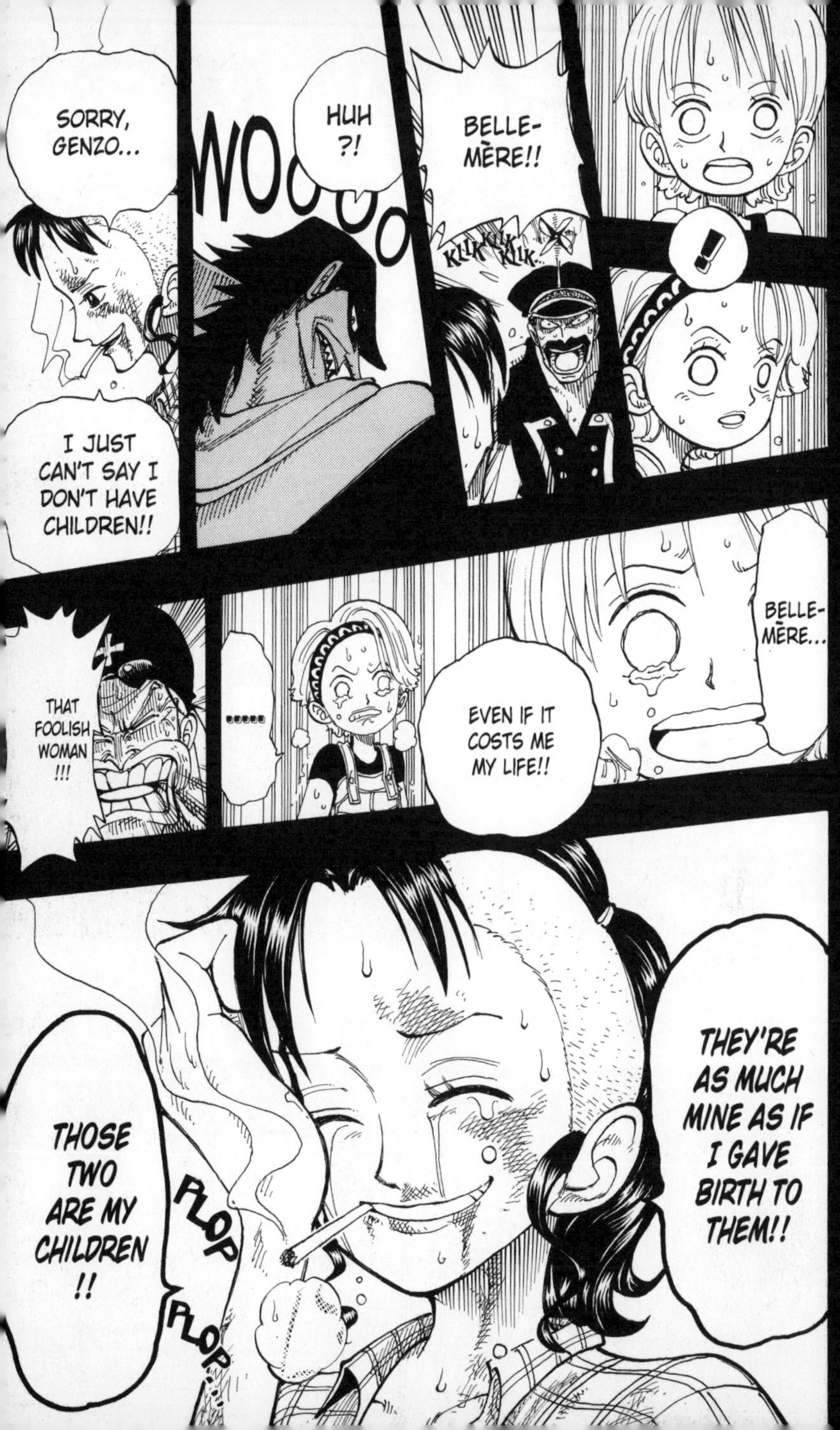
!
BELLE-MÈRE!!
KLIK KLIK KLIK KLIK...
HUH ?!
WOOOOO
SORRY, GENZO...
I JUST CAN'T SAY I DON'T HAVE CHILDREN!!
BELLE-MÈRE...
EVEN IF IT COSTS ME MY LIFE!!
.....
THAT FOOLISH WOMAN !!!
THEY'RE AS MUCH MINE AS IF I GAVE BIRTH TO THEM!!
THOSE TWO ARE MY CHILDREN !!
PLOP
PLOP
PLOP

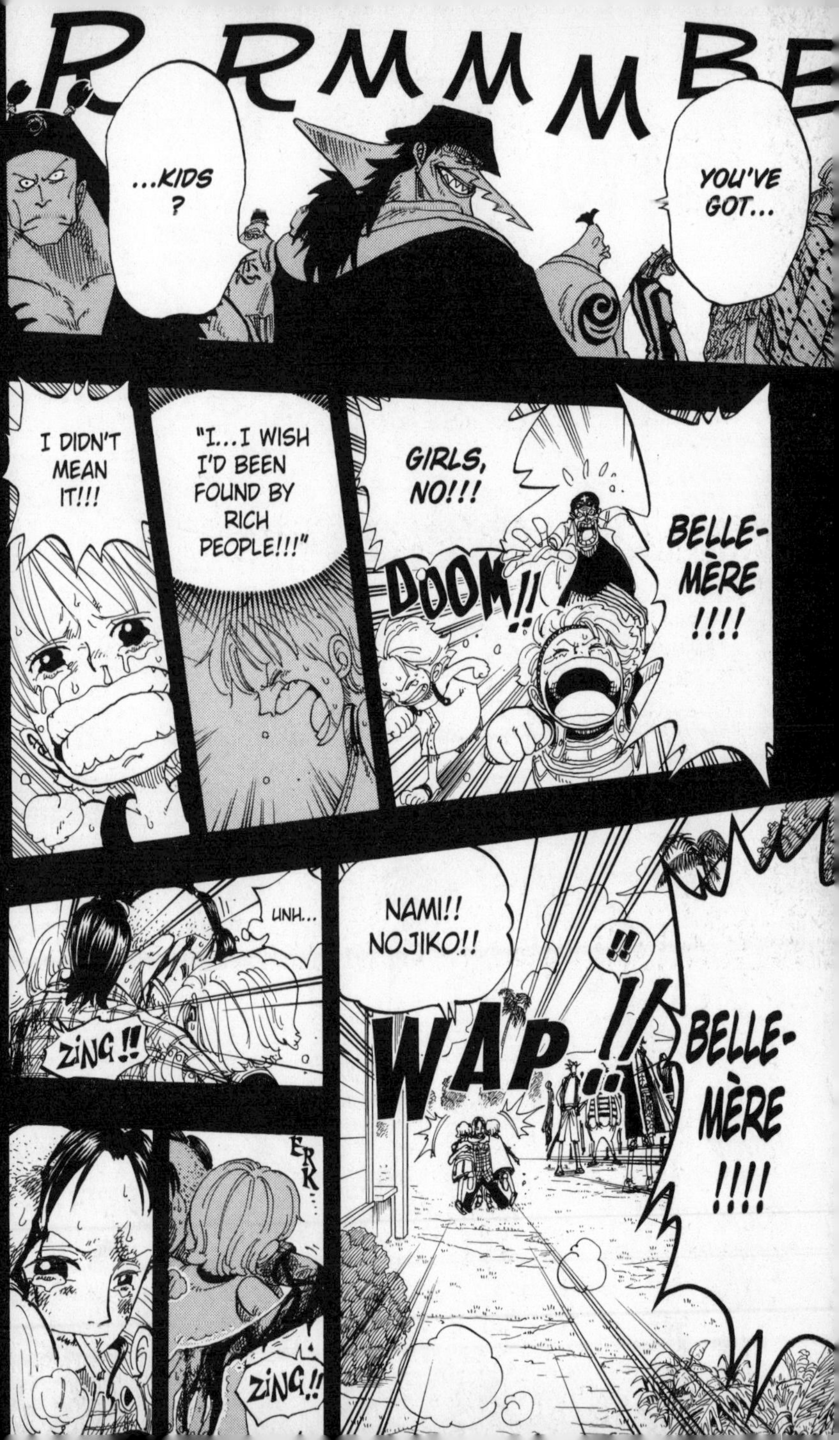
RRMMMBE
YOU'VE GOT...
...KIDS ?
GIRLS, NO!!!
BELLE-MÈRE !!!!
DOOM!!
"I...I WISH I'D BEEN FOUND BY RICH PEOPLE!!!"
I DIDN'T MEAN IT!!!
BELLE-MÈRE !!!!
NAMI!! NOJIKO!!
!!
WAP!!
UNH...
ZING!!
ERK...
ZING!!

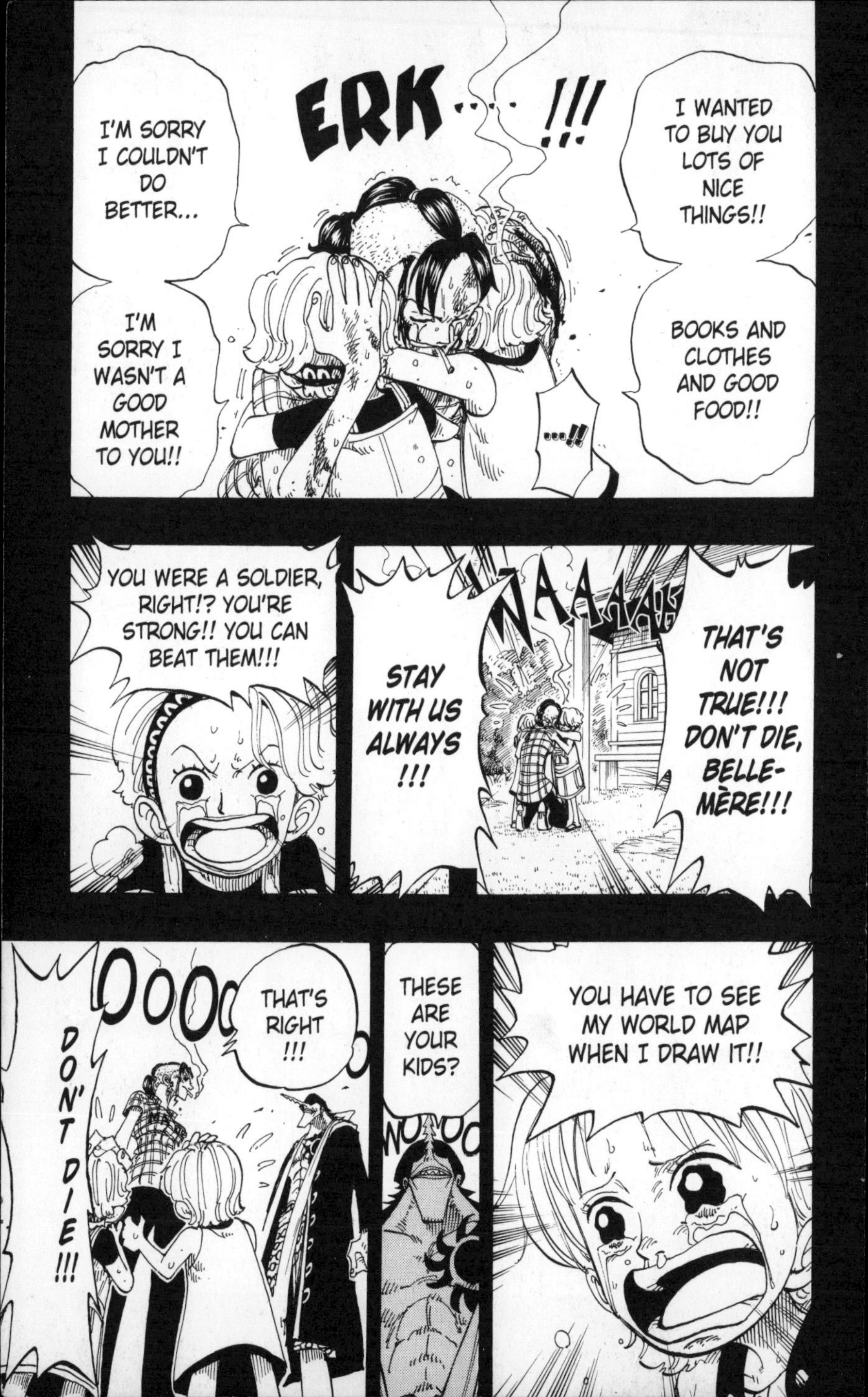
I WANTED TO BUY YOU LOTS OF NICE THINGS!!
BOOKS AND CLOTHES AND GOOD FOOD!!
ERK...!!!
...!!
I'M SORRY I COULDN'T DO BETTER...
I'M SORRY I WASN'T A GOOD MOTHER TO YOU!!
THAT'S NOT TRUE!!! DON'T DIE, BELLE-MÈRE!!!
WAAAAH
STAY WITH US ALWAYS!!!
YOU WERE A SOLDIER, RIGHT!? YOU'RE STRONG!! YOU CAN BEAT THEM!!!
YOU HAVE TO SEE MY WORLD MAP WHEN I DRAW IT!!
THESE ARE YOUR KIDS?
WOOO
THAT'S RIGHT!!!
OOOO
DON'T DIE!!!

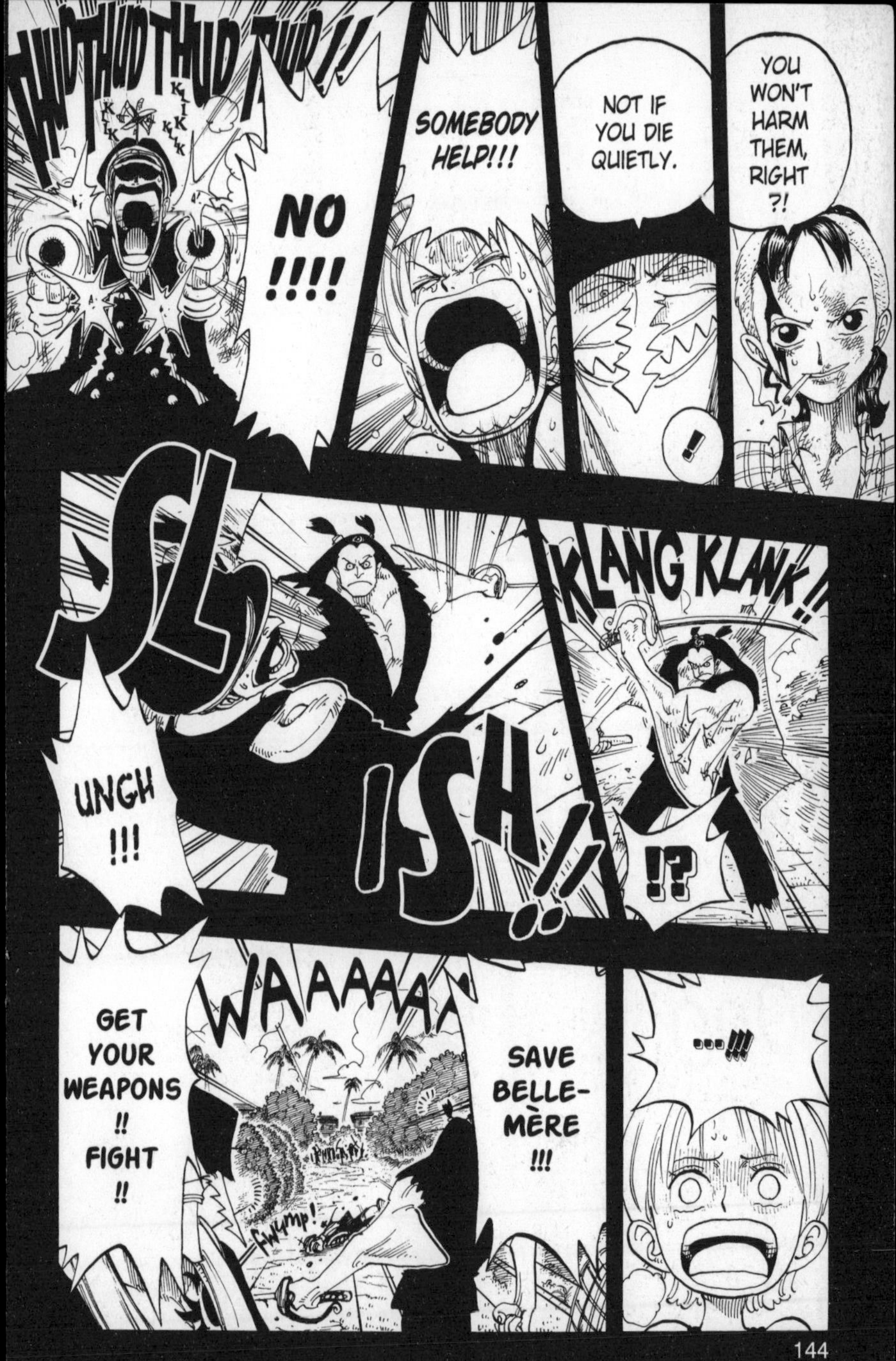
YOU WON'T HARM THEM, RIGHT ?!
NOT IF YOU DIE QUIETLY.
!
SOMEBODY HELP!!!
NO !!!!
THUD THUD THUD THUD!!
KLANG KLANK!!
!?
SLISH!!
UNGH !!!
...!!!
SAVE BELLE-MÈRE !!!
WAAAAA
GET YOUR WEAPONS !! FIGHT !!
fwump!

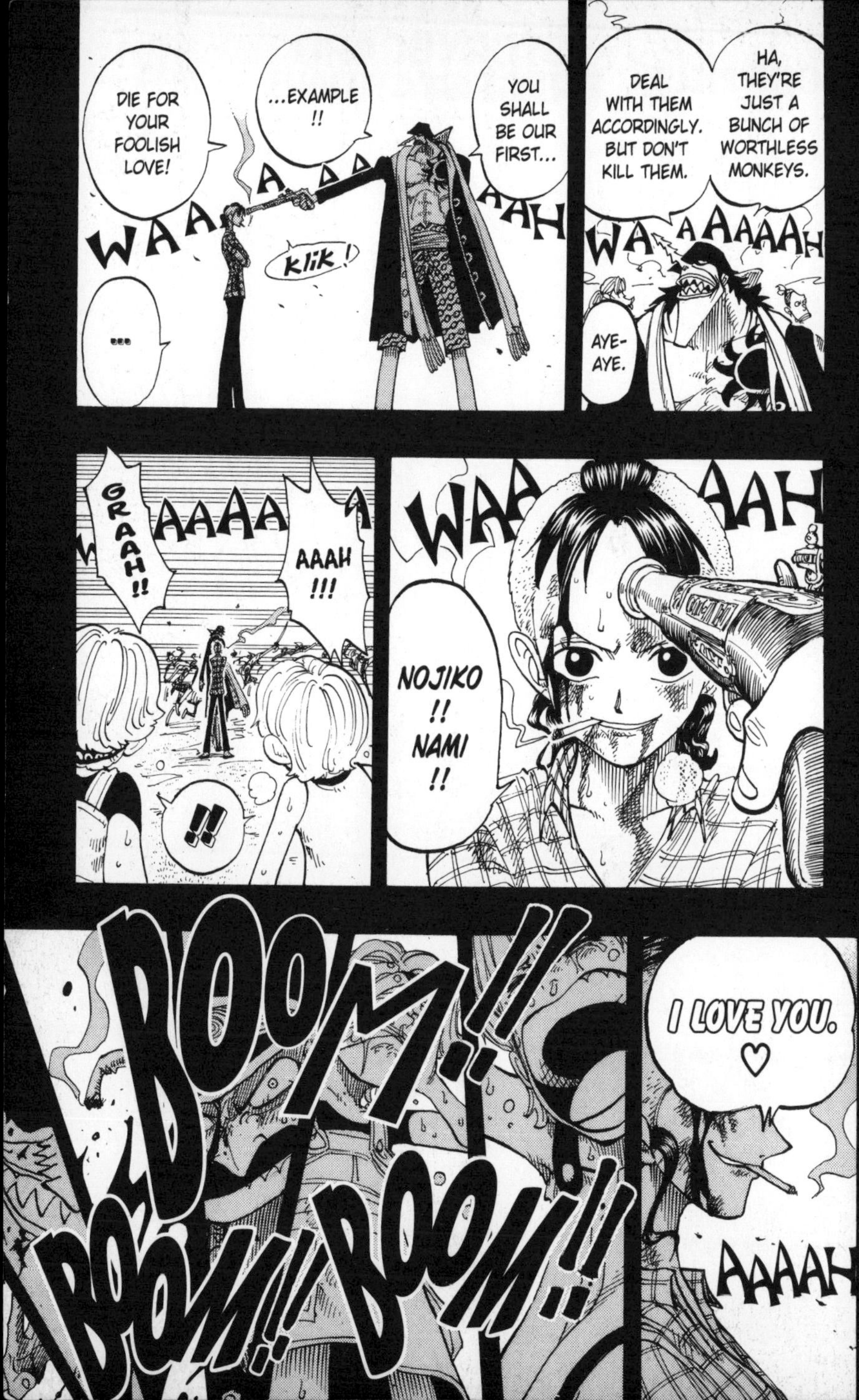
HA, THEY'RE JUST A BUNCH OF WORTHLESS MONKEYS.
DEAL WITH THEM ACCORDINGLY. BUT DON'T KILL THEM.
WAAAAAAH
AYE-AYE.
YOU SHALL BE OUR FIRST...
...EXAMPLE !!
DIE FOR YOUR FOOLISH LOVE!
WAAAAAAAH
klik!
...
WAAAAH
NOJIKO !! NAMI !!
GRAAAH!!
AAAAA
AAAH !!!
!!
I LOVE YOU. ♥
AAAAH
BOOM!!
BOOM!!
BOOM!!

ONE PIECE **STORYBOARD PRESENTATION!!** #11

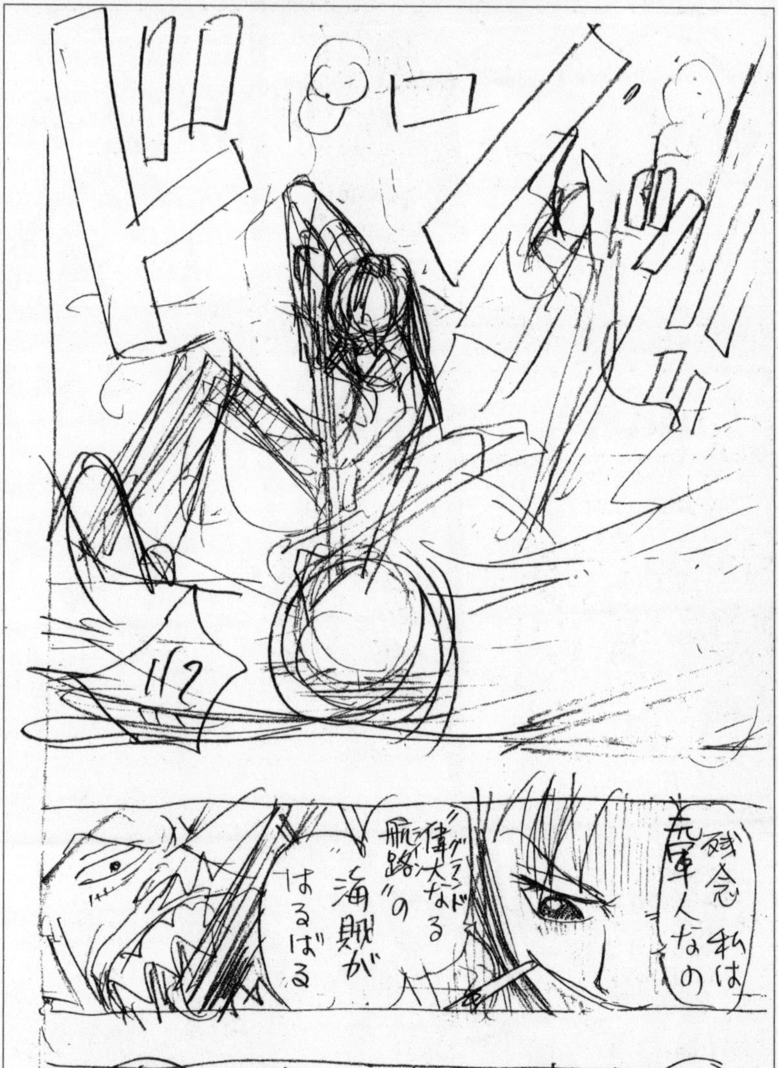
残念 私は海軍人なの
“偉大なる航路(グランドライン)”の海賊がはるばる
この村に
オォオオォ
何の用?

Chapter 79: TO LIVE

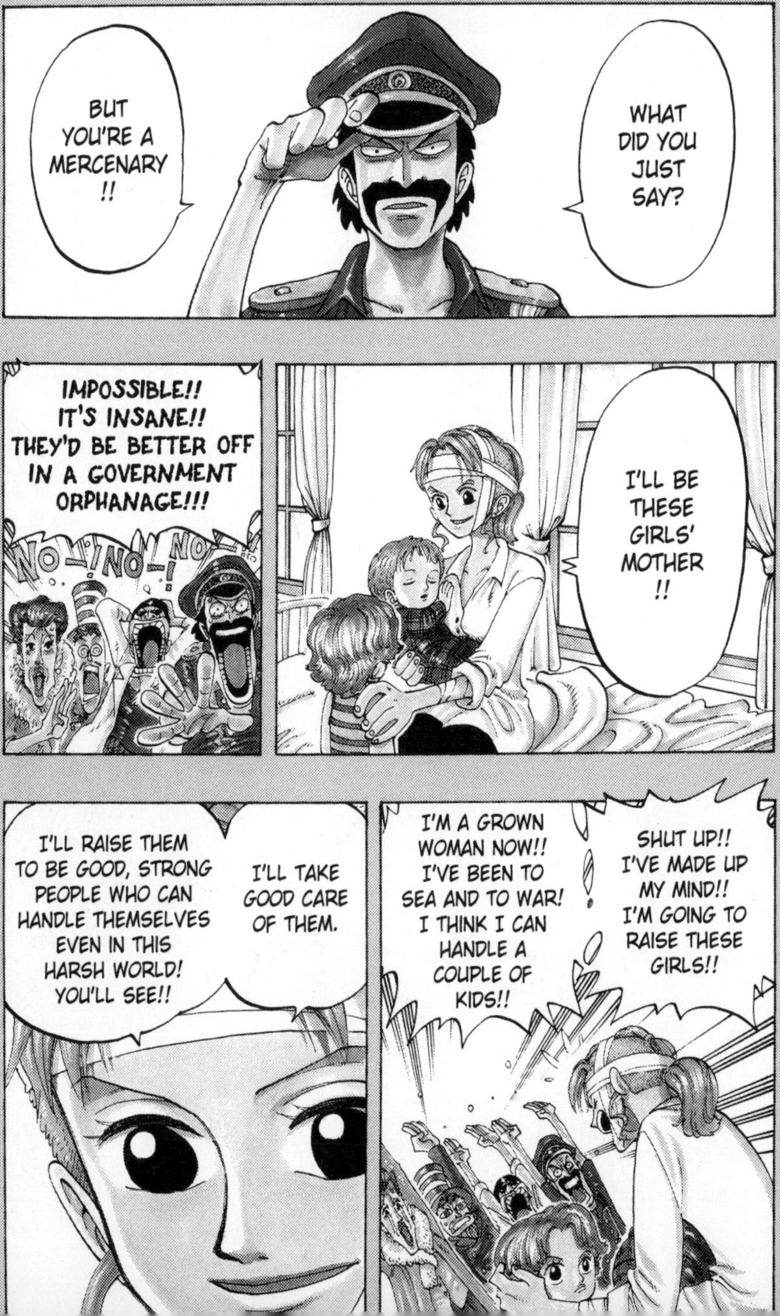
WHAT DID YOU JUST SAY?
BUT YOU'RE A MERCENARY!!
I'LL BE THESE GIRLS' MOTHER!!
IMPOSSIBLE!! IT'S INSANE!! THEY'D BE BETTER OFF IN A GOVERNMENT ORPHANAGE!!!
NO--!! NO--!! NO--
SHUT UP!! I'VE MADE UP MY MIND!! I'M GOING TO RAISE THESE GIRLS!!
I'M A GROWN WOMAN NOW!! I'VE BEEN TO SEA AND TO WAR! I THINK I CAN HANDLE A COUPLE OF KIDS!!
I'LL TAKE GOOD CARE OF THEM.
I'LL RAISE THEM TO BE GOOD, STRONG PEOPLE WHO CAN HANDLE THEMSELVES EVEN IN THIS HARSH WORLD! YOU'LL SEE!!

Chapter 79: TO LIVE

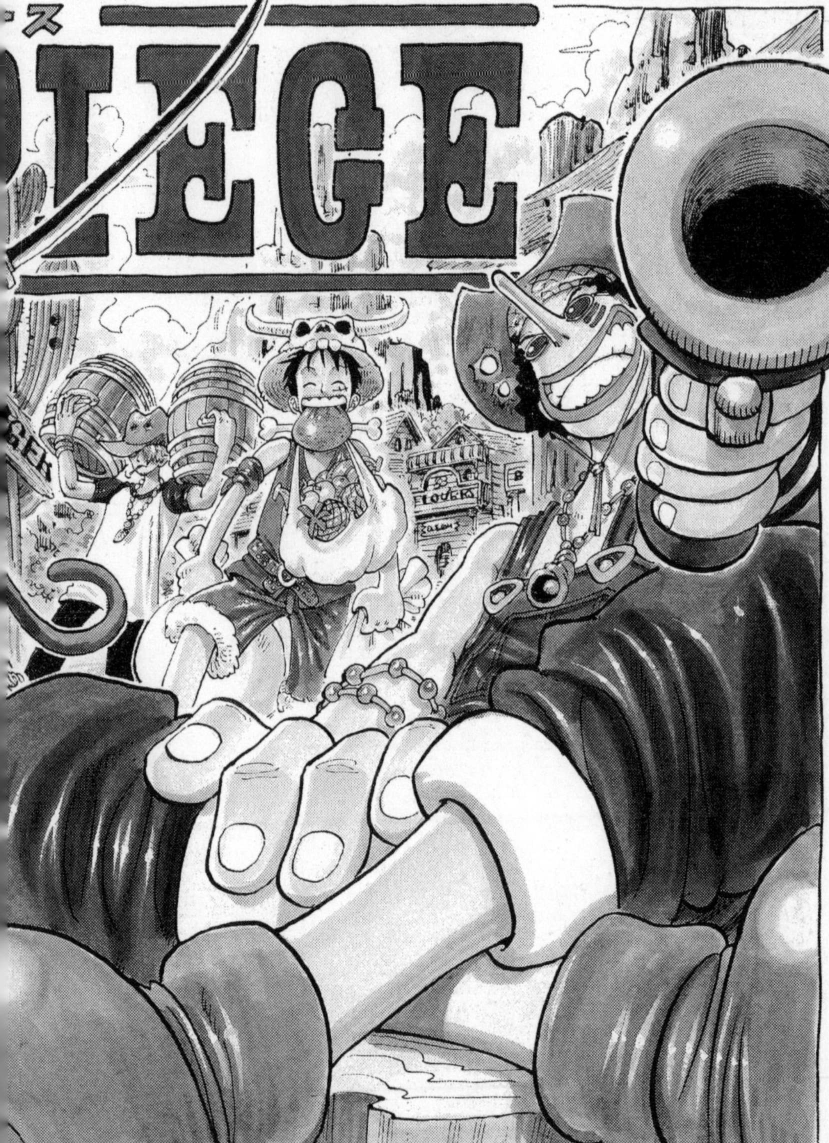

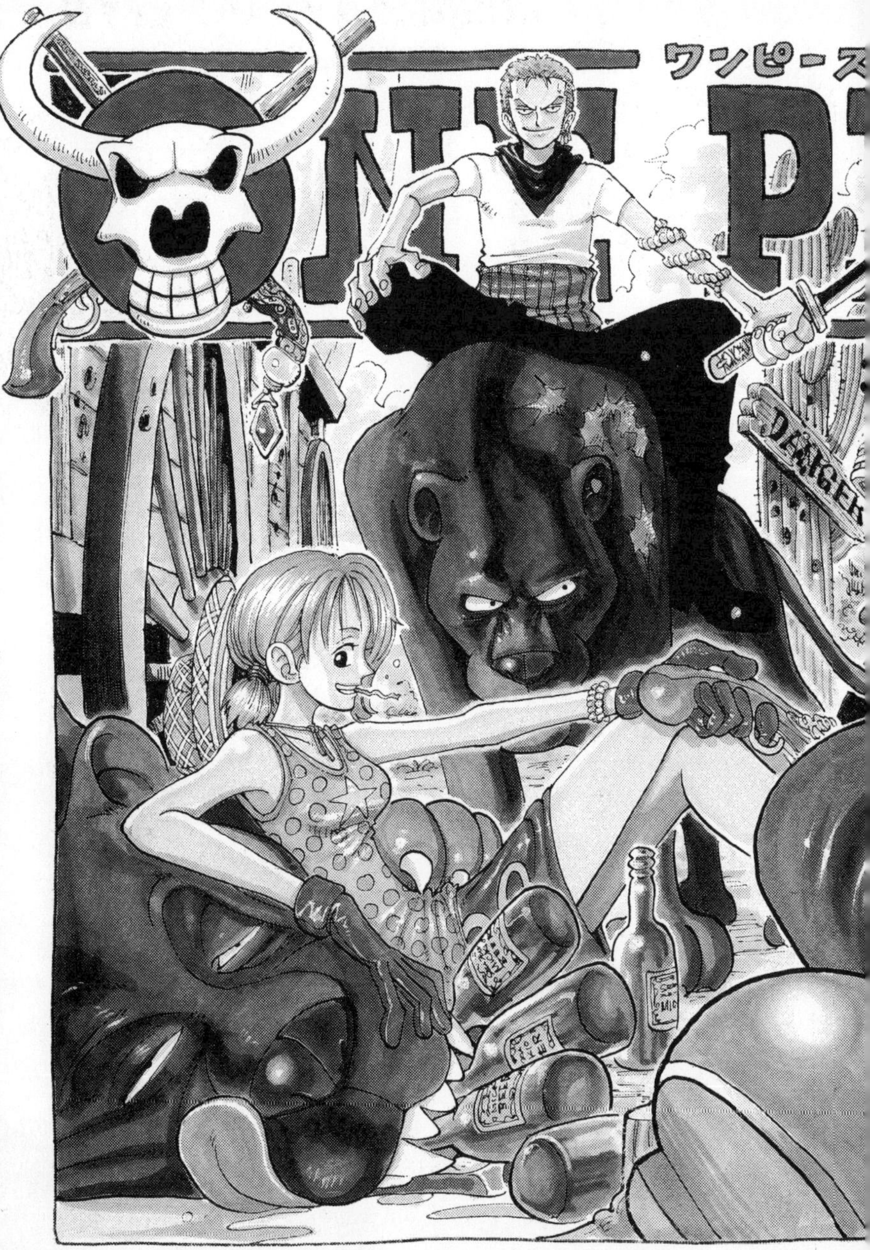
DANGER

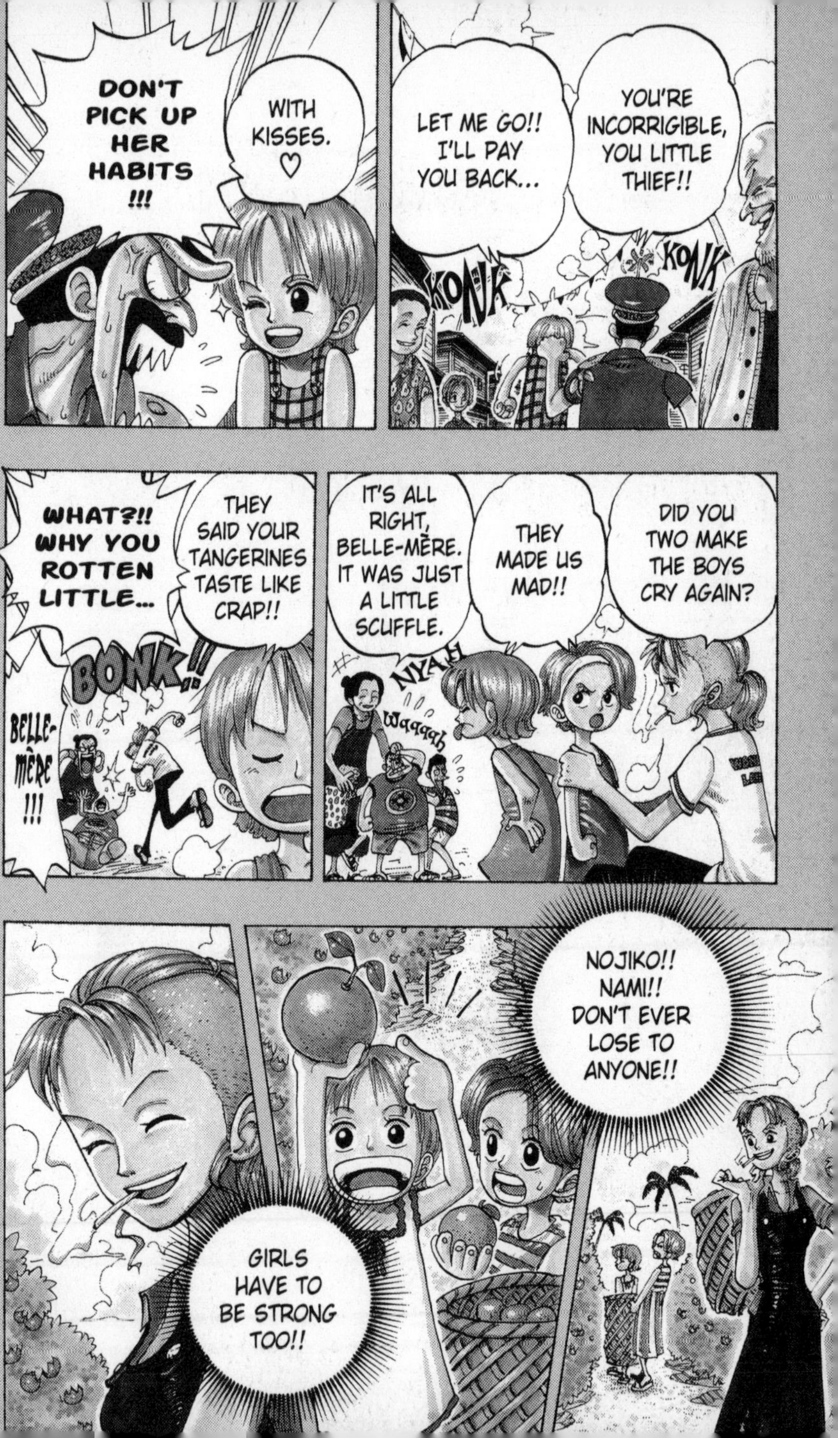
YOU'RE INCORRIGIBLE, YOU LITTLE THIEF!!
LET ME GO!! I'LL PAY YOU BACK...
KONK
KONK
WITH KISSES. ♡
DON'T PICK UP HER HABITS!!!
DID YOU TWO MAKE THE BOYS CRY AGAIN?
THEY MADE US MAD!!
IT'S ALL RIGHT, BELLE-MÈRE. IT WAS JUST A LITTLE SCUFFLE.
NYAH
Waqqqh
THEY SAID YOUR TANGERINES TASTE LIKE CRAP!!
WHAT?!! WHY YOU ROTTEN LITTLE...
BONK!!
BELLE-MÈRE!!!
NOJIKO!! NAMI!! DON'T EVER LOSE TO ANYONE!!
GIRLS HAVE TO BE STRONG TOO!!

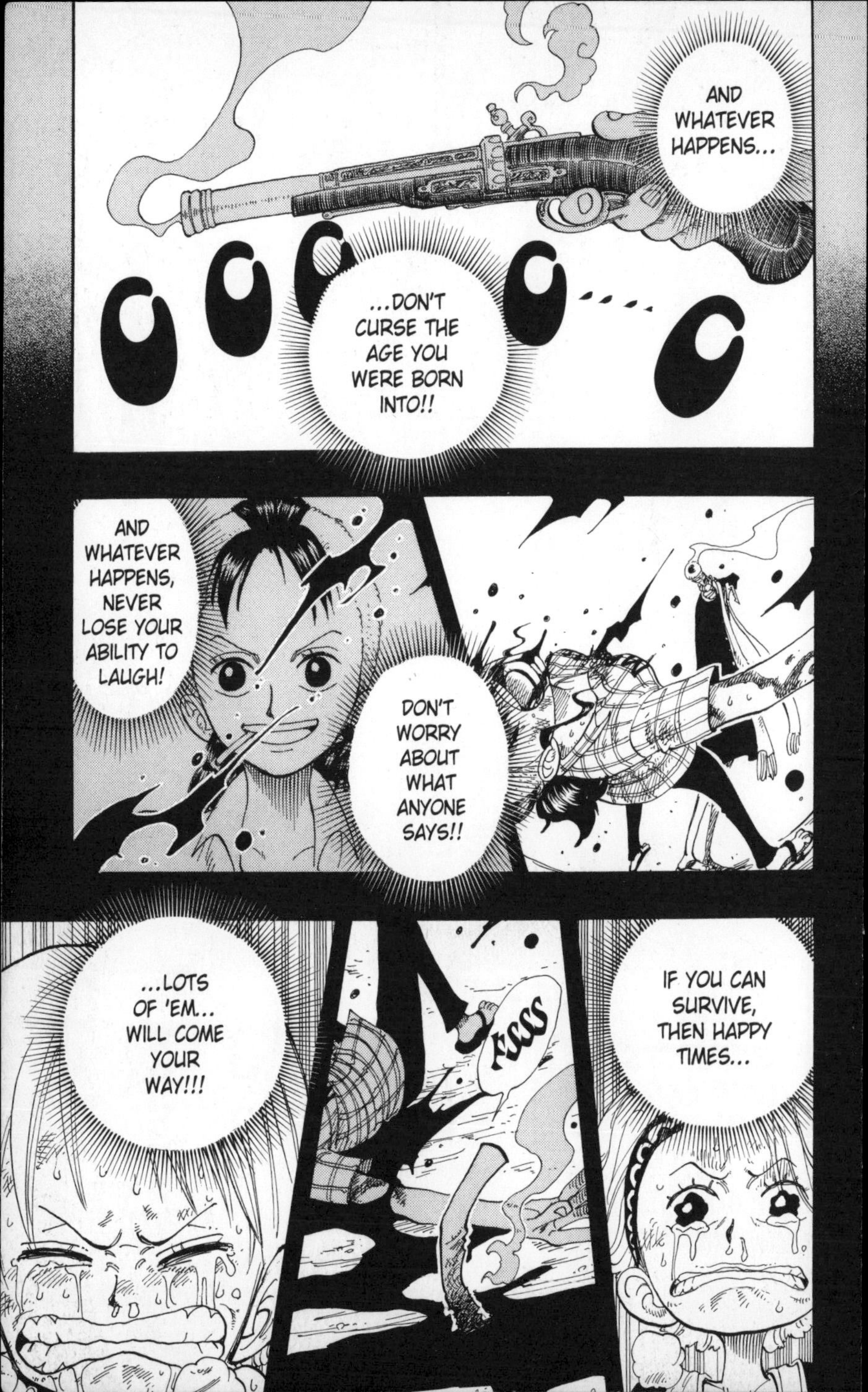
AND WHATEVER HAPPENS...
...DON'T CURSE THE AGE YOU WERE BORN INTO!!
DON'T WORRY ABOUT WHAT ANYONE SAYS!!
AND WHATEVER HAPPENS, NEVER LOSE YOUR ABILITY TO LAUGH!
IF YOU CAN SURVIVE, THEN HAPPY TIMES...
FSSS
...LOTS OF 'EM... WILL COME YOUR WAY!!!

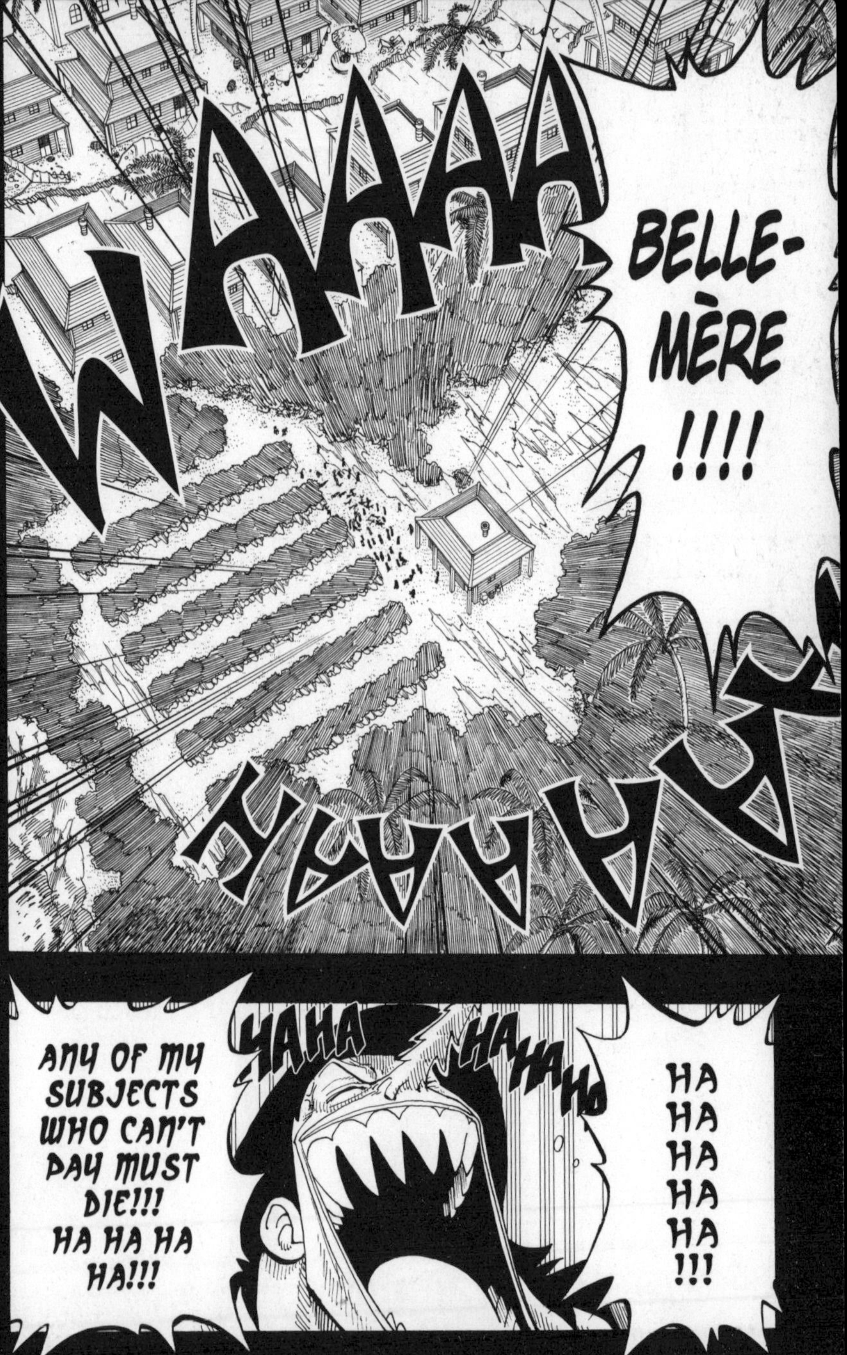
BELLE-MÈRE!!!!
HAHAHA
HAHA
HA HA HA HA HA HA!!!
ANY OF MY SUBJECTS WHO CAN'T PAY MUST DIE!!! HA HA HA HA!!!

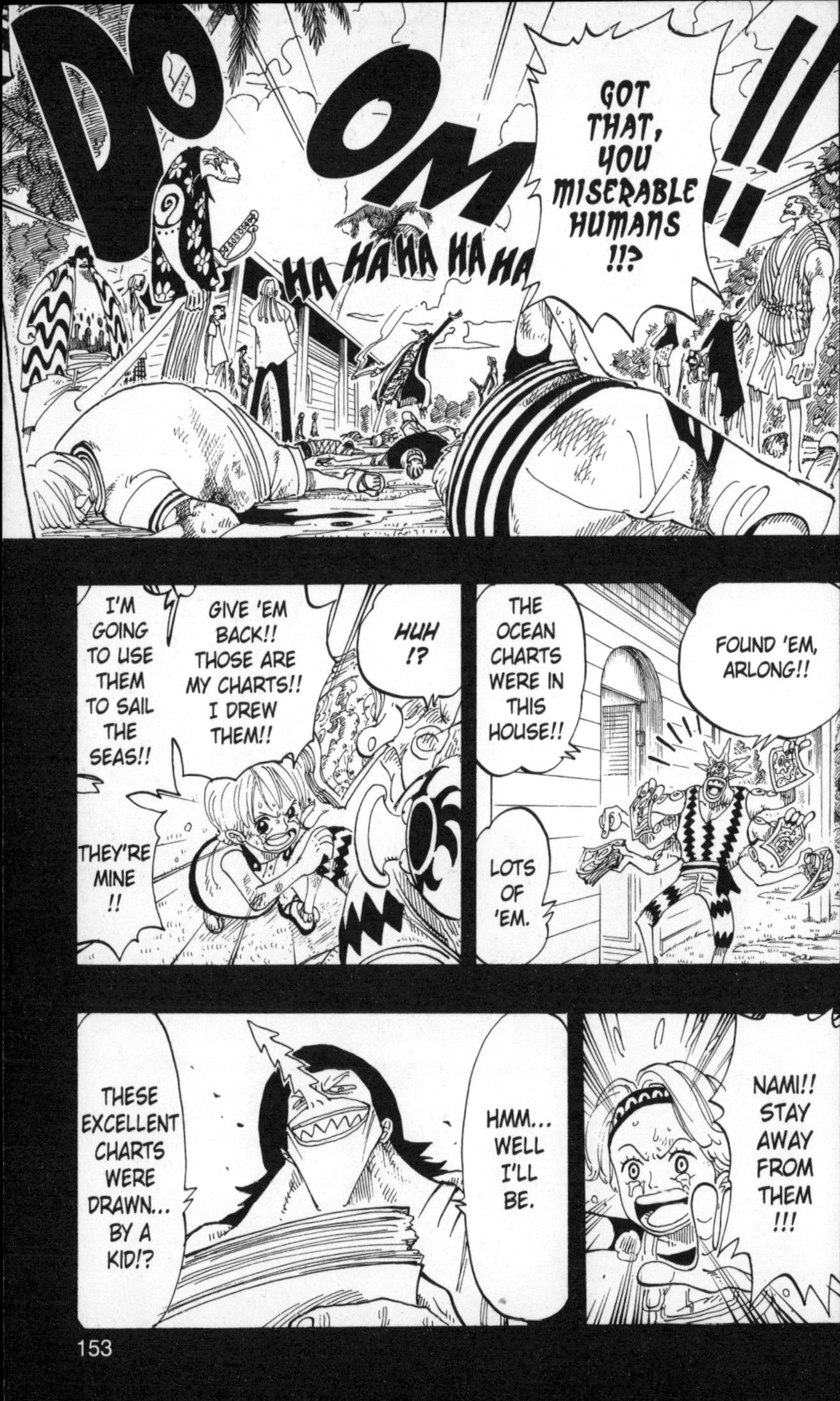
GOT THAT, YOU MISERABLE HUMANS!!?
DOOM!!
HA HA HA HA HA
FOUND 'EM, ARLONG!!
THE OCEAN CHARTS WERE IN THIS HOUSE!!
LOTS OF 'EM.
HUH!?
GIVE 'EM BACK!! THOSE ARE MY CHARTS!! I DREW THEM!!
I'M GOING TO USE THEM TO SAIL THE SEAS!!
THEY'RE MINE!!
NAMI!! STAY AWAY FROM THEM!!!
HMM... WELL I'LL BE.
THESE EXCELLENT CHARTS WERE DRAWN... BY A KID!?

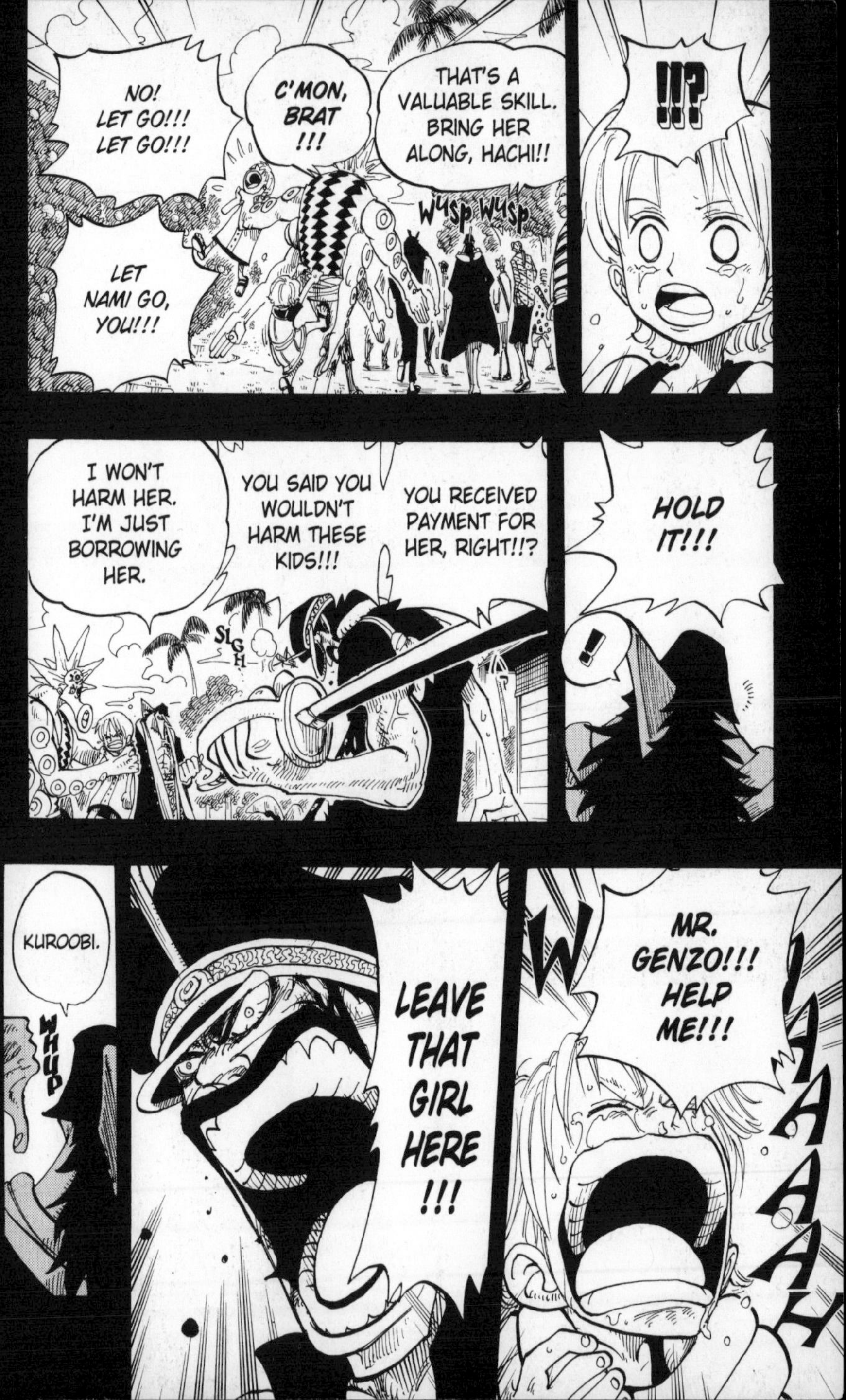
!!?
THAT'S A VALUABLE SKILL. BRING HER ALONG, HACHI!!
C'MON, BRAT!!!
NO! LET GO!!! LET GO!!!
WUSP WUSP
LET NAMI GO, YOU!!!
HOLD IT!!!
!
YOU RECEIVED PAYMENT FOR HER, RIGHT!!?
YOU SAID YOU WOULDN'T HARM THESE KIDS!!!
I WON'T HARM HER. I'M JUST BORROWING HER.
SIGH
MR. GENZO!!! HELP ME!!!
LEAVE THAT GIRL HERE!!!
KUROOBI.
WHUP

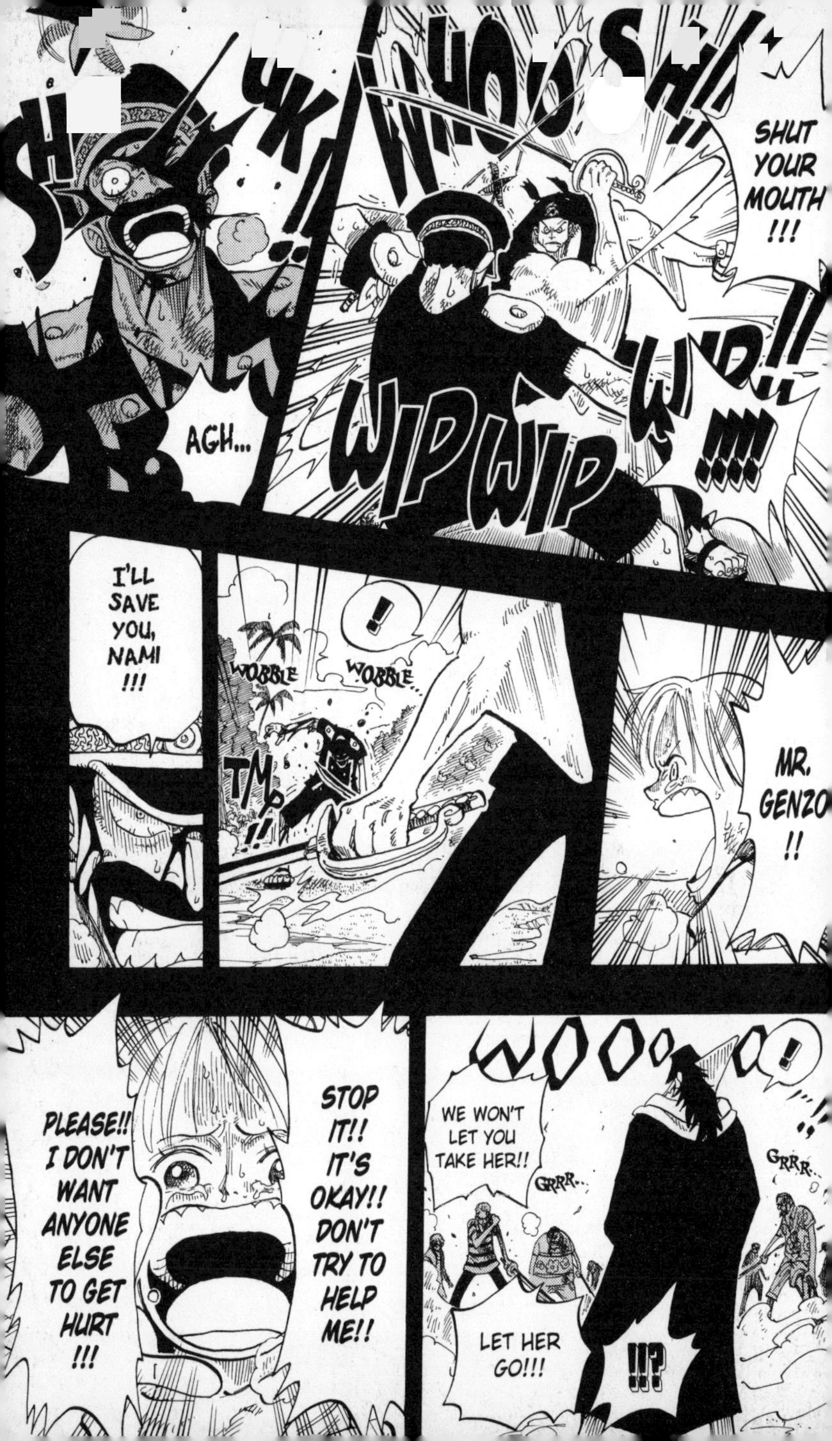
SHUT YOUR MOUTH!!!
WIPWIP
!!!!
AGH...
MR. GENZO!!
!
WOBBLE
WOBBLE
TMP!!
I'LL SAVE YOU, NAMI!!!
WE WON'T LET YOU TAKE HER!!
GRRR..
GRRR..
LET HER GO!!!
!!?
STOP IT!! IT'S OKAY!! DON'T TRY TO HELP ME!!
PLEASE!! I DON'T WANT ANYONE ELSE TO GET HURT!!!

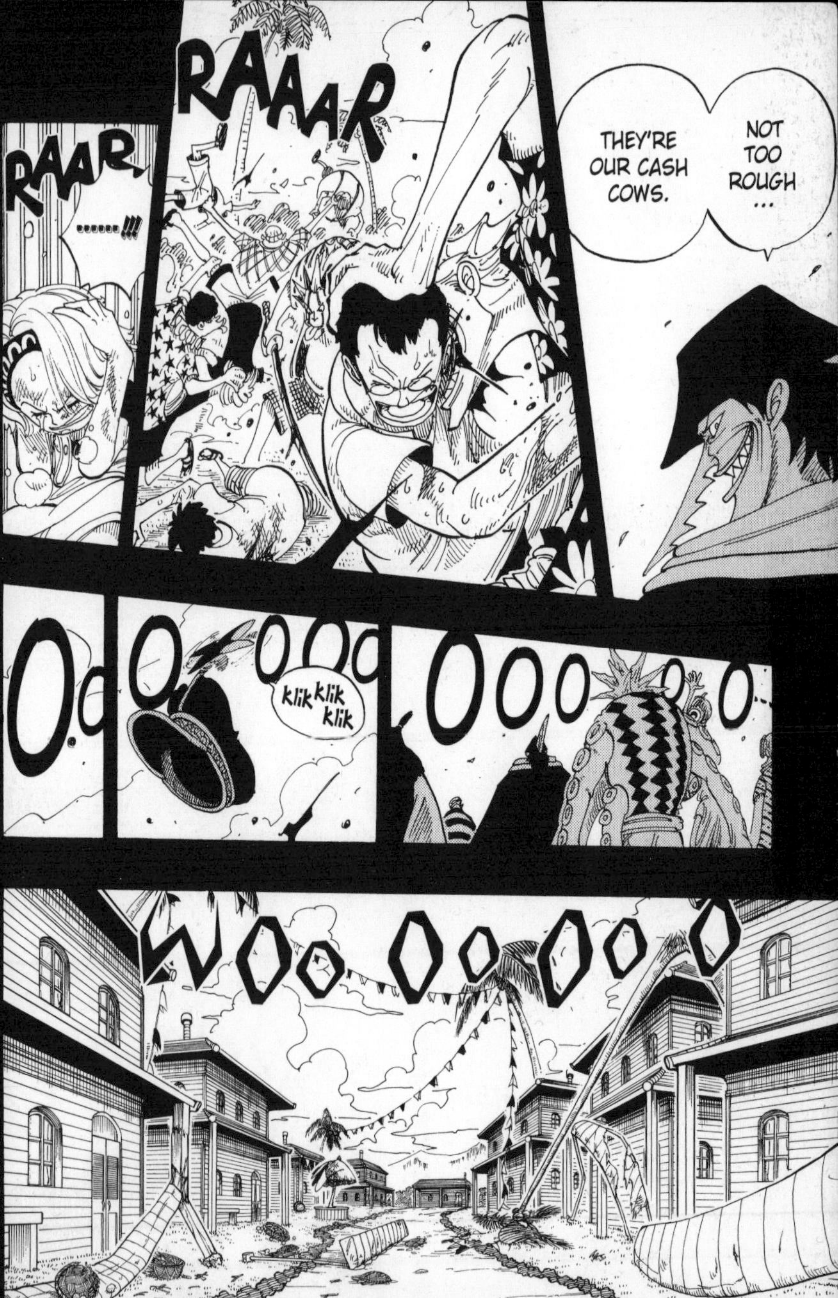
NOT TOO ROUGH ...
THEY'RE OUR CASH COWS.
RAAAR
RAAR
......!!!
OOOOO...
klik klik klik
OOO
OO
WOOOOOOO

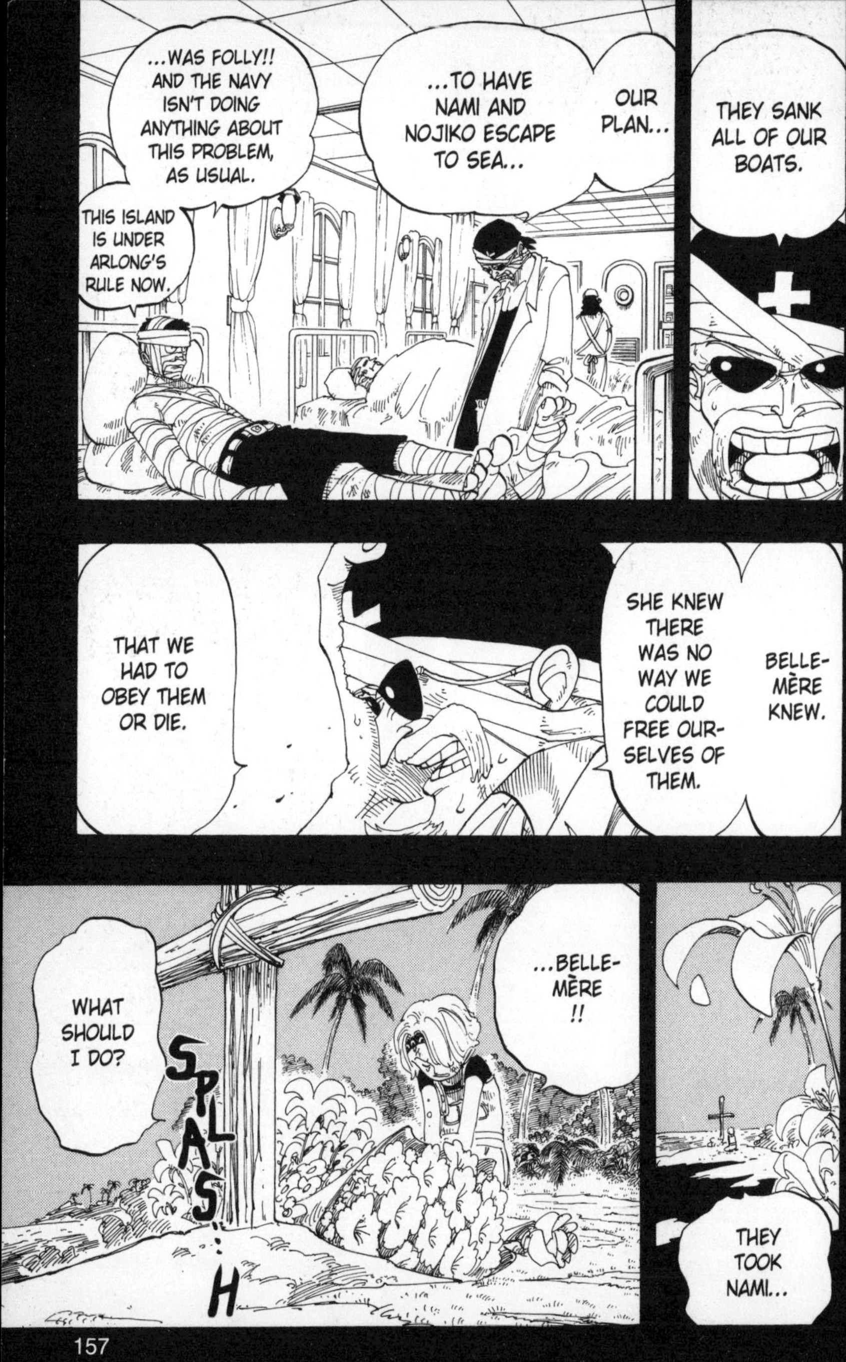

THEY SANK ALL OF OUR BOATS.
OUR PLAN...
...TO HAVE NAMI AND NOJIKO ESCAPE TO SEA...
...WAS FOLLY!! AND THE NAVY ISN'T DOING ANYTHING ABOUT THIS PROBLEM, AS USUAL.
THIS ISLAND IS UNDER ARLONG'S RULE NOW.
BELLE-MÈRE KNEW.
SHE KNEW THERE WAS NO WAY WE COULD FREE OUR-SELVES OF THEM.
THAT WE HAD TO OBEY THEM OR DIE.
THEY TOOK NAMI...
...BELLE-MÈRE !!
WHAT SHOULD I DO?
SPLASH

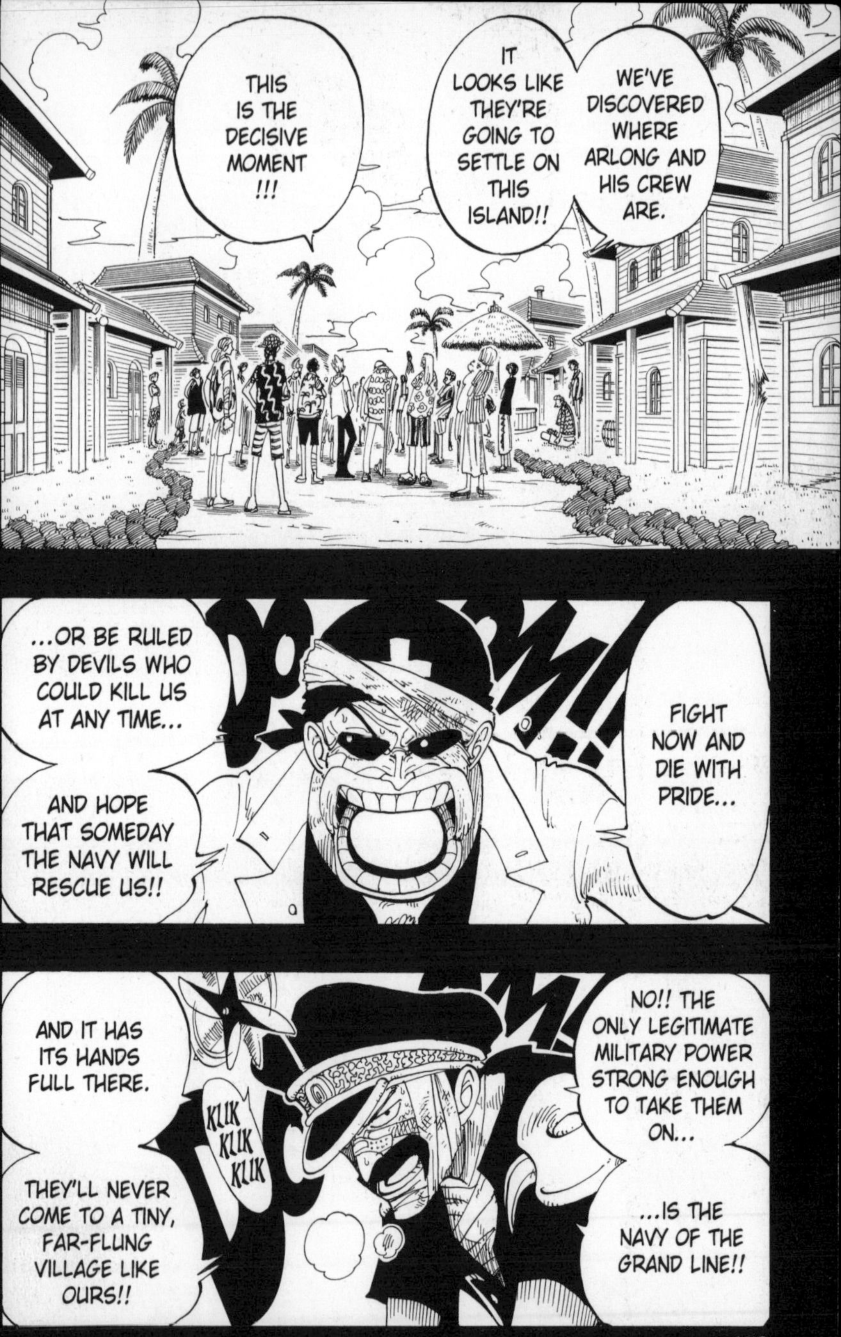
WE'VE DISCOVERED WHERE ARLONG AND HIS CREW ARE.
IT LOOKS LIKE THEY'RE GOING TO SETTLE ON THIS ISLAND!!
THIS IS THE DECISIVE MOMENT!!!
FIGHT NOW AND DIE WITH PRIDE...
...OR BE RULED BY DEVILS WHO COULD KILL US AT ANY TIME...
AND HOPE THAT SOMEDAY THE NAVY WILL RESCUE US!!
NO!! THE ONLY LEGITIMATE MILITARY POWER STRONG ENOUGH TO TAKE THEM ON...
...IS THE NAVY OF THE GRAND LINE!!
AND IT HAS ITS HANDS FULL THERE.
KLIK KLIK KLIK
THEY'LL NEVER COME TO A TINY, FAR-FLUNG VILLAGE LIKE OURS!!

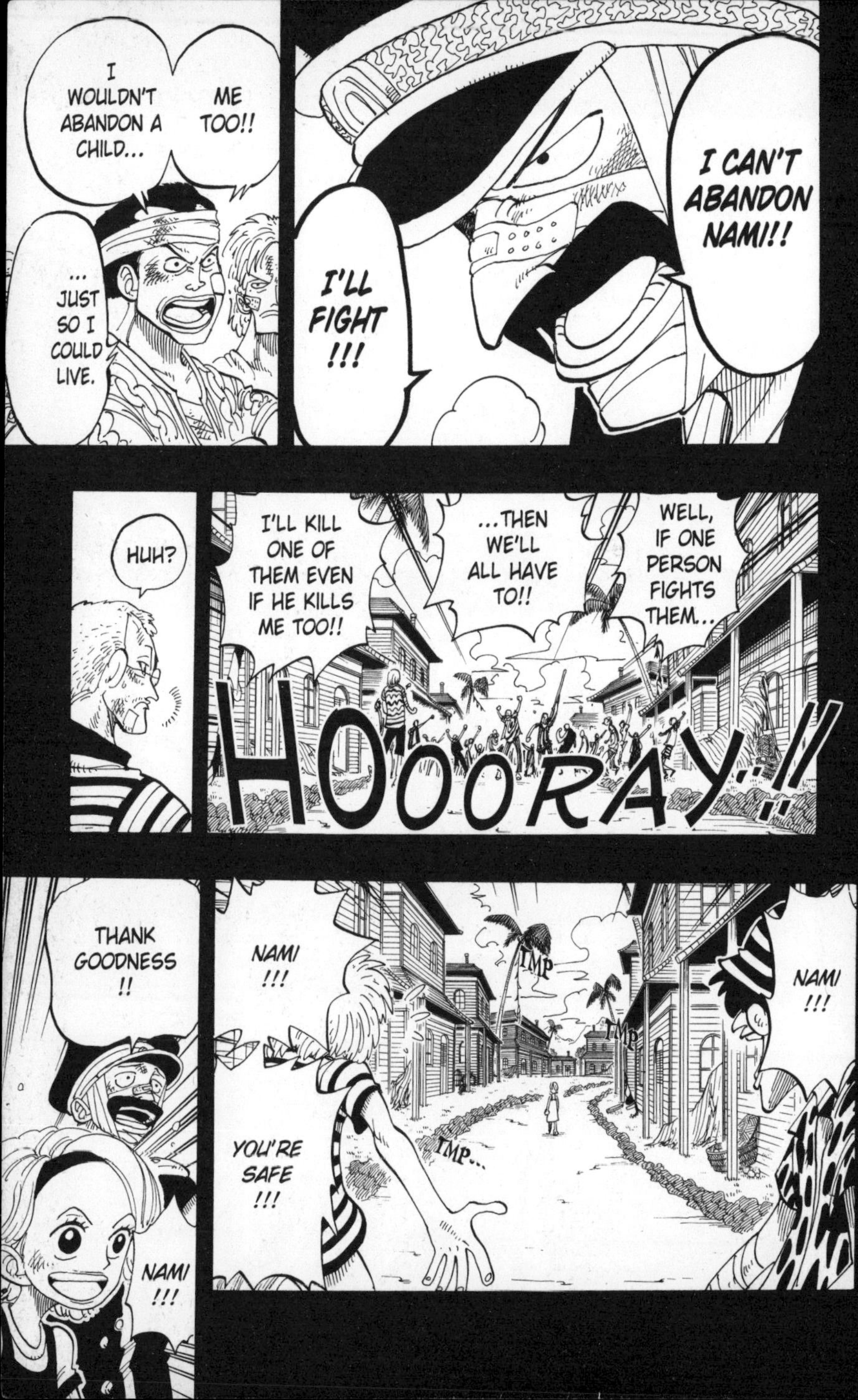
I CAN'T ABANDON NAMI!!
I'LL FIGHT !!!
I WOULDN'T ABANDON A CHILD...
... JUST SO I COULD LIVE.
ME TOO!!
WELL, IF ONE PERSON FIGHTS THEM...
...THEN WE'LL ALL HAVE TO!!
I'LL KILL ONE OF THEM EVEN IF HE KILLS ME TOO!!
HOOORAY..!!
HUH?
NAMI !!!
TMP
TMP
NAMI !!!
YOU'RE SAFE !!!
TMP...
THANK GOODNESS !!
NAMI !!!

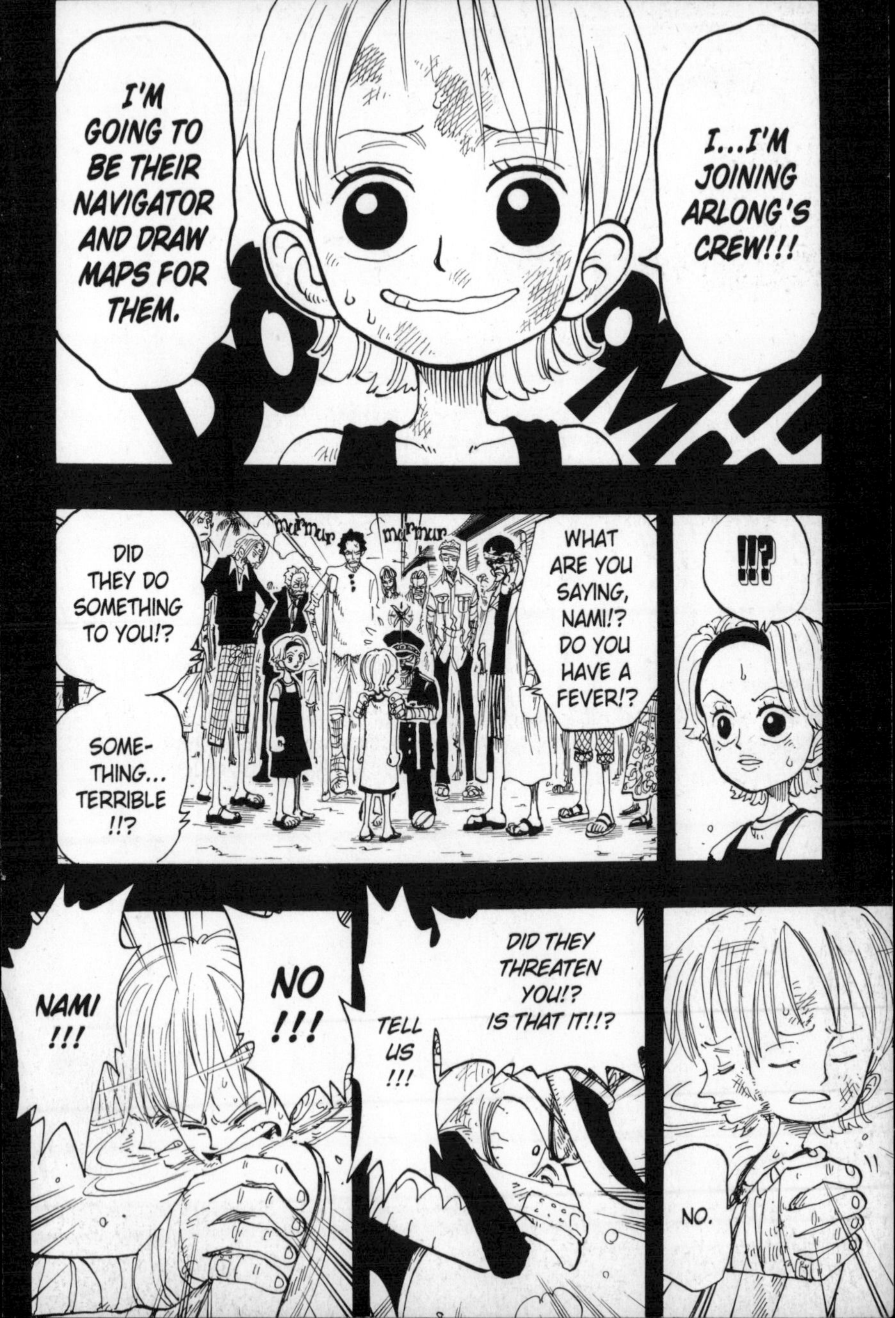
I...I'M JOINING ARLONG'S CREW!!!
I'M GOING TO BE THEIR NAVIGATOR AND DRAW MAPS FOR THEM.
!!?
WHAT ARE YOU SAYING, NAMI!? DO YOU HAVE A FEVER!?
murmur
murmur
DID THEY DO SOMETHING TO YOU!?
SOME-THING... TERRIBLE!!?
NO.
DID THEY THREATEN YOU!? IS THAT IT!!?
TELL US!!!
NO!!!
NAMI!!!

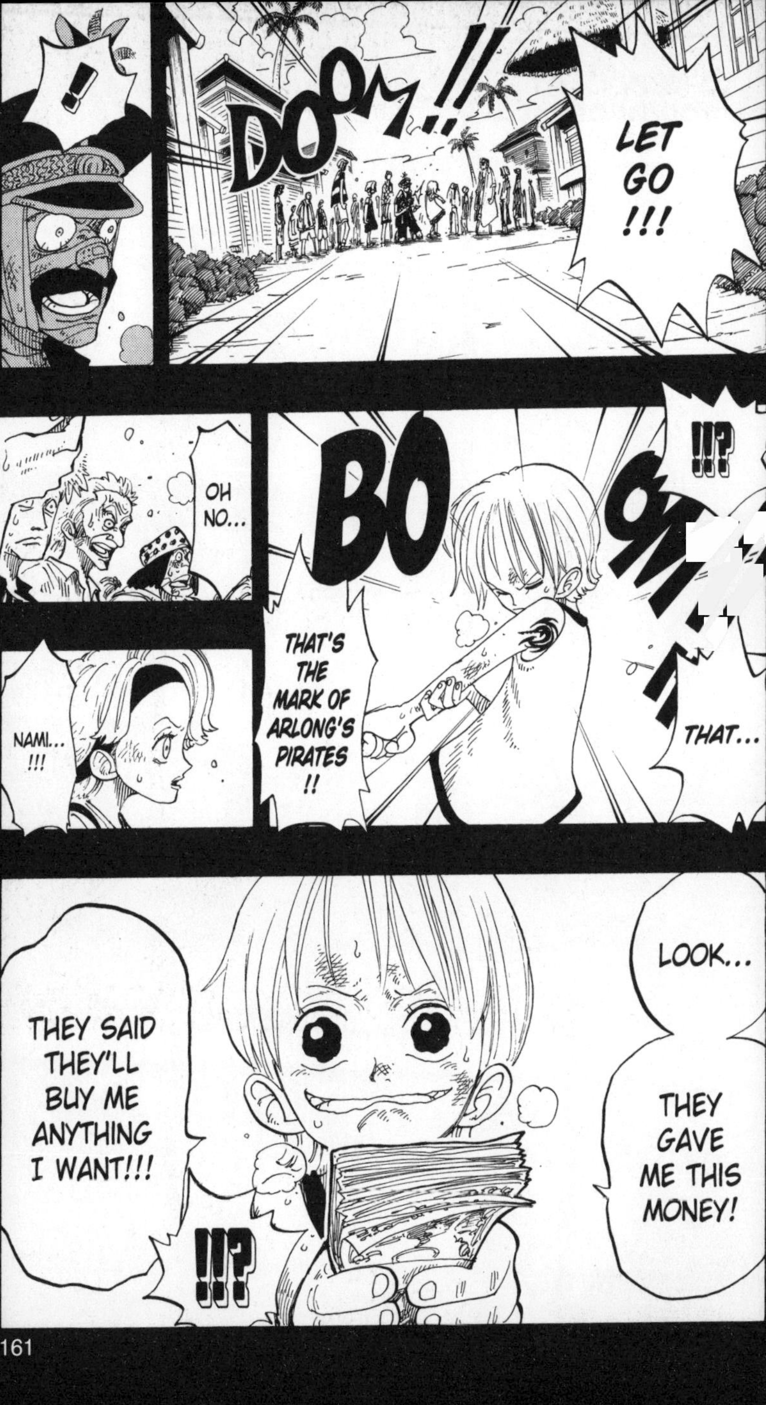
LET GO !!!
DOOM!!
!
!!?
BOOM
THAT...
THAT'S THE MARK OF ARLONG'S PIRATES !!
OH NO...
NAMI... !!!
LOOK...
THEY GAVE ME THIS MONEY!
THEY SAID THEY'LL BUY ME ANYTHING I WANT!!!
!!?

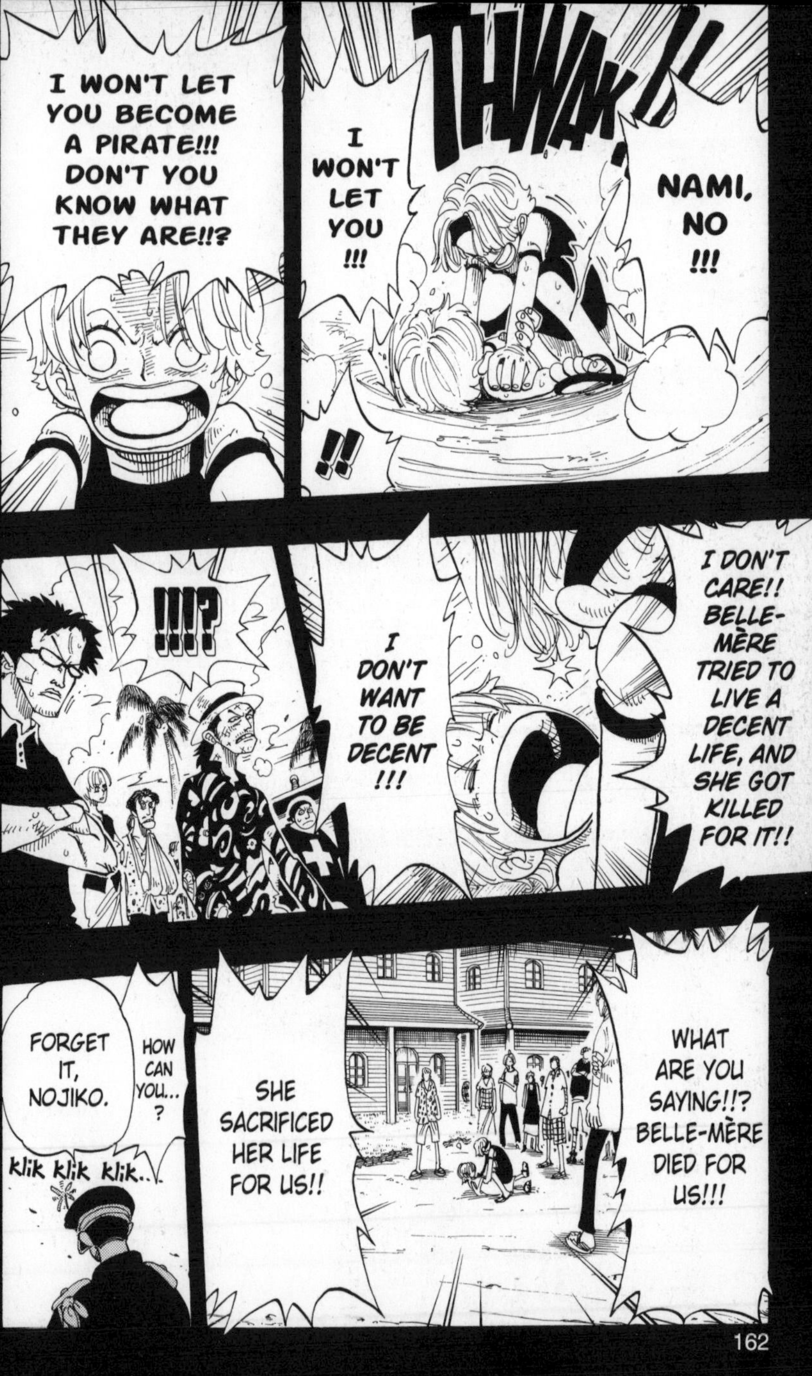
THWAK!!
NAMI, NO !!!
I WON'T LET YOU !!!
!!
I WON'T LET YOU BECOME A PIRATE!!! DON'T YOU KNOW WHAT THEY ARE!!?
I DON'T CARE!! BELLE-MÈRE TRIED TO LIVE A DECENT LIFE, AND SHE GOT KILLED FOR IT!!
I DON'T WANT TO BE DECENT !!!
!!!?
WHAT ARE YOU SAYING!!? BELLE-MÈRE DIED FOR US!!!
SHE SACRIFICED HER LIFE FOR US!!
HOW CAN YOU... ?
FORGET IT, NOJIKO.
klik klik klik..

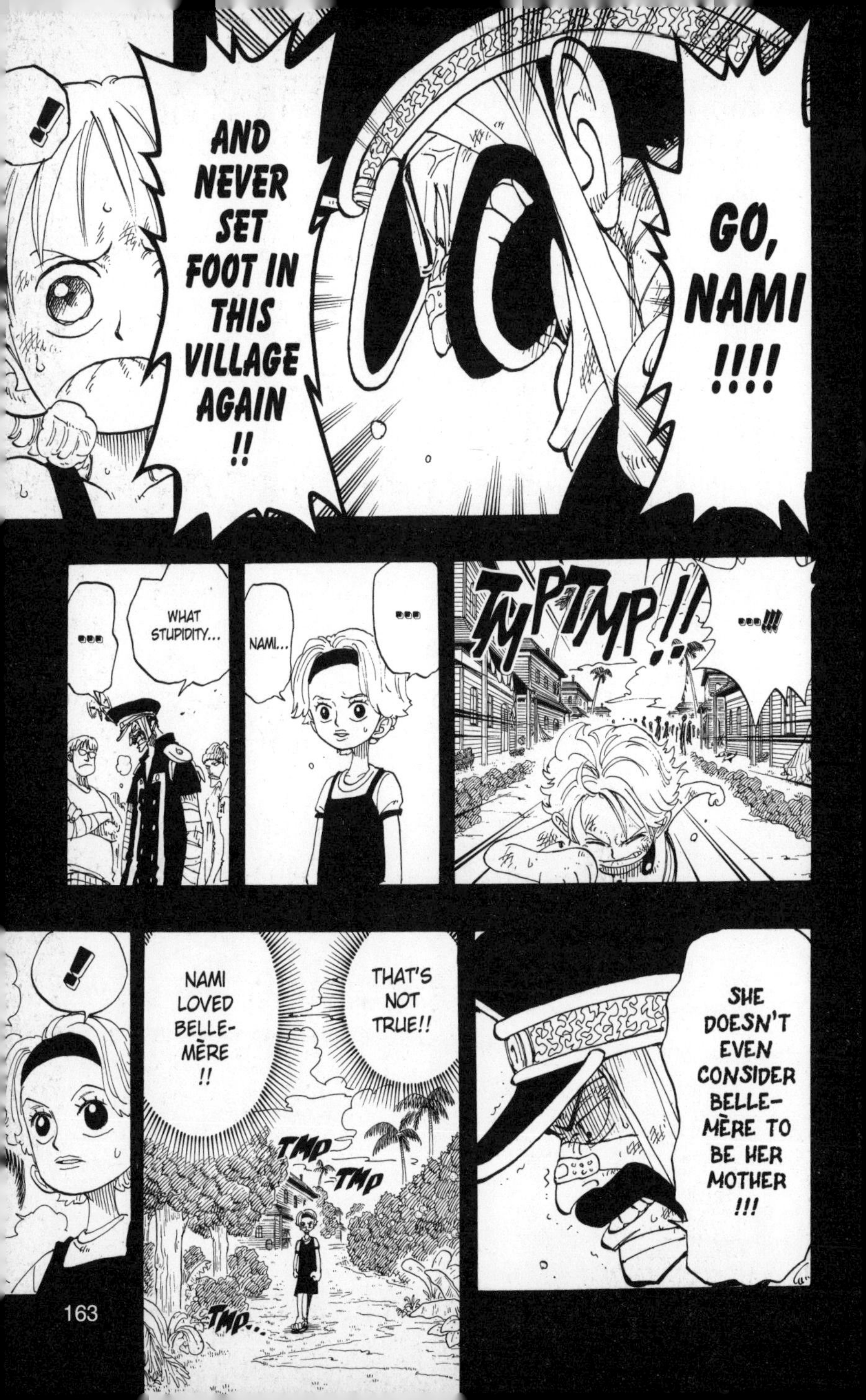
GO, NAMI!!!!
AND NEVER SET FOOT IN THIS VILLAGE AGAIN!!
!
TMPTMP!!
...!!!
...
NAMI...
WHAT STUPIDITY...
...
SHE DOESN'T EVEN CONSIDER BELLE-MÈRE TO BE HER MOTHER!!!
THAT'S NOT TRUE!!
NAMI LOVED BELLE-MÈRE!!
TMP
TMP
TMP...
!

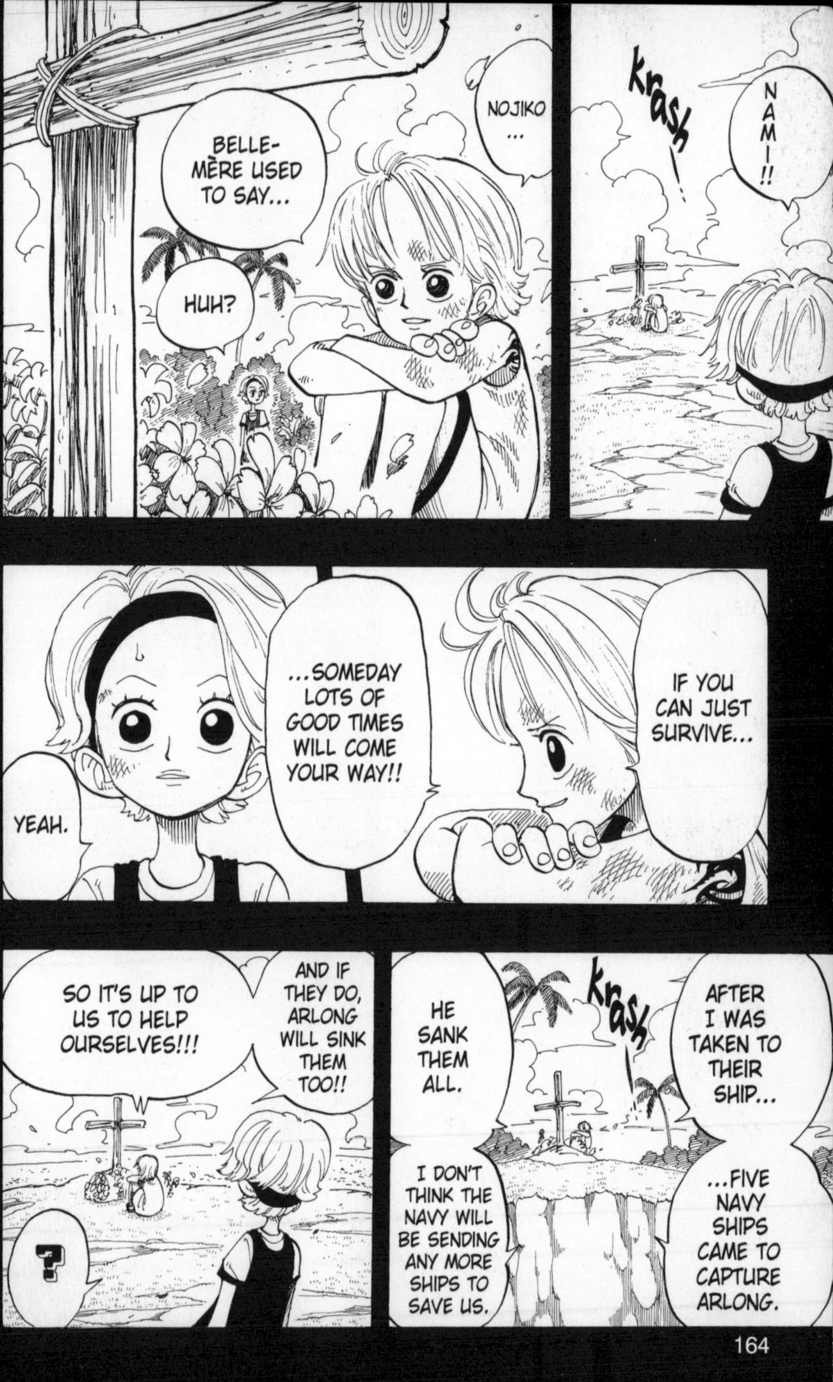
krash
NAMI!!
NOJIKO ...
BELLE-MÈRE USED TO SAY...
HUH?
IF YOU CAN JUST SURVIVE...
...SOMEDAY LOTS OF GOOD TIMES WILL COME YOUR WAY!!
YEAH.
AFTER I WAS TAKEN TO THEIR SHIP...
...FIVE NAVY SHIPS CAME TO CAPTURE ARLONG.
krash
HE SANK THEM ALL.
I DON'T THINK THE NAVY WILL BE SENDING ANY MORE SHIPS TO SAVE US.
AND IF THEY DO, ARLONG WILL SINK THEM TOO!!
SO IT'S UP TO US TO HELP OURSELVES!!!
?

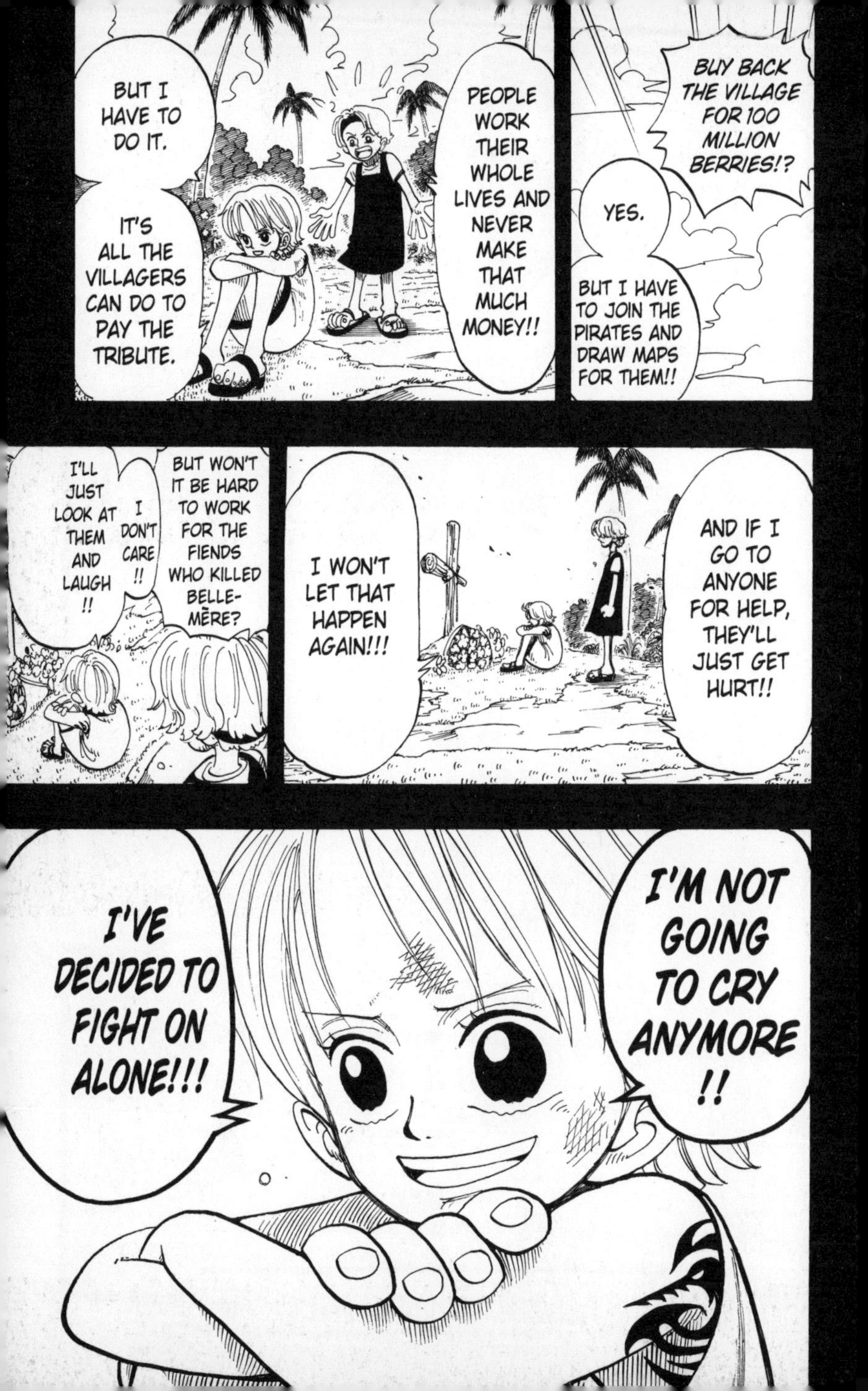
BUY BACK THE VILLAGE FOR 100 MILLION BERRIES!?
YES.
BUT I HAVE TO JOIN THE PIRATES AND DRAW MAPS FOR THEM!!
PEOPLE WORK THEIR WHOLE LIVES AND NEVER MAKE THAT MUCH MONEY!!
BUT I HAVE TO DO IT.
IT'S ALL THE VILLAGERS CAN DO TO PAY THE TRIBUTE.
AND IF I GO TO ANYONE FOR HELP, THEY'LL JUST GET HURT!!
I WON'T LET THAT HAPPEN AGAIN!!!
BUT WON'T IT BE HARD TO WORK FOR THE FIENDS WHO KILLED BELLE-MÈRE?
I DON'T CARE!!
I'LL JUST LOOK AT THEM AND LAUGH!!
I'M NOT GOING TO CRY ANYMORE!!
I'VE DECIDED TO FIGHT ON ALONE!!!

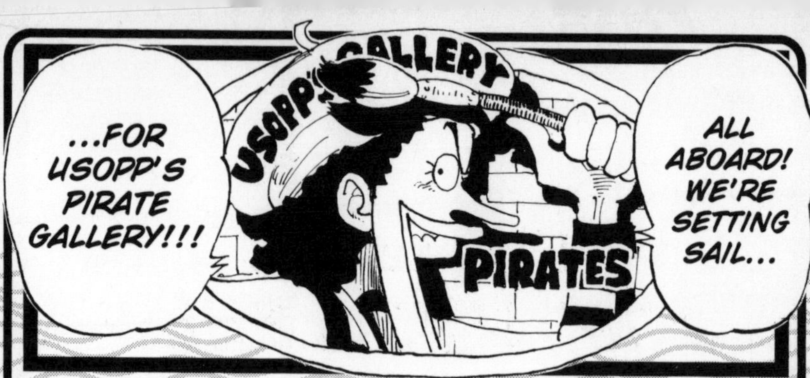
USOPP'S GALLERY PIRATES
ALL ABOARD! WE'RE SETTING SAIL...
...FOR USOPP'S PIRATE GALLERY!!!

IT'S ALL FUN AND GAMES TO LUFFY!

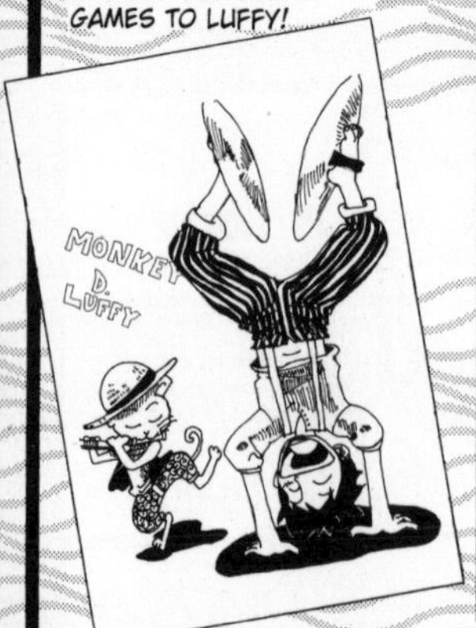
MONKEY D. LUFFY

ASHLEY, 13

OUR HERO LOOKS LOST.

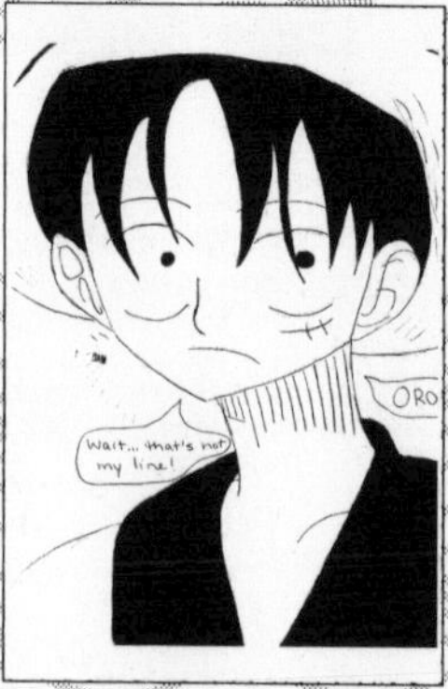
Wait... that's not my line!

ALLISON, 14

WHAT'S ON YOUR MIND, USOPP?

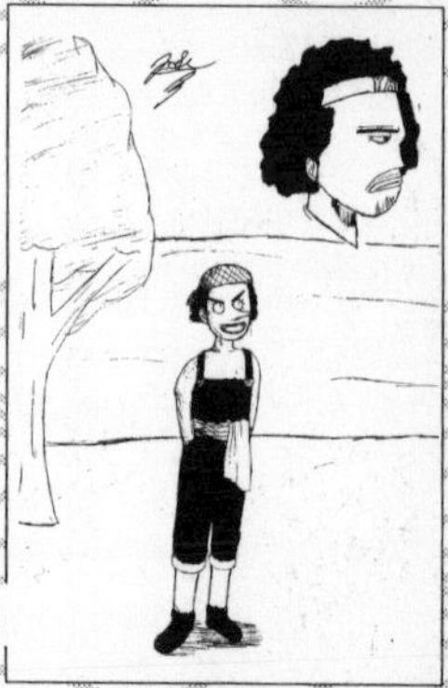

JORDAN, 13

AND THAT'S A FACT.

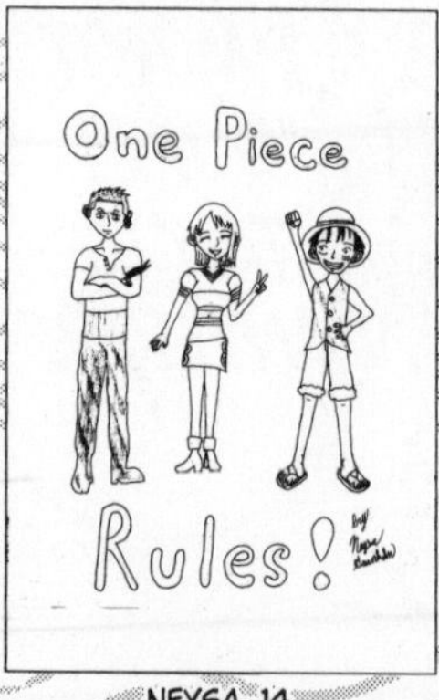
One Piece
Rules!

NEYSA, 14

TWO TOUGH COOKIES.

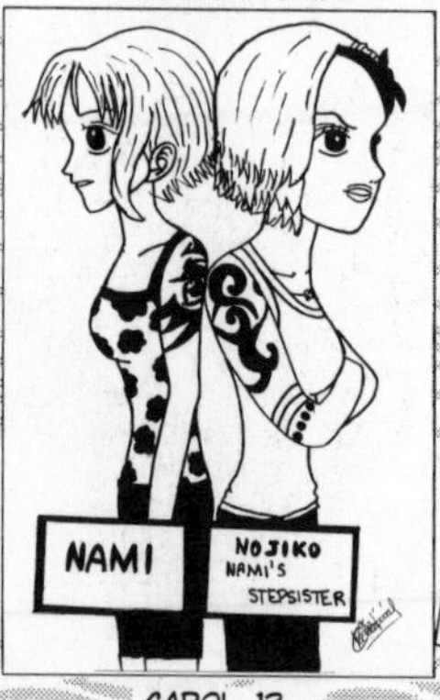
NAMI
NOJIKO NAMI'S STEPSISTER

CAROL, 13

THE FUTURE KING OF THE PIRATES.

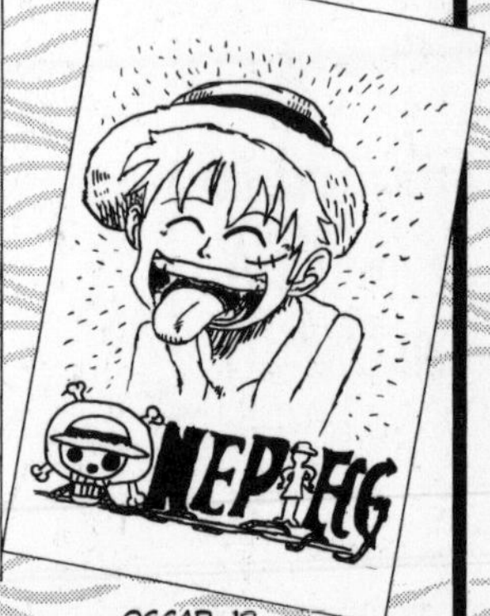

OSCAR, 13

SUBMIT YOUR FAN ART TO:
SHONEN JUMP C/O VIZ MEDIA, LLC P.O. BOX 77010, SAN FRANCISCO, CA. 94107
REMEMBER TO INCLUDE YOUR NAME AND AGE!!

USOPP'S COMMENTS WERE TRANSMITTED THROUGH THE U.S. SHONEN JUMP TEAM—*EDITOR*

Chapter 80:
A THIEF IS A THIEF

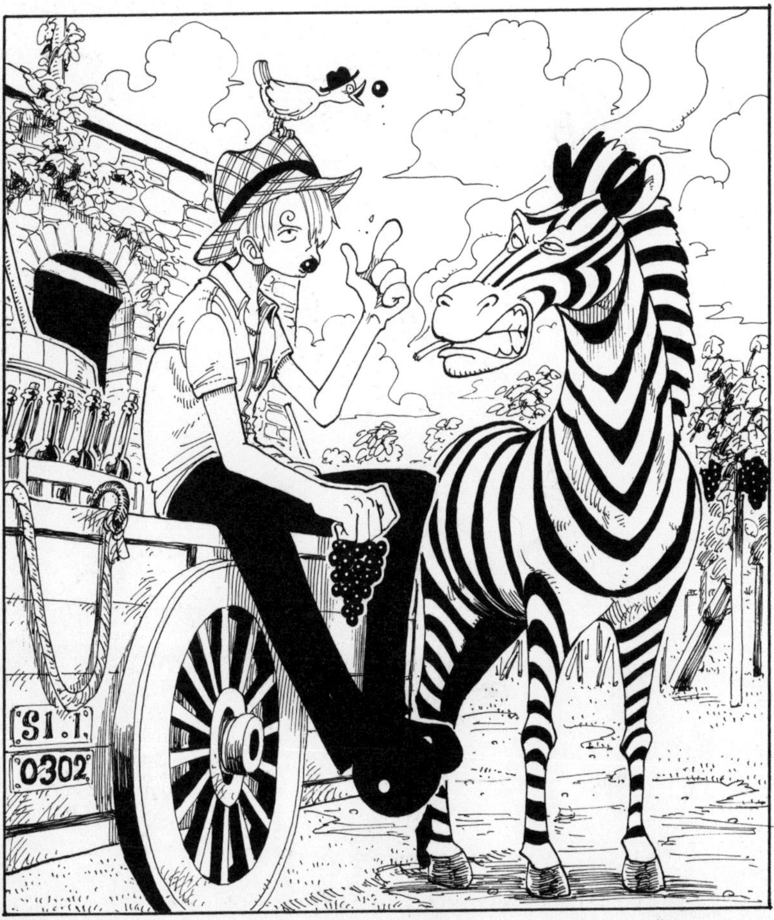
S1.1.
0302

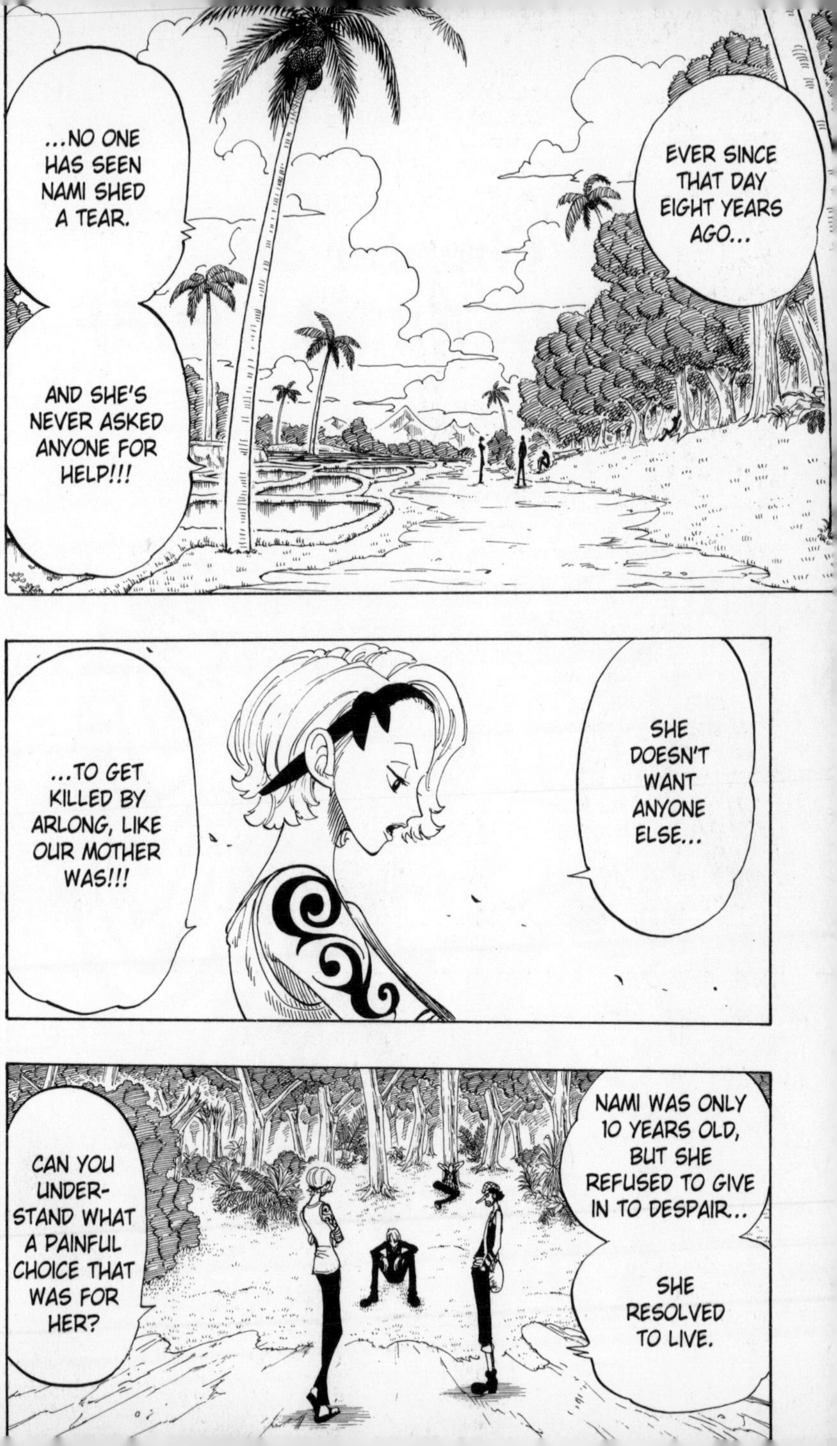
EVER SINCE THAT DAY EIGHT YEARS AGO...
...NO ONE HAS SEEN NAMI SHED A TEAR.
AND SHE'S NEVER ASKED ANYONE FOR HELP!!!
SHE DOESN'T WANT ANYONE ELSE...
...TO GET KILLED BY ARLONG, LIKE OUR MOTHER WAS!!!
NAMI WAS ONLY 10 YEARS OLD, BUT SHE REFUSED TO GIVE IN TO DESPAIR..
SHE RESOLVED TO LIVE.
CAN YOU UNDER-STAND WHAT A PAINFUL CHOICE THAT WAS FOR HER?

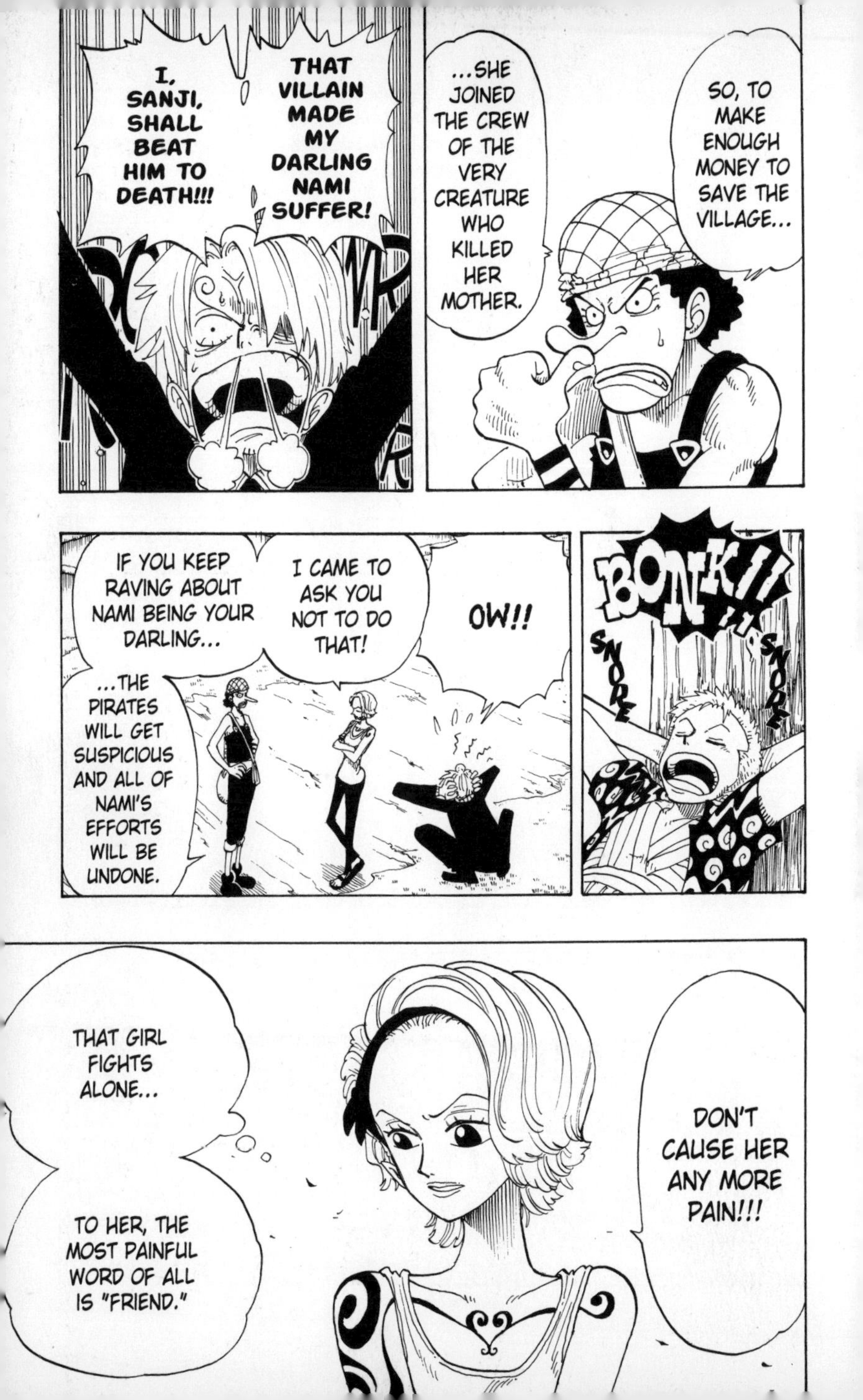
SO, TO MAKE ENOUGH MONEY TO SAVE THE VILLAGE...
...SHE JOINED THE CREW OF THE VERY CREATURE WHO KILLED HER MOTHER.
THAT VILLAIN MADE MY DARLING NAMI SUFFER!
I, SANJI, SHALL BEAT HIM TO DEATH!!!
BONK!!
SNORE
SNORE
OW!!
I CAME TO ASK YOU NOT TO DO THAT!
IF YOU KEEP RAVING ABOUT NAMI BEING YOUR DARLING...
...THE PIRATES WILL GET SUSPICIOUS AND ALL OF NAMI'S EFFORTS WILL BE UNDONE.
DON'T CAUSE HER ANY MORE PAIN!!!
THAT GIRL FIGHTS ALONE...
TO HER, THE MOST PAINFUL WORD OF ALL IS "FRIEND."

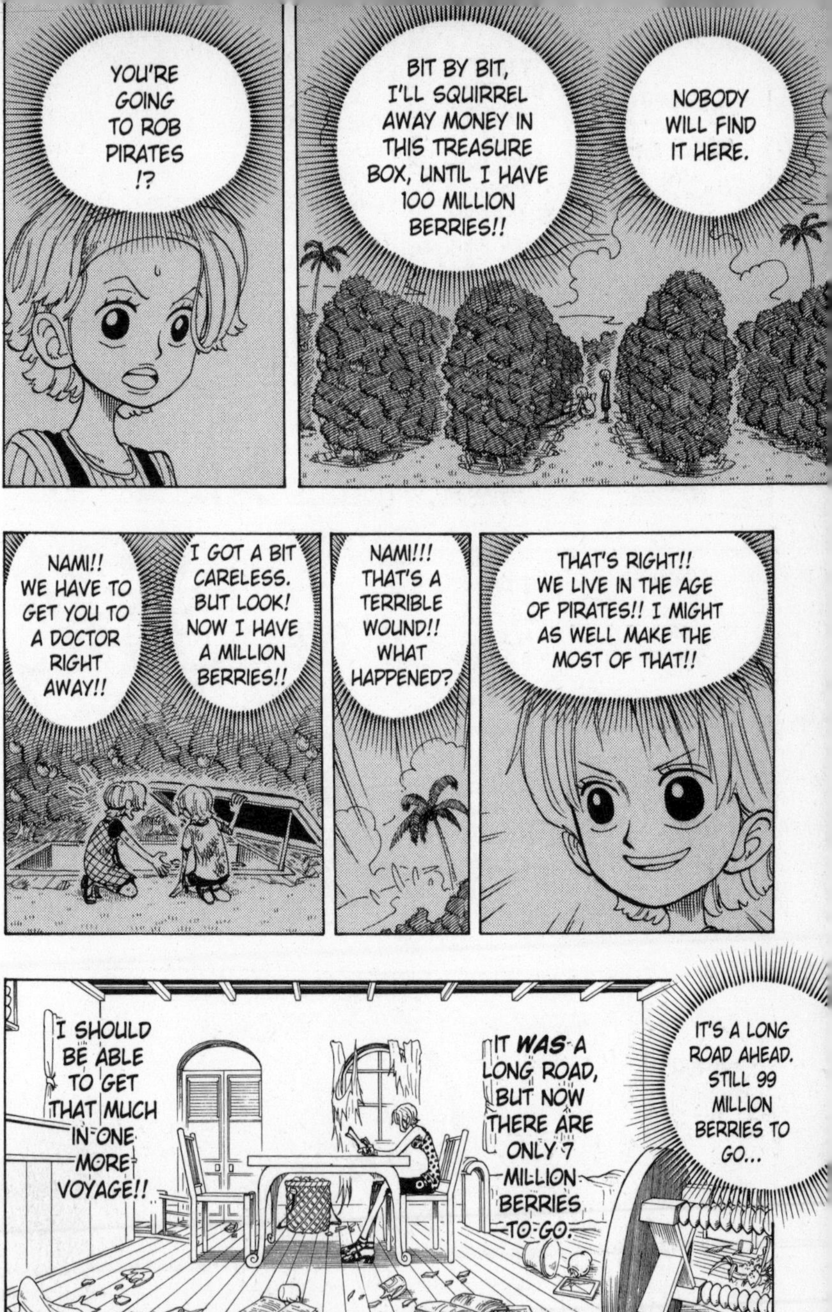
NOBODY WILL FIND IT HERE.
BIT BY BIT, I'LL SQUIRREL AWAY MONEY IN THIS TREASURE BOX, UNTIL I HAVE 100 MILLION BERRIES!!
YOU'RE GOING TO ROB PIRATES!?
THAT'S RIGHT!! WE LIVE IN THE AGE OF PIRATES!! I MIGHT AS WELL MAKE THE MOST OF THAT!!
NAMI!!! THAT'S A TERRIBLE WOUND!! WHAT HAPPENED?
I GOT A BIT CARELESS. BUT LOOK! NOW I HAVE A MILLION BERRIES!!
NAMI!! WE HAVE TO GET YOU TO A DOCTOR RIGHT AWAY!!
IT'S A LONG ROAD AHEAD. STILL 99 MILLION BERRIES TO GO...
IT *WAS* A LONG ROAD, BUT NOW THERE ARE ONLY 7 MILLION BERRIES TO GO.
I SHOULD BE ABLE TO GET THAT MUCH IN ONE MORE VOYAGE!!

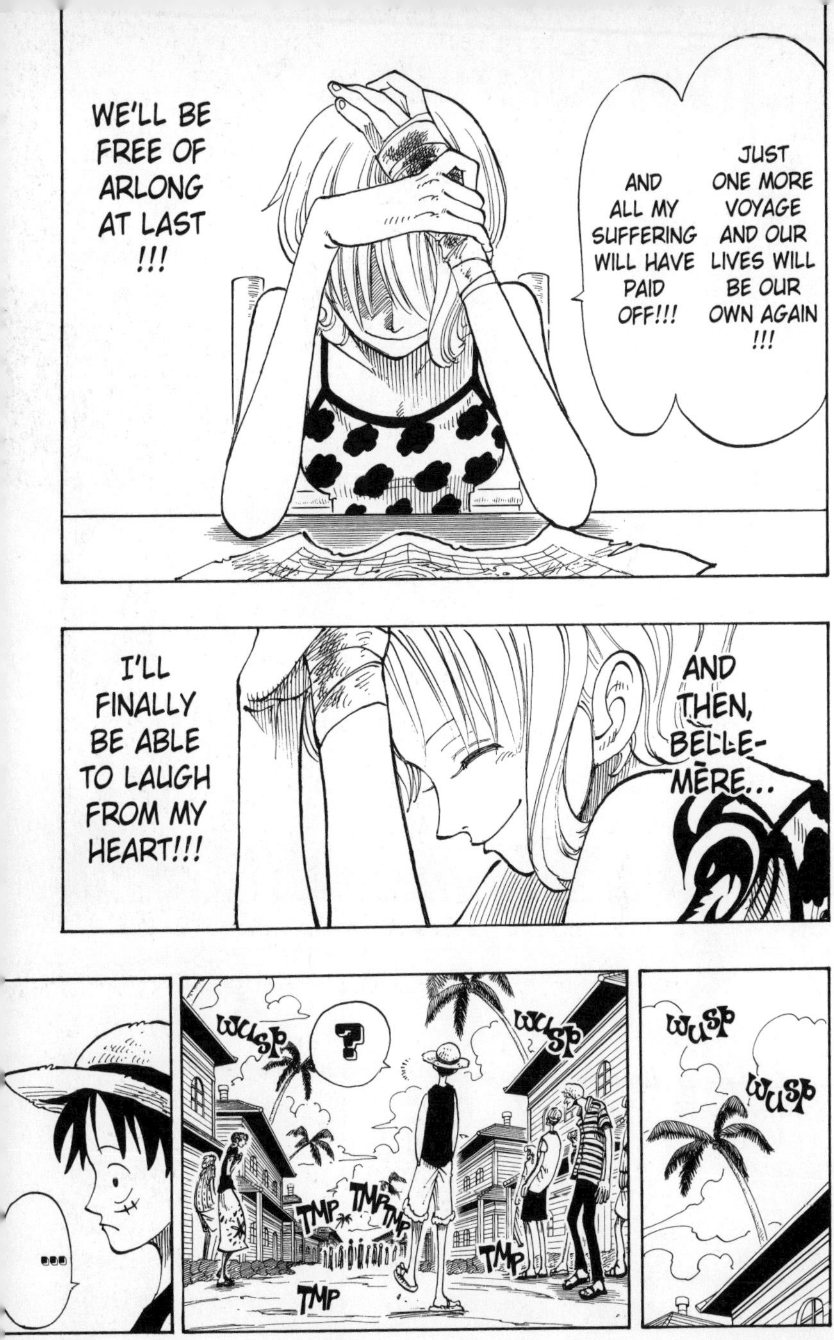
JUST ONE MORE VOYAGE AND OUR LIVES WILL BE OUR OWN AGAIN !!!
AND ALL MY SUFFERING WILL HAVE PAID OFF!!!
WE'LL BE FREE OF ARLONG AT LAST !!!
AND THEN, BELLE-MÈRE...
I'LL FINALLY BE ABLE TO LAUGH FROM MY HEART!!!
WUSP
WUSP
WUSP
?
WUSP
TMP TMP TMP
TMP
TMP
TMP
...

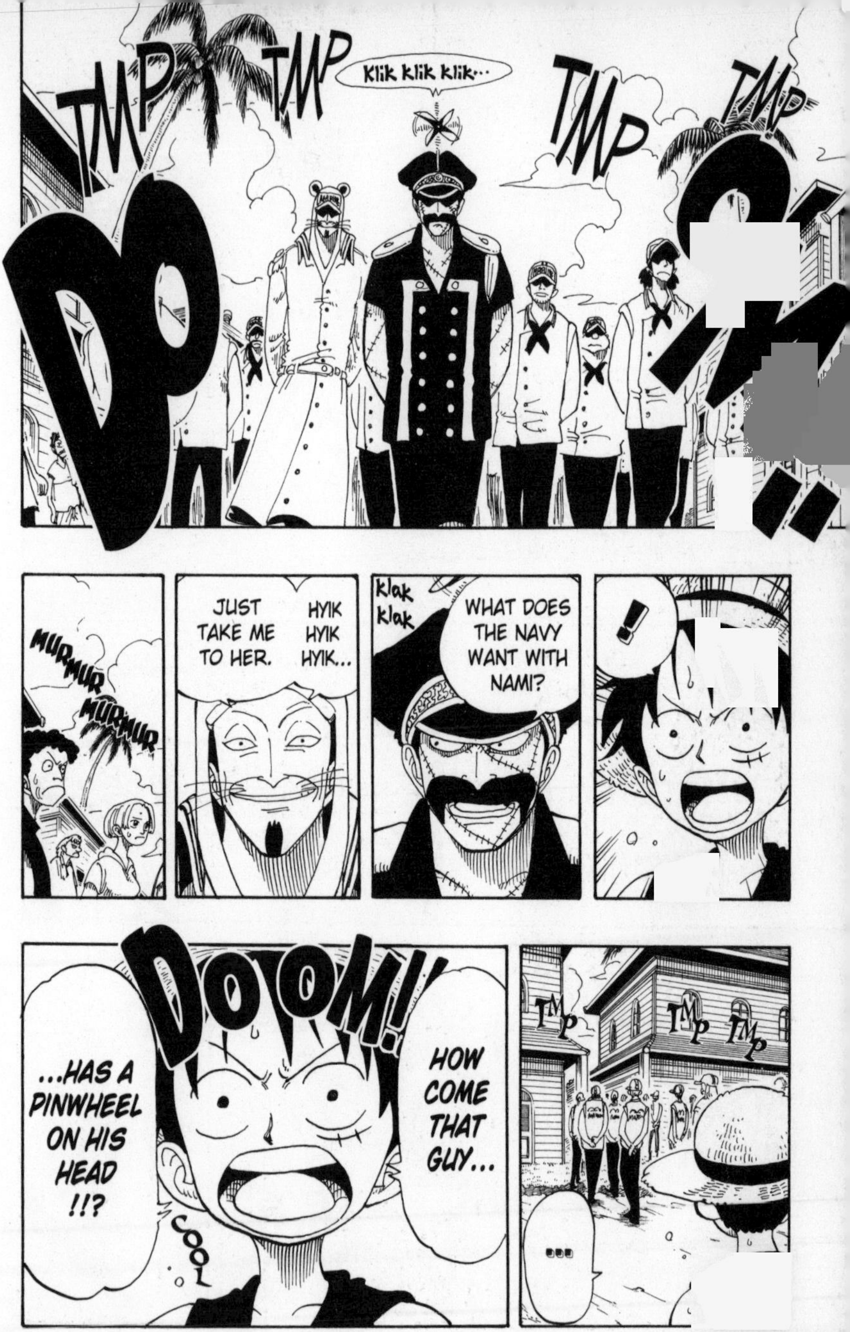
TMP
TMP
Klik klik klik...
TMP
TMP
DO
!
klak klak
WHAT DOES THE NAVY WANT WITH NAMI?
HYIK HYIK HYIK...
JUST TAKE ME TO HER.
MURMUR
MURMUR
TMP
TMP
TMP
...
DOOM!!
HOW COME THAT GUY...
...HAS A PINWHEEL ON HIS HEAD!!?
COOL

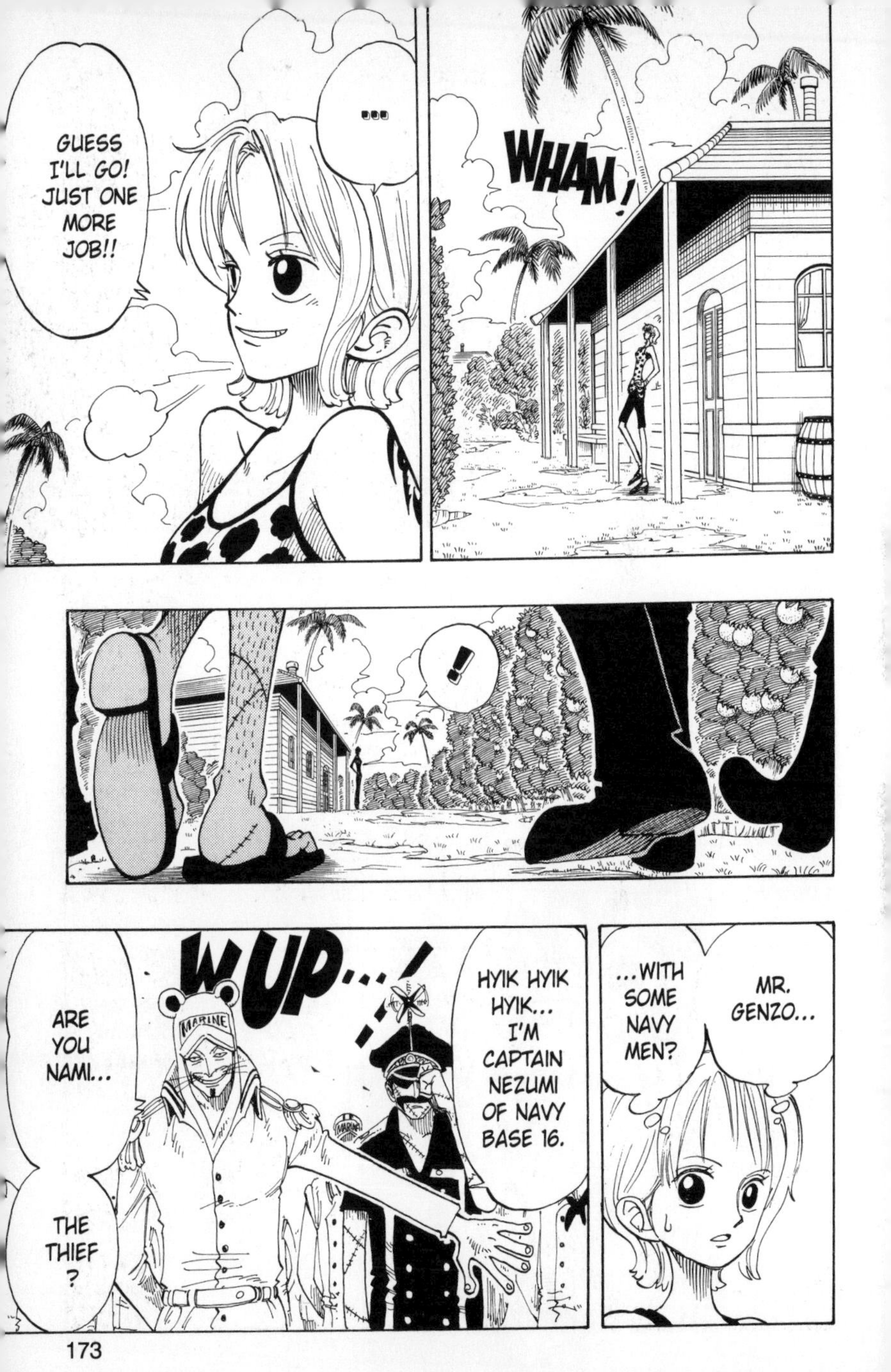
WHAM!
...
GUESS I'LL GO! JUST ONE MORE JOB!!
!
MR. GENZO...
...WITH SOME NAVY MEN?
WUP...!
HYIK HYIK HYIK... I'M CAPTAIN NEZUMI OF NAVY BASE 16.
ARE YOU NAMI...
THE THIEF?

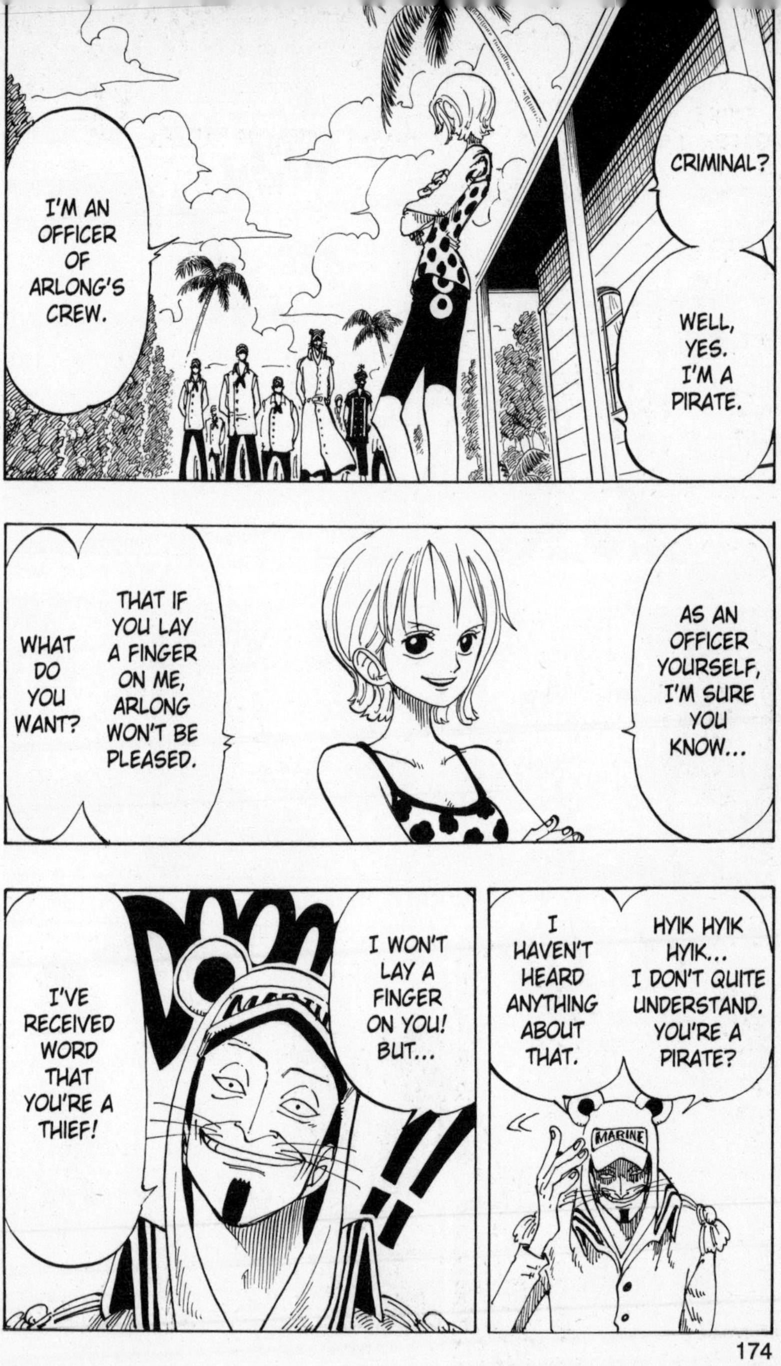
CRIMINAL?
WELL, YES. I'M A PIRATE.
I'M AN OFFICER OF ARLONG'S CREW.
AS AN OFFICER YOURSELF, I'M SURE YOU KNOW...
THAT IF YOU LAY A FINGER ON ME, ARLONG WON'T BE PLEASED.
WHAT DO YOU WANT?
HYIK HYIK HYIK... I DON'T QUITE UNDERSTAND. YOU'RE A PIRATE?
I HAVEN'T HEARD ANYTHING ABOUT THAT.
MARINE
I WON'T LAY A FINGER ON YOU! BUT...
I'VE RECEIVED WORD THAT YOU'RE A THIEF!

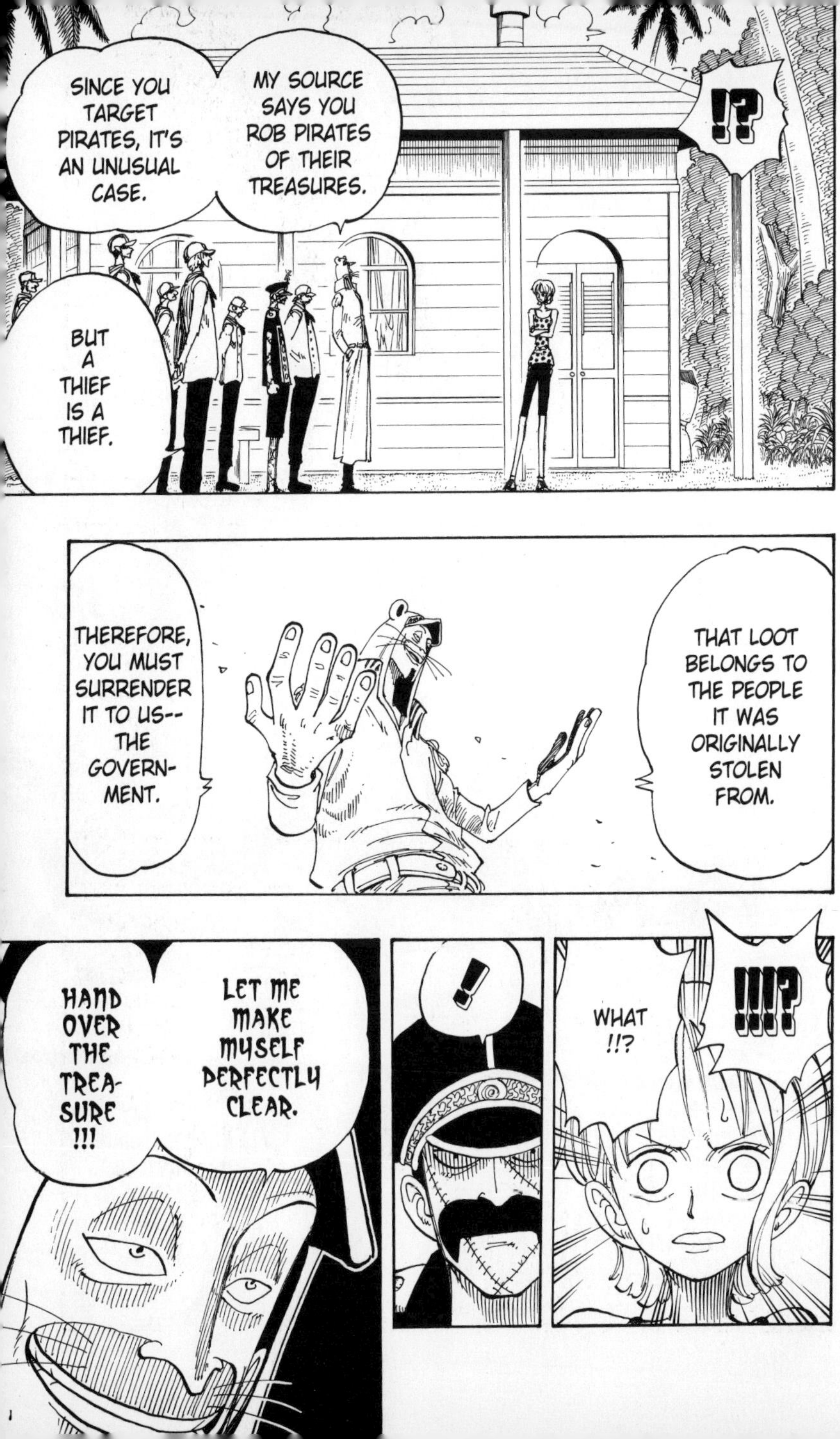
!?
MY SOURCE SAYS YOU ROB PIRATES OF THEIR TREASURES.
SINCE YOU TARGET PIRATES, IT'S AN UNUSUAL CASE.
BUT A THIEF IS A THIEF.
THAT LOOT BELONGS TO THE PEOPLE IT WAS ORIGINALLY STOLEN FROM.
THEREFORE, YOU MUST SURRENDER IT TO US-- THE GOVERNMENT.
!!!?
WHAT !!?
!
LET ME MAKE MYSELF PERFECTLY CLEAR.
HAND OVER THE TREA-SURE !!!

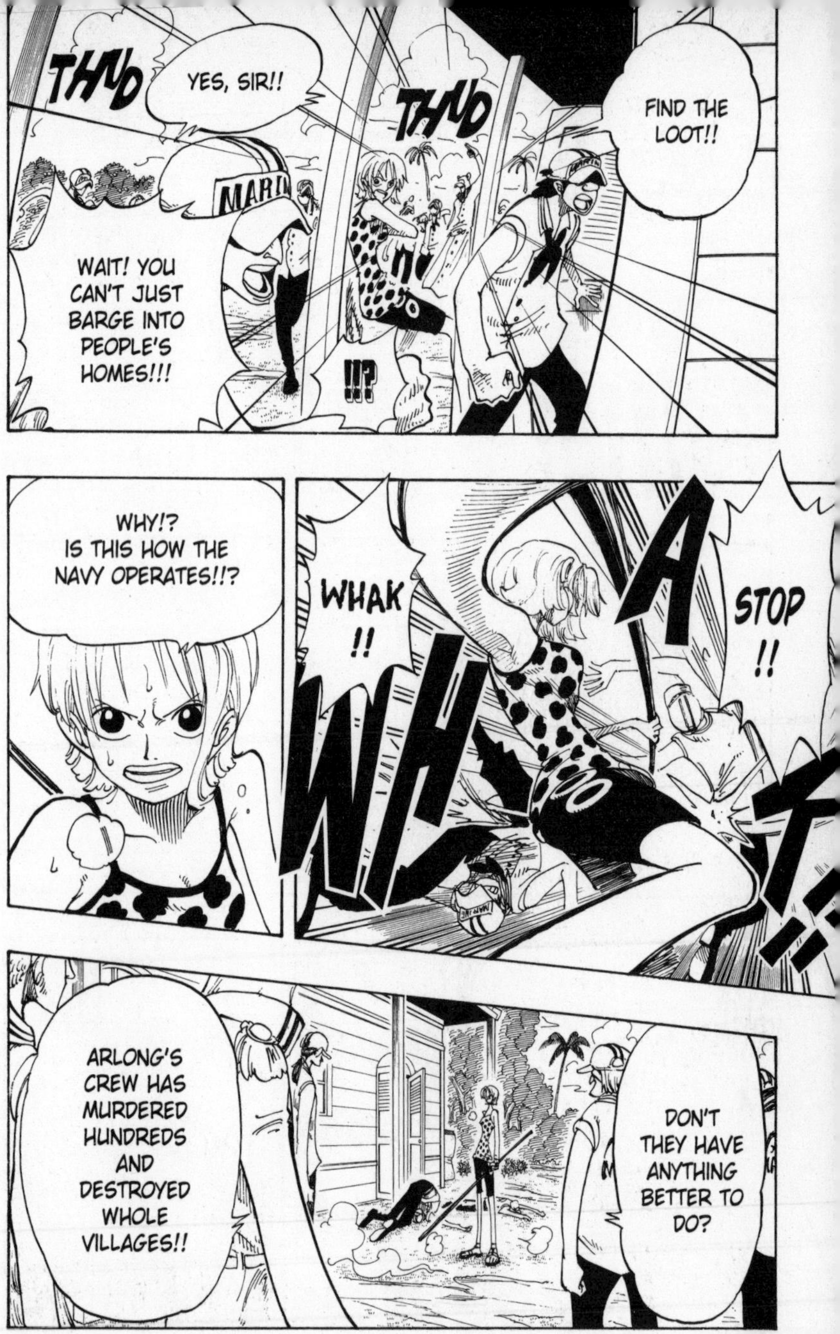
FIND THE LOOT!!
THUD
YES, SIR!!
THUD
WAIT! YOU CAN'T JUST BARGE INTO PEOPLE'S HOMES!!!
!!?
STOP!!
WHAK!!
WHY!? IS THIS HOW THE NAVY OPERATES!!?
DON'T THEY HAVE ANYTHING BETTER TO DO?
ARLONG'S CREW HAS MURDERED HUNDREDS AND DESTROYED WHOLE VILLAGES!!

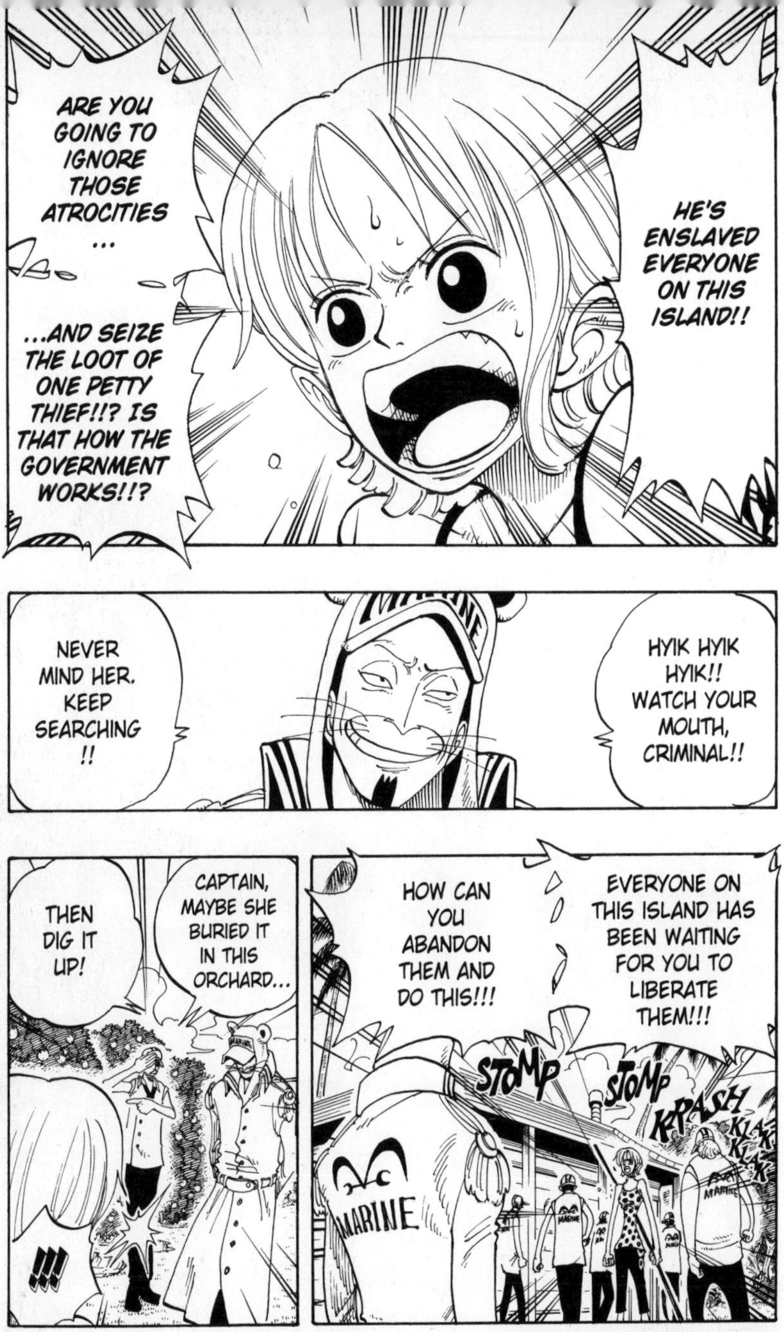
HE'S ENSLAVED EVERYONE ON THIS ISLAND!!
ARE YOU GOING TO IGNORE THOSE ATROCITIES ...
...AND SEIZE THE LOOT OF ONE PETTY THIEF!!? IS THAT HOW THE GOVERNMENT WORKS!!?
HYIK HYIK HYIK!! WATCH YOUR MOUTH, CRIMINAL!!
NEVER MIND HER. KEEP SEARCHING !!
EVERYONE ON THIS ISLAND HAS BEEN WAITING FOR YOU TO LIBERATE THEM!!!
HOW CAN YOU ABANDON THEM AND DO THIS!!!
STOMP
STOMP
KRASH
KLAK KLAK
MARINE
CAPTAIN, MAYBE SHE BURIED IT IN THIS ORCHARD...
THEN DIG IT UP!
!!!

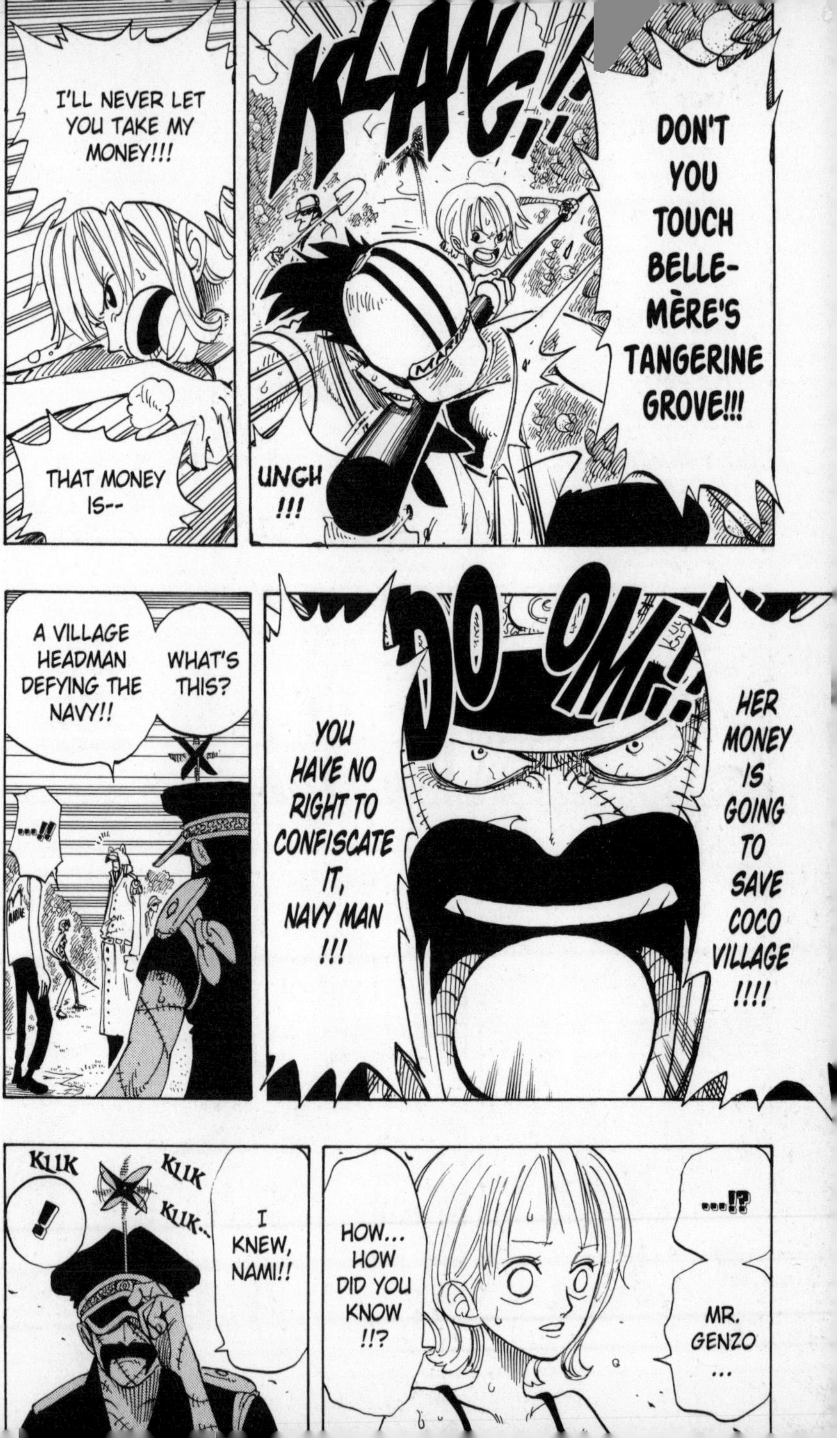
KLANG!!
DON'T YOU TOUCH BELLE-MÈRE'S TANGERINE GROVE!!!
UNGH!!!
I'LL NEVER LET YOU TAKE MY MONEY!!!
THAT MONEY IS--
DO-OM!!
HER MONEY IS GOING TO SAVE COCO VILLAGE!!!!
YOU HAVE NO RIGHT TO CONFISCATE IT, NAVY MAN!!!
WHAT'S THIS?
A VILLAGE HEADMAN DEFYING THE NAVY!!
...!!
...!?
MR. GENZO...
HOW... HOW DID YOU KNOW!!?
I KNEW, NAMI!!
KLIK
KLIK
KLIK..
!

READ THIS WAY

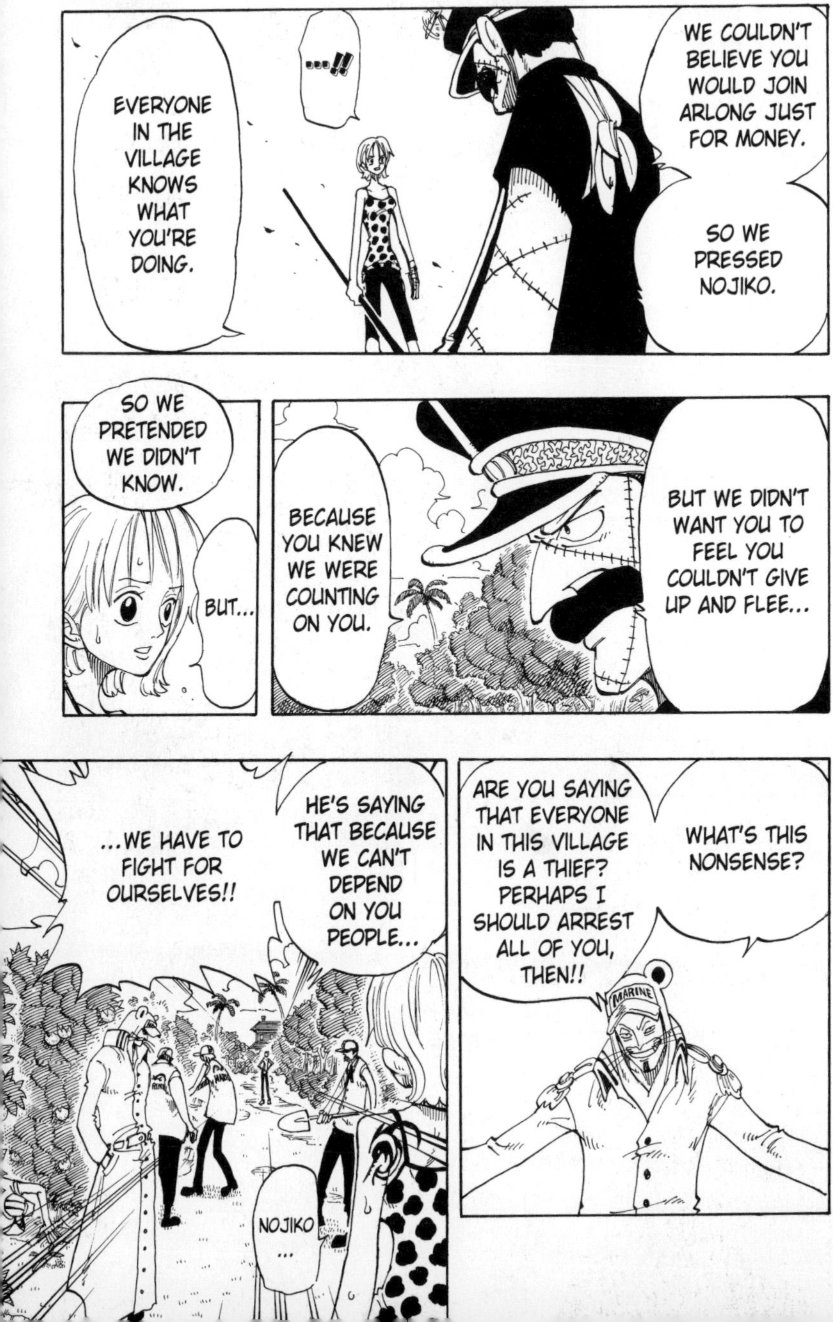
WE COULDN'T BELIEVE YOU WOULD JOIN ARLONG JUST FOR MONEY.
SO WE PRESSED NOJIKO.
...!!
EVERYONE IN THE VILLAGE KNOWS WHAT YOU'RE DOING.
BUT WE DIDN'T WANT YOU TO FEEL YOU COULDN'T GIVE UP AND FLEE...
BECAUSE YOU KNEW WE WERE COUNTING ON YOU.
SO WE PRETENDED WE DIDN'T KNOW.
BUT...
WHAT'S THIS NONSENSE?
ARE YOU SAYING THAT EVERYONE IN THIS VILLAGE IS A THIEF? PERHAPS I SHOULD ARREST ALL OF YOU, THEN!!
MARINE
HE'S SAYING THAT BECAUSE WE CAN'T DEPEND ON YOU PEOPLE...
...WE HAVE TO FIGHT FOR OURSELVES!!
NOJIKO ...

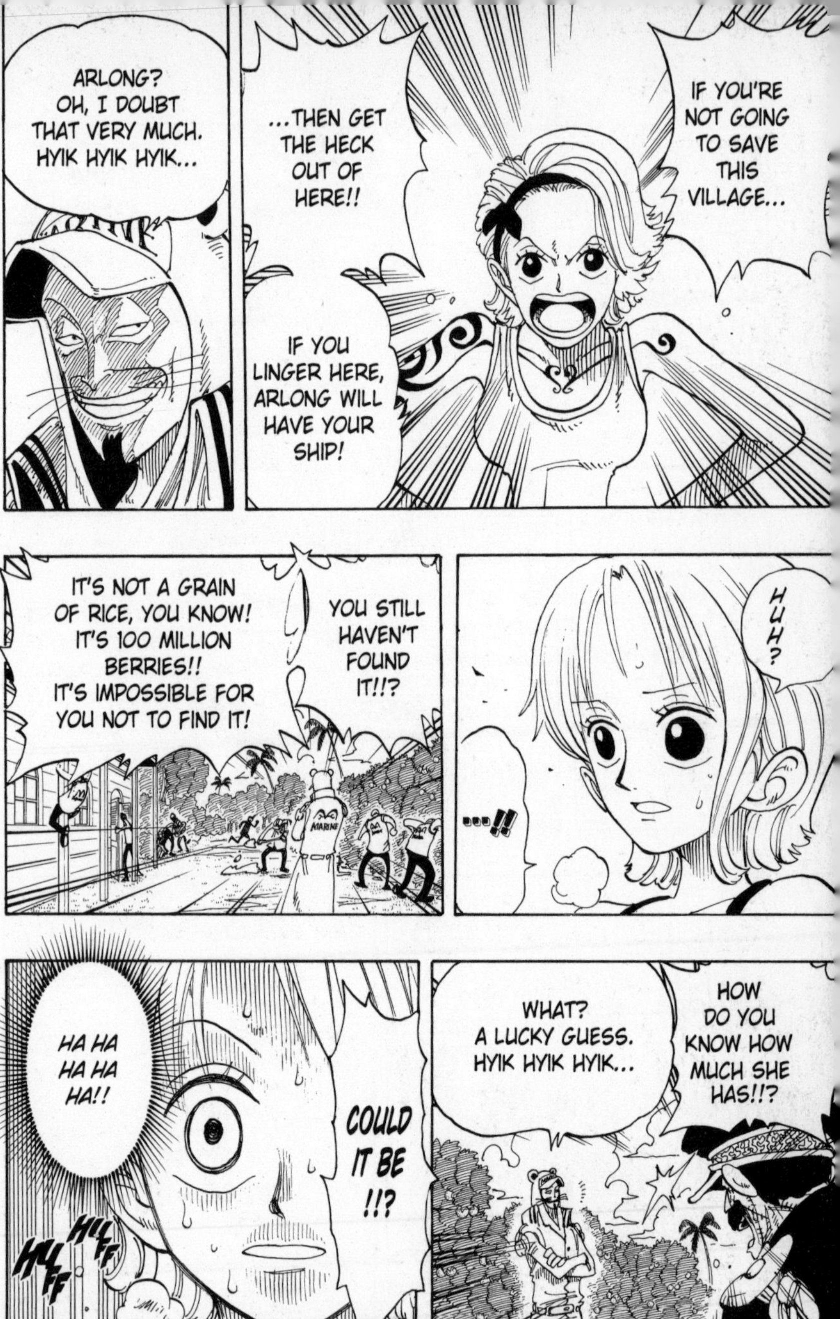
IF YOU'RE NOT GOING TO SAVE THIS VILLAGE...
...THEN GET THE HECK OUT OF HERE!!
IF YOU LINGER HERE, ARLONG WILL HAVE YOUR SHIP!
ARLONG? OH, I DOUBT THAT VERY MUCH. HYIK HYIK HYIK...
HUH?
...!!
YOU STILL HAVEN'T FOUND IT!!?
IT'S NOT A GRAIN OF RICE, YOU KNOW! IT'S 100 MILLION BERRIES!! IT'S IMPOSSIBLE FOR YOU NOT TO FIND IT!
HOW DO YOU KNOW HOW MUCH SHE HAS!!?
WHAT? A LUCKY GUESS. HYIK HYIK HYIK...
COULD IT BE !!?
HA HA HA HA HA!!
HUFF HUFF

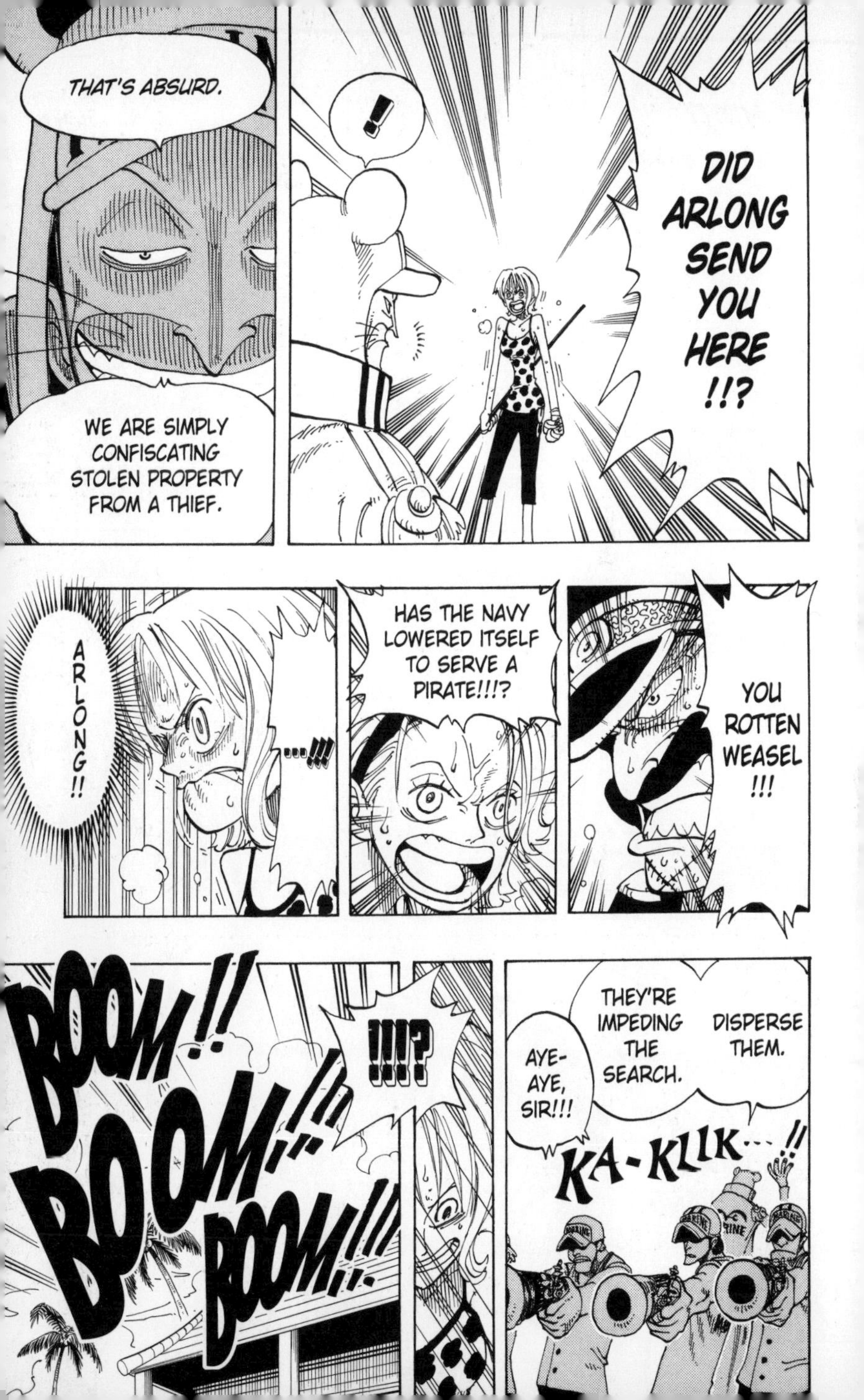
DID ARLONG SEND YOU HERE!!?
!
THAT'S ABSURD.
WE ARE SIMPLY CONFISCATING STOLEN PROPERTY FROM A THIEF.
YOU ROTTEN WEASEL!!!
HAS THE NAVY LOWERED ITSELF TO SERVE A PIRATE!!!?
...!!!
ARLONG!!
DISPERSE THEM.
THEY'RE IMPEDING THE SEARCH.
AYE-AYE, SIR!!!
KA-KLIK...!!
!!!?
BOOM!!
BOOM!!
BOOM!!

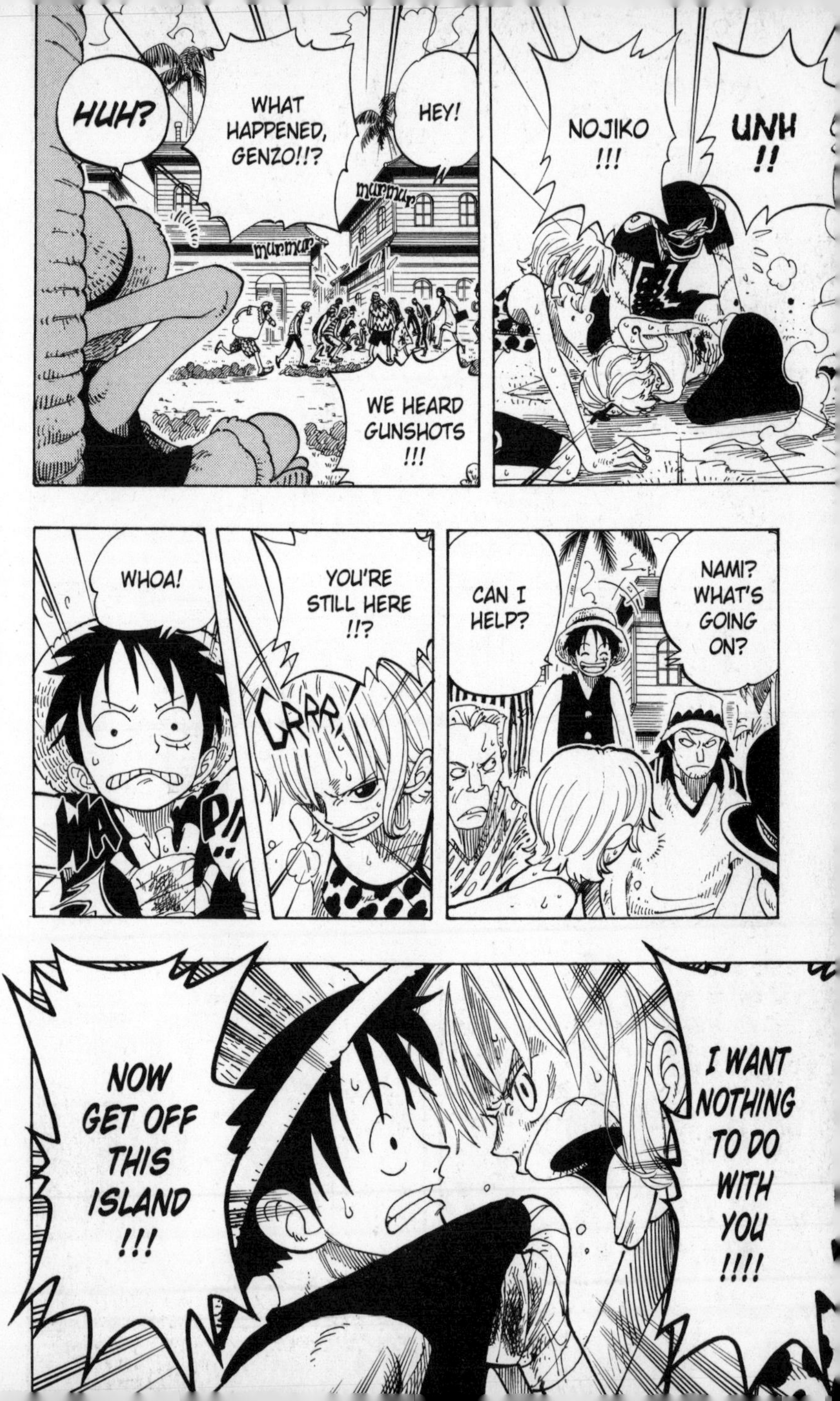
UNH !!
NOJIKO !!!
HEY!
WHAT HAPPENED, GENZO!!?
murmur
murmur
HUH?
WE HEARD GUNSHOTS !!!
NAMI? WHAT'S GOING ON?
CAN I HELP?
YOU'RE STILL HERE !!?
GRRR
WHOA!
I WANT NOTHING TO DO WITH YOU !!!!
NOW GET OFF THIS ISLAND !!!

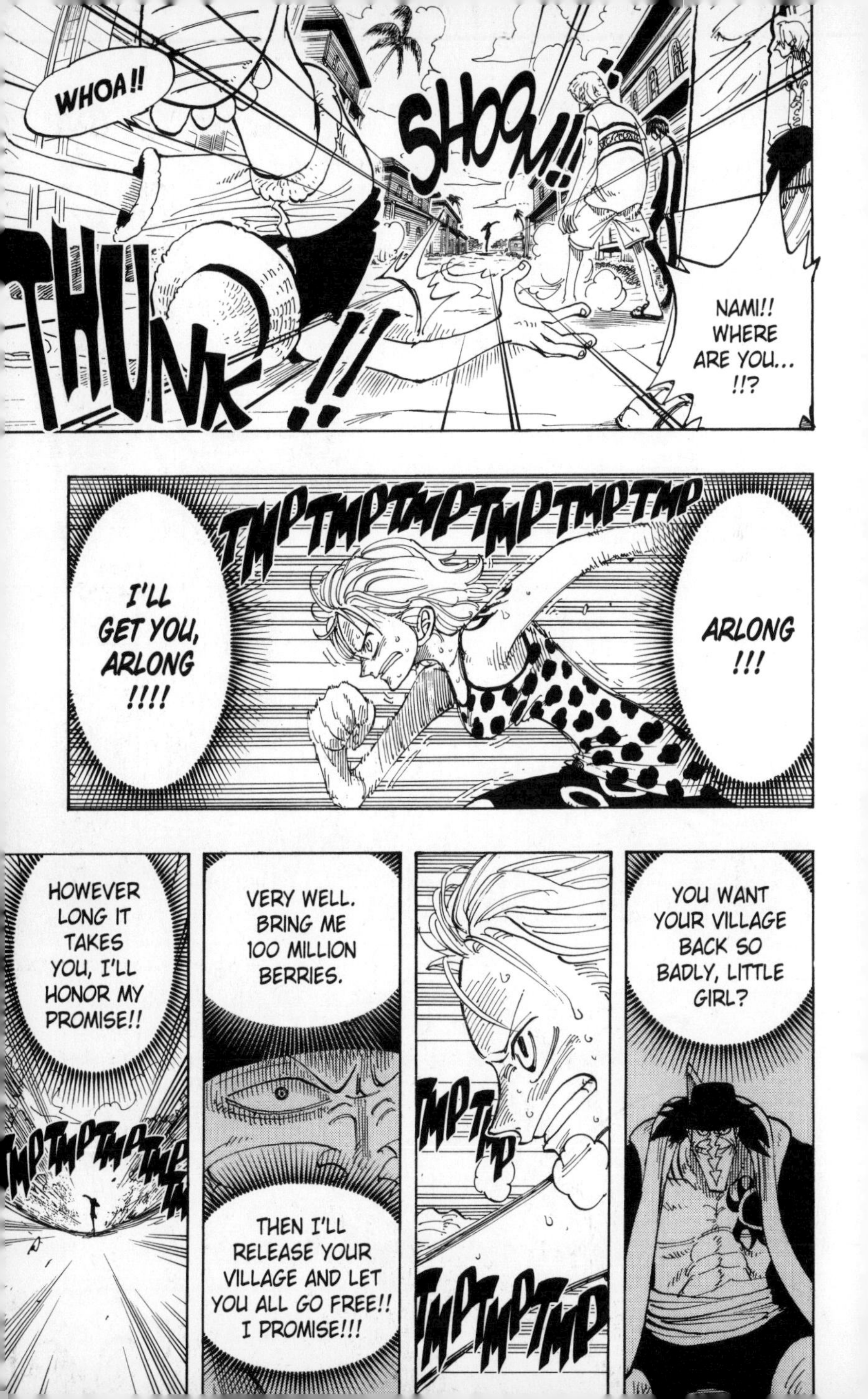
NAMI!! WHERE ARE YOU... !!?
SHOOM!!
WHOA!!
THUNK!!
ARLONG !!!
TMP TMP TMP TMP TMP TMP TMP
I'LL GET YOU, ARLONG !!!!
YOU WANT YOUR VILLAGE BACK SO BADLY, LITTLE GIRL?
TMP TMP TMP
TMP TMP TMP
VERY WELL. BRING ME 100 MILLION BERRIES.
THEN I'LL RELEASE YOUR VILLAGE AND LET YOU ALL GO FREE!! I PROMISE!!!
HOWEVER LONG IT TAKES YOU, I'LL HONOR MY PROMISE!!
TMP TMP TMP TMP TMP

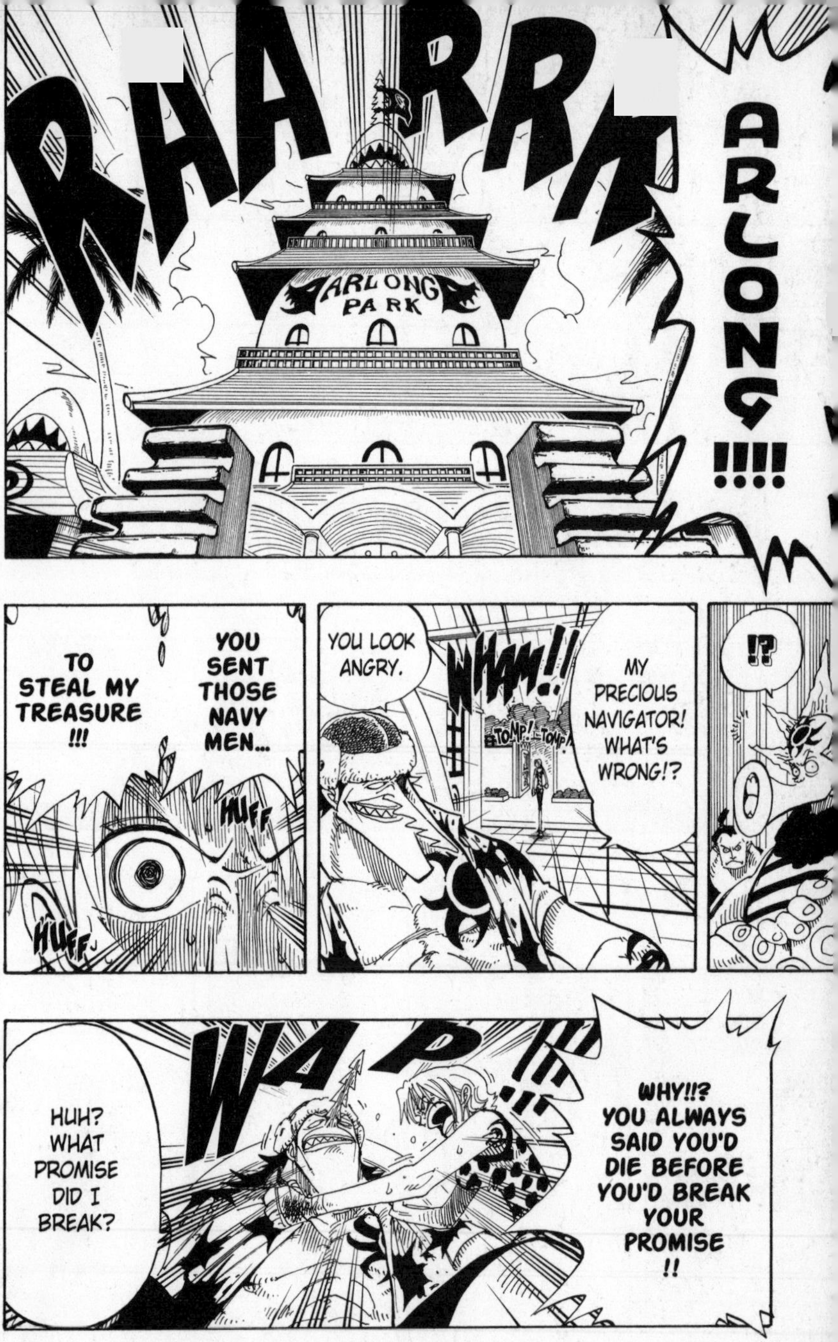
RAARR
ARLONG!!!!
!?
WHAM!!
MY PRECIOUS NAVIGATOR! WHAT'S WRONG!?
TOMP! TOMP!
YOU LOOK ANGRY.
YOU SENT THOSE NAVY MEN...
TO STEAL MY TREASURE !!!
HUFF
HUFF
WHY!!? YOU ALWAYS SAID YOU'D DIE BEFORE YOU'D BREAK YOUR PROMISE !!
WAP!!!
HUH? WHAT PROMISE DID I BREAK?

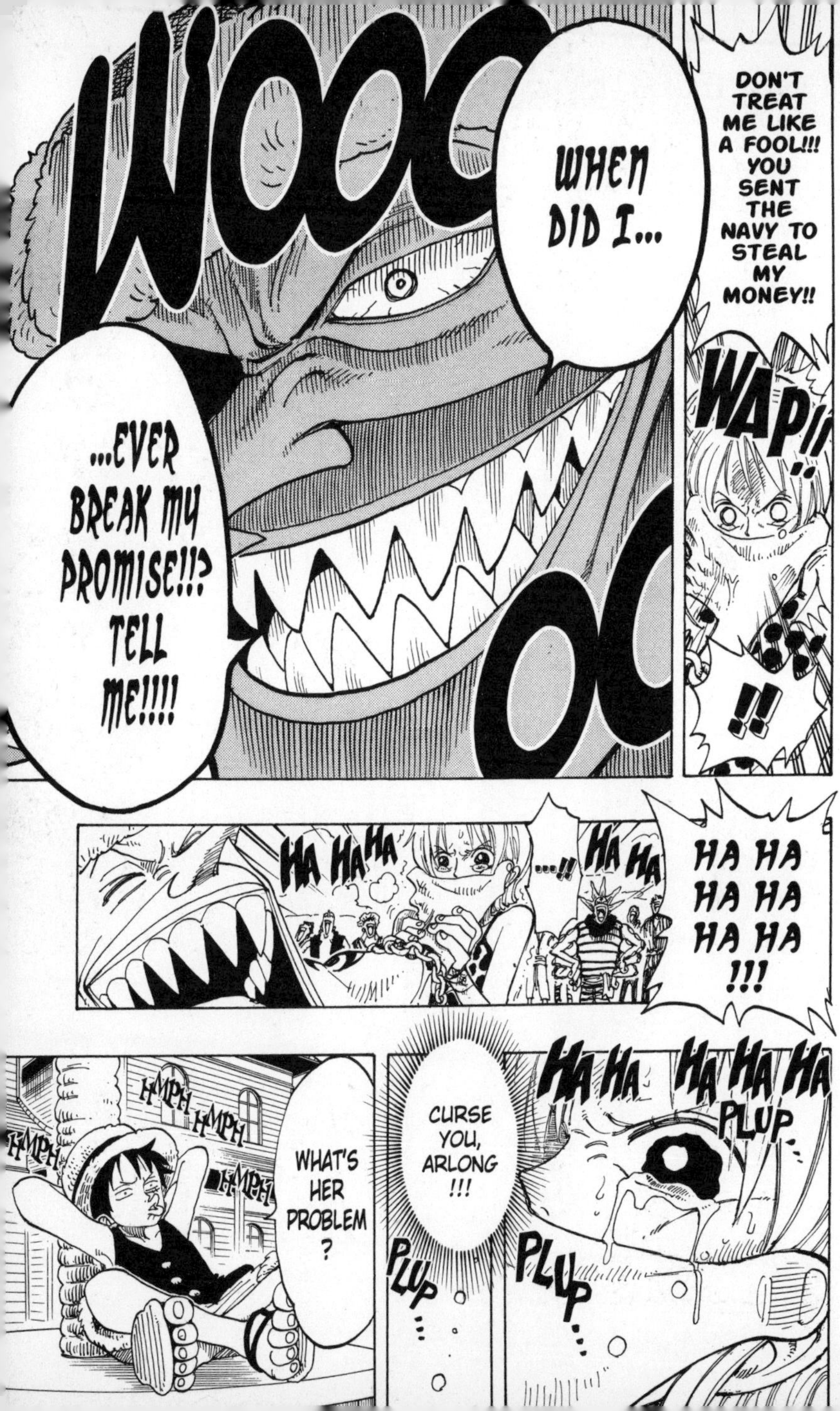
DON'T TREAT ME LIKE A FOOL!!! YOU SENT THE NAVY TO STEAL MY MONEY!!
WAP!!
!!
WOOOO
WHEN DID I...
...EVER BREAK MY PROMISE!!? TELL ME!!!!!
HA HA HA HA HA HA !!!
HA HA
...!!
HA HA HA
HA HA HA HA HA
PLUP
CURSE YOU, ARLONG !!!
PLUP...
PLUP...
WHAT'S HER PROBLEM ?
HMPH
HMPH
HMPH
HMPH

ONE PIECE **STORYBOARD PRESENTATION!!** #12

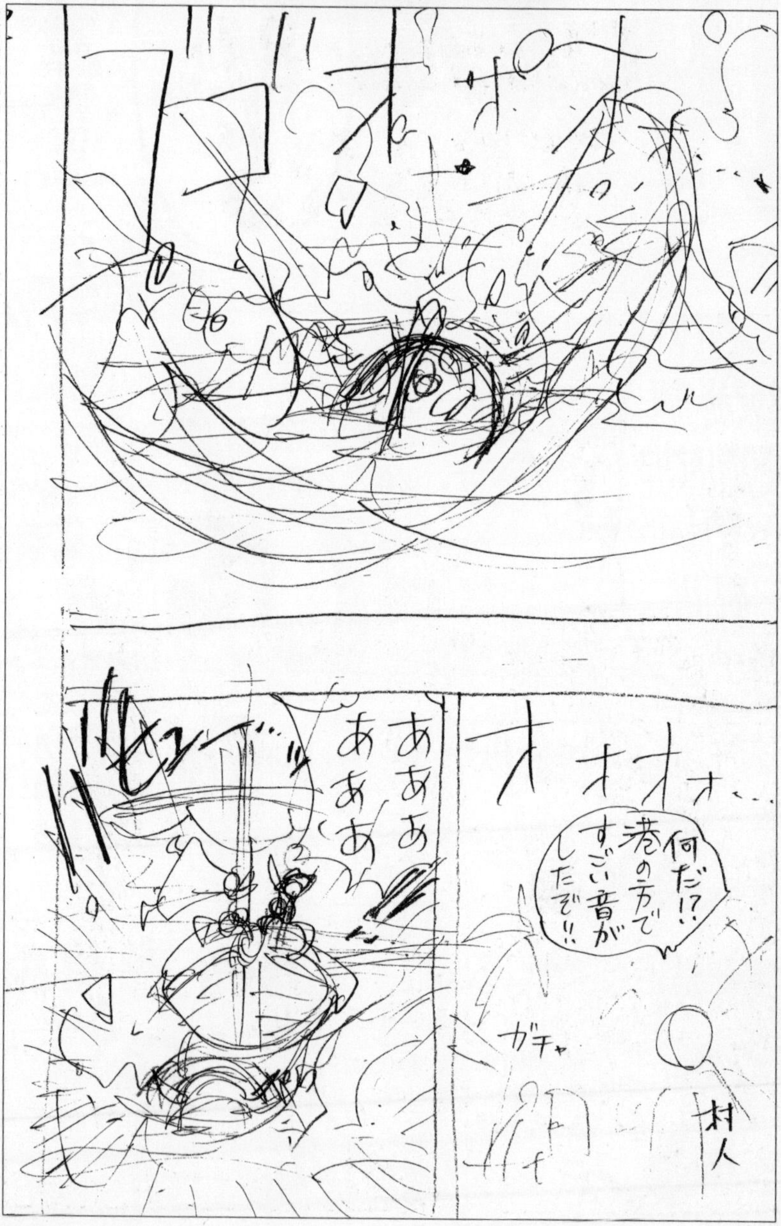
オオオオ…
何だ!? 港の方ですごい音がしたぞ!!
ガチャ
村人
あああああああ

Chapter 81:
TEARS

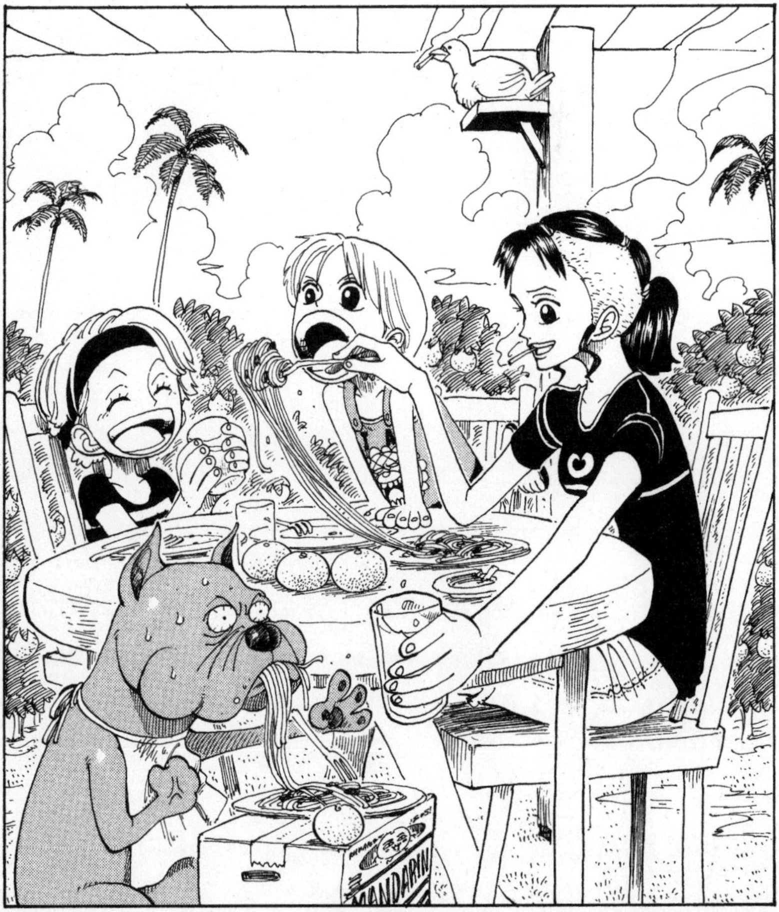
MANDARIN

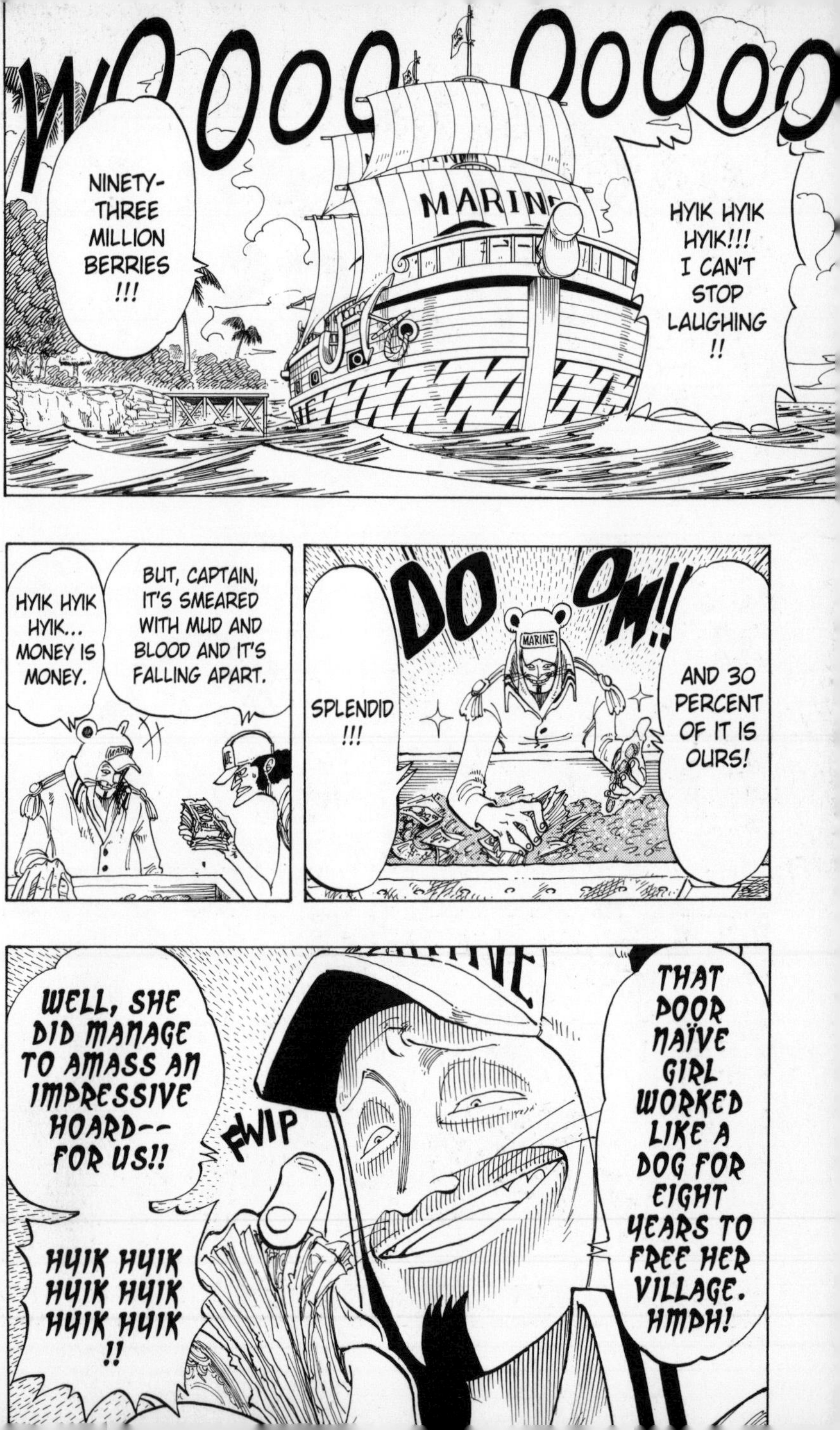
WOOOOO OOOOOO
MARINE
HYIK HYIK HYIK!!! I CAN'T STOP LAUGHING !!
NINETY-THREE MILLION BERRIES !!!
DOOM!!
AND 30 PERCENT OF IT IS OURS!
SPLENDID !!!
BUT, CAPTAIN, IT'S SMEARED WITH MUD AND BLOOD AND IT'S FALLING APART.
HYIK HYIK HYIK... MONEY IS MONEY.
THAT POOR NAÏVE GIRL WORKED LIKE A DOG FOR EIGHT YEARS TO FREE HER VILLAGE. HMPH!
WELL, SHE DID MANAGE TO AMASS AN IMPRESSIVE HOARD-- FOR US!!
FWIP
HYIK HYIK HYIK HYIK HYIK HYIK !!

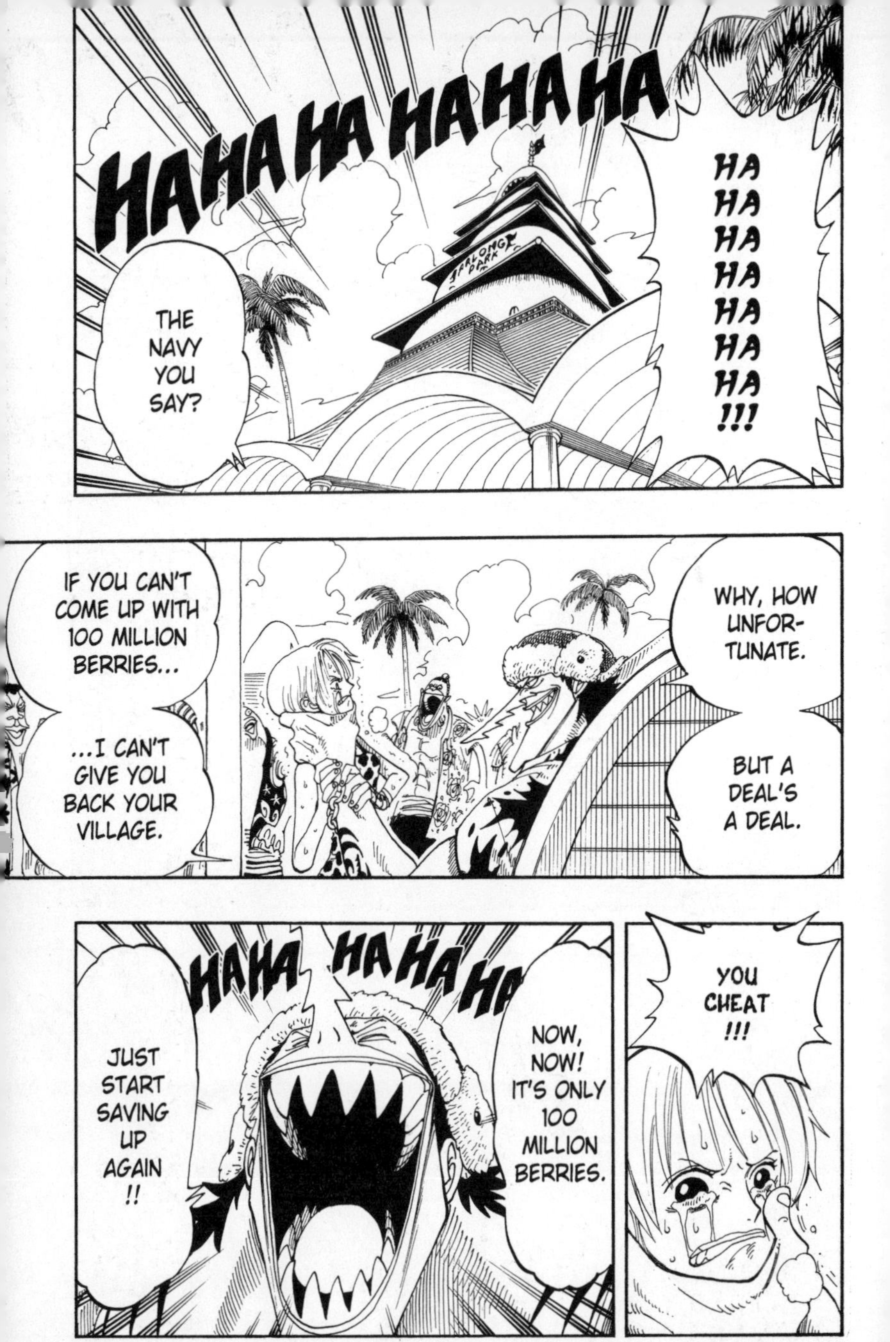
HAHAHA HAHAHA
HA HA HA HA HA HA HA!!!
THE NAVY YOU SAY?
WHY, HOW UNFORTUNATE.
BUT A DEAL'S A DEAL.
IF YOU CAN'T COME UP WITH 100 MILLION BERRIES...
...I CAN'T GIVE YOU BACK YOUR VILLAGE.
YOU CHEAT!!!
HAHA HAHAHA
NOW, NOW! IT'S ONLY 100 MILLION BERRIES.
JUST START SAVING UP AGAIN!!

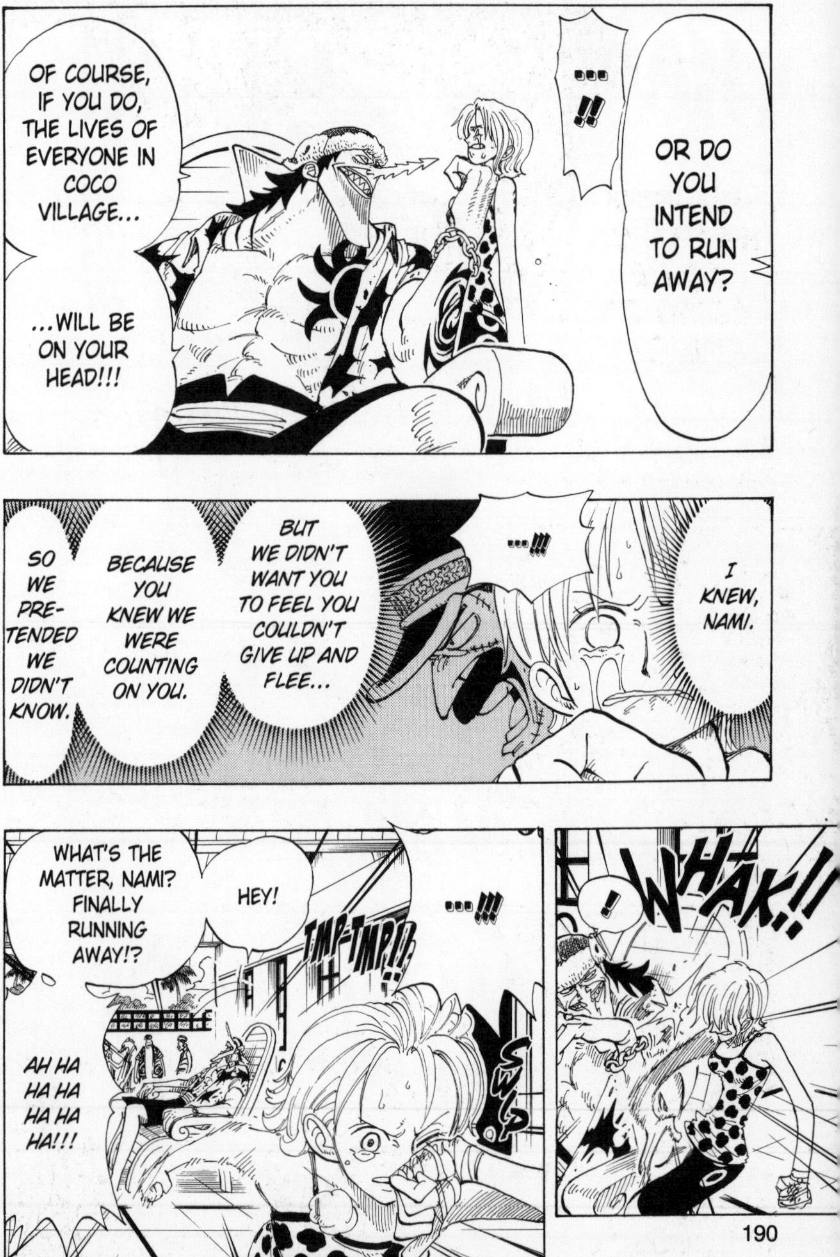
OR DO YOU INTEND TO RUN AWAY?
...!!
OF COURSE, IF YOU DO, THE LIVES OF EVERYONE IN COCO VILLAGE...
...WILL BE ON YOUR HEAD!!!
I KNEW, NAMI.
...!!!
BUT WE DIDN'T WANT YOU TO FEEL YOU COULDN'T GIVE UP AND FLEE...
BECAUSE YOU KNEW WE WERE COUNTING ON YOU.
SO WE PRE-TENDED WE DIDN'T KNOW.
WHAK!!
!
...!!!
TMP TMP!!
HEY!
WHAT'S THE MATTER, NAMI? FINALLY RUNNING AWAY!?
SWIP
AH HA HA HA HA HA HA!!!

READ THIS WAY

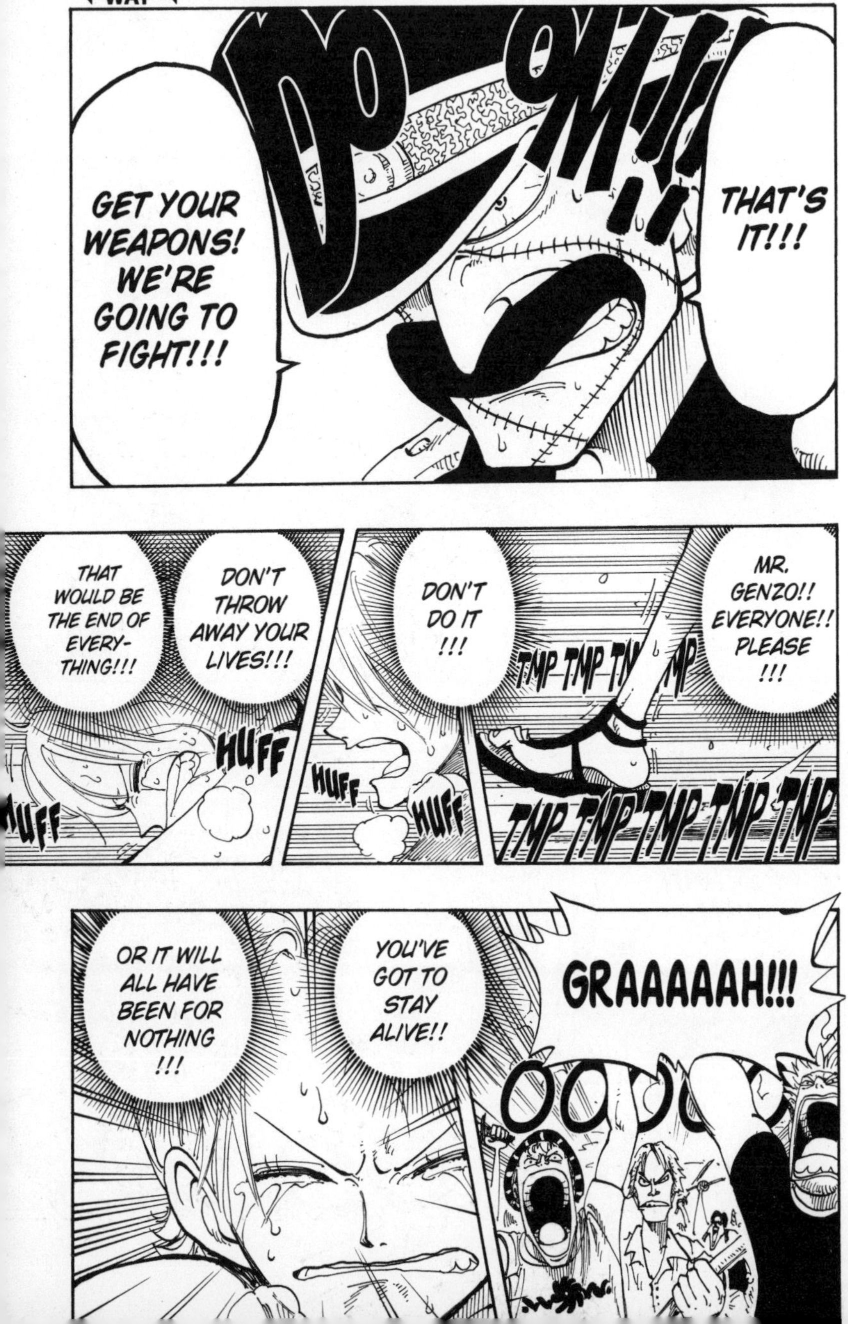
DOOM!!
THAT'S IT!!!
GET YOUR WEAPONS! WE'RE GOING TO FIGHT!!!
MR. GENZO!! EVERYONE!! PLEASE !!!
TMP TMP TMP TMP
TMP TMP TMP TMP TMP
DON'T DO IT !!!
HUFF
HUFF
DON'T THROW AWAY YOUR LIVES!!!
THAT WOULD BE THE END OF EVERY-THING!!!
HUFF
HUFF
GRAAAAAH!!!
YOU'VE GOT TO STAY ALIVE!!
OR IT WILL ALL HAVE BEEN FOR NOTHING !!!

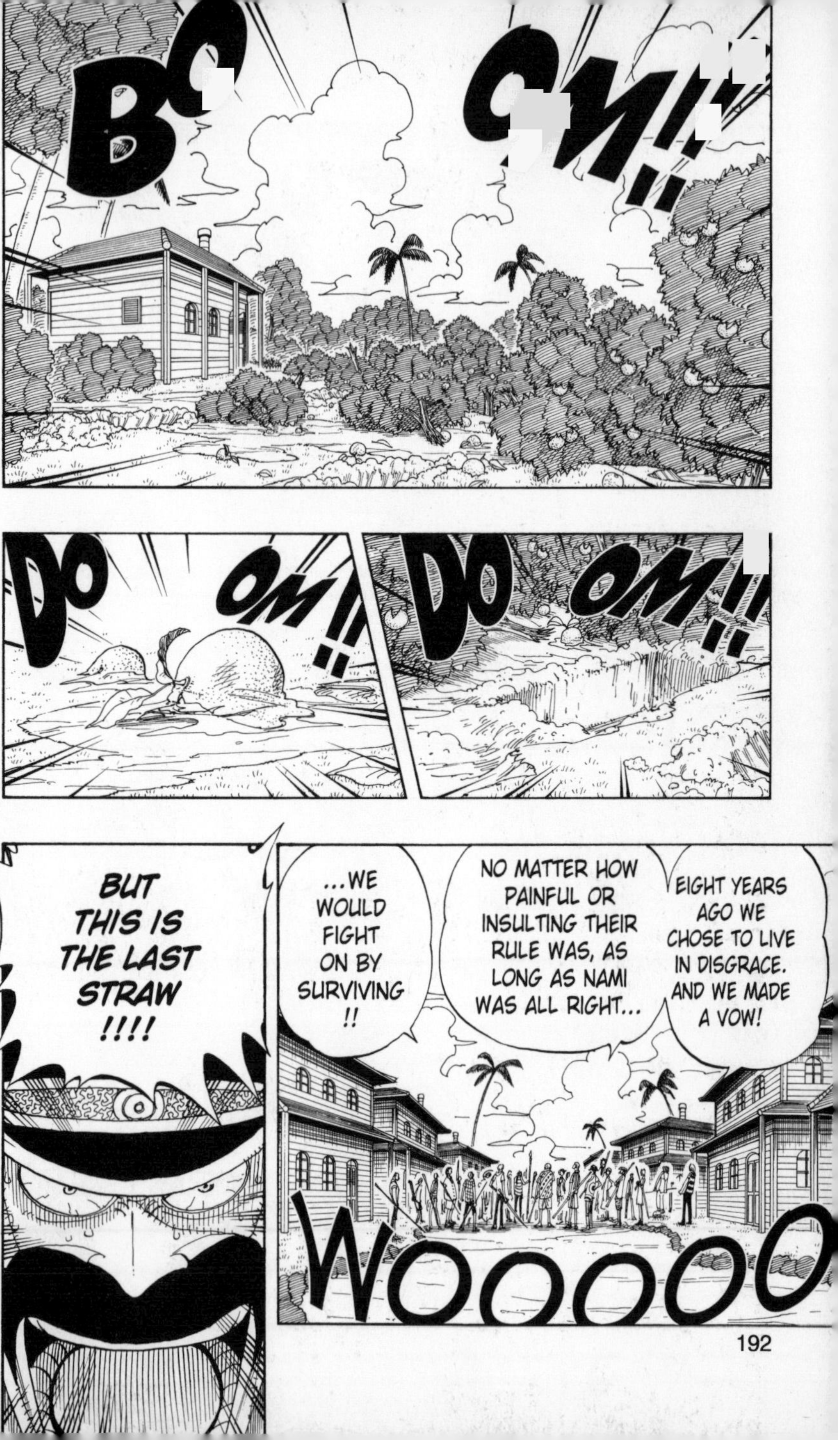
BOOM!!
DOOM!!
DOOM!!
EIGHT YEARS AGO WE CHOSE TO LIVE IN DISGRACE. AND WE MADE A VOW!
NO MATTER HOW PAINFUL OR INSULTING THEIR RULE WAS, AS LONG AS NAMI WAS ALL RIGHT...
...WE WOULD FIGHT ON BY SURVIVING!!
WOOOOOO
BUT THIS IS THE LAST STRAW!!!!

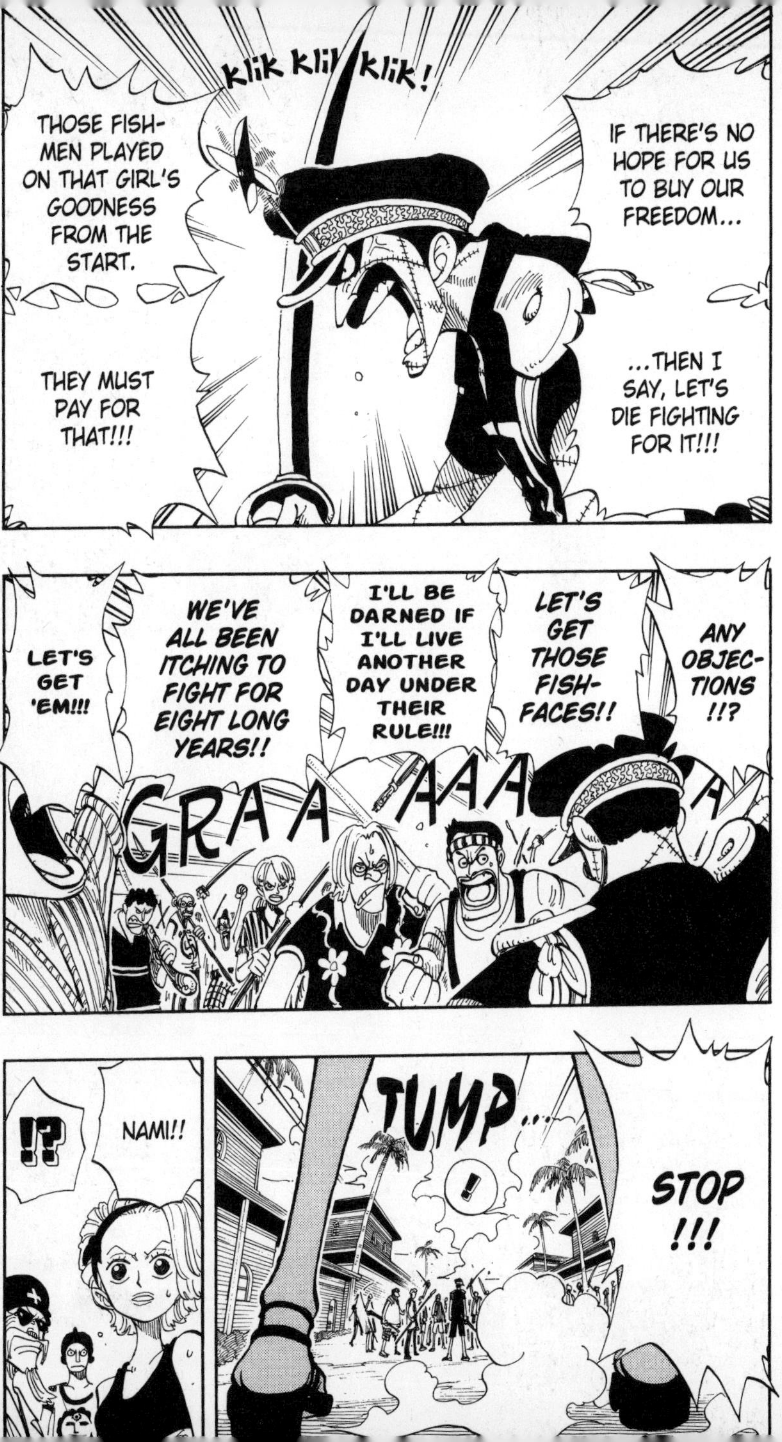
KLIK KLIK KLIK!
IF THERE'S NO HOPE FOR US TO BUY OUR FREEDOM...
...THEN I SAY, LET'S DIE FIGHTING FOR IT!!!
THOSE FISH-MEN PLAYED ON THAT GIRL'S GOODNESS FROM THE START.
THEY MUST PAY FOR THAT!!!
ANY OBJEC-TIONS!!?
LET'S GET THOSE FISH-FACES!!
I'LL BE DARNED IF I'LL LIVE ANOTHER DAY UNDER THEIR RULE!!!
WE'VE ALL BEEN ITCHING TO FIGHT FOR EIGHT LONG YEARS!!
LET'S GET 'EM!!!
GRAAAAAA
TUMP...
!
STOP!!!
NAMI!!
!?

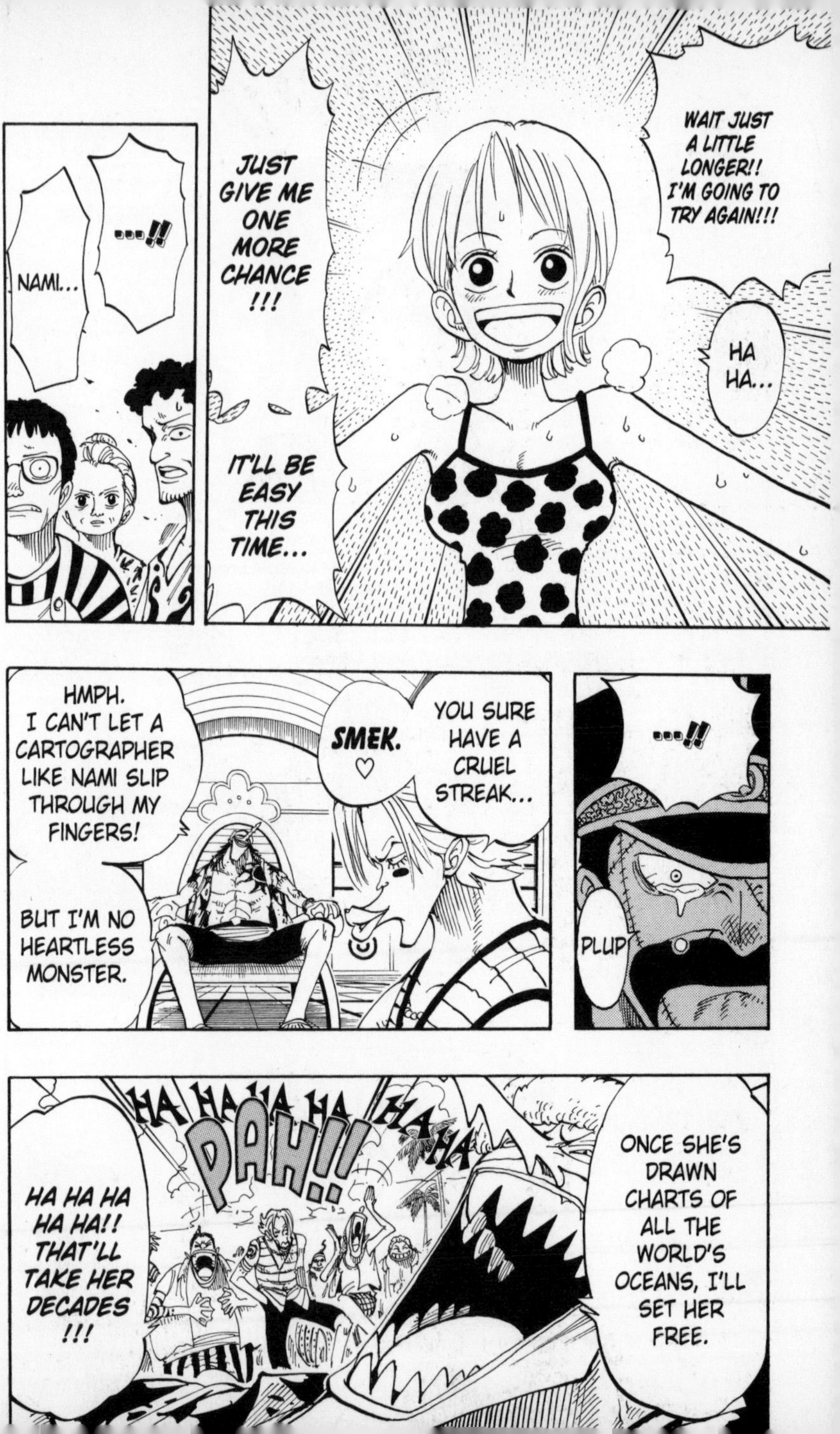
WAIT JUST A LITTLE LONGER!! I'M GOING TO TRY AGAIN!!!
HA HA...
JUST GIVE ME ONE MORE CHANCE!!!
IT'LL BE EASY THIS TIME...
...!!
NAMI...
...!!
PLUP
YOU SURE HAVE A CRUEL STREAK...
SMEK. ♡
HMPH. I CAN'T LET A CARTOGRAPHER LIKE NAMI SLIP THROUGH MY FINGERS!
BUT I'M NO HEARTLESS MONSTER.
ONCE SHE'S DRAWN CHARTS OF ALL THE WORLD'S OCEANS, I'LL SET HER FREE.
HA HA HA HA HA HA HA
PAH!!
HA HA HA HA!! THAT'LL TAKE HER DECADES!!!

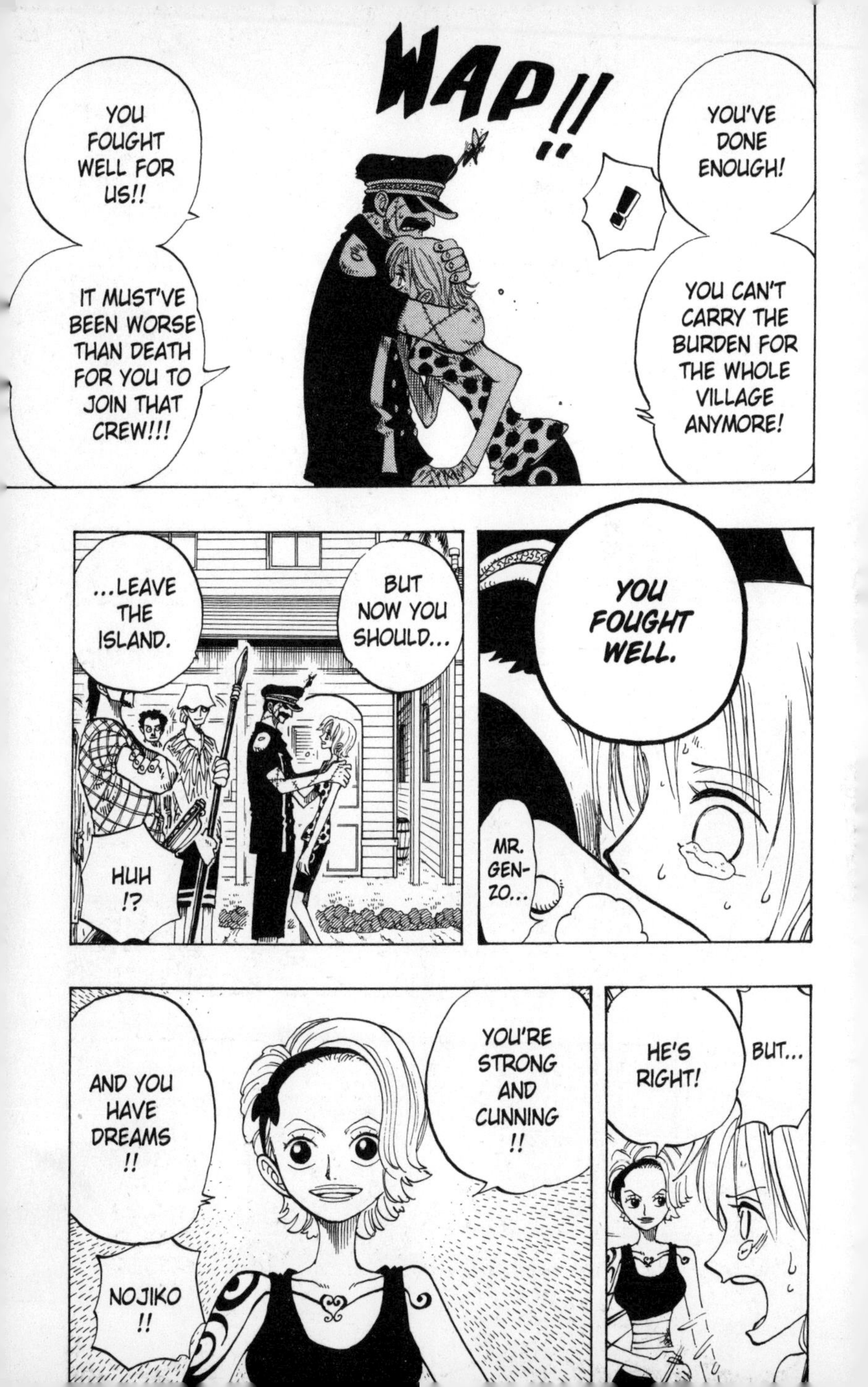
WAP!!
YOU'VE DONE ENOUGH!
!
YOU CAN'T CARRY THE BURDEN FOR THE WHOLE VILLAGE ANYMORE!
YOU FOUGHT WELL FOR US!!
IT MUST'VE BEEN WORSE THAN DEATH FOR YOU TO JOIN THAT CREW!!!
YOU FOUGHT WELL.
MR. GEN-ZO...
BUT NOW YOU SHOULD...
...LEAVE THE ISLAND.
HUH !?
BUT...
HE'S RIGHT!
YOU'RE STRONG AND CUNNING !!
AND YOU HAVE DREAMS !!
NOJIKO !!

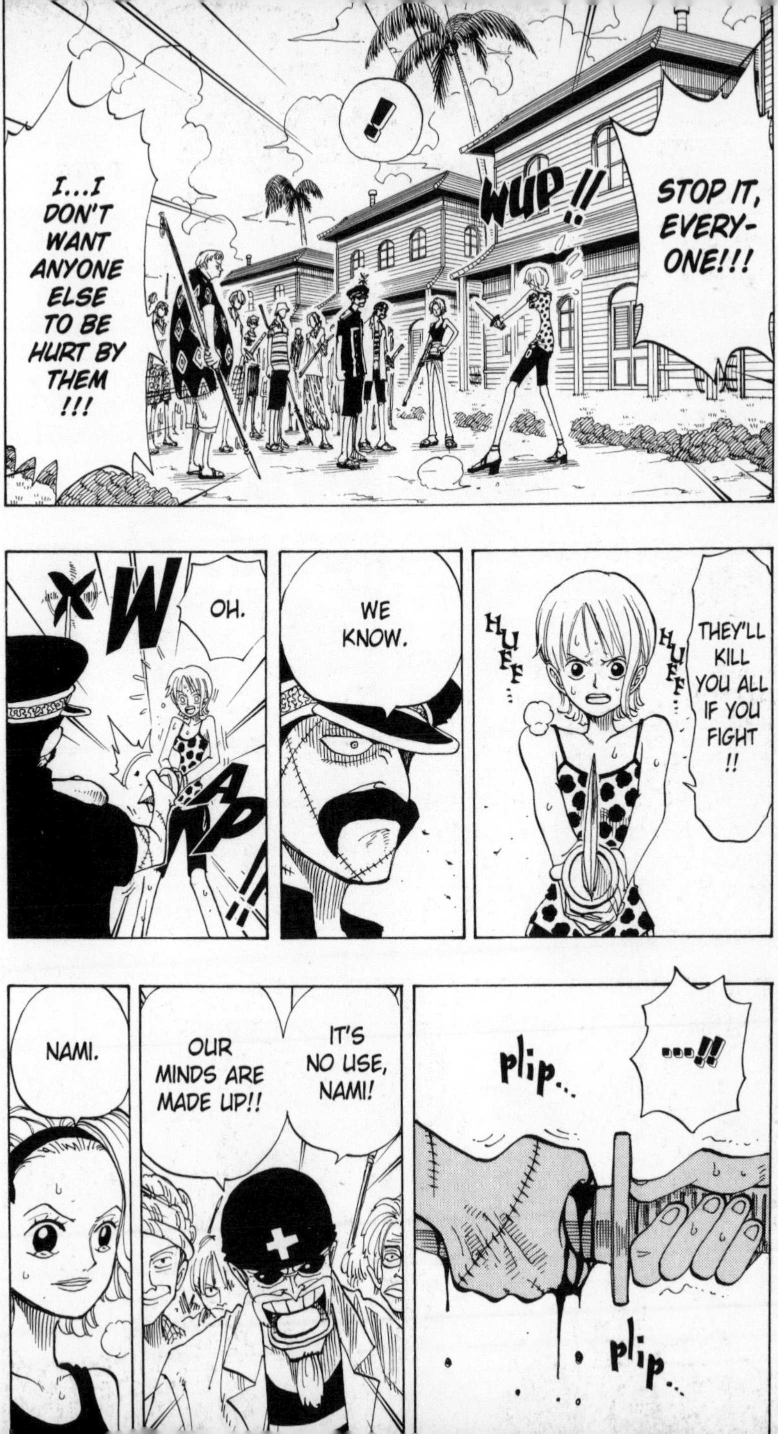
STOP IT, EVERY-ONE!!!
WUP!!
!
I...I DON'T WANT ANYONE ELSE TO BE HURT BY THEM !!!
HUFF HUFF...
THEY'LL KILL YOU ALL IF YOU FIGHT !!
WE KNOW.
OH.
...!!
plip...
plip...
IT'S NO USE, NAMI!
OUR MINDS ARE MADE UP!!
NAMI.

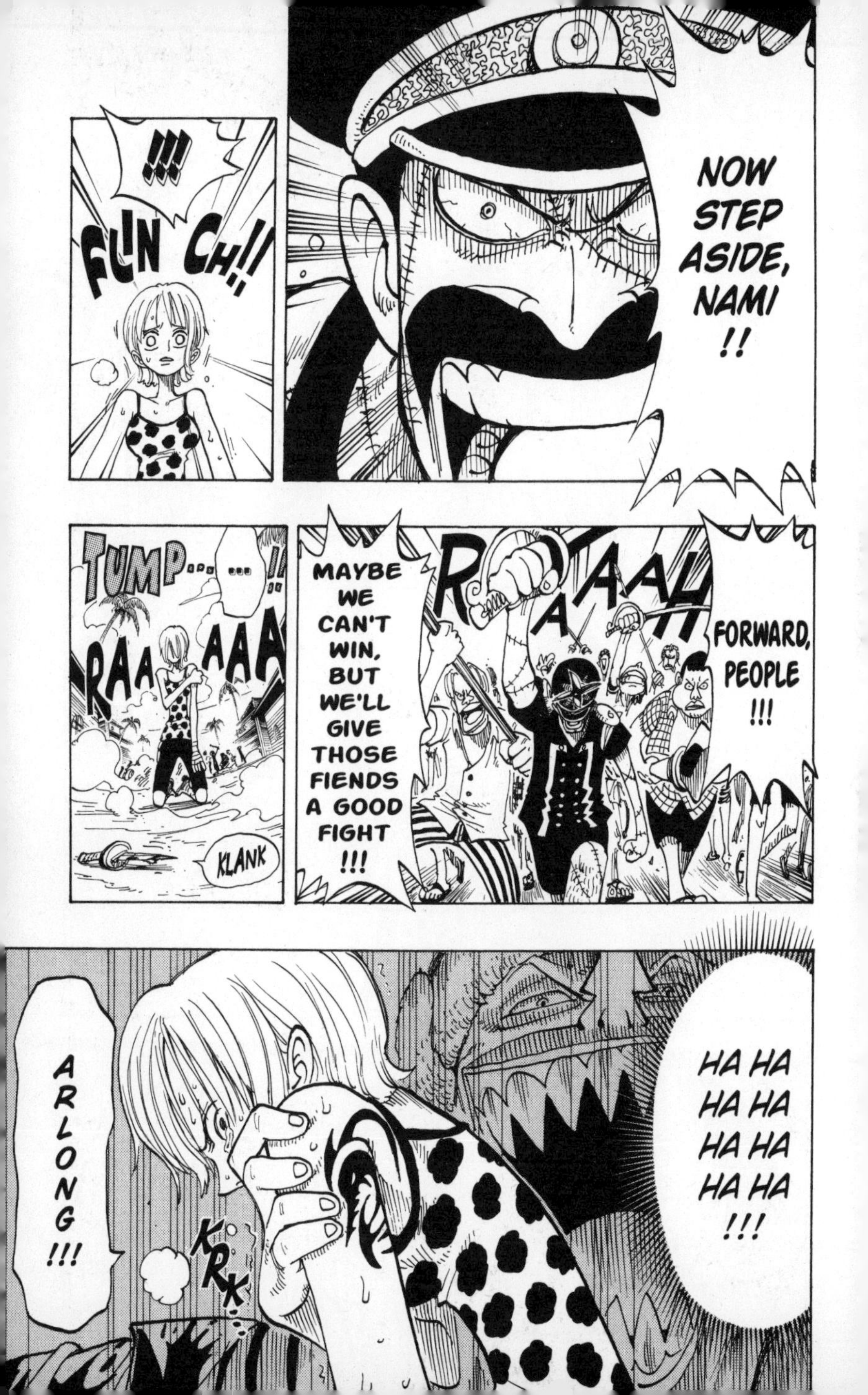
NOW STEP ASIDE, NAMI !!
!!!!
FLINCH!!
FORWARD, PEOPLE !!!
RAAAAH
MAYBE WE CAN'T WIN, BUT WE'LL GIVE THOSE FIENDS A GOOD FIGHT !!!
TUMP...
...
!!
RAAAAA
KLANK
HA HA HA HA HA HA HA HA !!!
ARLONG !!!
KRK

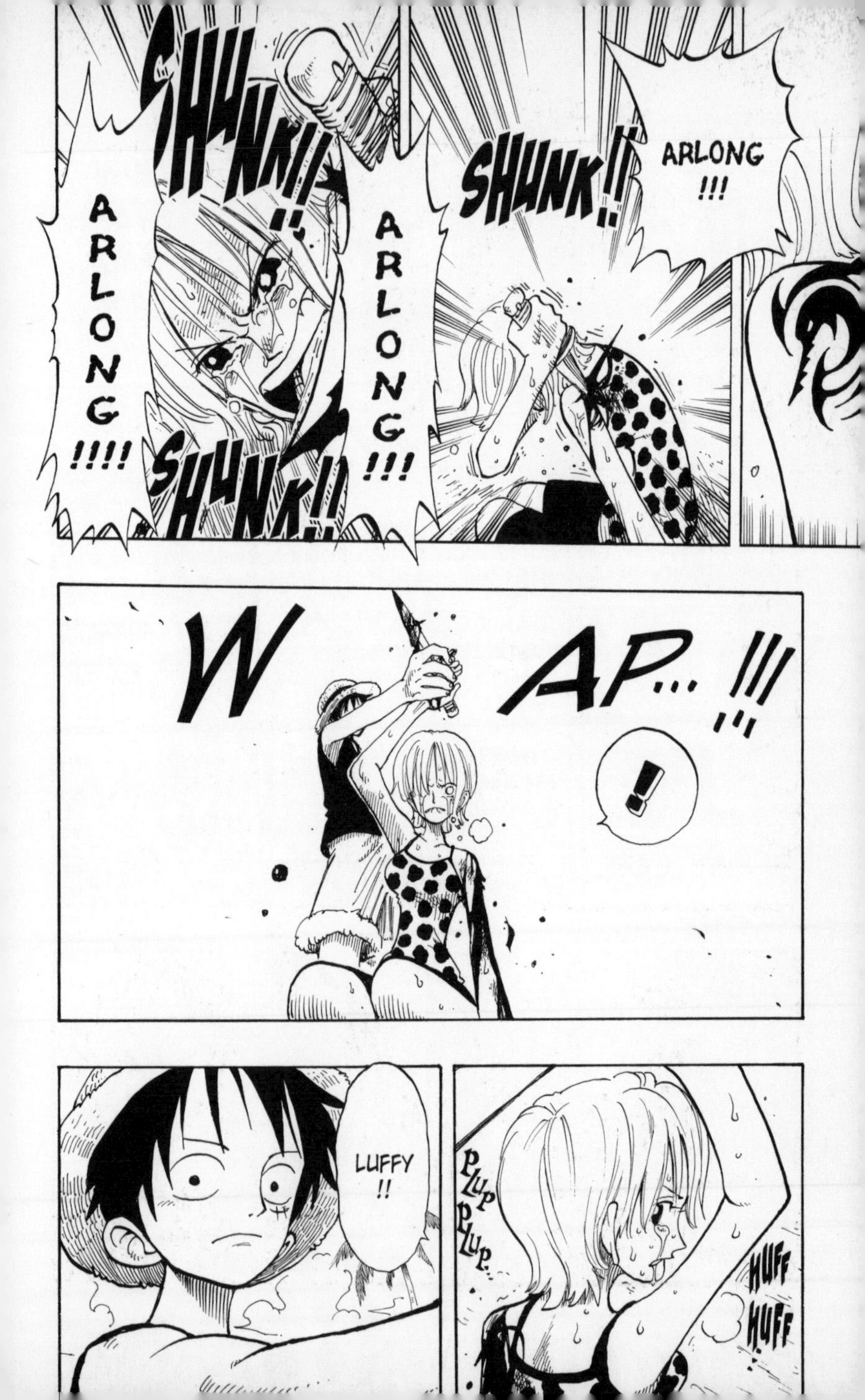
ARLONG !!!
SHUNK!!
ARLONG!!!
SHUNK!!
ARLONG!!!!
SHUNK!!
W AP...!!!
!
HUFF HUFF
PLUP PLUP...
LUFFY !!

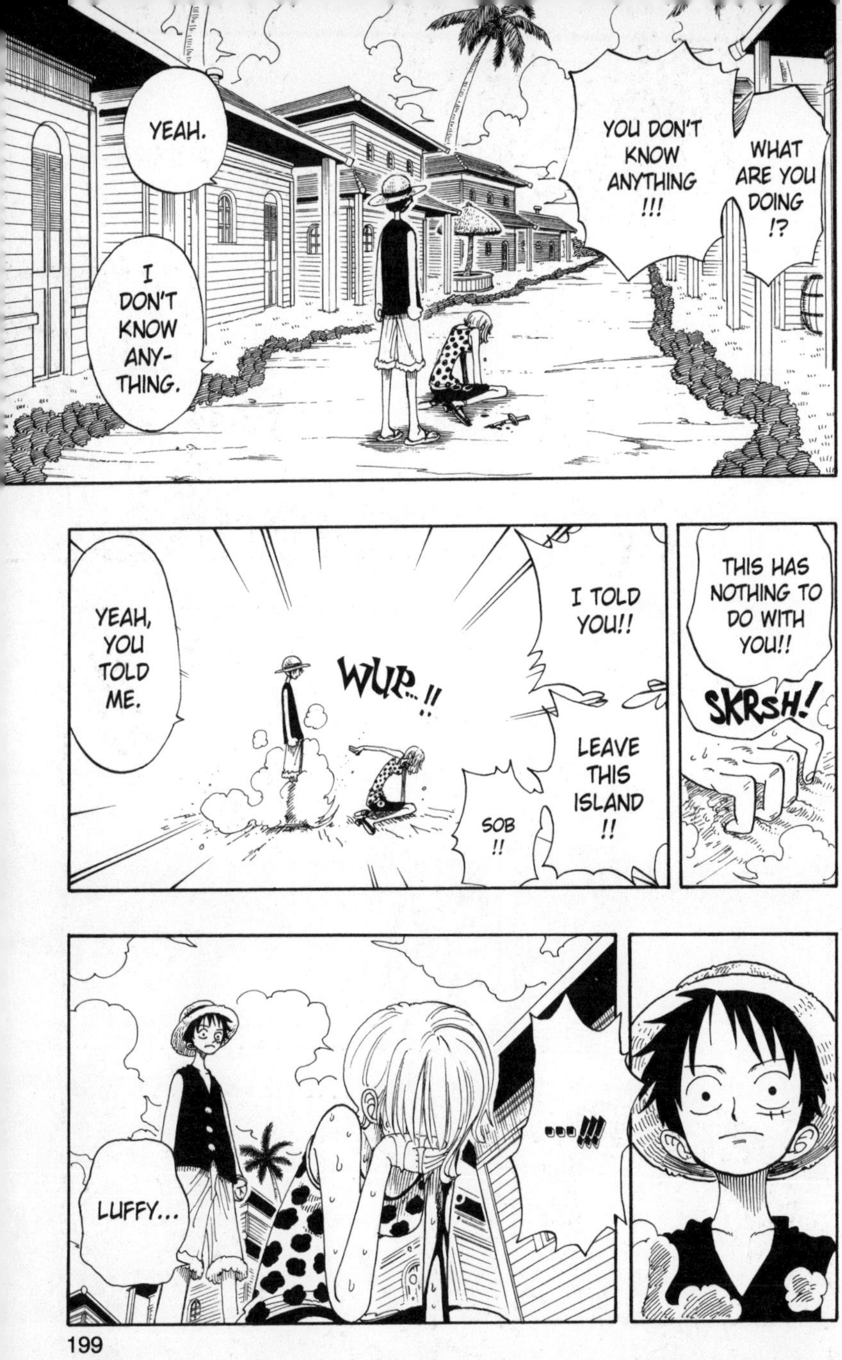
WHAT ARE YOU DOING !?
YOU DON'T KNOW ANYTHING !!!
YEAH.
I DON'T KNOW ANY-THING.
THIS HAS NOTHING TO DO WITH YOU!!
SKRSH!
I TOLD YOU!!
LEAVE THIS ISLAND !!
SOB !!
WUP..!!
YEAH, YOU TOLD ME.
...!!!
LUFFY...

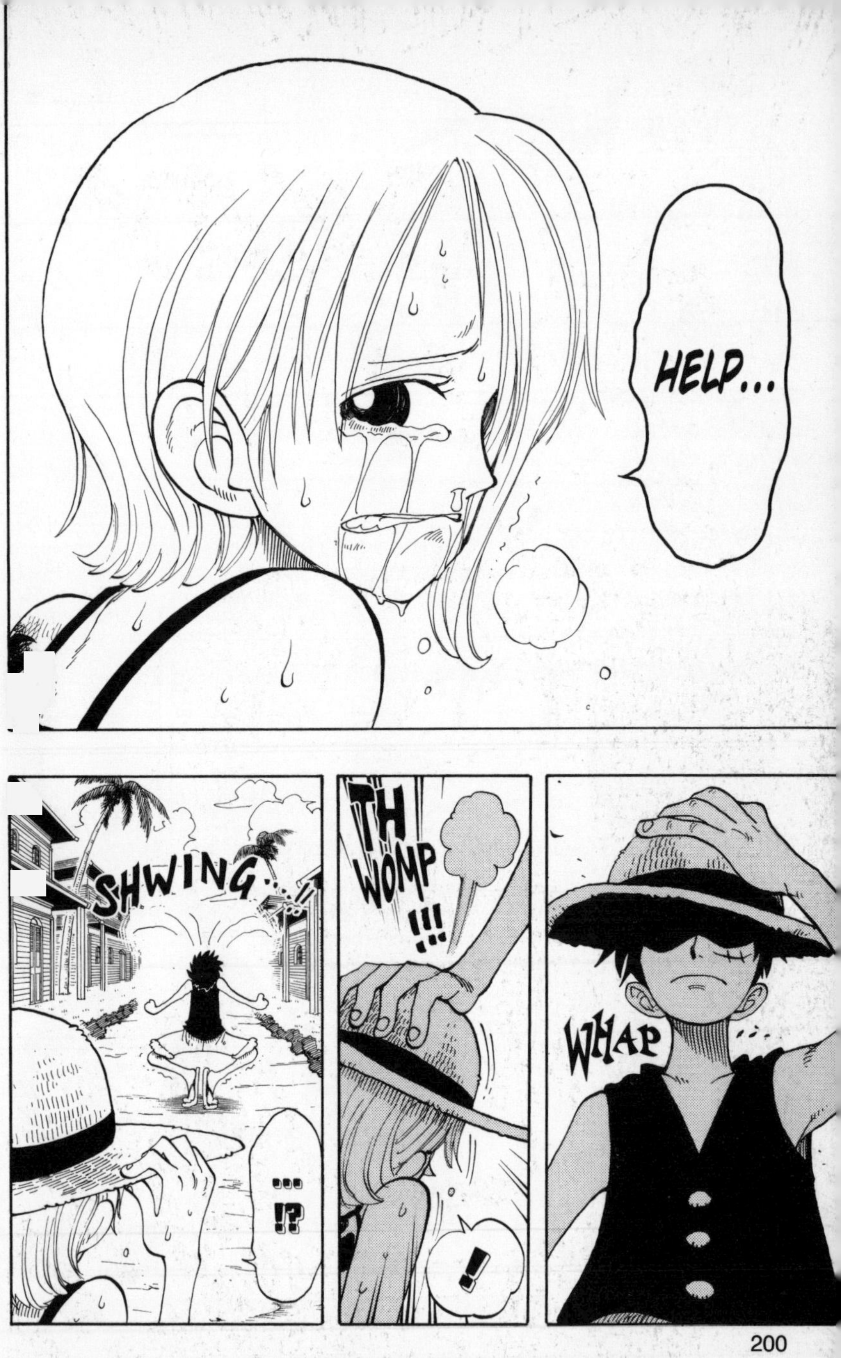
HELP...
WHAP
TH WOMP !!!
!
SHWING...!!
...!?

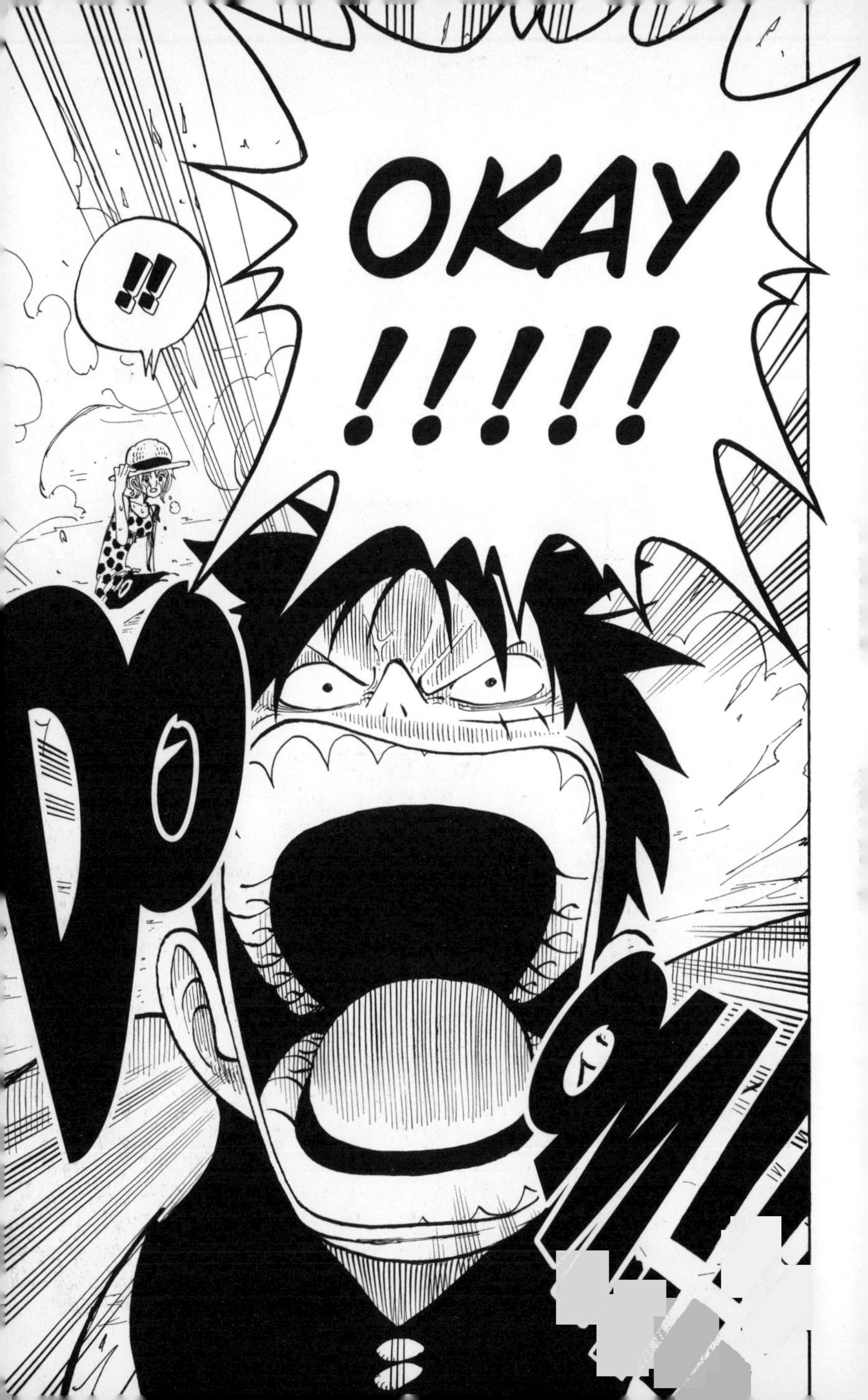
OKAY
!!!!!
!!

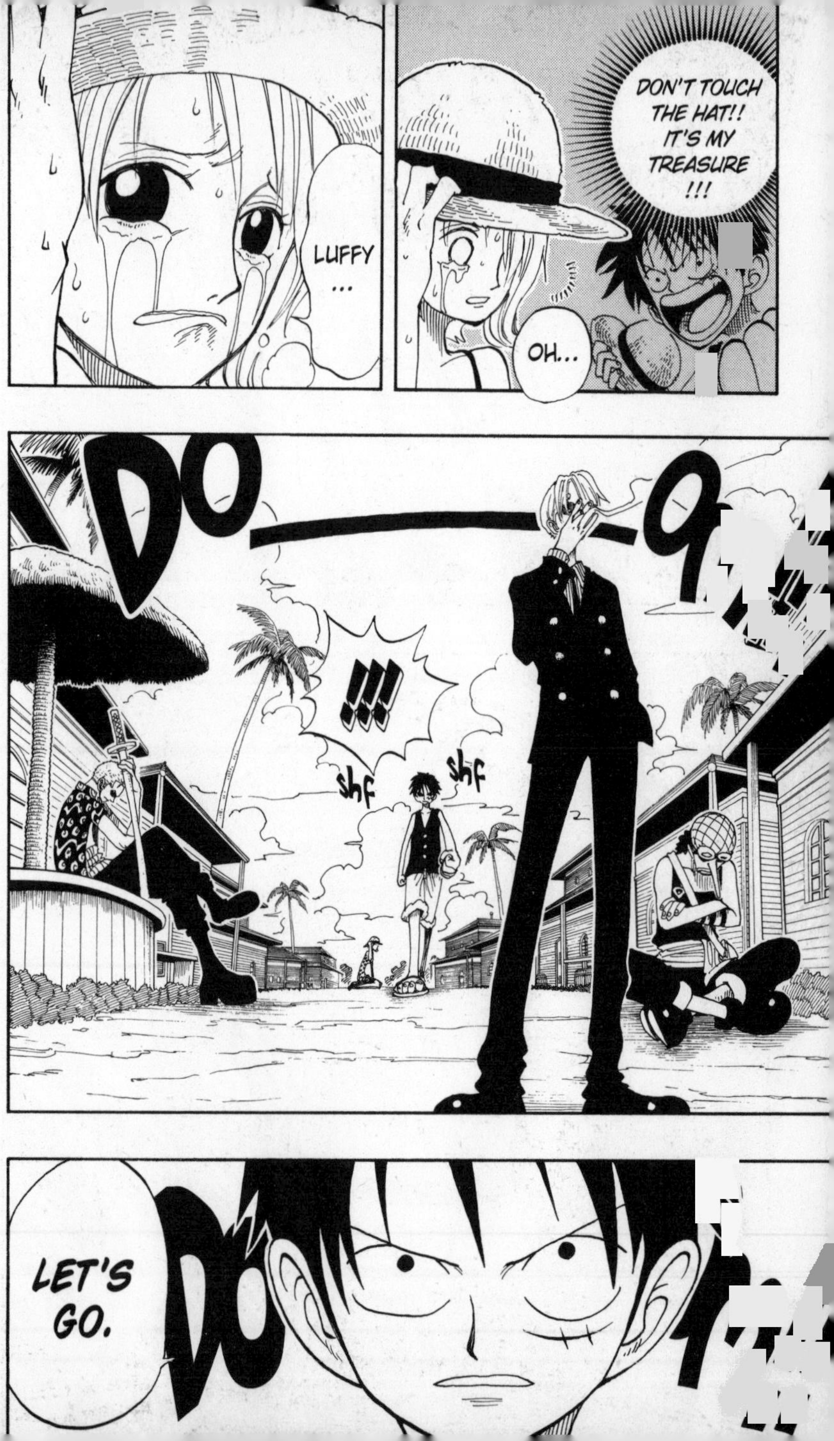
DON'T TOUCH THE HAT!! IT'S MY TREASURE !!!
OH...
LUFFY ...
DO
!!!!
shf
shf
LET'S GO.
DO

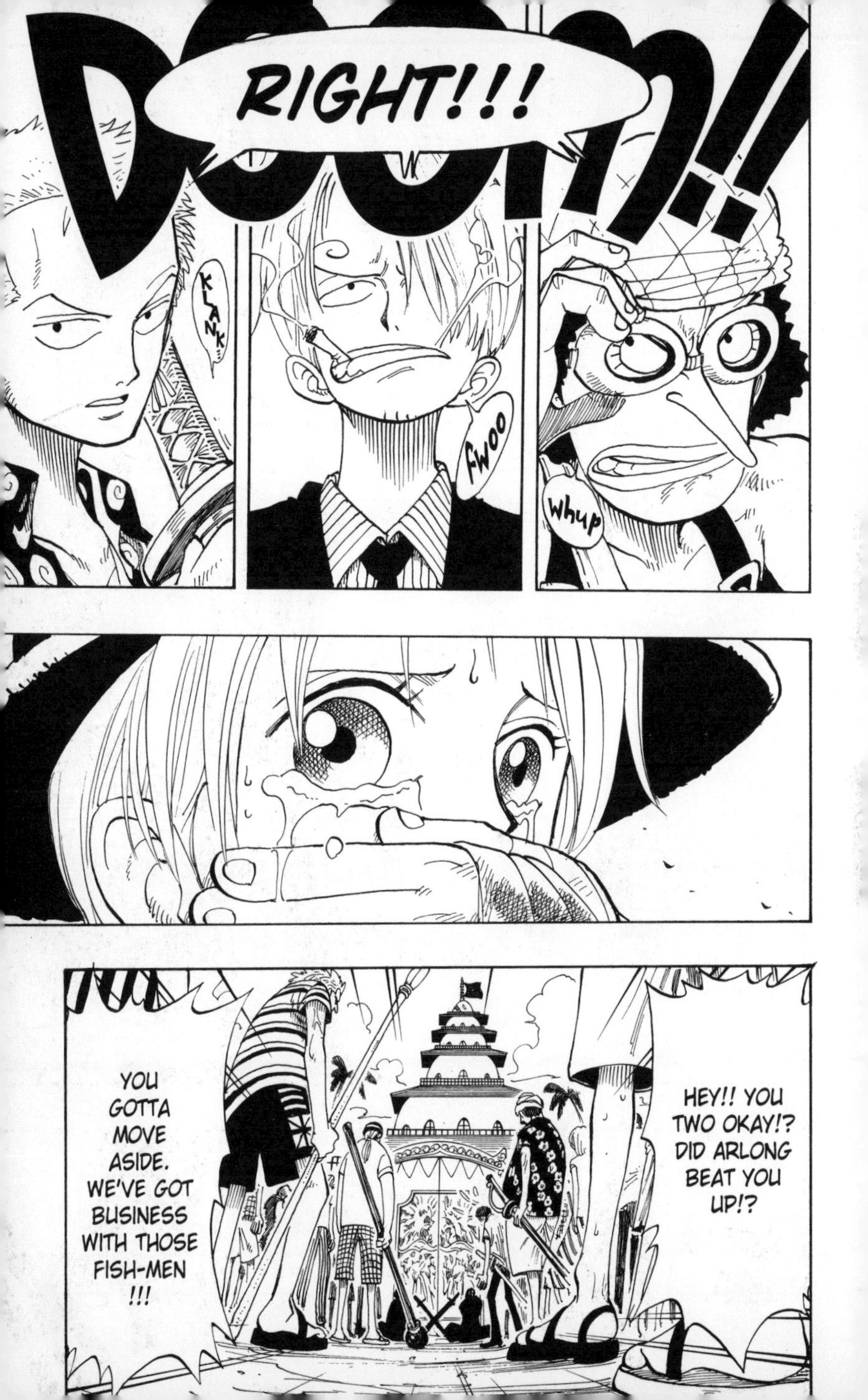
RIGHT!!!
whup
fwoo
KLANK
HEY!! YOU TWO OKAY!? DID ARLONG BEAT YOU UP!?
YOU GOTTA MOVE ASIDE. WE'VE GOT BUSINESS WITH THOSE FISH-MEN!!!

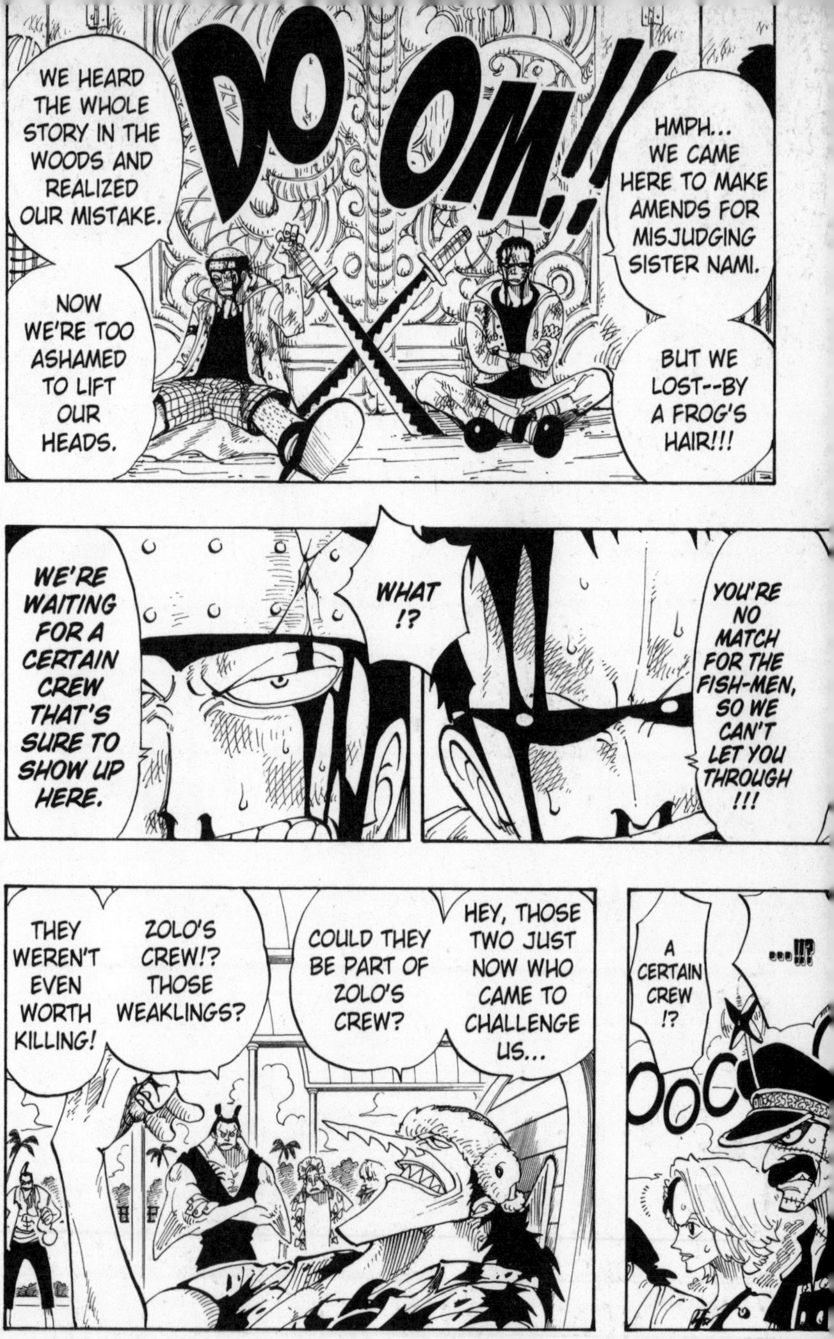
DOOM!!
HMPH... WE CAME HERE TO MAKE AMENDS FOR MISJUDGING SISTER NAMI.
WE HEARD THE WHOLE STORY IN THE WOODS AND REALIZED OUR MISTAKE.
BUT WE LOST--BY A FROG'S HAIR!!!
NOW WE'RE TOO ASHAMED TO LIFT OUR HEADS.
YOU'RE NO MATCH FOR THE FISH-MEN, SO WE CAN'T LET YOU THROUGH !!!
WHAT !?
WE'RE WAITING FOR A CERTAIN CREW THAT'S SURE TO SHOW UP HERE.
...!!?
A CERTAIN CREW !?
HEY, THOSE TWO JUST NOW WHO CAME TO CHALLENGE US...
COULD THEY BE PART OF ZOLO'S CREW?
ZOLO'S CREW!? THOSE WEAKLINGS?
THEY WEREN'T EVEN WORTH KILLING!

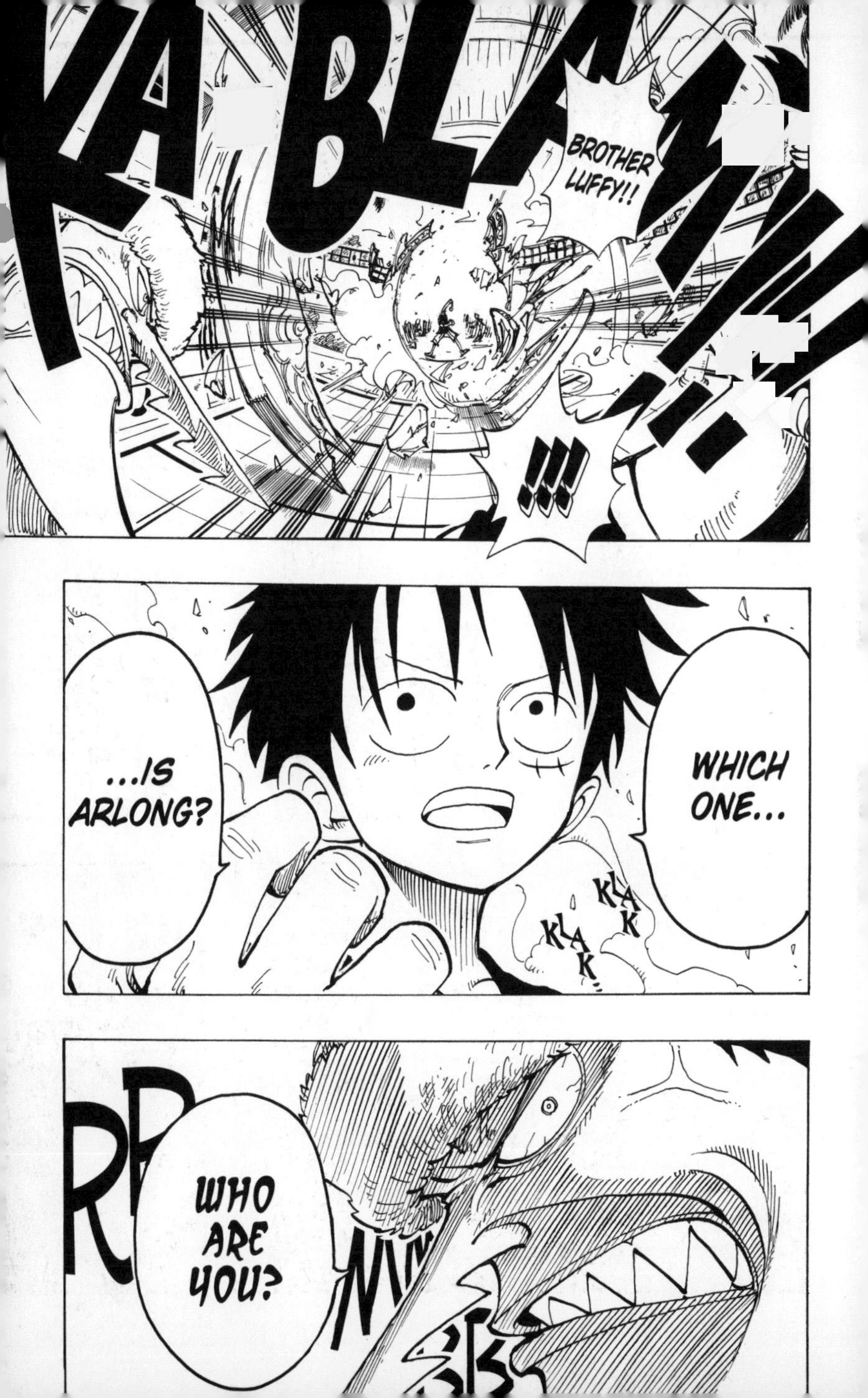
BROTHER LUFFY!!
!!!!
WHICH ONE...
...IS ARLONG?
KLAK
KLAK...
WHO ARE YOU?

COMING NEXT VOLUME:

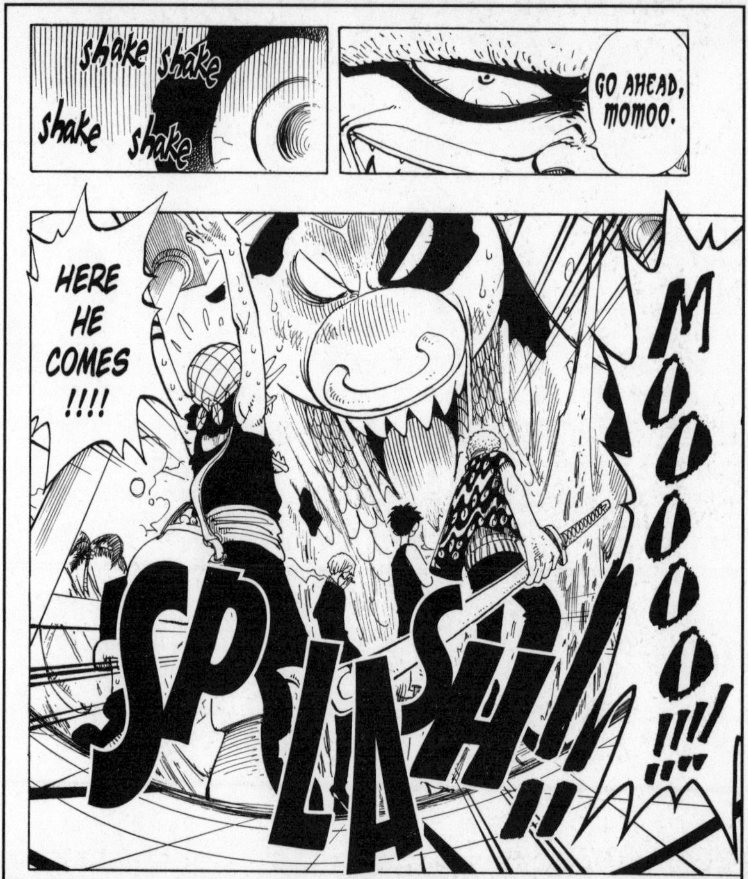
GO AHEAD, MOMOO.
shake shake
shake shake
MOOOOO!!!!!
HERE HE COMES!!!!
SPLASH!!

Luffy marches straight to Captain Arlong's lair for a showdown with the cold-blooded pirate. Before he gets down to business, however, the Fish-Men call on the ferocious sea monster from the Grand Line, Momoo, to turn Luffy and his crew into fish paste. But then Luffy loses his cool and makes a move that has *everyone* running for cover!

ON SALE NOW!

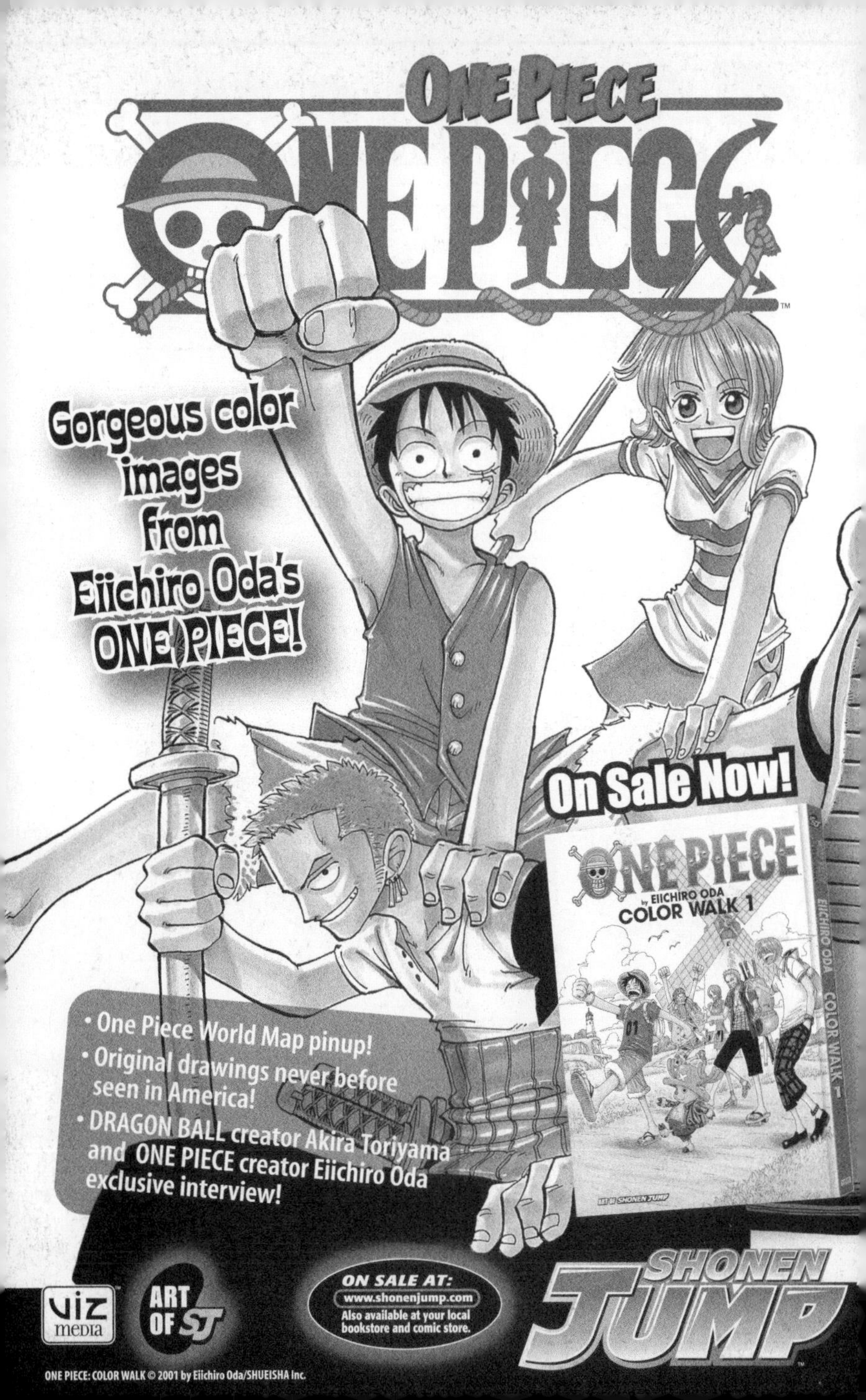
ONE PIECE
ONE PIECE™
Gorgeous color images from Eiichiro Oda's ONE PIECE!
On Sale Now!
ONE PIECE by EIICHIRO ODA COLOR WALK 1
EIICHIRO ODA COLOR WALK 1
ART OF SHONEN JUMP
• One Piece World Map pinup!
• Original drawings never before seen in America!
• DRAGON BALL creator Akira Toriyama and ONE PIECE creator Eiichiro Oda exclusive interview!
viz media
ART OF SJ
ON SALE AT:
www.shonenjump.com
Also available at your local bookstore and comic store.
SHONEN JUMP™
ONE PIECE: COLOR WALK © 2001 by Eiichiro Oda/SHUEISHA Inc.

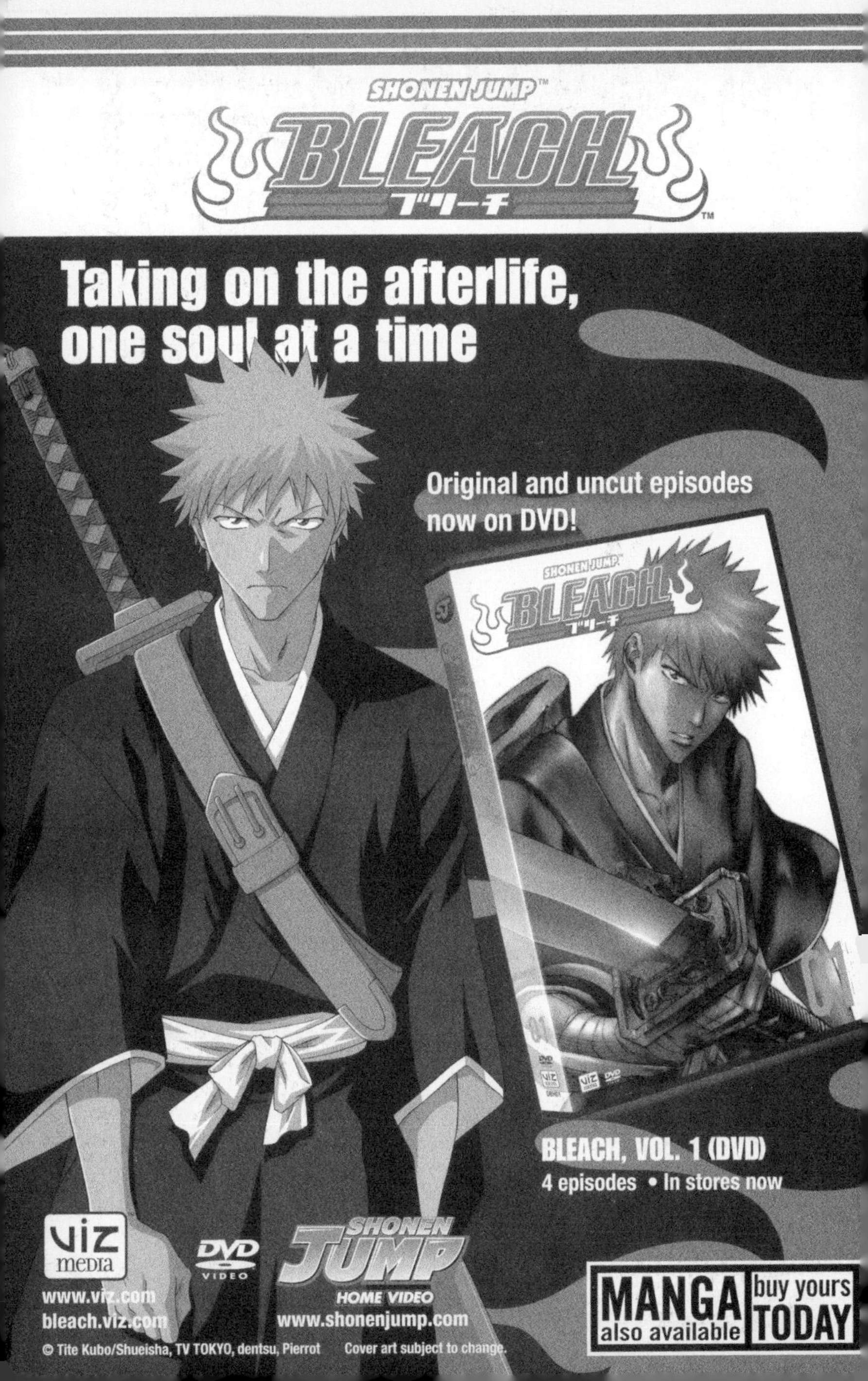

A BRUSH WITH THE AFTERLIFE

All Colour But The Black

THE ART OF BLEACH

By Tite Kubo, creator of *ZOMBIEPOWDER*.

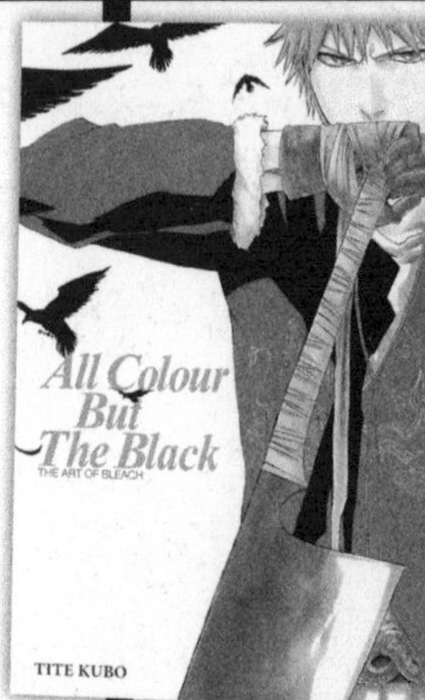
All Colour
But
The Black
THE ART OF BLEACH
TITE KUBO

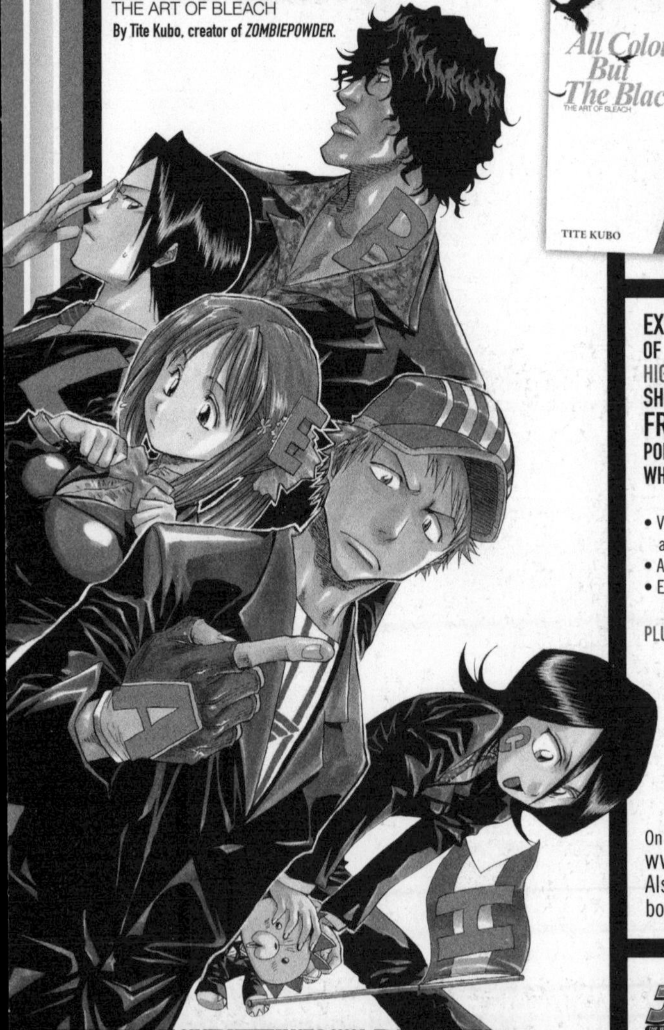

EXPLORE THE WORLD OF *BLEACH* THROUGH THIS HIGH-QUALITY ART BOOK SHOWCASING ARTWORK FROM TITE KUBO'S POPULAR MANGA SERIES, WHICH INCLUDES:

- Vibrant illustrations, including art from volumes 1-19
- An annotated art guide
- Extra character information

PLUS, AN EXCLUSIVE POSTER!

COMPLETE YOUR *BLEACH* COLLECTION WITH *THE ART OF BLEACH: ALL COLOUR BUT THE BLACK*— GET YOURS TODAY!

On sale at www.shonenjump.com
Also available at your local bookstore and comic store.

THE WORLD'S MOST POPULAR MANGA
www.shonenjump.com

www.viz.com

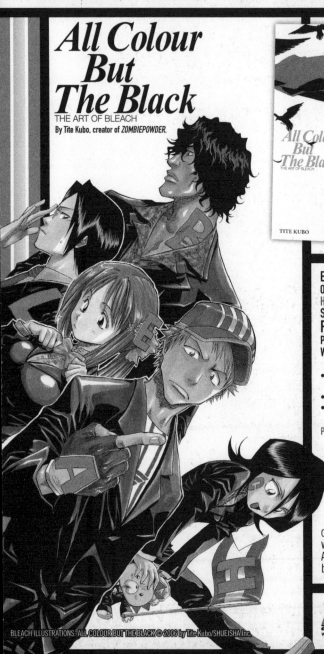

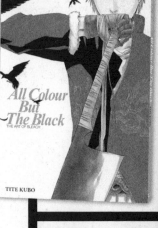

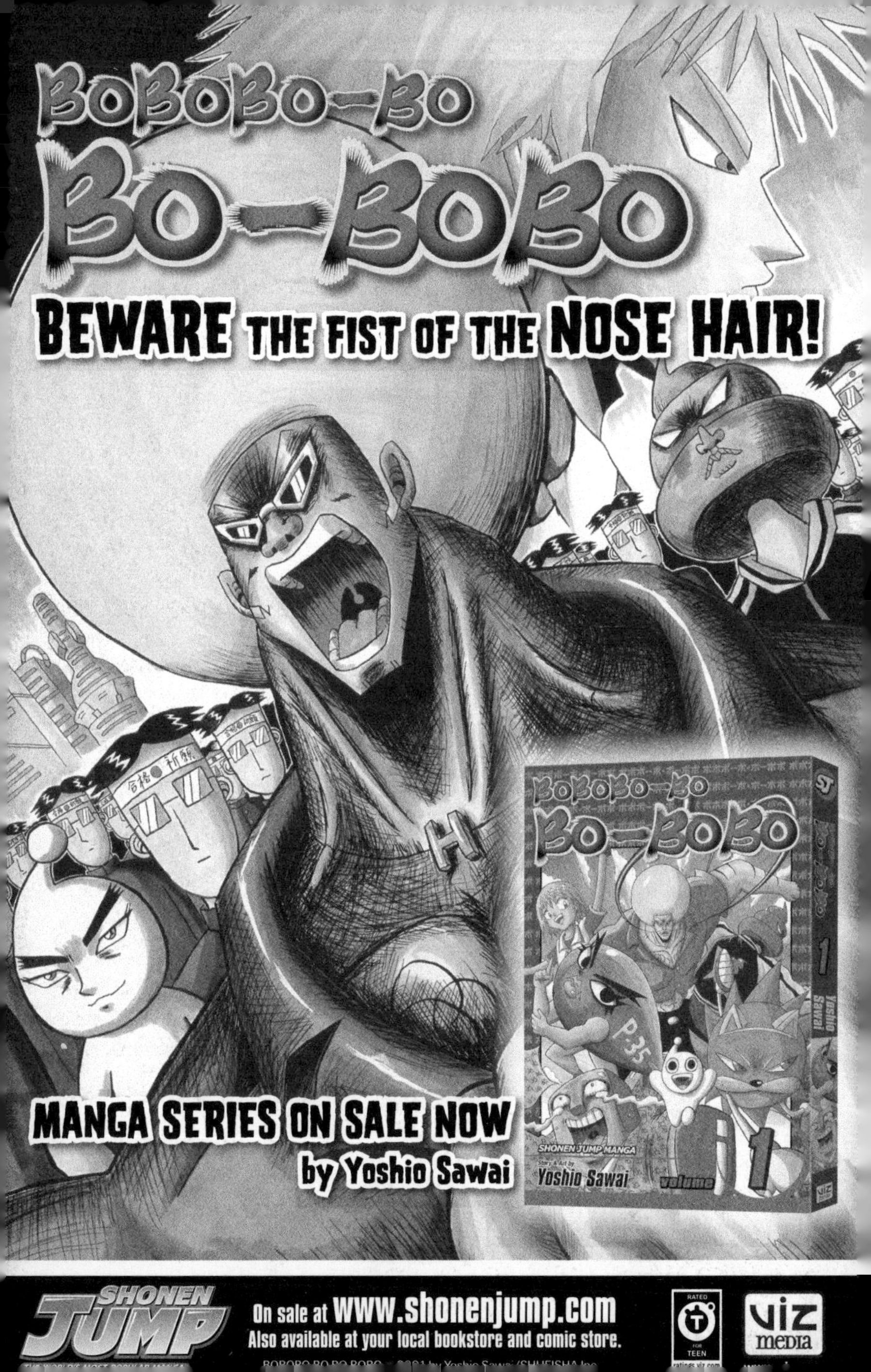
BOBOBO-BO
BO-BOBO
BEWARE THE FIST OF THE NOSE HAIR!
BOBOBO-BO BO-BOBO
SHONEN JUMP MANGA
Story & Art by
Yoshio Sawai
volume 1
MANGA SERIES ON SALE NOW
by Yoshio Sawai
SHONEN JUMP
On sale at www.shonenjump.com
Also available at your local bookstore and comic store.
RATED T FOR TEEN
VIZ media

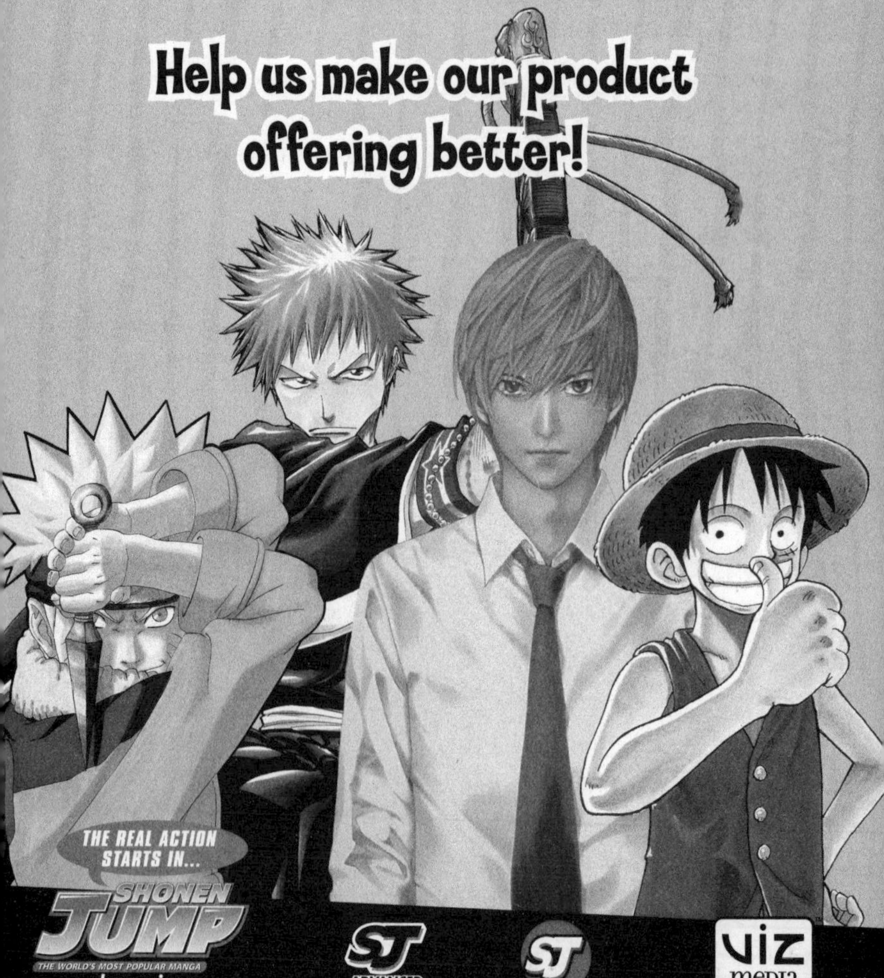
THE REAL ACTION STARTS IN...
SHONEN JUMP
THE WORLD'S MOST POPULAR MANGA
www.shonenjump.com
SJ ADVANCED
SJ
viz media